DUB IN BABYLON

Studies in Popular Music

Series Editors: Alyn Shipton, journalist, broadcaster and
former lecturer in music at Oxford Brookes University
and
Christopher Partridge, Professor of Religious Studies, Department
of Politics, Philosophy and Religion, Lancaster University

From jazz to reggae, bhangra to heavy metal, electronica to qawwali,
and from production to consumption, *Studies in Popular Music* is a
multi-disciplinary series which aims to contribute to a comprehensive
understanding of popular music. It will provide analyses of theoretical
perspectives, a broad range of case studies, and discussion of key issues.

Published:

Open Up the Doors
Music in the Modern Church
Mark Evans

Technomad
Global Raving Countercultures
Graham St. John

Forthcoming:

Send in the Clones
A Cultural Study of Tribute Bands
Georgina Gregory

DUB IN BABYLON

UNDERSTANDING THE EVOLUTION AND
SIGNIFICANCE OF DUB REGGAE IN JAMAICA
AND BRITAIN FROM KING TUBBY TO POST-PUNK

CHRISTOPHER PARTRIDGE

LONDON   OAKVILLE

Published by

UK: Equinox Publishing Ltd., 1 Chelsea Manor Studios, Flood Street, London SW3 5SR
USA: DBBC, 28 Main Street, Oakville, CT 06779

www.equinoxpub.com

First published 2010 by Equinox Publishing Ltd.

British Library Cataloguing-in-Publication Data
A catalogue record for this book is available from the British Library.

Library of Congress Cataloging-in-Publication Data
Partridge, Christopher H. (Christopher Hugh), 1961-
  Dub in Babylon : understanding the evolution and significance of dub
reggae in Jamaica and Britain from King Tubby to post-punk / Christopher
Partridge.
    p. cm. -- (Studies in popular music)
  Includes bibliographical references and index.
  ISBN 978-1-84553-311-3 (hb) -- ISBN 978-1-84553-312-0 (pb) 1. Dub
(Music)--Jamaica--History and criticism. 2. Dub (Music)--Great
Britain--History and criticism. I. Title.
  ML3532.P37 2010
  781.646--dc22
                            2009035241

ISBN-13   978 1 84553 311 3   (hardback)
          978 1 84553 312 0   (paperback)

Typeset by CA Typesetting Ltd, www.publisherservices.co.uk
Printed and bound in Great Britain by Lightning Source UK Ltd., Milton Keynes and
Lightning Source Inc., La Vergne, TN

IN MEMORIAM
Mark Dickinson
10 May 1959–18 September 2000

Contents

Acknowledgements

This book is, of course, indebted to several people, most of whom are, as is usually the case, those closest to me. First and foremost, as always, my sons, Tom, Sam, and Jordan are the most important. While they have benefited from a large dub and roots reggae collection in the house, they have repaid me many times over, not only with a vibrant, friendly home, but also by introducing me to much dubstep, electronica and drum 'n' bass. My growing music collection is large because of my addiction to music, but interesting because of their recommendations. (It's particularly pleasing that, as I finish this book, my youngest son, Jordan (aka Decyfer), has just released his first contribution to dubstep on the Studio Rockers label.)

I am particularly blessed to share my life with a partner who has a keen interest in and extensive knowledge of popular music. Few partners would have so willingly endured so much conversation about popular music. Thank you Marcia.

Of my close friends, with whom I have spent more hours than is perhaps healthy 'dubbed out' in the North West over the past three decades, four deserve a special mention: Crossy, Alex, Jeff, and Mark. Mark, who died on 18 September 2000, is greatly missed by us all and still fondly remembered for his outrageous humour and his devotion to reggae. It is now difficult for me to think of Misty in Roots and Bob Marley without also thinking of Mark. He was a good, gentle human being who made our lives that little bit brighter during the too short time he was with us. This book is for him.

While, of course, all those partners who have put up with us listening to dub and reggae over the years deserve a mention, Mark's partner, Diane, deserves a special mention. They were a genuinely lovely couple, which is why it was they who most often hosted our late-night dub sessions in the early 1980s. Another reason was Diane's cheesecake…

I am also enormously grateful to one of those dubheads, Jeff, for so enthusiastically agreeing to design such an outstanding cover.

I am indebted to the guidance I've had from academics and writers over the years, particularly Sara Cohen and Anahid Kassabian at the Institute of Popular Music, Liverpool University, Jason Toynbee at the Open University, and the independent scholar Erik Davis.

Finally, I want to thank the many people in the dub and dance communities with whom I have spoken over the years for offering help, answering my questions and correcting my recollections and perceptions of reggae in the 1970s. Particular thanks are due to Linton Kwesi Johnson for allowing me to use excerpts from his poetry in Chapter 4.

Publisher's Note
Every effort has been made to trace all the copyright holders, but some have proved untraceable. The publishers will be pleased to make the necessary arrangements at the first opportunity.

Introduction

Dub is, in many ways, the 'unsung hero' of contemporary dance, electronica, and remix culture. Indeed, it's surprising that it is rarely referenced in books on music, one dictionary simply identifying 'dub' as a 'tabor' – 'a small drum used in medieval times to accompany folk dancing' (Kennedy 2005: 212). Whilst this is true of course, the term also refers to something far more significant in the history of music than a small medieval drum. From the backstreets of Kingston to the dancefloors of Ibiza, from John Lydon to Bill Laswell, from Morocco's Aisha Kandisha's Jarring Effects to France's Brain Damage, from Germany's Rhythm and Sound to North America's Sub Oslo, and from ambient to illbient, dub has been a creative and influential force.

While a general study of the history of dub would have been interesting – and to some extent has been provided in the following chapters – a particular aim of this book is to contribute to the history of reggae 'outernational' (i.e. Rasta and reggae argot meaning, essentially, 'beyond the shores of Jamaica') by exploring the social, political, and, to some extent, religious significance of the genre in 1970s Britain, which was a particularly fertile period for the genre and the principal country within which it was initially developed outside Jamaica. Hence, beginning in Part One with the Jamaican religio-cultural background – which is necessary for understanding the cultural significance of dub – and the advent of reggae and dub, Part Two traces its reception in 1970s Britain, examining its musical, cultural and political importance for both African-Caribbean and, particularly, white subcultures. In other words, Part One analyses its relationship to Rastafarian culture – the history and central beliefs of which are related to reggae and examined in Chapter One – and the reception of that culture in the UK. Following the outernational development of these themes and ideas, Part Two discusses dub's cultural and musicological influence on punk and post-punk, the principal political music in late-1970s Britain. Finally, moving into the period of the decline of dub's influence in Britain in the early 1980s, dub is theorized in terms of post/modernism.

Hence, while the primary aim of the book is to contribute to popular music history, it is actually a confluence of several lines of thought. Firstly, as a historiographical project, it provides a cultural and musical history of dub from its origins in Jamaica to the decline of post-punk in early-1980s Britain. However, it seeks to be more than pure historiography, in that, secondly, it examines the religio-political ideas within dub and traces these through to the ideologies informing the subcultures of the late-1970s. Moreover, from the outset the discussion is punctuated with several case studies in order to demonstrate how these various lines of thought converged in particular settings and personal histories. Generally speaking, of course, a case study is used in the social sciences because it allows for more in-depth analysis, encouraging a systematic approach to the observation of ideas in specific contexts. It limits the variables, tightens the focus, and tests theories. Concerning this project, the approach suggested a finer understanding of how dub developed and the various social and cultural forces that shaped it. For example, in focusing on the work of Lee Perry, we will see the peculiar extent to which dub was influenced by North American popular culture, West African religion, Rastafarianism and the Jamaican social context. Again, we will see that while King Tubby might be understood as 'the father of dub', his work was the product of a particular culture and benefited from the confluence of several streams of influence, not least that of Lee Perry.

Thinking in terms of what might be understood as a 'dub methodology', having examined the principal ideological themes informing reggae and Rastafarian discourse in Part One, the book follows the echoes of those themes as they were received and reflected in another quite distinct context beyond that in which the original sound was created. In other words, in terms of reverb and delay, the book can be understood, to some extent, as a 'dubbed' history, in that, in Part One the creation of the sound is examined, as is the history of the ideas with which it was invested and the social context within which it emerged. In Part Two the book goes outernational and examines the reflection of the sound, its reception by listeners who are hearing it after a period of delay and the consequences of that delay on the sound and the ideas with which it was originally invested. That is to say, if an echo can, technically, be explained as a wave that has been reflected by a discontinuity in the propagation medium and returns with sufficient magnitude and delay to be perceived, Part Two of the book examines the nature of this discontinuity and the ideological and musicological effects it has had on dub. For example, it is argued that, in going outernational, there is, within the reception of dub, a shift in signification and meaning. Hence, to go to the chronological conclusion of the book, there are echoes of the original Jamaican social and ideological context within post-punk dub, but, it is argued, the signification has shifted and, more specifically, the religio-political charge with which it was originally animated has been weakened. While of course it might not have been completely divested of this charge, there was a process of ideological dilution. Survivals of it remained in the mix, as it were, but, in travelling to Britain, the emphasis shifted.

We will see in Chapter Four that it was received quite differently in the mid-1970s by punks, who were, to a large extent, politicized by reggae. Whereas in Chapter Three it is argued that it was received by 'hippie'/progressive rock subcultures in the same way that, for example, Gong or Tangerine Dream or various ambient musics were received (i.e. internally and, to an extent, spiritually, as part of an inner, psychedelic soundscape), in the following chapter we see that it moved from the beanbags and scented bedsits of suburbia to political rallies and to the streets of the inner city. Again, while the signification had undoubtedly shifted, the ideological echoes from the backstreets of Kingston were relatively loud and pronounced, the delay was minimal, the religio-political discourse foregrounded. However, in the final chapter it is argued that the shift of signification in the post-punk period meant that the strength of these echoes progressively declined; they receded into the distance, became distorted, and obscured.

As to why I decided to write the book, firstly, and, I suppose, primarily, since the mid-1970s I have been a fan of the genre and have followed its progress in the UK over the years. I listen to a lot of reggae and dub, whether on vinyl/CD or live. Secondly, I am also interested in punk and post-punk and, therefore, like many white music fans who grew up in the 1970s – including many of the key figures in contemporary dub, such as Adrian Sherwood – was introduced to the genre within the musical and social contexts that the book investigates. Finally, as well as having an academic interest in Popular Music Studies *per se*, I am a Religious Studies scholar with an interest in the media and cultures of everyday life. I am, however, fully cognizant of the implications of my position as a middle-class, white, male, academic fan who was introduced to dub reggae during the period which is the focus of the research. That is to say, I am keenly aware that this raises a number of well-known methodological issues relating to subjectivity and objectivity in research. Hence, I have sought, throughout, to take account of my peculiar perspective, being explicitly conscious of issues relating to, following Pierre Bourdieu, 'the objectification of objectification' (1990: 59) – the practice of the researcher must be subjected to the same critical scrutiny and sceptical eye as that which is researched. Bourdieu and Wacquant were quite right to insist that, 'as soon as we observe the social world, we introduce in our perception of it a bias due to the fact that, to study it, to describe it, to talk about it, we must retire from it more or less completely' (1992: 69). In other words, in such research a methodological distance can be produced which has the potential to distort. Consequently, the theoretical gaze or 'contemplative eye' needs to be acknowledged and the researcher should try to mitigate the effects of that which is 'injected into [one's] perception of the object by virtue of the fact that [one] is placed outside of the object, that [one] observes it from afar and from above' (Bourdieu and Wacquant 1992: 70). Again, Bourdieu and Wacquant wisely warn that researchers are in danger of failing to realize that 'what their apparently scientific discourse talks about is not the object of research, but their relation to the object'. Hence, they insist, 'a genuine reflexive sociology must constantly guard itself against epistemocentrism and the ethnocentrism of the scientist' (1992: 68–69). Similarly, thinking of my own research into the history and sociology of dub, Bourdieu's work has also been useful in alerting me to the possibility of reification. That is to say, I have been careful not to define the field of research, so to speak, rigidly as 'a set objective, historical relations between positions anchored in certain forms of power (or capital)' (Bourdieu and Wacquant 1992: 34–35), but rather more in terms of, as in my other work (e.g. 2005), 'habitus', or a set of historical relations in the form of 'mental and corporeal schemata of perception, appreciation and action' (Bourdieu and Wacquant 1992: 35). Without going into methodological detail, the point is that whereas 'field' suggests that researchers are in a place of privilege observing activities and, in this case, music reception and subcultural involvement, habitus suggests that which is more dialogical and reflexive. Hence, in the final analysis, I have sought at all times to be reflexive about my own involvement in the research and also to approach it with an attitude free of preconceived notions – guided, to some extent, by the ideals of phenomenology as developed within the discipline of Religious Studies. On the other hand, again, in the spirit of reflexivity and guided by the ideals of phenomenology, I have appreciated my emic standpoint as an aid to 'dialogical reflexivity' (see Flood 1999) which encourages empathy and understanding.

Finally, I am fully aware that a text cannot do justice to the sonic alchemy that is dub, particularly an academic text. Hence, I suggest that readers take time, firstly, to *listen* to dub and, secondly, to watch the excellent film by Bruno Natal, *Dub Echoes* (Soul Jazz Films, 2009). Nevertheless, my hope is that this book will convey just enough of dub's enchantment to ignite your interest if you are one of the unconverted and increase your devotion if you are one of the converted.

PART ONE

Dub JA: From the Days of Slavery to the Creation of Dub

1 Roots and Culture

In order to understand the emergence and significance of dub reggae in Jamaica something needs to be said about the context in which it evolved. While it would take us too far out of our way to trace the roots of Jamaican indigenous music through ska to mento and back into nineteenth-century folk traditions (see White 1983a), or even to comprehensively map the more recent evolution of reggae *per se* – the latter having been done adequately by others (see Katz 2004; Bradley 2000; Hebdige 1987; Jones 1988; Davis and Simon 1983) – some understanding of the evolution of the genre within which dub evolved and the socio-religio-cultural contours which have shaped it will be helpful. Certainly when we come to look at some of the key social and spiritual themes expounded by producers of dub, an understanding of the historical and cultural soil which gave it life is necessary.

There is now a substantial volume of research demonstrating that African-Caribbean cultures draw significantly on their African cultural heritage, particularly in relation to religion, politics, language, and music. More particularly, we now have a good understanding of, as Simon Jones comments, 'the mechanisms of retention and adaptation under slavery by which key aspects of [West African] cultures were preserved, blended with European forms and maintained in a whole array of practices and beliefs in the New World' (1988: 3).

Of course European, Christian hegemony was maintained through the granting of concessions in order to secure consensus. For example, in Jamaica the British sought to secure control over the slaves transported from West Africa by the imposition of the English language and Christianity. However, what actually emerged from this political and cultural struggle was not merely English and Christianity, but Jamaican Creole and Afro-Christianity. This new African-influenced language and religion is the consequence of a hegemonic 'negotiation' between the dominant and subordinate cultures in Jamaica. While the religion and language allowed some separation from the dominant culture, expressing resistance, and asserting the dignity of the African slave in an oppressive context, they nevertheless constitute an expression of incorporation into the dominant culture. Hence, what emerged was not wholly English, Christian or African, but rather a negotiated position. A cultural struggle took place, but the hegemony remained. It did so largely because the subordinate groups were allowed to incorporate something of their own culture in the dominant culture. Reggae and dub need to be understood in this context.

The aim of this initial chapter is simply to excavate and expose some central historical, political and religious features of this context in order to enable us to locate ideas as we travel into the cultural hinterland of dub. Hence, what follows is a discussion of the salient and relevant musical survivals, tracing these through to the emergence of dub reggae in Jamaica.

Do You Remember the Days of Slavery?

Jamaica, the third largest island in the West Indies, has more than 2.5 million inhabitants and is commonly known as a popular tourist destination. It is also widely known for its culture, particularly its popular music and the Rastafarianism to which it is related. This millenarian sectarian tradition (to which we will return below) and the distinctive culture to which it has become allied emerge out of a history of social activism of which many Jamaicans are proud. Hence, honoured by Jamaicans for their contribution to democracy and black liberation, several of their national heroes were, as well as being religious leaders and artists, prominent social activists. Notable among these are Marcus Garvey, Leonard Howell, Joseph Hibbert, Archibald Dunkley, Paul Bogle, George Gordon, Bob Marley,[1] and Claude McKay.

Arguably, democracy and liberation are far closer to the Jamaican heart than they are to many a white Western heart, in that they are viewed and cherished against a background of slavery and oppression. Indeed, Leonard Barrett's seminal study of Rastafarianism argues that the very psyche of Jamaican people is a product of their history:

> Jamaicans are by nature some of the most fun loving, hardworking, and gregarious people in the Caribbean. Treated with kindness and respect, they are likely to remain the most confident and dependable friends on earth. But if treated with impunity and disrespect, all the rage of a deep psychic revenge may surface with unpredictable consequences. This calm-and-storm personality of contemporary Jamaicans is a direct inheritance of that group of Africans who suffered the most frustrating and oppressive slavery ever experienced in a British colony (1997: 29).

It is little surprise, therefore, that numerous indigenous Jamaican folk songs, particularly reggae songs, are, in effect, liberation theologies, which recall the days of slavery.[2] Indeed, there is a sense in which the spirit of George Santayana's famous dictum permeates the religio-cultural milieu of reggae: 'those who do not remember the past are condemned to repeat it'.[3] As with other persecuted peoples, the Jewish community particularly – which has established Holocaust Memorial Days and Holocaust museums (notably, Yad va-Shem in Israel) – there is a commitment not to forget. Never again will African-Caribbeans submit to the yoke of the oppressor; there is a duty to remember their persecution by a dominant white society and to resist any attempts to repeat it; they must protect their freedom; they must recover and celebrate their roots and culture. The call to 'remember the days of slavery' is a consistent theme of particularly 'roots reggae' – reggae which focuses on religious and cultural history. Typical is the evocative 'Slavery Days' by the British band Misty in Roots – from their seminal album *Wise and Foolish* (1981) – which includes the refrain 'Let them remember the days of slavery'. More famously, the musician Winston Rodney (Burning Spear) – who has dedicated his work to the articulation of Rastafarianism and particularly to the memory and the message of the Jamaican social activist Marcus Garvey[4] – also wrote a song entitled 'Slavery Days' (*Marcus Garvey*, 1975). The song, which includes the refrain 'Do you remember the days of slavery?', discusses the plight of African slaves and the abuses they suffered. Not only does it demand that people remember their histories, but it defiantly asserts that they have survived and have not been defeated. Indeed, there are few, if any, roots reggae artists who have not reflected upon the days of slavery and articulated liberationist ideologies to some extent.

The overall point is that the religion and culture with which we are concerned is an outgrowth of the colonial and postcolonial experiences associated with plantation society in Jamaica, or what is sometimes termed 'Plantation-America' (see Wagley 1957). The concept of Plantation-America was developed to refer to societies which had been moulded by the rigidly stratified plantation system within which African slave labour was used to produce mainly sugar cane (Craton 1978; Burton 1997: 13–46). Although this model has been critiqued and refined, 'if viewed in a provisional and non-deterministic way', it does enable one, as Jack Johnson-Hill argues, 'to focus attention on the importance of both social and racial stratification in the development of modern Jamaican society' (1995: 9). The argument is that slavery and the plantation system have shaped Jamaican society and consciousness. Indeed, throughout Jamaica there are place names and large plantation mansions that serve to remind the people that their land was, up until 1962, a British colony and, until 1 August 1838, a slave colony.

Jamaica, of course, had an aboriginal population prior to the emergence of plantation society. The Taíno (often referred to as Arawak Indians) had migrated to the island between 650 and 900 CE. However, following the arrival of Columbus in 1494 – after discovering several other West Indian Islands in

1492 – Jamaica was transformed. (With particular reference to the Arawak Indians, this is commented on by Burning Spear in the song 'Columbus' on *Hail H.I.M.*). While this change was initially slow, being confined principally to trading, in the 1600s demographic and ecological change significantly accelerated when European landowners began cultivating sugar for the rapidly emerging markets in their homelands. To enable them to run these newly established plantations efficiently, they needed a large, disciplined workforce. This they found in West Africa. Hence, very quickly, sugar was not the only international trade to experience substantial growth. The increasingly lucrative slave trade opened up as large numbers of Africans were transported to the New World (Alleyne 1988: 69–75; Curtin 1968: 23–41; Hurwitz and Hurwitz 1971: 16–86; Zips 1999: 23–37) – the brutality of which is powerfully expressed by Bob Marley in the song 'Slave Driver' (on *Catch a Fire*, 1973). Although the Portuguese were the first to exploit West Africa, it was the British who became the principal transporters of human cargo. Captured by other Africans in tribal war or by Arab slave traders and sold to the British, they would be packed into slave ships, chained together, exported to the Americas, sold in auctions to plantation owners, and set to work either as servants in the Europeans' large houses or in gangs on the plantations. Many slaves died either during transportation (some traders allowing for half of their cargo to die on the voyage) or from unfamiliar West Indian diseases against which their bodies had little immunity.

The year 1655 is particularly important in Jamaican history, in that this was the year when England, under the leadership of Oliver Cromwell, decided to extend its global influence by seizing lands held by its weaker European neighbours. In particular, Cromwell promoted a scheme, known as 'the Western Design', which sought to capture Spanish territory in the Caribbean (Hurwitz and Hurwitz 1971: 11). On 10 May 1655, 38 warships lowered their anchors off the coast of Morant Bay. The few hundred Spanish settlers, led by General Arnaldo Isasi, presented little resistance against the 4000-strong British army. Although they sought to defend their property by releasing around 1500 slaves, unsurprisingly, few of them chose to support the Spanish, most fleeing to the hills in Jamaica's interior to settle with the *palenques* – who seem to have been freed African slaves or, perhaps, escaped indigenous Taíno slaves. Growing in strength, these former slaves, living in the hills of Clarendon, Guanana Vale, and Rio Juana, later became famous as 'the Maroons' (from the Spanish term for runaway slaves, *cimárron*), skilled guerrilla fighters who proved to be a formidable challenge to British colonial forces (Barrett 1997: 30–38; Campbell 1988; Schafer 1981). Eventually, in 1670, under the Treaty of Madrid, Spain officially transferred Jamaica to British rule.

The ink on the treaty had hardly dried before the dire effects of British rule were felt. Very quickly Jamaica was transformed from a small-scale, cocoa-based economy, run by numerous landowners with small plots of land and few slaves, into a massive sugar-producing plantation society. No longer did Europeans work next to their slaves on smallholdings. 'England sought to solidify white control further in 1662 by granting full British citizenship to Jamaica's white settlers. As citizens of the British Crown they were able to make their own laws and establish a political system that would exclude nonwhites for more than 200 years' (Robinson 1999: 1027). Business and investment in both the slave trade and the sugar trade boomed, with (it is estimated) more than 10 million slaves being sold in the New World. Jamaica was central to this trade, being a major British port for slavers. 'Nearly 2 million African slaves were transported through Jamaican ports alone' (Robinson 1999: 1027), and while, in 1677, there were around 9000 whites and 9000 black slaves working in Jamaica, by 1739 the number of whites had risen by only 1000, whereas the number of African slaves had risen to 100,000. Moreover, the working conditions for these slaves became increasingly harsh and brutal. Those who sought liberation were whipped severely and even lynched, many being gibbeted in a barbaric attempt to deter other slaves.

Nevertheless, as indicated above, running through this dark history of brutality and suffering there is a proud thread of resistance, one of the most significant early manifestations of which was the 'Maroons' who carried out guerrilla campaigns against the British (Zips 1999: 69–126; see also Assembly of Jamaica 1970 [1796]). Led by revered fighters such as Cudjoe (Cujo/Kwadwo), leader of the Clarendon maroon community, militias were highly effective against the colonial forces (see Barrett 1997: 30–38). It is perhaps not surprising, therefore, that, as Stephen Foehr found when he visited Jamaica in the 1990s, Cudjoe is still celebrated within some sections of Jamaican society as a symbol of black resistance. Indeed, within this tradition, reggae itself is often understood in terms of a manifestation of a history and culture of resistance (e.g. Campbell 1997: 133–40). It is warrior music and it is to Cudjoe and other 'freedom fighters' that many contemporary Jamaicans look for inspiration (see Zips 1999). 'We Africans here fight for our rights, including our African cultural rights. These deep-down type of Africans, such as Nanny, Cudjoe, Bogle – they were heroes. They fight for justice. They need justice and that's what they fight for' (Foehr 2000: 79). Again, with this historical context in mind, Bob Marley and the Wailers begin their album *Burnin'* (1973) with a song which has since been used by other liberationist organizations, such as Amnesty International, 'Get Up, Stand Up':

Get up, stand up,
stand up for your right
Get up, stand up,
don't give up the fight.

Indeed, with songs such as 'Rebel Music' and album titles such as *Uprising* and *Confrontation*, Marley makes this theme explicit in his work – as do numerous other reggae musicians.

The Maroons occupy a prominent place in Jamaican history. That said, as Alonford Robinson comments, 'freedom was not limited to maroon communities. A small and politically powerless free black and free coloured (a term used in Jamaica referring to people of partial African descent) community existed in the decades immediately preceding emancipation' (1999: 1027). Indeed, one of the biggest blows to slavery came at the hands of a black Native Baptist freed slave by the name of Samuel Sharpe.[5] In 1831, Sharpe organized more than 20,000 slaves into a formidable movement against slavery (Barrett 1997: 38–51). In what was to become known as 'the Baptist War' or 'the Christmas Rebellion', the insurrection he ignited was so violent that it sent shock waves around the British Empire (Burton 1997: 83–89). Hence, along with the political efforts of the abolitionists in Britain, this Jamaican rebellion served to increase the pressure on the British Parliament sufficiently to move it to abolish slavery in 1834. Although Sharpe did not live to see the fruit of his labours, having been executed in Montego Bay on 23 May 1832, 311,000 slaves were eventually freed in Jamaica alone.

This, however, did not actually improve the lot of many African Jamaicans. Although they were technically no longer slaves, neither were they full British citizens. Indeed, although white slave owners in Jamaica collectively received compensation of more than six million pounds, their former slaves were also required to remain in their employ as 'apprenticed labourers' in order to soften the economic impact of emancipation. Fieldworkers, for example, were required to work a further six years for their masters as 'apprentices' – others were required to work for four years. Hence, as far as the slaves were concerned, and as British abolitionists pointed out, their newly liberated existence was hardly better than the days of slavery. Moreover, during the apprenticeship period many landowners imposed stringent labour contracts on their workers, paid low wages, and imposed high taxes, making it difficult for former slaves to pursue alternative employment, thereby effectively tying them into working for their former masters. Consequently, in 1865 another rebellion arose within the Native Baptist community, led by one of its preachers, namely Paul Bogle – with the help of another minister, George William

Gordon. Bogle organized small, armed black militias and trained them in the hills above Morant Bay. After a rebellion in which 28 people were killed, colonial officials captured and whipped more than 500 African-Caribbeans, burned down almost 1000 of their homes, and executed over 500 protestors, including Bogle, who was hanged along with Gordon. Although it would be nearly another century before Jamaicans would finally see their independence from colonial control, Gordon and particularly Bogle have since become important icons of black resistance and liberation in Jamaica.

As noted above, while life has, in many ways, changed dramatically since the nineteenth century, as Dick Hebdige comments, 'the days of slavery have left an indelible mark on the island. Even in present-day Jamaica there are social and economic problems which can be traced back directly to the old plantation system. Jamaica's poverty, unemployment and racial and social inequality are all largely inherited from the past' (1987: 25). As is often pointed out, there have always been two Jamaicas, a minority, 'multiracial bourgeois society of about 100,000 people', and 'a nation of about two million people – who are poor, Black and uneducated' (*Jamaica Daily News*, quoted in Johnson-Hill 1995: 11; see also Curtin 1968: 101–21). That the lot of the slaves' descendents, whilst improved, is still poor, is graphically illustrated in the reggae film, *The Harder They Come*, starring Jimmy Cliff. Life is lived out, not on tropical sun-kissed beaches and in the Caribbean opulence of the travel brochures, but, for a large percentage of the black population, in ghetto conditions of poverty and hardship – in what Bob Marley referred to as a light-deprived 'concrete jungle' in which day-to-day life is hard (*Catch a Fire*, 1973). Indeed, the influence of life in the slums and shantytowns, in which many reggae artists spent their childhoods, is evident in much of the music produced particularly during the 1960s and 1970s. Again, as Hebdige comments, 'reggae has done much to publicise this image abroad. For reggae isn't just a set of highly danceable rhythms. The lyrics of reggae hits often stray far from the concerns of rock and pop music – problems with parents, boyfriends and girlfriends. The message is about poverty and inequality and black identity' (1987: 22).

Afro-Christianity

By 1838, the majority of Jamaican slaves had become at least nominally Christian as a result of the proselytizing efforts of black Baptist preachers, rather than the activities of their white counterparts who, as Richard Burton comments, 'began serious missionary work on the colony only in the 1820s, almost forty years after the first wave of slave converts had been made by black missionaries' (1997: 97). One such preacher was George Liele who travelled to Jamaica in 1783 following the American Revolution. In fact, white Christianity really only began to shape African Jamaican religion following emancipation in 1838. Furthermore, the years between 1838 and 1865 were marked 'not merely by a conflict for economic and social survival between ex-slaves and ex-masters but also by a cultural (and by extension social and political) struggle between the white missionaries on the one hand and, on the other, the freed community and its black preachers over the *kind* of Christianity that was to hold sway in Jamaica' (Burton 1997: 97; emphasis mine). Essentially, what had emerged as a result of the fifty or so years of black proselytism was a confluence of West African indigenous and Christian traditions – what some have referred to as 'Afro-Christianity' (Edmonds 2003: 32; Burton 1997: 97). This continuity with West African culture is hardly surprising since, as Barrett has argued, the Africans who were brought to Jamaica were

> not just thousands of black bodies known as slaves but, indeed, were culture bearers from highly developed cultural communities where *religion* was the strongest motivating force... Contrary to the *tabula rasa* hypothesis promulgated by slave philosophers and historians of Jamaica...the people who became slaves were the 'cream' of Africa between the ages of 16 and 30. As such they were important carriers of African culture (1978: 7; original emphasis).

Of particular note at this time was an unstable mix of Myalism and Christianity. With roots in West African religion, *myal* and *obeah* were techniques which enabled a person to communicate with the spirit world. Generally speaking, Obeah was used to curse individuals and to manipulate events malevolently, and Myalism was understood to be the remedy, in that it enabled one to remove hexes and provide immunity to spiritual attack. This is important because, again, it needs to be understood in terms of a culture of resistance. It was believed, for example, that slavery, understood as an evil with origins in white sorcery, could be countered by Myalistic techniques. In effect, the rationale was that white slavers were able to wield such power as a result of some form of Obeah and that this could be removed by the practice of Myalism (see Curtin 1968: 29). The point is that, even when Africans converted to Christianity, they carried with them into their new faith Myalistic elements (see Burton 1997: 99–101). Moreover, these elements were central to belief and practice, their Christian identity being moulded by African religion and culture, with its myths, values and rituals: belief in spirits of the dead, dancing, drumming, prophesying, glossolalia, trance, possession, and apocalypticism. Indeed, Malcolm Calley has argued that 'possibly the most important role of slavery in the West Indies was to hinder the diffusion of a detailed knowledge of Christianity to the slaves, thus stimulating them to invent their own interpretations and their own sects' (quoted in Cashmore 1983: 16). Again, this is significant, for, quite apart from the Myalistic counter offensive, Afro-Christian religion was perceived to be a manifestation of resistance, in that it represented a continuity with a traditional African cosmology that defined social realities in ways quite different from those that their white masters were seeking to impose upon them (see Barrett 1978: 9–13; Burton 1997: 97–103). As Ennis Edmonds comments, 'even when Africans converted to Christianity, the elements of Christianity to which they showed the greatest affinity were those that reinforced their Afrocentric worldview, informed their struggle for liberation, and promised them eventual freedom from and redress of the evil perpetrated against them by the colonial system' (2003: 33). Sharpe himself, for example, was not unusual in being both a Baptist preacher and also a 'daddy' (i.e. leader or priest) within West African slave religion.[6] (The key features to note here are those of Afro-centrism, liberationist spirituality and politics, and opposition to oppressive white society, all of which we will see articulated and developed in roots reggae culture.)

In the years immediately prior to the emergence of Rastafarian thought in Jamaica, not only Afro-centric beliefs, but apocalyptic beliefs had become more or less commonplace. That said, as Burton comments, 'it took the career of the remarkable Alexander Bedward (ca. 1859–1930) to bring the radical energies of Jamaican Afro-Christianity to their peak, whereafter it was superseded as the main challenge to the colonial order by the newly emergent millennialist cult of Rastafarianism' (1997: 116). Interestingly, while Bedward was vigorously anti-colonial, Barry Chevannes has argued that he accepted the colonialist theological premise that God was white and, also that, 'during the post-apocalyptic millennial period of the new heaven and new earth, blacks would become white' (1994: 28, 109). That said, as far as Bedward was concerned, the white people of the world were destined for destruction. Moreover, there is evidence that, in 1920, Bedward himself declared that, not only was he the harbinger of their end, but he would be the instrument of their destruction. Indeed, he seems to have declared that he was actually the returned Christ. As such, he would, like Elijah, ascend to heaven in a flaming chariot (on Friday 31 December 1920) and, after three days, return for his flock, take them to glory, and then begin the events of the apocalypse and the destruction of the white race. Perhaps needless to say, at the appointed time and date, in front of thousands of followers, no flaming chariot appeared. Following three subsequent predictions, each with the same earthbound result, the cognitive dissonance of his remaining followers was assuaged a little when he declared that God had commanded him to remain on the earth to preach. However, in 1921, following his alleged claim to be Christ and incendiary declarations suggesting the overthrow of the colonial authorities, he was arrested and interned in Kingston Lunatic Asylum, where he died in November 1930, a few weeks after the coronation of Emperor Haile Selassie I in Ethiopia.

Not only is Bedward still remembered fondly by some Jamaicans, but, interestingly, references to him have surfaced in British dub. Released in 1983, 'Bedward the Flying Preacher' is a thoughtful reflection on him by Prince Far I (backed by the loose collective known as Singers and Players), which respectfully and wittily remembers his claims and his demise (released on Singers and Players' *Staggering Heights*). Then, over a decade later, in 1996, 'Bedward', a popular remix of the song, was released by the British dub collective Zion Train on Dub Syndicate's *Research and Development*. Hence, regardless of his idiosyncratic millenarian beliefs, it would seem that Bedward is part of an Afro-centric stream of resistance to European colonial power that many still find inspiring and refreshing. (That said, we will need to question the significance, in dub 'outernational', of figures from Jamaican history such as Bedward. His name, like that of others, has continued within the tradition, but beyond Jamaican Rastafarianism, particularly as a result of the transition to post-punk dub, there is a sense in which it has become little more than a free-floating signifier, a simulacrum.)

Returning, however, to the Jamaican religio-cultural context, the coronation of Haile Selassie, along with Bedwardist millennialism, subversive slave political thought, Ethiopianism, and other streams of Afro-Christianity, paved the way for the still more subversive ideas of Rastafarianism, which emerged out of this milieu. Certainly Afro-Christian activists, Sharpe and Bogle particularly, are cited by Rastas as inspirational examples in their struggle against 'Babylon'. Moreover, we will also see that certain elements of Myalist and Afro-Christian worship contributed to the early development of Rasta music – and, indeed, dub.[7] However, before turning specifically to Rastafarianism, a little more needs to be said about a form of religio-political utopianism which emerged within Afrocentric thought.

The Emergence of Ethiopianism

As time passed, and as new Jamaican-born generations reflected on their history, this longing had a sacralizing effect on their perception of Africa. In other words, Africa gradually came to be understood as a promised land, the biblical Zion. As Patrick Taylor puts it, 'a past African Golden Age becomes a future millennial Zion' (1991: 102–3). Thinking from a more explicitly political perspective, from the late eighteenth century onwards, Jamaica witnessed the emergence of a back-to-Africa movement, which followed a pattern that can be observed within other histories of the oppressed. That is to say, it is not uncommon for peoples who have migrated from their homelands, usually as a result of force, to develop religio-political zionisms. As with other migrant communities, the African diaspora came to understand itself as an exiled people living in a hostile land ('Babylon'). This in turn led to an understanding of their homeland as pure and sacred (see Barrett 1997: 115–17; Daynes 2004).[8] Interestingly, much of the terminology used to describe such peoples and their experiences is taken from the Hebrew Bible and Jewish history. Whereas this might not always be appropriate, in the case of the African slave communities – and thinking particularly of the development of Rastafarianism and the key ideas articulated within reggae and dub – it is. While there is much that is Christian in African-Caribbean religion, it is suffused with Jewish theological ideas. For example, reinterpreting the story of the Israelites' journey from Egypt to the promised land, as detailed in the Pentateuch, not only did Jamaican Africans think of Africa in terms of the divinely ordained promised land, Zion, but they understood the Atlantic Ocean in terms of the River Jordan which needed to be crossed. In other words, as Dick Hebdige discovered, 'the Bible is a central determining force in both reggae music and popular West Indian consciousness in general... It is the supremely ambiguous means through which the black community can most readily make sense of its subordinate position within an alien society' (1979: 32, 33–34). More specifically, the biblical material is detraditionalized – removed from its original context and explicitly reinterpreted according to a new, largely self-oriented, religio-cultural philosophy (on detraditionalization *per se*, see Heelas, Lash and Morris 1996; Heelas 1996: 155–59; Partridge 2005). (Such detraditionalization is, we will see, a process evident within much roots reggae and dub.) For example, the following all include material which explicitly articulates a detraditionalized understanding of the dualism of 'Zion' and 'Babylon': Jah Warrior, *Great King's of Israel in Dub*; Prince Far I, *Message From the King*; Ijahman Levi, *Haile I Hymn*; The Wailers, *Burnin'*; Bob Marley, *Exodus*; Dreadzone, *Second Light*.

As to the emergence of an identifiable back-to-Africa movement (and of Ethiopianism generally – to which we'll return), perhaps the key early influence was Edward Wilmot Blyden (1832–1912) – now considered the pioneer of Pan-Africanism (Lynch 1967). Born into a middle-class free black family in Charlotte Amalie, St. Thomas, in the United States Virgin Islands, he was conscious that his upbringing was very much the exception for black people. From an early age he was recognized as a talented student, particularly in languages, literature, and oratory. So much so that a white clergyman, John Knox, took him under his wing and encouraged him to become a Christian minister. In May 1850, Blyden travelled to the United States to enrol in Knox's *alma mater*, Rutgers Theological College. In so doing he realized just how sheltered his upbringing had been, for it was here that he first encountered racism. Despite his obvious academic ability, purely on the grounds of his skin colour he was refused admission. Disappointed, but not deterred, he applied to two further theological seminaries, both of which turned him down for the same reason. He was now feeling the pressure of 'Babylon', a pressure which was about to be increased with the passage of the Fugitive Slave Law in September 1850. The effects of this law were that free black people could be mistaken for fugitive slaves and thus arrested and sold into slavery.

It was around this time that he encountered the American Colonization Society,[9] which, as part of their repatriation programme, offered to finance his passage to Liberia, the oldest republic in West Africa and one of only two African countries never colonized by a European power – the other being Ethiopia (see Grierson and Munro-Hay 1999; Mack 1999: 141). Indeed, Liberia's modern political foundations rest on the work of freed slaves who sailed there in the early nineteenth century. Blyden's interest in both the offer and the project was immediate. Within a couple of months, in December 1850, he travelled to Liberia's capital, Monrovia. He enrolled at the city's Alexander High School and by 1858 had become its Principal. Also during this time he was ordained into the Presbyterian Church, he served as editor of the *Liberian Herald*, and he published the first of his many pamphlets, *A Vindication of the Negro Race* (1857), in which he stridently attacked theories of black inferiority. In 1861 he made the first of seven journeys back to the United States in order to encourage more blacks to return to Africa, arguing that racial supremacy was so much part of the white psyche that it was doubtful that blacks would ever progress beyond being second-class citizens in Western societies.

Blyden's obvious intelligence, his forthright and articulate critiques of European and American cultures, and his promotion of the virtues of his new country led to a steady progression through Liberian corridors of power: President of Liberia College; Secretary of the State of Liberia; Liberian Commissioner to Britain and the United States; Liberian Ambassador to the British Court of St. James; Minister of the Interior. His position within Presbyterianism, however, took a quite different turn. In 1886 he resigned and a year later published a pamphlet that essentially detailed why he had done so. In *Christianity, Islam, and the Negro Race* (1967) he argued that Africans had suffered far more under Christianity than they had under Islam and that, therefore, the Christian faith *per se* was problematic for blacks. Indeed, like Rastarianism many years later, he claimed that Western Christianity had hindered the development of the African personality. Although not all his ideas – such as his defence of polygamy – were well-received, by the time of his death in 1912 his influence was beginning to be felt. Not only had the first Pan-African conference – which was, to a large extent, shaped by his thinking – been held in London in 1900, but his ideas on black identity began to take hold as the twentieth century progressed. In particular, he argued a thesis that is now at the heart of Rastafarian thought, namely that Ethiopia represents the pinnacle of civilization and learning. Indeed, Ethiopia and the celebration of its supremacy became identified with Africa *per se*. That is to say, for many within the African diaspora, Ethiopia became a synonym for the entire African continent; it was the heart of Africa; it was a powerful symbol of a free, sovereign, and sacred Africa; it was, therefore, as Neil Savishinsky has argued, 'a potent source of inspiration for African nationalist leaders, many of whom chose the "pan-African" colours of the Ethiopian flag as a symbol for their emerging political parties and newly independent states' (1998: 135). In short, Ethiopianism 'espoused a vision of African liberation and a future Ethiopian empire' (Edmonds 2003: 34).

It should be noted, however, that, in developing Ethiopianism – and thereby laying the intellectual foundations for back-to-Africa political and religious thought – Blyden was actually developing an idea, the embryo of which was already present in African-American culture. Indeed, significantly, the slave preacher George Liele had himself adopted the idea and in 1784 founded in Jamaica, what he initially called, the Ethiopian Baptist Church. As Barrett comments,

> by the time of the emergence of the Black churches, Africa (as a geographical entity) was just about obliterated from their minds. Their only vision of a homeland was the biblical Ethiopia. It was the vision of a golden past – and the promise that Ethiopia should once more stretch forth its hands to God – that revitalized the hope of an oppressed people. Ethiopia to the Blacks in America was like Zion or Jerusalem to the Jews (1997: 75).

As has been noted, for many it became a focal point on the eschatological horizon, the Zion to which they were being called to return. It was this emergent Ethiopianism that Blyden developed from a Pan-Africanist perspective.[10] Drawing on classical sources, he argued that, rather than being the barbaric, dark continent described by white Christians and, perhaps most eloquently and influentially, in Joseph Conrad's 1902 novel *Heart of Darkness* (1994), Africa was actually the cradle of civilization.

Ethiopianism, however, didn't develop into the culture of resistance in America that Blyden and many others hoped it would. Nevertheless, although disappointed, he was optimistic and looked forward to the day when a 'black Moses' would lead the dispersed peoples of African origin back to their homeland. Drawing again on imagery from the Hebrew Bible, he prophesied the following: 'The Negro leader of the Exodus who will succeed will be a Negro of Negroes, like Moses was a Hebrew of the Hebrews – even if brought up in Pharaoh's palace [i.e. at the heart of the land of oppression] he will be found. No half Hebrew and half Egyptian will do the work...for this work heart, soul and faith are needed' (quoted in Lynch 1967: 121). If, at this time, there was little sign of Blyden's hope coming to fruition in North America, this was not the case in Jamaica. Largely because of its more militant history, the embers of radical political Ethiopianism were smouldering and simply needed someone to fan them. That person was Marcus Garvey. He would be the 'Negro of the Negroes'. As Barrett argues, 'the movement that was to embody the Ethiopian ideology par excellence was the Back-to-Africa Movement of Marcus Garvey. It was in Garvey – the prophet of African redemption – that the spirit of Ethiopianism came into full blossom' (1997: 76–77).

Marcus Mosiah Garvey (1887–1940), born in St Ann's Bay, Jamaica, was the leader of the first genuine large-scale black movement and, with reference to Blyden's 'prophecy', was popularly referred to during his lifetime as 'Black Moses'. However, unlike Blyden, his early life did not especially indicate the illustrious, Mosaic path his life would follow. He left school at the age of 14 to serve as an apprentice in his godfather's printing business. Two years later, aged 16, he decided to move to Kingston, where his initial interest in politics was stimulated by the anti-nationalist and anti-colonial thought he encountered there. However, he didn't stay long in Kingston, moving first to Costa Rica, then through Central America, and eventually, in 1913, to England in search of work. In England he met up with the enigmatic Dusé Mohammed Ali, who had in the previous year founded the *Africa Times and the Orient Review*, which quickly became the most influential international platform for Pan-African and Pan-Oriental thought during this period. A direct response to Universal Races Congress held in London in 1911, it was a truly Pan-African endeavor. Moreover, it was in this journal (October 1913) that the young Garvey published his first important article – 'The British West Indies in the Mirror of Civilization: History Making by Colonial Negroes' – in which he predicted that West Indians would become instrumental in founding an empire equivalent to the 'Empire of the North' (Garvey 1983: 27–32). In 1914 he returned to Jamaica and, on 20 July that year, founded the Universal Negro Improvement Association (UNIA) in Kingston. Very quickly the UNIA, and Garveyism in general, became influential and international, being the movement for African repatriation and self-government that many oppressed and depressed Africans had, since Blyden, been longing for. As Peter Clarke points out, 'The Garvey movement, like the Rastafarian movement, was born perhaps as much from despair of ending injustice and discrimination in America as it was from a vision of Africa as a "Land without Evil"' (Clarke 1994: 37).

Like Blyden before him, central to his teaching and that of the UNIA was the return of Africans to Africa, the only place, he believed, where black people would truly be at home and be respected as a race. Indeed, arguably the largest project of the UNIA was the founding of the Black Star Steamership Line.[11] Owned solely by blacks, and thus a source of great pride, it was a project which was intended to encourage trade between black communities around the Atlantic and also, arguably, to provide the means for Africans to return to Africa.[12] However, as far as we are concerned, the point is that, again, like Blyden (but unlike Bedwardist Afro-Christian teaching), Garvey is significant for insisting that Africans should be proud of their blackness, consider returning to their homeland, lay the foundations for a new superior African civilization, correct the prejudiced white histories of Africa, recognize African civilization as the world's first and greatest, and worship a black God 'through the spectacles of Ethiopia':

> We, as Negroes, have found a new ideal. Whilst our God has no colour, yet it is human to see everything through one's own spectacles, and since the white people have seen their God through white spectacles, we have only now started out (late though it be) to see our God through our own spectacles. The God of Isaac and the God of Jacob let him exist for the race that believe in the God of Isaac and the God of Jacob. We Negroes believe in the God of Ethiopia, the everlasting God – God to Son, God the Holy Ghost, the one God of all ages. That is the God in whom we believe, but we shall worship him through the spectacles of Ethiopia (Garvey 1986: 34).

Having said that, it is rather surprising that Garvey himself never visited Africa. Indeed, his vision of Africa was based less on actual knowledge of the continent and more on the Bible and was, therefore, largely romantic – in the sense that aspects of his thought are strongly reminiscent of the 'noble savage' imagined by Jean-Jacques Rousseau. Nevertheless, while his dream of physical repatriation was not realized, he did succeed in focusing the minds of Africans on issues which were to become central to the Rastafarian movement. Indeed, for many Rastas this very focusing of the mind can be understood in terms of a return to Africa and thus as Garvey's fulfilment of his Mosaic calling. Psychologically, emotionally, culturally, and spiritually Garvey has led his people back to the promised land. He has raised the African consciousness and ensured that Ethiopia is the focal point for many African minds. Moreover, in this sense, reggae is a superb example of what Garvey achieved, for through it the significance of Ethiopia has become apparent, not only to Africans, but to peoples of many races and cultures.

Of particular importance, however, especially for Rastafarianism, were Garvey's comments concerning an African redeemer. For example, he interpreted Psalm 68:31 as follows: 'We go from the white man to the yellow man, and see the same unenviable characteristics in the Japanese. Therefore, we must believe that the Psalmist had great hopes of the race of ours when he prophesied "Princes shall come out of Egypt and Ethiopia shall stretch forth his [*sic*] hands to God"' (Garvey 1986: 61). Indeed, while there is little evidence for the claim, many Jamaicans also believe him to have prophesied the following: 'Look to Africa for the crowning of a Black King; he shall be the Redeemer' (Barrett 1997: 81) or 'Look to Africa when a black king shall be crowned for the day of deliverance is near' (Clarke 1994: 36).[13] Who would this royal redeemer be? The answer, for Garvey and for many Jamaican Garveyites, came in 1930 with the enthronement of Haile Selassie I. Several days after the coronation, on 8 November 1930, Garvey published an article in his Jamaican newspaper *The Blackman*, which referred back to his earlier comments:

> The Pslamist prophesied that Princes would come out of Egypt and Ethiopia would stretch forth her hands unto God. We have no doubt that the time has now come. Ethiopia is now really stretching forth her hands. This great kingdom of the East has been hidden for many centuries, but gradually she is rising to take a leading place in the world and it is for us of the Negro race to assist in every way to hold up the hand of the Emperor Ras Tafari (Lewis 1998: 145–46).

That said, it should be noted that, unlike Rastafarians, Garvey later became disillusioned with Haile Selassie, referring to him as 'a cowardly lion' for fleeing to Britain in 1936 following the Italian invasion of Ethiopia in 1935 (Spencer 1998: 370). Haile Selassie's army, of course, was no match for the Italian forces and, although he did attempt to repel them and even gave an impassioned speech before the League of Nations pleading for assistance, when none arrived exile seemed his only option. For Garvey, however, this was not the action of an Ethiopian warrior and certainly not that of the coming deliverer prophesied by the Psalmist.

Leonard Howell and the Advent of Rastafari in Jamaica

On 2 November 1930, Ras (meaning 'Prince') Tafari Makonnen (1892–1975), the great grandson of King Saheka Selassie of Shoa, was crowned Negus of Ethiopia. Declaring himself to be in the line of King Solomon and taking the name Haile Selassie I (Might of the Trinity), as well as 'King of Kings' and 'Lion of the Tribe of Judah' – which are important biblical references – it is not surprising that when he was crowned in St George's Cathedral in Addis Ababa in front of representatives from many nations (see Waugh 2005), those who had been inspired by Garvey's teaching saw more than the accession of another Ethiopian ruler. In Haile Selassie I/Ras Tafari many saw the Messiah, the fulfilment of biblical prophesy, even God incarnate (Wint 1998). This interpretation of the events was particularly taught by Leonard Howell, who, with Joseph Hibbert, Archibald Dunkley, and Robert Hinds, was one of the principal architects of emergent Rastafarian religio-political thought (Hill 1983; Spencer 1998). However, the scholarly consensus would seem to be that it was Howell who first taught the divinity of Haile Selassie, which was to become a central tenet of much (not all[14]) Rastafarian theology (Campbell 1997: 71, 144; Cashmore 1983: 22; Chevannes 1994: 121; Hill 1983: 28; Smith, Augier and Nettleford 1960: 6; Spencer 1998: 361). We have seen that the deification of prominent leaders was not novel in Jamaican religious history. As such, these seeds of Rastafarian doctrine did not fall on stony ground.

It should be noted that, while Howell was clearly one of the original preacher's of the deity of Haile Selassie, not only is this early period a little obscured, but there is some indication that the Rastafarian movement might be the product of several independent charismatic personalities preaching a similar doctrine (see Edmonds 2003: 36, 147). For example, in the same period Hibbert began preaching almost the same theology in rural Jamaica. Having returned from Costa Rica in 1931 – to which he had migrated at the age of 17 and where he had been a member of a Masonic Lodge called the Ancient Mystic Order of Ethiopia – he began preaching a form of Christian millenarian Ethiopianism. Following Haile Selassie's accession, he quickly became convinced that Ras Tafari was indeed the divine coming deliverer. After moving to Kingston and making contact with Howell, Hibbert eventually established the Ethiopian Coptic Church, which was influenced very much by his former involvement with the Ancient Mystic Order of Ethiopia. Moreover, as noted above, Hibbert and Howell were not the only preachers to be convinced of Ras Tafari's divinity. Having worked as a seaman for the United Fruit Company, Dunkley, like Howell and Hibbert, returned to Jamaica in the early 1930s with very definite ideas about the significance of events in Ethiopia. Also like Howell and Hibbert, his Rastafarian preaching quickly found a following within the religious milieu of Jamaica. However, the main point to note is that, regardless of who was the first to proclaim his divinity, within perhaps three years of his coronation, devotion to Ras Tafari as the Ethiopian messiah had taken root. The seeds of Rastafarianism had been planted and were beginning to grow rapidly in their native Jamaican soil.

It is perhaps not surprising that Howell has been singled out as the earliest exponent of the deity of Ras Tafari, for while it is difficult to assess the impact of each early Rastafarian preacher, it does seem clear that the most important and influential was Howell. That said, to some extent, a mist of mythology (some being of Howell's own devising) obscures our understanding of his early history. For example, it is quite widely claimed (even amongst scholars) that, in 1896, he served in the Ashanti Wars[15] and learned several African languages (Edwards 1999: 645). However, others, most notably the historian Robert Hill, have argued that he was born on 16 June 1898 (Hill 1983: 28). What does seem to be clear though is that he was born at May Crawle in the Bull Head Mountain district of upper Clarendon, Jamaica, that he travelled to Colon, Panama, and the United States, that he enlisted in the US Army Transport Service as a cook, and that he arrived in New York on 28 October 1918. In May 1924 he signed his first papers for US citizenship. Following his time in the army, he worked as a construction worker in New York, where it is very likely that he encountered the Trinidadian American Communist Party Leader George Padmore, who seems to have had a formative impact on his thinking and with whom he later corresponded from Jamaica (1938–39). In the early 1930s, shortly after the accession of Haile Selassie I – which some claim Howell attended – he returned to Jamaica and began preaching Rastafari to all who would listen. Other significant influences on his thought at this time were Garvey (whom he had also encountered in New York) and, more enigmatically, a book published in 1924 by Robert Athlyi Rogers called *The Holy Piby* (Rogers 2000).[16] The founder of the Afro Athlican Constructive Church, Rogers argued that Ethiopians were the chosen people of God and that Garvey was his apostle. Indeed, it would seem that Howell's own influential pamphlet, *The Promised Key* (reproduced with commentary in Spencer 1998: 364–86) – written under the pseudonym G. G. Maragh and claiming to have been published in Ghana – simply plagiarized significant parts of both *The Holy Piby* and another Jamaican work by Fitz Balintine Pettersburgh, *The Royal Parchment Scroll of Black Supremacy* (see Spencer 1998: 362; Hill 1983: 27; Clarke 1994: 46). However, whatever its value as an original work, there is little doubt that *The Promised Key* occupies a significant place in Rastafarian history as a summary of the key themes preached by Howell (Spencer 1998: 385).

Howell's uncompromising declaration of Haile Selassie's divinity, his insistence that his arrival was a clear sign that Africans would soon return to the land of their fathers, and his conviction that Africa itself would soon gain a position in the world long denied by whites soon attracted the attention of Jamaicans at all levels of society. Indeed, everything about him was beginning to attract attention of, not only ordinary Jamaicans, but also of the police: 'With the burgeoning of his movement, Howell was able to purchase a plantation great house called Pinnacle Hill, which was raided by police and from which Howell and his followers were eventually evicted for a variety of provocations, including the cultivation of ganga (cannabis), stockpiling of weapons, and the reported harassment of neighbours' (Spencer 1998: 361). As indicated above, he also appears to have assumed the title 'Gangungu Maragh'[17] – sometimes referred to as 'Gangunguru' or 'Gong' (e.g. Collingwood 2005: 67) – a non-African, possibly Hindi-derived neologism, which he possibly picked up from Indian labourers in Jamaica. Whatever the etymology, Howell understood it to indicate something of his mystical status, as well as his role as a great leader and teacher of wisdom and virtue (see Hill 1983: 35–36; Spencer 1998: 386; A. Mansingh and L. Mansingh 1985: 109).[18]

In 1934 Howell and Hinds were charged with sedition and imprisoned for two years. On his release from prison he founded the Ethiopian Salvation Society and developed his commune on the abandoned Pinnacle plantation in the hills outside Kingston (see Bishton 1986: 94–95; Foehr 2000: 25–38). As Johnson-Hill writes, 'Howell paid taxes on the acreage and redistributed plots of land amongst his followers. At different times between six hundred and sixteen hundred Rastas lived rent-free at Pinnacle, cultivating cash crops, especially ganga' (1995: 18). It is likely that it was during this period that the spiritual practice of smoking ganga was introduced, one which has since become a significant component of much (but by no means all) Rastafarian religious practice (Barrett 1997: 128).

He also developed a strongly immanentist theology, in which the divine was understood to be present within all people. It is, it seems to me, important to grasp the implications of this immanentism, since it may account for his often misunderstood declarations that he was himself Haile Selassie. That is to say, although we have seen that such a claim would not have been novel in Jamaica – in that, around this time, Bedward had become popular as one who believed himself to be Jesus Christ – in actual fact Howell's thesis makes some theological sense in the context of a spirituality which claims both the divinity of Haile Selassie and the presence of the divine within each person. Indeed, it may have been the logical outworking of this theology that led him to the same fate as Bedward. In 1960 he was committed to a psychiatric hospital for reportedly insisting on his own divinity (Spencer 1998: 361). His son, however, has always insisted that he 'didn't think he was God, and the people didn't think of him as God' (quoted in Foehr 2000: 28). Nevertheless, whatever his intended meaning, we will see that this form of theological immanentism has since become important within mainstream Rastafarian thought.

By the 1960s, the Rastafari movement, which Howell had done so much to promote, was waxing, while his own influence was waning. Other Rastafarians, such as Count Ossie (to whom we'll return), were beginning to take his place, as he was quickly losing credibility as a stable and trustworthy leader. That said, it is beyond dispute that if, as Cashmore argues, 'every element of the Rastafarian belief system could be found in Garvey's philosophy' (1983: 24), Howell was the principal Rastafarian interpreter of those elements. He laid solid foundations on which Rastafari could now build.

Having said that, significant though Howell was, as we have seen, he was not the only reason for the rise of Rastafarianism in Jamaica. Clarke, for example, makes an important point when he argues that 'the creation by Haile Selassie in 1937 of the Ethiopian World Federation (EWF), a branch of which was opened in Jamaica by Paul Earlington in 1938...gave considerable impetus to the Rastafarian movement' (1994: 47). Although it is not entirely clear that the EWF was the direct creation of Haile Selassie, it did support his cause. Indeed, it was established in New York as a lobbying organization with the primary aim of soliciting aid and goodwill for a country resisting Italian colonialism. However, it also had the broader Garveyite aims to 'unify, solidify, liberate, and free the Black people of the world in order to achieve self determination, justice and maintain the integrity of Ethiopia – which is the divine heritage of the black race' (Barrett 1997: 89; see also Cashmore 1983: 53). Although the organization was not strictly Rastafarian (in that it did not, for example, promote the divinity of Haile Selassie or physical repatriation), and although it suffered from schism several times, it was nevertheless an important focus for Jamaican Rastas. By the 1950s it became clear to observers that Rastafarianism in Jamaica was a religo-cultural force to be reckoned with. It had begun to grow rapidly, particularly amongst the poor and disaffected who were inspired by its Ethiopianist teachings, its emphasis on black superiority, its commitment to the overthrow of white colonial oppression, and its millenarianism, which taught the apocalyptic end of the present era, the judgement of 'Babylon', and the dawning of a new age of peace and love in which Africa would receive its rightful place of eminence among the nations. It was also clear in the 1950s that its influence was beginning to reach beyond Jamaican shores. It spread to other parts of the Caribbean, to the United States, and was beginning to be felt in Britain.

That beating within this new Jamaican religion was a millenarian heart is hardly surprising bearing in mind the Christian apocalyptic milieu in which it emerged. Indeed, it could be argued that millenarianism has been a key force in the shaping of the Jamaican religio-political psyche, particularly that of the poor and oppressed, who longed for liberation and an end to the current world order. As a millenarian belief system, Rastafarianism likewise appealed to the poor and disaffected in Jamaican society. However, the point I want to make here is simply that this apocalyptic critique of the current world order and its accompanying semiotic promiscuity[19] led many Rastas to be distrustful, not only of those in governmental and ecclesiastical authority, but particularly those in law enforcement. Quite simply, they were living in Babylon and the forces of Babylon could not be trusted (see Johnson 1976a: 397ff.). Hence, as Clarke points out, 'the police and the law enforcement agencies in general became a special object of hatred as members began to be jailed in increasing numbers for ganga (marijuana) offences and, in particular, members of the Nyabinghi section of the movement, for resorting to violence as a means of resolving poverty and discrimination' (1994: 49). That said, violence actually ran counter to mainstream Rastafarian millenarianism, which, as with mille-narian thought generally (see Partridge 2005: 279–327), emphasized change as a result of divine intervention, rather than human effort. Indeed, during the 1940s and 1950s this distinction tended to separate mainstream Rastafarian belief from that of the Garveyites, who were less inclined to wait for a super-natural solution to racial discrimination and suffering. However, while this is true, it should also be noted that, as became increasingly clear, one cannot generalize about Rastafarianism. As it is not a hierarchical institution with system-atically worked out orthodoxies and orthopraxies, there are many versions of belief and practice. Hence, while some Rastas could be described as politically quietist, others have sought to stimulate the process of change by engagement in politics. Indeed, as the movement expanded and evolved, particularly during the 1960s, it became more political, and thus, inevitably, attracted the atten-tion of Babylon. Its strident critiques of established religion, the government, the professional classes, and indeed any form of authority which maintained the status quo and thus effectively supported Babylon, 'the system', led to a common perception that it was dangerous. And, as noted above, sometimes this perception was not mistaken, in that there were militant Rastafarian fac-tions which instigated significant social unease and violent confrontation with the police (see Cashmore 1983: 29–33).

As the 1960s progressed the complexity of the movement increased with its appeal broadening. Gradually more privileged social groups, including par-ticularly students, joined the movement. This broadening of appeal led to an evolution of thinking. In particular, because such privileged social groups lived relatively comfortable lives, while they were committed to notions of black power and Pan-Africanism, they were also reluctant to adopt ideologies com-mending a return to Africa. Indeed, some were openly hostile to the idea of physical repatriation. For example, in the 1970s, the British dub poet Linton Kwesi Johnson argued that it would be a very good thing for all Rastas who want to go back to Africa to do so. They will then be awoken unto reality. Many of them would suffer culture shock. I know that for sure. Many of them would probably have nervous breakdowns when they see the conditions of existence that the African masses have to live under. Rastas think England is Babylon, but Nigeria is Babylon, Ghana is Babylon... 'Back to Africa', you know, that dream died with Marcus Garvey (Johnson in interview with MacKinnon 1979).

While Johnson is not a Rasta,[20] he provides a good illustration of the type of thinking that led to a strengthening of theories of *symbolic* repatriation within Rastafarianism. As in much Pan-Africanism and Rastafarianism today, although some (including a *white* Rasta I have spoken to) maintained the hope that they would one day relocate to Africa, many began to think in terms simply of a return to African consciousness. In other words, the rhetoric shifted towards a focus on 'mental decolonization, a process of deconversion, of turning away from the ethos, mores, and values of colonial society and a reconversion to the African view and way of life' (Clarke 1994: 51). In short, it was argued that the mind of Babylon needed to be replaced by an Ethiopian mind. This, in many ways, was an important theological and ideological shift, which has had significant practical implications. Rastas were not now thinking in eschatological terms of leaving their corrupt, oppressive societies for a better life in the promised land – often identified as Shashamane.[21] If they were going to stay where they were, the life here and now needed to be improved. Hence, along with the nurturing of an African consciousness, the oppressed were politicized. Increasingly, the true Rasta felt it a duty to challenge the social, spiritual and intellectual structures of Babylon from within. That said, although there were intellectuals – particularly the Guyanese historian Walter Rodney (see Rodney 1969; Campbell 1997: 128–33) – who were challenging the colonial government in Jamaica, it was quickly becoming apparent to many Rastas that it would be the artists and musicians who would be central to the mobilization of the forces of good and most effective in 'chanting down Babylon' (Marley). Hence, as we will see, 'roots reggae' was understood, not only as spiritual music, but also as a political, liberationist, anti-establishment, countercultural force. Another British dub poet, Benjamin Zephaniah, makes these points very forcefully:

Rastafari is a form of black liberation theology. Although we say that we shall be liberated in heaven, Rastafarians insist that we must also be liberated here on earth. Rastafarian liberation theology has no party manifesto. It is not political in that sense. Rather, it is about social responsibility; and if that means speaking out about the misuse of power in society, then so be it. I see it as my duty to take a stand and to help those who are struggling to help themselves. Rastafari has given purpose to my writing. I am a scribe of Rastafari bearing witness and writing the third testament. I am full of this sense of purpose. In interviews I have no problem answering that often asked question, 'What is the poet's role in society?' The amount of books I sell or my popularity is of little importance to me. Making sure that what I write is written is far more important (2005: 447; see also Jones and Zephaniah 2005).

By the early 1970s, reggae and Rastafarianism had emerged as an important factor in Jamaican politics. As Anita Waters comments, 'beginning in 1972... Jamaican political parties have frequently used Rastafarian symbols and reggae music in their electoral propaganda' (1985: 3). Most notably, in the 1972 elections, Michael Manley, the Prime Minister of Jamaica (1972–1980), explicitly courted Rastafarian support (King 2002: 105–20; Waters 1985: 140–98; Denselow 1989: 128–33). Not only did he advocate socialist policies and the redistribution of wealth, which appealed to the Rastas, but, as Denselow comments, 'he carried the "rod of correction", the staff that Emperor Haile Selassie himself had given to him when he arrived in Jamaica' (1989: 128). Hence, while many Rastas distanced themselves from any involvement in party politics and the 'Babylon system', Manley's reception of the 'rod' made him special – as is made explicit on Clancy Eccles' 'Rod of Correction' (available on the retrospective *Joshua's Rod of Correction*, the cover of which has a photograph of Manley holding up the staff). Hence, encouraged by Rastafarian millennial discourse, it was widely believed that Manley's election would usher in the dawning of new era, an easier life and, of course, the legalization of cannabis. Hence began his successful 'reggae election', with Delroy Wilson's 'Better Must Come' (1971) adopted as the official theme song for his People's National Party (PNP). However, perhaps inevitably, Manley did not live up to expectations. Not only did he conveniently forget to legalize 'the herb', but, more worrying, social conditions deteriorated. Hence, not unreasonably, reggae musicians began to critique his government. For example, two years into his premiership, Marley complained about growing social inequity in his 'Them Belly Full (But We Hungry)' and also about the continued oppression of Rastas in his 'Rebel Music' (both on *Natty Dread*). Indeed, his album *Rastaman Vibration* (1976) is particularly scathing. That said, although the country gradually declined into crisis under the PNP, with a State of Emergency being declared in 1976, the elections of that year saw Manley returned to power. Although some reggae songs were banned and Manley responded harshly to his musical critics,

> as the election approached, one reggae song in particular was not
> banned from the radio, but given saturation airplay. 'Smile Jamaica'
> by Bob Marley was quite unlike the angry songs on *Rastaman Vibra-*
> *tion*, for it was actually optimistic, with lines like 'Smile, natty dread,
> smile, you're in Jamaica now'. Was it a song of support for the PNP?
> Many Jamaicans thought so (Denselow 1989: 130).

It would appear, therefore, that Marley had settled many of his differences
with Manley's government and, in a subtle fashion, had begun to support
him. Of course, as a national and, indeed, international star, his influence was
considerable. However, it is unsurprising that not everyone agreed with his
involvement in party politics and, three days prior to a free concert at National
Heroes Park, gunmen (whose identity has never been discovered) broke into
his premises in Hope Road, Kingston, and made an attempt to silence him.
The assassination attempt failed, the concert went ahead, and Manley and the
PNP were returned to power.

The point is, however, that, whether Marley's influence was decisive or not
– and it's difficult to think that it was not – it is certainly true that reggae has
helped to mould the contours of contemporary Jamaican politics and society.
As Linton Kwesi Johnson has commented, 'In Jamaica, the politicians have to
listen to the songs. The musicians are powerful' (quoted in Denselow 1989:
133). More particularly, as will become increasingly clear, the articulation of
religio-political themes by reggae musicians has had considerable social and
political significance, not only in Jamaica, but throughout the Western world,
particularly in Britain.

Rastafarianism in Britain

Rastafarianism seems to have first appeared in Britain in the early 1950s.
Sheila Patterson, for example, found evidence of an abortive attempt, in 1955,
to establish a Rastafarian organization called the United Afro-West Indian
Brotherhood (1967: 360). However, the movement's presence in the UK did
not begin seriously to coalesce until the end of the 1960s when the Universal Black Improvement Organization (UBIO) began meeting in London. The
UBIO attempted, as Cashmore says, 'to satisfy the conditions of a mass all-
black enterprise, sanctioned by supernatural power but with inherent potential for collective action'. He continues, 'modelled basically on Garveyite lines,
the Universal Black Improvement Organization had as its main architects two
Jamaican-born London residents, Immanuel Fox and Gabriel Adams, both of
whom were familiar with the growing importance of Ras Tafari to blacks in
Jamaica' (1983: 51). Hence, whilst Fox and Adams (a name he later changed
to Wold) were primarily interested in Garveyite black consciousness raising,

they developed their thought with reference to key Rastafarian themes. They also established a political wing of the UBIO, the People's Democratic Party. That said, it would seem that, at this early stage, the organization had no clear programme: 'it was not strictly Rastafarian in doctrine, philosophy or ambition; nor was it a straightforward political interest group. It was literally a mixture of Rastafarian concepts and themes built on to a neo-Garveyite structure' (Cashmore 1983: 51). This lack of direction within the movement, perhaps inevitably, limited any success and influence it might have had. What it did do, however, was inspire interest in Rastafarianism. So much so that its founders decided to travel to Jamaica to suggest to the leaders of the principally Rastafarian organization, the Ethiopian World Federation (EWF), that a branch be established in London. Although the influence of the EWF was waning, nevertheless it still 'maintained a thoroughly Rastafarian character and was without doubt the single most impressive African-centred organization displaying the important features of centralised authority and, therefore, a degree of social control over its members' (Cashmore 1983: 52). Moreover, although it was not a religious organization as such, there was official recognition of the Ethiopian Orthodox Church, to which many Jamaican Rastafarians belonged. Hence, on returning to London, not only did Fox and Adams bring the EWF, they also brought Ethiopian Orthodoxy.

According to Cashmore's research, in 1972 Claudius Haughton, a Jamaican living in Birmingham, visited the fledgling London 'Local' (as EWF branches are termed) having been impressed by some of their literature. After discussions with the leadership, he returned to Birmingham to found the second British Local. However, according to my own research, the origins of the current Birmingham EWF Local lie, not in 1972, but in early 1981, when a meeting was convened at Brixton Town Hall under the stewardship of Pepe Judah (Ras Melenik). The aim of this meeting was 'to identify the correct structure for the unification of Black people and the Rastafari Movement' (EWF, Local 111, 2005). After further meetings and the presentation of the constitution of the EWF by Ras Pinto Foxe (a former President of Local 33 in Ladbroke Grove, London), the Birmingham Local was established in September 1981, in Muntz Street Community Centre, Small Heath, Birmingham (EWF, Local 111, 2005).

Without going into the details of the organization, the point to note is that, by 1973, Rastafarianism had begun to take root in Britain. However, as Cashmore comments,

> while interest in the EWF and its Rastafarian themes was spiralling, the membership itself was a more or less temporary association of enthusiasts organised around a common interest, its belief system was a broadly based synthesis of ideas and practices gleaned from

whatever sources were available (often supplemented by individualistic interpretations) and its leadership was dispersed, thus denying the movement any formal locus of final authority (1983: 53).

Consequently, the movement became vulnerable to schism. For example, Cashmore comments that one of the founders, who he simply refers to as 'Pepe', left and established a branch of another Jamaican Rastafarian sect, namely the Twelve Tribes of Israel – now the largest Rastafarian organization in Britain (and, indeed, anywhere outside Jamaica).[22] However, it would appear that he is referring to Pepe Judah who continued his commitment to the EWF. In other words, the founding of the Twelve Tribes was simply a development of the Rastafarian presence in the UK, rather than competition as such.

Moreover, it should be noted of Rastafarianism that, while such organizations grew as the 1970s progressed, their membership never reflected the true extent and influence of the movement in Britain. This is simply because many Rastas deliberately choose not to belong to a particular religious group. With its particular focus on self-spirituality and the immanence of the divine, many prefer not to join organizations, but rather to pursue a path of personal devotion. Nevertheless, whether Rastas chose to practise their faith as part of a recognized organization or not, 1973 did seem to be the pivotal year for the movement in Britain. Cashmore even goes so far as to refer to the beginning of a 'Rastafarian renaissance': 'great chunks of the West Indian community were swallowed up in enthusiasm as Ras Tafari manifested itself in England' (1983: 54).

It is worth noting at this point that, not only was Rastafarianism relatively inconspicuous in the UK at this time, but it was actually perceived to be consonant with certain streams of white British society and culture. On the surface at least, politically, culturally and aesthetically, Rastafarianism merged with the counterculture. Indeed, for many young whites, Rastafarianism carried significant subcultural capital. The use of cannabis, countercultural politics, anti-authoritarianism, alternative spirituality, and long hair were almost de rigueur within the 'cool' communities of Britain's major cities. Although Rastas were, of course, distinctive in many respects, and their specific beliefs and ideals rather different from those who had been influenced by North American hippie culture, radical leftwing politics, and the process of Easternization (Campbell 1999; Partridge 2004a: 87–118), there were areas of overlap which enabled a certain level of continuity with the countercultural milieu. This is clearly evident in the reflections of those recorded by Jonathon Green in his illuminating oral history, *Days in the Life: Voices from the English Underground 1961–1971*. One interviewee, Miles, recalls the following:

> The hip society in Notting Hill in those days was basically very involved with West Indians. They were the only ones around who had good music, they knew all about jazz and ska and bluebeat. They also smoked rather good dope... We also knew a lot of black guys like Michael de Freitas and Asiento Fox, known as Priest, who was the head of the Rastafarians. A whole bunch of really nice guys who used to hang out in the apartment and sometimes stay for three or four days, sitting around smoking enormous spliffs (Green 1998: 10).

Similarly, another interviewee, Courtney Tulloch, makes the following significant comment, which is worth quoting in full:

> The underground didn't draw everything from America. People like Hoppy came into contact with Rastafarians before they came into contact with white beats. The Rastafarians were the first group in the Western world to actually drop out of white society, saying, 'This is Babylon, we don't want anything to do with it.' There was a grouping of Rastafarians in Ladbroke Grove and people like Hoppy met them in the early days around Notting Hill. He'd have seen black people with long, long hair before any single white person had long hair. That's not to say that the influences from America or wherever didn't influence white youth – their long hair may have been copied from somewhere else – but the truth is that Rastafarians were the first to drop out of western society. And this was the flavour that was represented in the contacts between blacks and the young whites; these were the type of blacks in the Notting Hill area who were also thinking, 'This society isn't right for me.' It's the white nigger syndrome. Norman Mailer's white nigger. Whites who declared dissatisfaction with their emotions, their personality, and their cultural identity. They stated it themselves: 'We are sick; we have to burn this thing out of ourselves, to make ourselves human beings.' That's basically what the whole hippy thing was about: rediscovering yourself, killing the machine man, the machine society, cleaning it out of your mind, looking at yourself. But that was for them. I'm not saying that there were no black people who took acid, but there were always Rastas like Priest saying, 'That's for *them*. Freaking out, you've got to freak out another way, you've got to rediscover your African-ness, not get like them (Green 1998: 10–11).

Although all the cultural details in this quotation might not be entirely accurate, the perception concerning the significance of Rastafarianism during this period is important. Certainly, that such continuities became increasingly significant and fluid as the 1970s progressed will become apparent in the following chapters.

Belief and Practice

Before turning to trace the musical roots of dub, a brief overview of five general areas of belief and practice will be helpful, in that some initial understanding of them will enable a fuller grasp of developments that will be explored in subsequent chapters. These areas, which have already been touched upon, are as follows: Babylon; immanentism and the authority of the self; dread; dreadlocks; the sacramental use of ganga.

Firstly, the concept of Babylon, central to Rastafarian discourse (see Davidson 2006), is ubiquitous within reggae and dub culture – whether Rastafarian or, increasingly, non-Rastafarian. Indeed, concerning the latter, in the late 1970s and early 1980s it was clear to many at the time (including myself) – and particularly those who supported the Rock Against Racism movement in Britain – that Rastafarian terminology, especially 'Babylon', was transcending not only Rasta culture, but black culture *per se*. For example, when, in 1979, the white punk group 'The Ruts' achieved chart success with their apocalyptic 'Babylon's Burning', some may have been bemused by the reference. Was it biblical? For many, who had, like The Ruts – Paul Fox, Malcolm Owen, Dave Ruffy, and John Jennings – become fascinated with reggae and the dub sound, the reference was obvious: Babylon was the oppressive, principally white establishment, which was, as many millenarian Rastas believed, due to experience an apocalyptic conflagration. Within two years, as if to confirm the stark message of 'Babylon's Burning', The Ruts released another Rasta-influenced single to coincide with London's Southall race riots of July 1981, namely 'Jah War'. Similarly, their heavily dubbed 'Give Youth a Chance' makes explicit reference to the evils of 'Babylon' and urges its audience to 'live in Jah'.[23] Hence, there is more than a little truth to Hebdige's thesis (1979) that British punk culture itself was a yearning for a 'white ethnicity' similar to Rastafarianism. However, the point here is that 'Babylon' has become one of Rastafarianism's more important contributions to much reggae-, punk-, post-punk-, and even cyberpunk-influenced countercultural thought.[24] Indeed, the Jamaican Rastafarian use of the term 'Babylon' to refer primarily to the police (Breiner 1985–86: 33; Pollard 1982: 29) quickly became the dominant subcultural understanding in Britain in the 1970s and 1980s – as indicated by the police sirens which introduce 'Babylon's Burning' by the Ruts and 'Riot' by Basement 5 (on *1965–1980*). As Linton Kwesi Johnson has put it, Babylon is 'police, oppressor, land of oppression' (1976a: 398). Again, Franco Rosso's film, *Babylon* (1980),[25] and Wolfgang Büld's 1978 documentary, *Reggae in a Babylon*, are excellent documents of the desperate plight of black youth in London during the late-1970s – poverty, police brutality, and racism shape the lives of those who sojourn in Babylon. As actor and Aswad guitarist Brinsley Forde (who played the leading role in *Babylon*) has commented,

> *Babylon* opened a lot of people's eyes to what was actually going on around them, as stuff like that had never been seen on the big screen before. Even some of the actors that were in it learned from it... After the riots in London, Lord Scarman asked to see *Babylon*, because it was very, very close to the mark of what was happening in London and the political problems and social problems that were happening in England (quoted in Bradley 2002: 115).

Regardless of its cultural influence and its interpretation beyond Rastafarianism, within the Rasta community the concept of 'Babylon' – and, of course, the related concept of 'Zion' (see Davidson 2006) – is of supreme doctrinal and ideological importance:

> Any interpretation of the significance of Rastafari must begin with the understanding that it is a conscious attempt by the African soul to free itself from the alienating fetters of colonialism and its contemporary legacies. To accomplish this freedom, Rastas have unleashed an ideological assault on the culture and institutions that have dominated the African diaspora since the seventeenth century. In Rastafarian terms, this consists of 'beating down Babylon'. They have also embarked on an ambitious endeavour of 'steppin' outa (out of) Babylon' to create an alternative culture that reflects a sense of their African heritage (Edmonds 1998: 23; see also Davidson 2006).

In a way not dissimilar to Martin Luther's understanding of 'the Babylonian captivity of the Church', Rastas think of themselves, their religion, and their culture in terms of captivity within an ungodly system. This, of course, is in keeping with Judeo-Christian apocalyptic discourse (Partridge 2005: 279–88). Throughout the Bible, and particularly in the Book of Revelation, Babylon functions as a symbol for all that is evil, brutal, oppressive, and, indeed, Satanic in the world. This understanding is regularly expounded in dub and roots reggae, the concern with Satan, for example, being particularly explicit in Max Romeo's 'Chase the Devil' (*War ina Babylon*, 1976). Hence, as in Christian eschatology, so also in Rastafarianism, the fall of Babylon is a central motif. Most Rastas will know by heart such biblical passages as the following: 'Fallen! Fallen is Babylon the Great, which made all the nations drink the maddening wine of her adulteries' (Rev. 14:8).

Also typical of Rastafarian millenarian thought is the belief that there are dark forces working against the 'people of Jah', systems that psychologically and culturally propagate values and beliefs antithetical to the good life. This, of course, is also true of other millenarian movements (see Partridge 2005: 279–327). Indeed, there is a sense in which Rastafarians work with understandings of sin and evil very close to those developed in liberation theologies, in that both understand sin to be corporate as well as personal. Just as individuals, according to Christian theology, are understood to be sinful, so political organizations, social structures, multinational companies, and world systems can also be understood as inherently evil – concrete manifestations of Babylon. Rastafarian cosmology, therefore, is often highly dualistic. The world is understood in terms of a cosmic struggle between the profane and the sacred, darkness and light, Babylon and Zion. It is not surprising, therefore, that Rastas believe themselves to be part of a sacred history leading to the fall of Babylon and eschatological victory.

Concerning the Rasta's artistic contribution to the collapse of Babylon, there is an emphasis on the supernatural efficacy of the spoken word – understood to be a manifestation of divine presence, with the power to create and destroy. Rastas can 'chant down Babylon'. That is to say, they can verbally contribute to the destruction of Babylon through protest, poetry, and, of course, popular music. Consequently, understood in these terms, Rasta music becomes a powerful religio-political tool with eschatological consequences.

It is, therefore, not surprising that, as Rastafarianism became embedded in British society, and as many white youths identified with at least some of the emotional frustration felt by the black community, its conceptual framework began to make sense of the world for them too. The following comment by Cashmore is worth quoting in full. However, first, it should be noted that the quotation appears in the 1983 edition of his important sociological analysis, *Rastaman: The Rastafarian Movement in England*, which was originally published in 1979. Between 1979 and 1983 Britain experienced significant social upheaval, including race riots. It is with this recent history in mind that he writes the following:

> ...the concept of 'Babylon' has provided a new, exhilarating awareness of the world for thousands.

> In Babylon, there is a theory of a world divided and a vision of how it will someday be totally transformed...Babylon is the system controlled by whites and perpetuated in such a way as to preserve their interests – at all costs. To do so, blacks have to be kept down and exploited, while whites keep their domination. It is a system that has its origins in the European expansion of the seventeenth and eighteenth centuries, yet remains intact in the present day. In the 1970s it was an idiosyncratic and maybe bizarre way of interpreting the world. In the 1980s, with blacks disproportion-

ately affected by spiralling unemployment and overrepresented in crime statistics, Babylon *is* the world. In fact, it is not even necessary to be black.

The riots of 1980 and 1981 gave some indication of the growing currency of Babylon as a way of interpreting the world. The young black's anger was directed not so much at specific people or groups of people, but at the system of Babylon, its institutions and symbols of exploitation; amongst them, the shops on which blacks depended for their food, the property in which they lived, the people who were meant to protect them. The rioters destroyed their own ghetto communities because those communities reminded them of the system of exploitation...

Even if the Rastas were not directly responsible for precipitating the riots, they certainly stimulated the kind of consciousness behind them (1983: vi).

While it is unlikely that all the disenfranchised young British black and white youths, for whom this consciousness was an inspiration, fully understood its implications, it is clear that, like The Ruts, they felt that it articulated ideas and frustrations with which they could identify. The Ruts' anthemic track 'Babylon's Burning' (on *The Crack*, 1979) is a particularly good example of a song that, using the argot of Rastafari, comments on the palpable 'anxiety' of the period and the violence that often erupted in the streets: 'You're burning the street, you're burning the ghetto'.

Secondly, for many Rastas, while there are some authorities that are important for determining correct belief and conduct, particularly the Bible, such authorities must submit to the authority of 'the self'. Religious doctrines, biblical ideas, and their correct interpretation must be personally verified by privately 'head resting' (meditating) with Jah or by communally 'reasoning' at 'groundings' (religious discussion sessions).[26] As indicated above, many Rastafarians do not feel the need for the usual apparatus of institutional religion and are suspicious of much biblical interpretation, particularly that of traditional, mainstream Christianity. Moreover, head resting and groundings, it is argued, lead to spiritual 'knowledge' rather than simply 'belief' – 'overstanding', rather than simply understanding. (This Rastafarian penchant for neologisms will be discussed below.) Moreover, trust in the judgement of 'the self' is supported by a strong immanentist theology which understands the divine to be *within* 'the self'. To 'know' the will of Jah and to know 'truth' one must meditatively turn within. This, in turn, has led to a certain spiritual eclecticism within Rastafarianism. That is to say, some Rastas will search for truth and enlightenment in all areas of human faith and endeavour. Zephaniah expresses this approach well:

> ...most importantly, [Rastafarianism made me] aware that I could find... Jah... by looking inwards. I learnt how to read any one of the many holy books, or any scientific book, and apply my own intelligence. I learnt that rituals may be of some use, but that there is a way to find a direct line to Jah through meditation and inner peace. I was no longer concerned with understanding the world, I was now able to 'overstand' it. For the Rastafarian, to overstand is to apply your mind to a subject and discern a greater meaning than the obvious one... In other words, overstanding goes beyond basic understanding... Rastafari has taught me to be at ease with my 'self' and not to fear silence, darkness, or solitude. Although I work for and celebrate the community, and value my relationship with others, there is also a great sense of liberation in not relying on the congregation to find strength. Nor do I feel the need for a building as a centre of worship. Jah is always with me. To be precise, Jah is part of me. So I have no real need to look outward for Jah. To find and worship Jah, I must look within (2005: 447).

Hence, although some organizations, such as the Twelve Tribes of Israel, will emphasize the role of a particular prophet and the importance of a particular set of sacred writings, for many there is no absolute authority to which one might turn in order to decide what is orthodox and what is heterodox.

Related to this understanding of the spiritual life is the concept of 'I' – 'the most important word and letter in the Rasta vocabulary' (Mulvaney 1990: 39) – and, in particular, 'I 'n' I' (the relational self and often simply a synonym for 'we') which is ubiquitous in Rasta argot or 'dread talk'. Indeed, it should be noted that such 'dread talk' or 'I-ance' is, as Velma Pollard comments, 'a comparatively recent adjustment of the lexicon of Jamaican Creole to reflect the religious, political and philosophical positions of the believers in Rastafari' (1982: 17; see also Pollard 1985; Homiak 1995). As such, at one level, it is a linguistic attempt at separation from the dominant culture of Babylon (see Hutton and Murrell 1998: 50–51), an expression of resistance that asserts the dignity of the Rasta in an oppressive context. Hence, whereas, in Jamaican creole, the first person singular is often expressed by the pronoun 'me', as Joseph Owens comments, Rastas 'would seem to perceive this creole pronoun "me" as expressive of sub-service, as representative of the self-degradation that was expected of the slaves by their masters. It makes persons into objects, not subjects. As a consequence, the pronoun "I" has a special importance to Rastas and is expressly opposed to the servile "me"' (1983: 62). However, at another level, it is also fundamentally theological. Johnson-Hill's analysis of 'I 'n' I' is particularly helpful in drawing out these deeper references:

> In the first instance it connotes a sense in which the self is believed to be inextricably linked with symbols of divine agency such as Selassie-I, Rastafarl, God or 'Jah'. For example, the 'I' of the self is fundamentally related to the 'I' in Selassie-I. That is, in the Rastafarian imagination the Roman numeral in the title 'Hailie Selassie I' does not connote 'the first' as much as it evokes the 'I' of the I-n-I relation (1995: 22).

More specifically, the expression I 'n' I (prominent within dub and roots reggae) suggests the collapse of the Christian creator–creature dualism. As Johnson-Hill puts it, 'by referring to oneself in the first person singular as I-n-I, there is a virtual equation between oneself and God' (1995: 22–23). Moreover, the emphasis on 'I' also assumes a basic theological anthropology that infers the unity of the human race, in that Jah's presence within all persons constitutes an ontological unity. Properly understood, therefore, I 'n' I is a theologically sophisticated way of emphasizing the immanence of the divine and the three-fold relationship between the self, other selves, and the divine Self. Indeed, the prefixing or suffixing of 'I' is used so frequently within Rasta argot that it appears almost arbitrary. However, while it may often be used simply to foreground their sense of difference, for others it actually expresses sacred-ness and/or the individual's ontological continuity with the referent: 'Ivine' (divine); 'Iration' (creation); 'Ises' (praises); 'Iman' (Rastaman); 'Ites' (heights – meaning spiritual highs); 'Ital' (vital – indicating a concern to live authenti-cally in relation to nature); 'Itals' (pure food, usually vegetarian – see Homiak 1995: 142–51); 'Ifrica' (Africa); 'Irie' (meaning both spiritually high and feeling good – a common Rasta greeting); 'Isus' (Jesus).

Thirdly, the Rastafarian understanding of truth is rooted in a particular kind of experience referred to as 'dread'. Dread is an important term, in that, while it is sometimes used as a synonym for 'Rasta', it is actually invested with mul-tiple levels of meaning. As Rex Nettleford comments, 'all the responses known to Jamaican history…psychological withdrawal, black nationalism, apocalyptic exultation, denunciation, and the bold assertion of a redemptive ethic…were… invoked by the Rastafarian and made to take form in one grand and awesome expression – dread' (Nettleford, in Owens 1979: viii). Others have described it as a term indicative of 'a serious political, economic, spiritual, cultural, or social situation' (Mulvaney 1990: 25), or 'the awful, fearful confrontation of a people with a primordial but historically denied racial selfhood' (Owens 1979: 3), or 'bad' and 'terrible' (Pollard 1982: 30). However, generally speaking, it is indicative of the righteous person in 'Babylon' – the 'true Rasta man'. Hence, again, it is the language of resistance. The Rasta is a dread, in a dread situation, using 'dread talk', and wearing dreadlocks.

Fourthly, concerning the last of these, again a range of cultural, religious, and political ideas are invested in the symbolism of 'dreadlocks', which, for a Rasta, 'is a sacred and inalienable part of his identity' (Chevannes 1994: 145; see also Chevannes 1995c). Most scholars agree that the hairstyle began in the early 1950s – possibly the late-1940s (see Chevannes 1994: 152). However, there is some disagreement over the origins of dreadlocks. Some, for example, have drawn attention to photographs in the Jamaican press of Africans with similar hairstyles, which may have influenced young black radicals (Campbell 1997: 95–96; Edmonds 2003: 58–59). It has also been noted that Howell's guardsmen at the Pinnacle commune adopted dreadlocks to accentuate their fierceness (Waters 1985: 46). This is related to the fact that for some Rastas dreadlocks are believed to resemble the mane of the lion, which is significant, not only because Ras Tafari is understood to be 'the Lion of the Tribe of Judah', but also because the lion is a cultural symbol of strength, vitality, superiority, and royalty (Clarke 1994: 90). Again, it has been persuasively argued by Barry Chevannes that dreadlocks were a trademark of the Youth Black Faith, a group of young radical Rastas founded in 1949, which exerted considerable influence on the movement up until the 1960s. 'They were young and on fire with the doctrine. They were, for the most part, men who entered adolescence in the late 1930s, who left the countryside for Kingston and embraced the faith' (1995b: 79). Certainly, for the 'locksmen' of the Youth Black Faith, matted long hair was a direct countercultural reaction to established social norms, in that they were aware that in wearing dreadlocks they were adopting the role of the outcast. Indeed, more specifically, they aligned themselves with the derelicts of Jamaican society who having 'lost touch with reality, had no reason to conform to the acceptable human standards of behaviour. They lived in the open on sidewalks or under trees, foraged among the refuse, talked only to themselves or not at all, were unwashed and foul-smelling' (Chevannes 1995b: 88). One such person who was well-known and a keen follower of Garvey was known as 'Bag-a-Wire' – celebrated by King Tubby in his 'Bag A Wire Dub' (available on King Tubby & Friends, *Dub Like Dirt*).[27] He was shunned by society and taunted by children. The Youth Black Faith identified with the plight of such individuals as Bag-a-Wire. Not only did they believe themselves to be outcasts, but they did not want to be part of the society that shunned the derelict. Hence, they became what society abhorred. Hence, in a similar way to punk styles in mid-1970s Britain, the wearing of dreadlocks was an active gesture of subcultural resistance to dominant cultural norms. More specifically, as Kobena Mercer has argued, 'the historical importance of Afro and Dreadlocks hairstyles cannot be underestimated as marking a liberating rupture, or "epistemological break", with the dominance of white-bias' (1994: 104). From a specifically Rastafarian perspective, the hairstyle declared that 'dreadness' was a way of life. Indeed, for a time the true Rasta was expected to wear dreadlocks: 'Many who did not embrace dreadness fell by the wayside, and by the 1970s, Rastafarl no longer recognized "combsomes" (i.e., those who combed their hair, depending on circumstances) as authentic members of the movement' (Rowe 1998: 76–77). Because the combing and straightening of hair, which was common at the time, was understood to be acquiescence to the norms imposed on blacks by white society, it was seen by some as a betrayal of black beauty and culture. Benjamin Zephaniah, for example, recalls that, as a young Rastafarian, he 'used to be very critical of Rastafarians who had children that did not wear dreadlocks' (2005: 447).

Whatever the actual origins of dreadlocks, most Rastas will provide biblical justification for the style, invoking the following passage from Numbers 6 concerning the Nazirite vow:[28]

> And the Lord said to Moses, 'Say to the people of Israel, when either a man or a woman makes a special vow, the vow of a Nazirite, to separate himself to the Lord...all the days of his vow of separation no razor shall come upon his head; until the time is completed for which he separates himself to the Lord, he shall be holy; he shall let the locks of the hair of his head grow long' (Num. 6:1, 5).

Hence, although there are those who wear dreadlocks simply to accrue a little subcultural capital – thereby, to some extent, defusing its ideological power – devout Rastas nowadays tend to understand their cultivation to be an act of both consecration and resistance. Hence, the cutting of a Rasta's locks is understood as an act of desecration – rendering the sacred profane (which, as Rastas will point out, is what Delilah and the Philistines did to the Nazarite Samson in order to remove his strength – Judges 16:19). Moreover, sometimes dreadlocks are also understood to be spiritual aids, 'psychic antenna' that establish a mystical link between the self and Jah, in that they facilitate communication with Jah and the mystical 'earthforce'.[29] Since dreadlocks 'connect Rastas with earthforce, the shaking of the locks is thought to unleash spiritual energy, which will eventually bring about the destruction of Babylon' (Edmonds 2003: 59–60). Consequently, in accordance with the millenarian milieu, dreadlocks symbolize the inevitable collapse of Babylon. As such, some Rastas believe that the very sight of dreadlocks generates fear and trembling in the Babylonian heart – hence the term '*dread*-locks' is invested with another more militant meaning.

Overall, however, dreadlocks signify obedience to Jah Rastafari, pride in African culture, a commitment to natural beauty (over against artificial beauty – which is often determined by white values and preferences), and opposition to the values and social mores of Babylon. Although this spectrum of meaning is greatly diluted for many in the West, particularly non-Rastafarians, dreadlocks are nevertheless understood to be a symbolic way of confronting and standing apart from mainstream society:

> the symbol of the dreadlocks became a lasting sign of black pride in Jamaica, a symbol which was to gain international significance after reggae artists took on the physical appearance of the Dreads and exposed this culture of the hills to the saloons of London, Frankfurt, and Amsterdam, to the big musical centres of Los Angeles and New York, and ultimately to the Independence celebration in Zimbabwe (Campbell 1997: 96).

Furthermore, as indicated above, the countercultural significance of dreadlocks has transcended Rastafarianism, becoming particularly significant in white subcultures such as, in the UK, the New Age travellers and 'crusties' of the late-1980s and 1990s rave scene (see Partridge 2006; Hetherington 2000). Again, following on from rave subcultures, within the contemporary dub scene, many white artists wear dreadlocks to indicate both continuity with Rasta culture and also, more broadly, countercultural commitment. Long hair, of course, had become a popular signifier of countercultural sympathies during the 1960s and, hence, dreadlocks which were, at least superficially, invested with like meanings were interpreted similarly by white hippies – just as the Afro was in the United States. However, this assimilation of dreadlocks into the dominant culture has led some black cultural theorists to question the significance of the hairstyle as a signifier of radical black pride and resistance. Mercer, for example, noting the political nature of *all* black hairstyles, in that they 'each articulate responses to the panoply of historical forces which have invested this element of the ethnic signifier with both social and symbolic meaning and significance' (1994: 104), makes the following worthwhile points. On the one hand, dreadlocks and Afros '*counter*politicized the signifier of ethnic and racial devalorization, redefining blackness as a desirable attribute. But, on the other hand...within a relatively short period both styles became radically *de*politicized and, with varying degrees of resistance, both were incorporated into mainstream fashions within the dominant culture' (Mercer 1994: 104–105; original emphasis). In seeking to understand this process of depoliticization, he makes a useful distinction between 'two logics of black stylization', namely, one which emphasized the *natural* and one which, as with 'combsomes' (i.e. those who straighten their hair), emphasized *artifice*. Concerning the latter, his point is that the process of straightening hair – and thereby acquiescing to the dominant culture – is a process of *cultivation*. To cultivate 'is to transform something found "in the wild" into something of social use and value, like domesticating a forest into a field. It thus implies that in its natural given state, black peoples' hair has no inherent aesthetic value: it must be worked upon before it can be beautiful' (1994: 105). Of course, he recognizes that all human hair is cultivated to some extent, 'shaped and reshaped by social convention and symbolic intervention'. However, the point is that the nature–culture relationship is important for understanding both the political significance of dreadlocks and also why they were absorbed into mainstream white culture. Both hairstyles signified an embracing of the 'natural' over against the conventional. The Afro, for example, became a symbol of black pride, of Black Power.

> By emphasizing the length of the hair when allowed to grow 'natural and free', the style countervalorized attributes of curliness and kinkiness to convert the stigmata of shame into emblematics of pride. Its name suggested a link between 'Africa' and 'nature' and this implied an oppositional stance *vis-à-vis* artificial techniques of any kind, as if any element of artificiality was imitative of Eurocentric, white-identified, aesthetic ideals (Mercer 1994: 106).

Of course, it is important to note that dreadlocks are not actually *natural*, in that they have to be carefully cultivated. In other words, it is a style constructed to look natural and alien. As such, it is a political statement, constructed in opposition to white, Eurocentric cultures and codes. Dreadlocks are explicitly constructed as ethnic and countercultural signifiers in *this* Western context. They would not be readily recognized as African in Africa. Although we have noted that there is some evidence of Africans adopting a similar hairstyle, it would appear that they did so tactically in order to appear alien. This seems to have been the case with the Mau Mau in Kenya in the 1950s. Hence, in contemporary Africa, not only would such styles *not* signify Africanness, but, on the contrary, they would, as Mercer argues, 'imply an identification with First World-ness' (1994: 112). However, as far as we are concerned, the point to note is that, while not explicitly African, the style spoke of naturalness (perhaps even drawing on European Enlightenment ideas such as Rousseau's Romanticist myth of 'the noble savage'); it spoke of freedom; and it functioned as a symbol of countercultural resistance in Babylon. To this limited extent, the meaning of the style was understood and appreciated by hippies and other counterculturalists. Indeed, by the late-1980s, inspired by the punk rejection of commodified hippie culture and the 1970s fashion of wearing combed hair long, some – particularly those inspired by green politics and some form of Paganism or other eco-spirituality (see Partridge 2005: 42–81; 2006; Hetherington 2000) – turned to dreadlocks to express both 'the natural' and also an attitude, if not an ideology, of resistance to dominant culture.

Finally, and perhaps most controversially, Rastafarians practise the sacramental smoking of ganga. Although not all Rastas smoke ganga,[30] there are a great many who do take 'the chalice' or 'kochi'/'cutchie'/'kouchie' (large water pipe) or 'chillum' (conical or cylindrical pipe) or 'spliff' (long cigarette). Seeking to ground their practice in sacred history, most find biblical warrant for the use of ganga in passages such as Gen. 1:29 ('And God said, Behold, I have given you every herb bearing seed, which is upon the face of the earth') and Rev. 22:2 ('And the leaves of the tree of life are for the healing of the nations'), and even apocryphal sources which, they believe, indicate that it grew on the grave of Solomon – thus supporting the belief that it engenders 'wisdom' (see Junique 2004: 16, 47). For example, the following words are printed on the album cover of Jah Power Band vs. Sly and the Revolutionaries, *Sensi Dub*, Vol. 7/1: 'The Herb of Wisdom which was found in the Tomb of Solomon is for the Healing of the Nation'. Moreover, many Rastas declare that not only does it have biblical support, but also that its value can be empirically verified, in that it is actually good for a range of physical maladies and particularly efficacious for spiritual healing. In other words, it not only relaxes, but, in a similar way to psychedelic religionists (see Partridge 2005: 121–22; 2003), they claim that 'the holy herb' is a source of inspiration, in that its use makes one more receptive to the divine within (see Bilby 1985: 86–89). It also liberates the oppressed mind: 'The proper use of herbs has a central role to play in freeing the mind from the *fuckery* of colonialism. It provides the inspiration necessary to transcend alienating structures of thought. Herbs...are the key to the lock of understanding; God chooses to reveal himself through herbs' (Yawney 1978: 169; original emphasis).

Using numerous terms and neologisms – e.g. collie herb, sensemina (sensemilla), lamb's bread, king's bread, Jerusalem bread, strength, kaya, maka, hola (holy) herb, weed, wisdom weed, and healing of the nations – the significance of ganga is conspicuously evident in reggae and dub, being frequently referenced in album artwork, lyrics, track titles, and during live performances (see Shapiro 2003: 209–22). Moreover, although we will be returning to the use of cannabis in relation to dub in a later chapter, it is worth noting here that, not only do the echo and reverb[31] of dub and its sonorous bass give it a mystical, ethereal quality, but (as many users have related to me) the genre seems to produce atmospheres conducive to the psychological effects of cannabis. The use of the offbeat opens up spaces that encourage states of mind very similar to those induced by cannabis. This, in turn, lends itself to spiritual interpretation. This particular quality of dub is identified in David Toop's eloquent description:

> Dub music is like a long echo delay, looping through time. Regenerating every few years, sometimes so quiet that only a disciple could hear, sometimes shatteringly loud, dub unpicks music in the commercial sphere. Spreading out a song or a groove over a vast landscape of peaks and deep trenches, extending hooks and beats to vanishing point, dub creates new maps of time, intangible sound sculptures, sacred sites, balm and shock for mind, body and spirit (1995a: 115).

Toop's description is significant because it is an emic appreciation of the genre – a view of dub from the inside. From this perspective it is not difficult to see why cannabis use might significantly contribute to the creation and appreciation of dub.

Moreover, we will see in the following chapter, that, because the relationship between counterculture, popular music, and spirituality had already coalesced in Western society during the late-1960s, Rasta culture and reggae found a receptive subculture when it went 'outernational'. Perhaps even more so than long hair, from the mid-1960s cannabis became increasingly de rigueur for many popular musicians, for those fascinated by alternative spiritualities, and for those with countercultural sympathies (see Sherman and Smith 1999: 81–117). Bearing this in mind, it is something of an omission that the few early academic discussions of reggae and race within the emerging discipline of cultural studies, which tended to be informed by neo-Marxist theorizing – as was particularly evident at the influential Centre for Contemporary Cultural Studies (CCCS), University of Birmingham, UK – underplayed the significance of ganga, spirituality, and, indeed, dub. Perhaps the most well-known CCCS theorist to write on reggae, Hebdige, provides little analysis in his *Cut 'n' Mix* (1987) of the significance of spirituality within roots culture and hardly mentions the ubiquitous use of ganga (see also Hebdige 1974, 1976b; Centre for Contemporary Cultural Studies, 1982). Of course, it was important for such theorists not to contribute to a tacit racism that simplistically linked drugs to black youth cultures. (As I have noted, Benjamin Zephaniah pointed out to me that this has been a particular concern of his.) However, to neglect fundamental emic elements – as if they are peripheral, insignificant, or not worthy of serious academic scrutiny – is not only patronizing, but perpetuates and, indeed, engenders basic misunderstandings.

Concluding Comments

As noted in the Introduction, much of this chapter might appear rather divorced from a discussion of dub, particularly dub in the UK. However, as well as providing general background information important for understanding the context in which the genre arose, it also introduces key concepts and themes which will be developed in subsequent chapters in order to explain the continuing significance and appeal of the genre within certain subcultures. Whether we think of the self-removal of the Maroons from the world of the plantation, or the culture of West African indentured labourers, or the millenarian themes of Afro-Christianity, or the Ethiopianism of Back-to-Africa politics, or the deification of Haile Selassie I, or the sacralized use of 'weed', or the I 'n' I mystical identity of the self and the divine, as I have indicated, they have all significantly contributed to the religio-political discourse of reggae and dub. Indeed, were it not for this history and culture, roots reggae and dub would never have appeared in the forms that they eventually did.

2 Rastafarian Music, Sound-System Culture, and the Advent of Dub

Focusing particularly on the development of popular music in Jamaica, this chapter continues the discussion in the previous chapter, in that it makes explicit the integration of Rastafarianism and reggae. Although reggae has rapidly evolved, for many musicians and listeners its connections with Rasta culture are central and thus hermeneutically important. Indeed, for many, roots reggae is explicitly religious music. This, we will see, becomes enormously important when considering the influence and significance of dub, much of which explicitly references spirituality.

Just as Rastafarianism has drawn on African, African-Caribbean and Judaeo-Christian traditions in the construction of its belief system, so also Jamaican popular music has drawn on these cultures and traditions (as well as specifically British music[1]). Afro-Christian worship, for example, which had much in common with traditional African forms of worship, had a formative impact on the development of Jamaican popular music. Indeed, the anthropologist I. M. Lewis has argued, in his influential study of shamanism and spirit possession, that almost everything that can be said of a West African indigenous religion, such as the *bori* cult, 'applies with equal force to the analagous Christianized slave cults of the Caribbean and South America' (2003: 93). As noted in the previous chapter, much Afro-Christianity encouraged dancing, verbal interaction with the preacher, glossolalia, drumming, and similar practices to those found in African ecstatic religion. Hence, it was, as Dick Hebdige has noted,

> easy for the slaves to insert the old African call and response pattern into the Christian service. Instead of just sitting quietly and listening to the minister, the congregation would add to or cut across his sermon with their own responses. In this way, the preacher would "ride" the developing mood. He could give voice to the feelings and fears and hopes of the people. And together, preacher and congregation formed a bond (1987: 47).

Furthermore, there is rhythm in this interaction, in that the speech 'ebbs and flows and builds up to a crescendo along the line of repeated phrases just like a talking blues or a rock song or a piece of improvised jazz' (Hebdige 1987: 49). His point is that this approach to worship has had an impact on the development of reggae: 'the talking back and forth between the preacher and his congregation, the "righteous" sermons, the use of a limited number of familiar stories (Moses, Daniel, etc.) – all these have been taken over and used in reggae music' (1987: 49; cf. Abrahams 1976). However, whilst this is true, it is African and early Rastafarian religious music that has had the biggest formative impact on the genre.

Nyabinghi and the Emergence of Rasta Drumming

Central to Rastafarianism in Jamaica is 'Nyabinghi'.[2] As with many Rastafarian terms, Nyabinghi has several meanings. Firstly, it was a term introduced into the movement by Howell. Possibly after reading a dubious newspaper article about a militia force led by Selassie called the Niyabingi Order of Ethiopia, he adopted the word as a rallying cry for Rastas, emphasizing that it meant 'death to black and white oppressors'.[3] Nyabinghi thus became code for the violent overthrow of the government (see Johnson-Hill 1995: 18–19). Secondly, it became an orthodox, primarily spiritual faction of Rastafarianism (Clarke 1994: 49). Thirdly, it is an official 'gathering of the brethren for inspiration, exhortation, feasting, smoking [ganga], and social contact' (Barrett 1997: 120–25). Finally, related to the latter, it is sometimes used of a genre of music that consists of chanting and drumming – so-called because it is played at Nyabinghi gatherings (Edmonds 2003: 100–102; Davis 1997: 254) – the most influential exponent of which was Count Ossie (Oswald Williams).

Showing the deep influence of African music (see Nagashima 1984: 56–57), Rastafarian music was (and still is today for many Rastas) Nyabinghi, a modified version of African drumming known as Burru (or Buru, Burra). Indeed, although overstating his point a little, James Davis nevertheless makes the following worthwhile comment: 'Ironically, reggae isn't authentic Rasta music – Nyahbinghi drumming is' (Davis 1997: 254). Of course, as we have seen, drumming was not unusual within Jamaican culture, having already been practised within the Maroon communities, within Myalism and, more broadly, within Afro-Christianity.[4] Indeed, many of the melodies and harmonies are drawn from Christian hymnody. However, scholars have tended to focus on Kumina – a Jamaican ancestor religion with roots in West African belief systems – and have sought to make explicit links between Nyabinghi drumming and that practised within Kumina (Bilby and Leib 1986; Burton 1997: 115, 123; White 1984).[5] However, not only has this connection been questioned (see Nagashima 1984: 72, 77–78), but the thesis is offensive to many Rastafarians. This is because, as Kenneth Bilby and Elliot Leib have found,

> in spite of a respect for the 'Africanity' of Kumina drumming, [Ras-
> tafarians] disapprove of certain fundamental aspects of the Kumina
> religious experience, such as ancestral spirit possession and the
> emphasis placed on the continuing participation of the dead in the
> affairs of the living. Many younger Rastafari today, and some elders
> as well, categorically reject the idea that Nyabinghi music has roots in
> Kumina (Bilby and Leib 1986: 23; Nagashima 1984: 78).

However, having said that, a survey of work done in the area, as well as an
evaluation of the significance of early figures, Count Ossie particularly, does
suggest some continuity. For example, there is clear evidence that Ossie, the
principal early influence on the development of Rasta drumming, was taught
by those steeped in the Kumina tradition. Consequently, it is difficult to argue
that Nyabinghi drumming was not, to some extent, influenced by Kumina
ritual drumming (Reckford 1977: 8–9; 1998: 239–40). Indeed, it has been
pointed out that

> West Kingston of the 1940s and 1950s – the period when Nyab-
> inghi drumming was born – was a cauldron of competing cultural
> and musical styles and forms, all of which were interacting with and
> influencing one another. The rural migrants who were flowing into
> Kingston from all over the island in search of opportunities gravitated
> mainly to West Kingston, bringing with them their varied musical
> traditions (Bilby and Leib 1986: 23).

These included both Burru and Kumina traditions. Hence, again, it is very
likely that there would have been at least some cross-fertilization. Indeed,
it has been persuasively argued that Howell's Pinnacle community regularly
used Kumina drumming during worship (Chevannes 1979: 151). Moreover,
that many Rastas migrated to the West Kingston slums of Back-O-Wall and
the Dungle (where much early Rasta music was developed) following the
destruction of the Pinnacle community by police in 1954 (Edmonds 2003: 38)
adds further support to the thesis linking Kumina to Rasta drumming.

Whatever the significance of Kumina ritual drumming for Nyabinghi,
there is some consensus concerning the influence of Burru drumming (Reckford 1977: 6–8; Hebdige 1974: 20–21; Edmonds 2003: 100–102). While many
Rastafarians insist that their music has its genesis within early Rastafarianism and is, therefore, unique to the movement, Verena Reckford has found
that even some Rasta musicians 'willingly admit that their music, the vital
drums and riddims, is an adoption, and that they were first the drums and riddims of *Burru* music' (1977: 6). Bearing in mind that much Jamaican popular
music was a development of that which emerged in Afro-Christian revival-

ist traditions, the rhythms of which were, to some extent, Eurocentric, it is perhaps not surprising that there was a strong desire within Rastafarianism for an authentically African music. This they found at the gatherings of the Burru men, who, they believed, had protected African ritual drumming from other cultural influences. Hence, it is worth noting at the outset that the use of drumming in Rastafarian music is invested with explicit political significance, in that it is understood to be an explicit and *undiluted* medium of African culture and, therefore, a challenge to the Eurocentric culture favoured by many middle-class Jamaicans.[6]

While little research has been produced on early Burru music, Reckford's work in the 1970s found oral traditions which suggested that Burru was popular during the years of slavery, it being one of the few forms of African-derived music allowed by the colonial masters – largely because of its function as a 'work metronome for the slaves' (1977: 6). That said, Yoshiko Nagashima discovered an oral tradition suggesting that Burru existed '*since* the emancipation of the slaves' (1984: 70; emphasis added) and was considered, not merely a musical genre and subculture, but, to some extent, a religion in its own right. However, whatever the precise history and religo-cultural significance of Burru, what is clear is that, following the abolition of slavery, Burru drummers moved into the poorer areas of the cities, particularly West Kingston, and eked out a living doing casual work. When the Rastas also moved into the area and began to form their own communities, they found that they had much in common with the Burru men: both were social outcasts, distrusted by mainstream Jamaican society and often treated as criminals by the police (Reckford 1977: 6); both were committed to the retrieval of African culture; both understood themselves in terms of cultures of resistance to the dominant Eurocentric Jamaican culture. Moreover, the Burru-Rasta relationship was mutually beneficial. Put simply, the Rastas had an ideology and a spirituality that appealed to the Burru men, and the Burru men had a musical tradition and a communal dance (the Burra) that appealed to the Rastas. However, it soon became apparent that the ideological and spiritual pole of this relationship was dominant, in that, by the late 1930s, many Burru men had become Rastafarians. Indeed, Burru culture itself began to evolve in a Rastafarian direction, their dance gatherings eventually becoming Nyabinghi sessions – large religious and cultural conventions at which there would be drumming, chanting and dancing (Barrett 1997: 120–25).

As to the nature of Burru drumming, there were three drums: the bass drum, the repeater (*peta*) and the *fundeh* (for photographs and illustrations, see Reckford 1977: 2–5, 7, 9). Although the drumming technique evolved within Rastafarianism, the three drums were kept – but were now called *akete* drums. The bass drum is much the same as a military band bass drum, although the skins are, ideally, those of a ram goat – because, according to Count Ossie, 'the ram goat is less vociferous than the ewe by nature, and its bleat is of a lower tone. Hence, the skin when hit is of a desirable low pitch' (Reckford 1977: 3). Held on the lap, the drum is hit with a padded stick. The *fundeh* is longer and narrower than the bass drum, with a body usually made of barrel staves or other strips of wood. Producing an alto pitch, it rests on the floor, is held between the knees, and is played with both hands, the fingers being kept in a closed position. Finally, producing a soprano pitch, the repeater is a shorter drum than the *fundeh*. It too rests on the floor, is held between the knees, and is played with the outer edges of the hand and the finger tips in an open position. Possibly the most difficult to master, as one Rasta commented, 'a man really have to have the music in him to really play that repeater well. As a matter of fact, him mus' really learn fi play the *fundeh* well good before him touch the repeater so him can know how fi work in the repeater on the other riddim them' (quoted in Reckford 1977: 6).[7]

Generally speaking, there are two forms of Rasta drumming. Related to the 'riddims'[8] (particularly the drumming patterns) in West African music, those that are slower and more reflective are used in 'churchical' (i.e. religious)[9] music and the faster and lighter riddims are typical of 'heartical' songs, which tend to be more socio-political. On the Wailers' album *Burnin'*, for example, 'I Shot the Sheriff' uses a heartical riddim, whereas 'Rastaman Chant' is an excellent example of a churchical drumming pattern, as, indeed, is much early Nyabinghi music – much of the singing of which is explicitly indebted to Christian worship. More generally, ska was influenced very much by non-religious, heartical riddims, whereas roots reggae tends to be slower and, therefore, more churchical in tone. As Hebdige comments, 'as the years went by, many younger reggae musicians and singers took up the religious ideals of the Rastafarian cult. Their music became heavier, slower, and more serious. And from that time on, the influence of the churchical riddims of Rastafarian drumming began to be heard in reggae music' (1987: 58). To some extent, this slower, heavier, more churchical trait within reggae is accentuated in dub. Indeed, there are several good examples of this within British dub. Noah House of Dread and African Head Charge in particular have developed churchical rhythms. For example, 'Far Away Chant', from African Head Charge's 1981 album *My Life in A Hole in the Ground*, places the emphasis firmly on the use of *akete* drums. More striking still, however, is their thoughtfully religious album *Songs of Praise* (1990), on which 'Free Chant (Churchical Chant of the Iyabinghi)' and 'Dervish Chant' are excellent examples of the development of churchical drumming patterns. Another good example, one which specifically uses a vocal introduction recorded at a 'grounation' camp in Jamaica, is Jah Shaka's 'Rastafari Dub', on *Dub Salute 2* (1994).

As noted above, a direct line of influence from Rastafarian drumming to reggae came in the form of Count Ossie (who died in a car crash in 1976), who has been described as 'a kind of living bridge between Rasta music and early ska' (Hebdige 1987: 58). Indeed, according to many (including Ossie himself), it was he who originated identifiably Rasta drumming (see Reckford 1977: 8). It all began, apparently, in the Salt Lane area of the Dungle, West Kingston, where groups of Rastas would meet to discuss the ideas of Garvey and Rastafarian spirituality. 'Yuh know', Ossie explained to Reckford, 'man was anxious them time to know the answers to puzzles 'bout himself and his race. Is during that time, down there at Salt Lane, under a tree, where we generally meet and reason, that the idea of the music come to me and I work at it, until we have what people call today *Rasta Music*' (Reckford 1977: 8). Having nurtured his interest in music in the Boys' Brigade, in the 1940s Ossie was drawn to the Burru drumming of 'Brother Job', who eventually became his mentor. However, as he couldn't afford his own drums, he had to practise the riddims he was being taught on upturned paint cans. Eventually, he had his own set of three drums made and began to develop his own riddims. By the late 1940s Rastafarian camps, 'grounations', were conspicuous events at which Jamaica's leading jazz musicians would often mingle with Ossie's drummers (see Katz 2004: 33). In the early 1950s Ossie set up a large Rasta camp at Adastra Road in Rennock Lodge, East Kingston. This quickly became the hub of the new musical movement. 'Anyone who wished to "talk" in music with Ossie and the others was free to come along and join in one of Ossie's long, open jamming sessions. Though no recordings of these original sessions have survived, the music broke new ground and was to prove extremely influential' (Hebdige 1987: 58–59). Notable musicians who attended these gatherings included Roland Alphonso, Tommy McCook, Don Drummond and Rico Rodriguez, all of whom were to become key influences on the development of ska. Indeed, Rodriguez (who was to become particularly important within British reggae) lived for long periods of time at Ossie's camp, was a close friend of the drummer, and a formative influence in his group, the Mystic Revelation of Rastafari (Katz 2004: 38–39). This eclectic mix of influences in early Rasta music is clearly evident on Ossie's seminal triple album *Grounation*. The album includes Rasta chants, drumming, jazz-based instrumental expositions, and even, as Steve Barrow and Peter Dalton comment, 'a couple of songs that sound akin to British folk airs' (1997: 163). Indeed, while this musical eclecticism is evident within reggae to some extent, we will see that it becomes particularly prominent again in dub.

Bearing these alliances in mind, it is perhaps not surprising that, as well as his development of Rastafarian religious music, Ossie is also known for his involvement with the emergence of ska. This, of course, is culturally significant, in that, largely as a result of Ossie's religious input, ska contributed both to the mainstream recognition of Rastafarianism within Jamaica and also to the later confluence of reggae and Rastafarian religio-political thought. Of particular importance was the decision of Prince Buster (Cecil Campbell) to include Ossie and his drummers on what was to be a hit single by the Folkes Brothers, 'O Carolina' (1960). In the face of increased competition in the sound-system scene, Buster was looking for something new and, in particular, wanted to develop/exploit the emergent penchant for retrieving African culture. Hence, as Lloyd Bradley comments, 'he dreamed up a scheme to bring the Rasta master drummer Count Ossie and his troupe into the recording studio. Buster had loved Ossie's drums since childhood, when, in the pre-sound-system days, dancehalls featured big bands, with Ossie's groups often performing during intervals, and would climb trees outside just to sneak a peek' (2000: 59). The increasing popularity of Rastafarianism's Afro-centric spirituality and Garvey-ite political thought within the ghetto communities (though not, at this early period, within the Eurocentric middle-class suburbs) and Ossie's significant standing within the Rasta community meant that, apart from anything else, it made good commercial sense to include him. Buster was not disappointed. As he recalls,

> Of course, the radio wouldn't play it, because society was so terrible against the Rastas. First, they said they couldn't play it because they didn't think it was a record, because it wasn't constructed in the way American music was constructed. Then they admit they were afraid that it would mess up their advertising because the Rasta involvement would cause people to back out. But because my sound was so popular and I was playing this music – constant play – they were forced to (quoted in Bradley 2000: 61).

Consequently, it wasn't long before other musicians began to see the value of including Ossie and his drummers (see Barrow and Dalton 1997: 24–25; Bradley 2000: 59–62). Rival producers, Coxsone Dodd and Harry Mudie particularly, also encouraged Ossie and his drummers to accompany bands in their recording studios. 'It is difficult to gauge the importance of Prince Buster's "O Carolina"', notes Bradley.

> While in terms of actual musical construction it probably wasn't that influential, as a piece of cultural legislation it was enormous. For the first time[10] in the nation's history one of the few surviving African-

based artforms – a true articulation of black Jamaicanness – had become involved with a commercially viable mainstream expression. It was a bond between Rastafari and the Jamaican music business that is still in place to this day (2000: 61).

The Rise of the Sound System

It is true that...many popular Jamaican artistes are untrained musicians whose crude musical offerings are an insult to the sophisticated ear... What should be taken into consideration when the criticisms are being made is that many listeners and practitioners of Jamaican pop music, especially in the area of 'dub' music, do not refer to their works as music or song, but as 'sound'. People will say that this or that artiste has released 'a great sound'; not a *song* but a *sound*, which does not necessarily have anything to do with pleasing melodic flow and so on (Reckford 1977: 4–5).

While we might want to question her understanding of the 'sophisticated ear' and, indeed, whether Jamaican music is as crude as she suggests, it is true both that many indigenous musicians were technically untrained and also that there is an emphasis on 'sound' within the culture. That said, this terminology derives less from the nature of the music than from the culture of the 'sound system' that had evolved since the mid-1940s in Jamaica. Indeed, the term 'sound system' became popular at a time when Jamaicans were listening to jazz and rhythm and blues – much of which could hardly be described as 'unsophisticated' or 'crude'.

In the 1940s and 1950s the principal musical genre in the ghettoes was mento, arguably Jamaica's first indigenous popular music (see Nagashima 1984: 81–82; Barrow and Coote 2004). Similar to up-tempo calypso, which became associated with it, the roots of mento can be traced back to nineteenth-century Jamaica. Essentially, mento emerged as a complex synthesis of Afro-European folk forms and Jamaica's quadrille bands. 'Unassociated with a church, ethnicity, or region, mento provided a common musical ground and quickly became Jamaica's national music' (Clayton 1999b: 1289). Indeed, like much contemporary reggae, it was frowned upon by the church and middle-class society because of its 'slack' lyrics, which were not only bawdy, but often explicitly sexual.[11] Although several mento songs were recorded during the 1920s by Carribean jazz musicians, and although the mento duo Slim and Sam, who performed in Kingston, increased the profile of the genre considerably, it was not until 1951 that true mento recordings first began to appear on 78 rpm discs, when Stanley Motta established his studio and began cutting local records. Indeed, largely as a result of Motta's entrepreneurial activity, the late 1940s and 1950s are often referred to as 'mento's golden age', in that increasing numbers of artists began to record mento songs in a broadening range of rhythms and styles. Moreover, this period is particularly significant, in that it witnessed not only the peak of mento's creativity and popularity in Jamaica, but also the birth of Jamaica's recording industry. That said, although these initial mento recordings were Jamaican, the records themselves were manufactured in London. Mento records were then shipped back to Jamaica and played on the radio alongside the increasing volume of North American jazz and rhythm and blues. Indeed, Jace Clayton makes the point that 'mento's grassroots popularity led Jamaicans to establish their own record labels and production facilities by the 1960s, in perfect time for Jamaica's independence in 1962 and the emergence of ska music' (1999b: 1289). However, the development was not quite as straightforward as he suggests.

By the early 1960s, mento was increasingly and disparagingly associated with its rural roots and unfavourably compared to the popular music being imported from Jamaica's largest and most influential northern neighbour, the United States. The music of such as Fats Domino and Louis Jordan increasingly appealed to an aspirational urban working class not wanting to be reminded of rural deprivation. Hence, as Winston Blake[12] comments concerning the early 1950s, 'Big band, that music was also our pop music here... That was the swing era, the big band era: Count Basie, Tommy Dorsey, Stan Kenton, Glenn Miller. The formative bands in Jamaica played that music as dance music' (quoted in Katz 2004: 2–3). Moreover, as a result of the development of radio technology, Jamaicans were, during the 1940s and 1950s, increasingly able to tune into transmissions from the southern United States. 'On a clear day these broadcasts could be picked up fairly easily, even on a battered transistor. And in West Kingston, the r&b [rhythm and blues] produced in New Orleans...became something of a craze amongst those rich enough or lucky enough to have access to a radio' (Hebdige 1987: 62; see also Katz 2004: 1–4; Beckford 2006: 29–30). This led to a growing fascination throughout Jamaican urban society with the music produced by particularly African Americans, especially jazz and rhythm and blues. However, as noted above, only relatively affluent, middle-class Jamaicans could afford both the radios and also access to venues where much of the jazz was being played. Indeed, it should be noted that, whereas mento was popular with many Jamaicans, there had been, since the 1930s, a thriving jazz scene and 'among the savvier of Jamaica's city-dwellers, jazz held greater currency'. Hence, Katz continues, 'in the economically buoyant post-war years big band jazz and swing groups remained the most popular music among the upper echelons of society' (2004: 2).

The point, however, is that a growing hunger for the authentically American product within the communities of the Jamaican poor, who could not afford the venues at which the best Jamaican bands played, led to the opening of a significant gap in the cultural market, which creative entrepreneurs such as Clement 'Sir Coxsone Downbeat' Dodd and Duke 'The Trojan' Reid could exploit. They assembled mobile audio units – which usually consisted of a turntable, a radio, and large speakers – in order to bring North American music to an infatuated public. These 'sound systems' played to increasingly large gatherings at dancehalls – the 'halls' usually being large, flattened, enclosed pieces of land (known as 'lawns'), which had been cleared for the purpose of dancing. As Steve Barrow comments, 'these dances in Jamaica are in the open. They're not in a hall. They call it "dancehall", but there's no hall. There's just the sky' (*Dub Echoes* DVD). At such venues, the music was heavily amplified in order, as Hebdige puts it, 'to convey the right sense of conviction'. Moreover, 'if people were to dance they had to hear the bass, which carried the important "shuffle" rhythm. So the systems got bigger, louder, and "heavier"' (Hebdige 1987: 62–63). These large and loud sound-system events became important social gatherings at which there would be stalls selling fruit juices, beer, and traditional Jamaican dishes. Owners of cafés, for example, ordered powerful amplifiers from North America or, increasingly, had systems built by local electricians in Jamaica. The sheer volume of such systems had the effect of rapidly drawing a large audience when played in the open air.

Central to sound-system gatherings, of course, were the disc jockeys, who were not only responsible for ensuring that the music played was the latest, but were also entertainers, performance artists, local superstars, concerned to foster larger-than-life personas. This reflected the fierce rivalry between sound systems. Although the entry fee to a sound-system event was low (about two shillings in the early 1960s), disc jockeys could make money. Moreover, there was significant kudos attached to attracting a greater following than one's rivals. Hence, much was invested in keeping fans loyal to sound systems through the playing of new and exclusive records.[13]

Such rivalry was – and still is to some extent – evident in the performances, pseudonyms and images cultivated by the disc jockeys. Names such as Duke Vin, Count Smith, Sir Nick the Champ, Tom the Great Sebastian, King Edwards, Duke Reid, Prince Buster, and King Tubby, and the wearing of crowns, long cloaks and other forms of power fashion is indicative of their self-dramatization and the culture to which they appealed. Indeed, some even sported weaponry. For example, Arthur 'Duke' Reid, a former police sergeant, was well known for wearing a .45 calibre magnum in a holster at his waist, a .22 pistol inside his waistcoat, and often carrying a loaded shotgun. Hence, not only were they cultural bricoleurs playing with symbols and styles of monarchy and aristocracy, but they often played with images of violence, presenting themselves as criminals, gangsters, and legendary outlaws.

Richard Burton's work on the significance of 'play' helps us to understand this element of Caribbean culture. Although writing more generally about styles of conversation and nicknames in the Caribbean, his comments are directly applicable to sound-system culture: 'this is a world of stylized, not actual, aggression, and while on the surface the men are affirming, or attempting to affirm, their superiority as *individuals*, deep down what they are acting out in the form of a competitive verbal ritual is their equality *as a group*. In the course of an evening's agonic exchange, male egos are both asserted and assuaged' (1997: 159; original emphasis). Informing this stylized violence, there was an indigenization of American screen images of 'heroism', gun cultures, and reconstructions of masculinity. For example, in the early 1960s the Skatalites were evoking other Western images of violence and masculinity when they entitled their major hit 'Guns of Navarone' (1964)[14] just as, a decade later, Bob Marley was very clearly evoking the gun culture of the Western in his 'I Shot the Sheriff' (1973). Indeed, that the Western became enormously popular within reggae culture indicates the direction in which the cultural winds were blowing.

> In the '60s, Jamaica was a nation with no television industry of its own, forcing it to rely on the United States for most of its screen entertainment. As is often the case when American movies are exported, the island received a steady diet of films short on refinement and long on action and cowboys. These films were enthusiastically embraced by Jamaicans, especially the working class of Kingston, who became serious connoisseurs of the spaghetti westerns made by directors such as Sergio Leone and Sergio Corbucci. By the late '60s Kingston open-air movie theatres, such as the Majestic and the Regal, would be packed for western double features, with the more emotional fans in the audience sometimes saluting on-screen heroics with live gunshots. Legend has it that one theatre was forced to show films on a cement screen after its regular one had been filled with bullet holes after one too many westerns (Morrow 1999: 64).

Not only did numerous reggae album covers depict artists as cowboys, but the artists and disc jockeys themselves took the names of characters and actors they had seen in the Westerns: Lone Ranger; Clint Eastwood; Lee Van Cliff (i.e. Cleef); Josey Wales; and Gregory Peck. Album titles included *The Good, the Bad, and The Upsetters* (1970), *How the West Was Won* (1981) – the cover of which was designed in the style of a 1960s film poster – *Clint Eastwood* (1969), *East-*

wood Rides Again (1970), and *Hot Shots* (1970) – the cover of which has a photograph of a woman wearing holsters and holding two six-shooters. Again,
when reggae artists perform and record together it is often described in competitive terms. Although the more irenic verb 'meets' is sometimes used to
describe the encounter, it is often used in the confrontational sense of 'versus',
which is also frequently used: *Scientist v Prince Jammy: Big Showdown* (1980);
Two Giants Clash: Yellowman Versus Josey Wales (1984); *Aggravators Meets the
Revolutionaries* (1987); *Kung Fu Meets the Dragon* (1975) – the last is one of
many titles reflecting the enormous interest in the martial arts engendered by
the Bruce Lee films, particularly *Enter the Dragon*. Similarly, within dub culture
there are numerous references to Hollywood movies and glamorized violence:
Sly and Robbie's *Raiders of the Lost Dub* (1981); Prince Jammy's *Kamikaze Dub*
(1979); Scientist's *Scientist Heavyweight Dub Champion* (1980), and *Scientist
Dubs Culture into a Parallel Universe* (2000) – the cover art of which mimics the
typical superhero comic duel.

Such posing is an example of performance rhetoric in which the signs and
codes used by artists are shared and understood by the audience. A similar
general point is made by Frith who, following Noël Carrol's analysis of 1960s
performance artists, comments that, on the one hand, the artist is *objectified*
as a medium of the art and, on the other hand, the artist is *subjectified* as the
site of the narrative. Concerning the latter,

> performance art described stage performers (actors, dancers) who
> now took themselves and their bodies as the objects or sites of nar-
> rative and feeling. Such performers no longer 'acted out' (or 'in') a
> playscript or choreographic score, but effectively *subjectified* them-
> selves: the implication of their work (which depended...on a degree of
> collusion from the audience) was that what was happening on stage
> was determined only by the nature, shape, technique, body, and will
> of the performers themselves, which meant...a new emphasis on the
> process of putting together and taking apart a *persona* (Frith 1996:
> 205; original emphasis).

Masculine, heroic, and often violent personas within reggae and dub were
powerful because they were interpreted by their initial audiences in terms
of their own, shared experiences living in poor, oppressed circumstances in
black, ghetto societies. They understood the rhetoric.[15]

Controversial though the emphasis on violence has become within Jamaican dancehall culture – particularly when articulated as part of homophobic
or misogynist discourse (see Boyne 2005; Cooper 2004: 145–78) – Carolyn
Cooper seeks to contextualize it. She argues that such rhetoric is part of 'an
indigenous tradition of heroic "badness" that has its origins in the rebellious

energy of enslaved African people who refused to submit to the web of bondage' (2004: 147). More particularly, in seeking to understand the rhetoric, we can understand such 'heroes' as rebel archetypes within a history of racial oppression and poverty. That is to say, as we have seen, there has been, within African-Caribbean history and culture, a celebration of the rebel and, more ideologically, of individual revolt against the system. However, as Hebdige has very helpfully argued, with the advent of dub and roots reggae, the rhetoric of rebellion was given a much wider currency, in that it was 'generalized and theorized'.

> Thus the rude boy hero immortalized in ska and rock steady – the lone delinquent pitched hopelessly against an implacable authority – was supplanted as the central focus of identity by the Rastafarian who broke the law in more profound and subtle ways. Not only did the Rasta fix the dreary cycle of solitary refusal and official retribution within the context of Jamaica's absent history, he broke that cycle altogether by installing the conflict elsewhere on the neglected surfaces of everyday life. By questioning the neat articulations of common sense (in appearance, in language etc.) the Rasta was able to carry the crusade beyond the obvious arena of law and order to the level of the 'obvious' itself. It was here, quite literally on the 'skin' of the social formation, that the Rastafarian movement made its most startling innovations, refracting the system of black and white polarities, turning negritude into a positive sign, a loaded essence, a weapon at once deadly and divinely licensed (1979: 37).

Hence, the transition from ska to roots and dub reggae saw the music become more self-consciously Afro-centric, the language more religio-political and less accessible, and, as Hebdige says, 'the menace more overt' (1979: 37). Songs about ghetto violence and street skirmishes were being replaced by songs such as Max Romeo's 'War ina Babylon'. In this sense, the words and themes themselves were being versioned, in that they were being deconstructed and reconstructed. There was a shift in signification. The violence became both ideological and spiritual, indeed eschatological. Hence, whether Max Romeo sang about 'War ina Babylon' or 'Chase the Devil' (both on *War Ina Babylon*) the meaning of the lyrics was deliberately ambiguous. Again, this is usefully indicated by Hebdige: 'it was fought around ambiguous terms of reference which designated both an actual and an imaginary set of relations (race–class nexus/Babylon; economic exploitation/biblical suffering), a struggle both real and metaphorical, which described a world of forms enmeshed in ideology where appearance and illusion were synonymous' (1979: 38).

The overall point, however, is that, whether the genesis of this particular form of rhetoric can be traced back to an energy inherited from Jamaican slaves and the idealization of the rebel, or needs to be understood in terms of play within Caribbean culture, or is simply the influence of North American popular culture, or, indeed, whether, as I have argued, it is a confluence of all of these streams of thought and action, such images of masculinity and stylized violence were clearly evident at an early period in the role-play of the first sound-system disc jockeys. Certainly much of this culture rose to prominence during the sound-system rivalry of the 1950s, emerging out of the desire to attract a large following. More significantly, however, this rhetoric then became sacralized and politicized within roots reggae and dub. That it did so is an important issue to which we will need to return, once we have outlined the rise and significance of the early sound systems.

In order to keep their sounds fresh, sound-system operators 'found that they needed to get their hands on particular records by lesser-known artists. Only outstanding tunes that were out of the ordinary would retain the dancers' interest and stop them from seeking more exciting sounds at an opponent's set' (Katz 2000: 11). Sound systems had employees who would seek out new records and also attend the rival dances in order to discover the nature of the competition. Each sound system would jealously guard their records, sometimes scratching off the title and artist's name, so that, even if rivals managed to get a look at the record, there would be no details to enable them to place an order. 'If they thought the artist on a new record sounded familiar, they would inform their bosses and immediate attempts were made to obtain a copy' (Clarke 1980: 58–59). Indeed, sometimes the efforts to remain popular by securing exclusive records went beyond merely staged violence and coercion. For example, it was generally known that Duke Reid's Trojan sound system (named after the Bedford Trojan truck) became one of the largest and most successful principally as a result of the intimidation and violence exercised by his henchmen. 'Reid was a large man who liked to throw his weight around, and had a legion of rough ghetto-dwellers and off-duty policemen who were always willing to lend a heavy hand' (Katz 2000: 12). Similarly, Vincent 'King' Edwards had a posse of unscrupulous minders on whom he could call to further his empire. Hence, rival sound systems without the muscle to defend their interests often found themselves intimidated or physically dismantled. For example, one of the earliest sound-system legends, Duke Vin, who had been 'the selector' (i.e. disc jockey) for Tom the Great Sebastian's sound system – the first to rise to prominence in Jamaica (Chang and Chen 1998: 19) – cut his losses and moved to London in 1954, where he established the first British sound system in Ladbroke Grove (Barrow and Dalton 1997: 12–13).[16]

The advent of the sound system was, as Katz points out, 'extremely important to Jamaica's popular culture, particularly as it was a defining element in setting-up the island's home-grown music industry' (Katz 2004: 3).[17] Overstating his significance somewhat, Kenneth Khouri claimed to be 'the complete pioneer of everything' (quoted in Katz 2004: 16). However, in terms of Jamaican record production, there is some truth to this claim, for it would seem that it was he who set up the first record-pressing and major recording business, the Federal Record Manufacturing Company. He had already, in 1954, established the Pioneer Company, which secured the Jamaican rights for the distribution of Mercury records. This was significant for sound-system culture, in that it hardly needs stating that purchasing records and even discovering new releases in Jamaica in the 1950s was far more difficult than it is nowadays. Although the major sound systems could afford to send people to North America to buy records, acquiring the latest rhythm and blues records was expensive.[18] Hence, once local talent could be recorded relatively cheaply, attention began to turn to the promotion of locally produced rhythm and blues. Although Bradley claims that Duke Reid was the first major sound-system man to 'dip his toe into recording when he began producing his own sessions in 1957' (2000: 41), there is evidence to suggest that Coxsone Dodd – who was making frequent record-buying trips to North America in the 1950s – had already begun making his own recordings at Federal by 1956 (see Katz 2004: 17). However, the key point to note is that by the close of the decade local Jamaican recordings were receiving an enthusiastic reception and all the major sound systems, some record shop owners, and other business entrepreneurs were manufacturing 45 rpm singles. Such entrepreneurs included, most notably, Edward Seaga, a Harvard-educated anthropologist, who would eventually become a prominent member of the Jamaican Labour Party and Prime Minister of the country (1980–1989), and Chris Blackwell – an aide-de-camp to the Governor General of Jamaica and the son of a wealthy, white English-born plantation owner and a Costa Rican-born Jewish mother with Jamaican ancestral roots going back to the seventeenth century – whose shrewd business acumen would lead, in 1959, to the founding of the enormously successful Island record label (named after Alec Waugh's 1956 novel, *Island in the Sun*), which was largely responsible for the initial globalization of reggae. In 1962, after securing licensing agreements with the leading producers, Blackwell moved to London in order to supply Jamaican releases to Britain's growing expatriate community. (Interestingly, one of the first records he released – 'Judge Not' – was produced by Leslie Kong and written by Robert Marley – though the surname was misspelled 'Morley'.)

These local records had also begun to be recorded at and played on Jamaica's first commercial radio station, RJR (Radio Jamaica Rediffusion), which had been established in 1950. In September 1959 a second Jamaican radio service was launched, the government-owned JBC (Jamaica Broadcasting Corporation). Moreover, whereas earlier in the 1950s few people could afford radios, by the end of the decade the situation had changed significantly.

> During the 1950s, Rediffusion introduced cable-fed wall boxes for their broadcasts, which were rented by the week and required neither electricity nor batteries, and when JBC went on air it was hooked up to this scheme. By 1960, 90 per cent of households in Jamaica had a working radio, a fivefold increase since 1945, a figure greatly assisted as the electrification of rural Jamaica progressed; by the early-1960s about three-quarters of this country was wired to the national grid (Bradley 2000: 91–92).

Furthermore, by the late-1950s, transmissions of jazz and rhythm and blues began to decline as another popular musical genre flooded the United States airwaves, namely rock 'n' roll. However, Jamaicans were not impressed with what they considered to be this less danceable form of music. Dodd's response was swift. Using local talent, he developed a homegrown synthesis of Jamaican mento and North American styles of music. One of the first bands to emerge playing this new hybrid music was Clue J and the Blues Blasters (Katz 2004: 32). Very quickly, there was a demand for original Jamaican dance music, a development which saw the evolution of what was known as 'blue beat', which the trombonist Don Drummond is credited with creating. The blue beat, as Reckford comments, 'was the Jamaican musician's interpretation of American rhythm-and-blues tunes with a mento flavour'. She continues, 'The combination worked, but the taste of success quickly erased the blues beat as Jamaicans began composing their own music, which became known as "ska"' (1998: 236).[19] However, the group that would eventually define the ska sound was formed by some of the principal musicians who had been meeting with and had been influenced by Count Ossie (McCook, Rodriguez, Alphonso, and particularly Drummond), The Skatalites. Moreover, while much of the lyrical content was, like that of mento, hardly 'churchical', there were a good many early ska songs that betrayed this later Rasta religious influence. Again, as noted above, the entrepreneurial Prince Buster was crucial here. Tapping into the growing influence of the Rastas' concern to promote that which was genuinely African and Jamaican, rather than American, his invitation to Count Ossie 'to participate in his sessions was always far more important than simply changing the beat' (Bradley 2000: 87).

Consequently, Jamaican rhythm and blues, which had incorporated elements from indigenous traditions (notably mento) and African rhythms, as well as European song patterns, gradually developed a distinctive sound. Moreover, the bass-heavy sound systems for which the records were produced also had a formative influence on the emerging genre. As Kevin O'Brian Chang and Wayne Chen comment, 'there seems to have been no conscious attempt to create anything definably Jamaican. The music simply evolved as the subtle difference from R&B became progressively more pronounced. No one can say when the first ska record was created, but it became progressively more obvious that the music the session men were playing just didn't sound like "regular" R&B anymore' (1998: 30). As well as the continuing popularity of the sound systems, the arrival of the jukebox in the late-1950s began to contribute to the dissemination and promotion of these new Jamaican rhythms. It is perhaps also significant that the arrival of ska coincided with Jamaican independence (6 August 1962), in that it was, in a sense, the advent of the island's musical independence. That is to say, the newly independent Jamaica now had a distinctive cultural export. Indeed, it is difficult to overestimate the impact of ska on the country's fledgling music industry. It was, as Katz has argued, 'a great creative stimulus to the island's musicians, as its emergence allowed for less curtailed and more honest musical expression. With the arrival of this uniquely Jamaican genre, the island's popular music had come of age' (2004: 29).

King Tubby and the Advent of Dub

The term 'dub' is now used widely and indiscriminately by producers of dance and ambient music. This is not entirely inappropriate, for, as the British postpunk producer Adrian Sherwood has commented, 'everything from hip-hop to techno and every other form of music right now has stolen ideas off dub, or incorporated those ideas' (quoted in Hawkins 1996). While there is obvious hyperbole here, the point is nevertheless an important one. The influence of dub permeates much contemporary electronica, dance, and urban music. Indeed, the phrase 'drum and bass', now the name of a particular genre of dance music, was originally coined by King Tubby. Dub was, as Mark Prendergast comments, 'hugely influential and in truth was the original Drum and Bass. Mixing, sampling, and rapping in truth all owe their origins to dub reggae' (2000: 457). The point is that there is an increasingly wide range of contemporary music that is explicitly and conspicuously indebted to dub, from the dance-oriented rock of a band like Death in Vegas to the indigenous Moroccan music of Aisha Kandisha's Jarring Effects,[20] to the more 'indie'[21] rock-oriented work of Primal Scream[22] and, of course, to the punk and post-punk music of bands such as The Clash, PIL, The Terrorists, Killing Joke, Bad Brains, and even the Welsh-speaking Anhrefn, some of whose album *BWRW CWRW* (1989) was mixed by the Mad Professor. Hence, Sherwood is right, the music industry owes much to the pioneers of dub. And, of course, thinking more broadly, reggae *per se* has influenced much contemporary popular music. Hip-hop, for example, is explicitly indebted to reggae. As DJ Kool Herc (Clive Campbell) – widely regarded as the founding father of hip-hop (e.g. Shapiro 2005: 212; Erskine 2003: 73; Prendergast 2000: 459–60; Veal 2007: 247–48) – has commented, 'ever since U Roy began this thing, it was just a matter of time before it got the international respect it deserved. Hip-hop and reggae are cousins' (quoted in Marley 2005: 42). Indeed, he himself was inspired by the Jamaican sound systems and deejays he had witnessed in Kingston during his youth. Having moved to New York in 1967 with his father, he continued to purchase imported Jamaican music, which directly influenced his own work with disco, funk and soul in the early 1970s. He wasn't alone of course, for, as Marley comments, many of the artists involved in the birth of rap were 'either born in Jamaica or had Jamaican parentage' (2005: 42; see also Shapiro 2000b). In more recent years, the streams of rap, reggae and dub have been very successfully reunited by such as the Asian Dub Foundation and Damian Marley, who worked with Method Man on 'Lyrical .44 (Dancehall Remix)', the 'AA Side' of his 2005 hit single, the superb 'Welcome to Jamrock' (for a useful introduction to the ubiquitous influence of the Jamaican system of recording and performance, see Manuel and Marshall 2006).

Before continuing with an overview and some analysis of the genesis of dub in Jamaica, it's worth noting that the term itself evolved out of earlier terminology used in the recording industry in the United States. This is significant because we will see that the genre has remained fundamentally related to recording technology. Traditionally known as 'black wax', 'soft wax', 'slate' or 'reference disc' – and in the manufacturing sector as an 'acetate' – the dub plate was a metal plate with a fine coating of vinyl. Recorded music would be pressed on to the dub plate, following which a 'stamper'[23] or metal master disc would be created in order to produce quantities of vinyl records. The process of transferring the music on to the vinyl-coated metal plate was known as 'dubbing' – just as adding sound to a film is also known as dubbing. Hence, the terms 'dub' and 'dub plate' are not solely allied to the genre of 'dub'. However, the point is that, with the demand for exclusive, unreleased music in Jamaican sound-system culture, the trade in 'pre-release' dub plates grew. And it is within this culture, hungry for new sounds and ideas, that the genre of 'dub' emerged.

The term dub, in the sense of a musical genre, was, therefore, originally applied to a remixing technique pioneered by Jamaican engineers and producers who were seeking novel and exclusive music (i.e. 'specials') for sound-system use. So successful was the technique that it quickly evolved as a relatively inexpensive and creative way of reusing rhythm tracks. Essentially, recording engineers produced tracks on which their efforts were often more evident than those of the original musicians. Indeed, the mixing desk and even the recording studio itself came to be understood as a musical instrument in that, in a similar way to a jazz musician's improvisation on a standard tune, the engineer is involved in the reconceptualization of a piece of music. As Jonathon Tankel puts it,

> remixing *is* recoding, the reanimation of familiar music by the creation of new sonic textures for different sonic contexts... The remix recording creates a new artefact from the schemata of previously recorded music. It is *prima facie* evidence of [Walter] Benjamin's contention that 'to an ever greater degree the work of art reproduced becomes the work of art designed for reproducibility' (quoted in Frith 1996: 242).

Indeed, in the final chapter it will be argued that it can be understood in terms of poststructuralism and postmodernism. However, the point here is that, to quote Simon Reynolds, 'what all [the] strands of dub theory share is the exaltation of producers and engineers over singers and players, and the idea that the studio effects and processing are more crucial than the original vocal of instrumental performances' (2000: 36). Indeed, Reynolds has even suggested that 'roots reggae is now almost exclusively valued for dub's legacy of disorienting studio techniques' (2000: 35). Similarly, Vivien Goldman insists that 'dub is Jamaica's greatest gift to the world' (2003: 2). Although these statements represent a rather Euro-centric, electronica-oriented perspective, with which many Jamaicans would not agree, they do indicate the wider cultural significance the genre has accrued since its humble Caribbean origins. Dub is now truly 'outernational'.

As to the history of dub in Jamaica, Barrow and Dalton have identified three phases through which it has progressed: firstly, the instrumental; secondly, the version; and finally, dub (1997: 199). Having said that, although some, such as Hebdige (1987: 82), wrongly conflate instrumentals and dub, the principal shift is between the instrumental and the version, dub being simply a later, more extreme and sophisticated development of the version (see Corbett 1994: 129). Indeed, the terms were almost synonymous, many dubs simply being referred to as 'versions'. This is still true today, a good example being the work of Ray Garza and Rob Hilton as The Thievery Corporation, particularly their *Versions* (2006). Similarly, the Berlin-based Mark Ernestus and Moritz von Oswald, who influenced the development of techno-house and electronica in the 1990s, have, since 1996, as Rhythm and Sound, released some striking roots reggae tracks with artists such as Sugar Minott and Cornell Campbell, most of which have B-side dubs, which they prefer to term 'versions' – the A-side tracks, which are already heavily dubbed, are stripped down even further into deep, bass-oriented 'versions' (e.g. *The Versions*; 'See Mi Version' on *See Mi Yah*).

The first phase of dub was the recording of 'instrumentals' principally for sound-system use. These were simply versions of reggae songs from which the vocals had been removed. This development, it appears, happened quite by accident. In the late-1960s, a wealthy and influential acquaintance of Duke Reid's, Rudolph 'Ruddy' Redwood, an entrepreneur who had, in 1957, established a record store and then a small four-speaker sound system (Ruddy's Supreme Ruler of Sound – SRS Sound System) in Spanish Town, was accidentally given a 'soft wax' (i.e. 'dub plate') without the vocals added. He quickly recognized a promising development. However, as is often the case with oral histories, there are several variations of this catalyzing event and the context that occasioned it. According to Bradley's sources, 'the music business was by now nationwide, and record men like Reid had to consider more than their immediate environment. Thus, they began doing what would have been unthinkable five years previously', namely 'giving unique, unreleased soft waxes to other sound systems' (2000: 312). In other words, according to Bradley, the previewing of 'dubs', which producers had formerly restricted to the patrons of their own sound systems, was now broadened to include other deejays, with whom, of course, they were not in competition. As Redwood himself put it, 'I get involve with Duke Reid, Coxsone, and then I started gettin' [exclusive] records from Duke Reid mostly – they call it dubs that time, yunno, special records' (quoted in Barrow and Dalton 1997: 200). It was this distribution of acetates prior to their commercial release that led to the revolutionary 'mistake'. The dubs were sent to Redwood via Byron Smith, one of Reid's Treasure Isle engineers.

> His Treasure Isle sound-system specials came via a disc cutter called Smith, who one day offered him a cut of The Paragons' 'On the Beach' (featuring John Holt) that he had, quite literally, forgotten to put the vocal track on. As he accepted the tune, Redwood was immediately aware of the possibilities of revisiting what was a proven popular record (it had already been released as a huge hit), and that night played the vocal and instrumental versions back to back. By the time the second record was a few bars in the entire lawn was singing along, and, according to those who were there, it was a totally spine-tingling moment (Bradley 2000: 312).

When Duke Reid, a gifted entrepreneur, heard of the success of this instrumental version, he was likewise not slow in recognizing the commercial opportunities this new development presented, and in the following year he reintroduced a stream of his old classics as instrumentals.

Bunny Lee, however, relates a slightly different version of the key event. Indeed, Lee's understanding is particularly appealing, since he claims to have been there at the time with King Tubby, who would later become the principal architect of dub.

> The first man who really start version by mistake is a man from Spanish Town named Ruddy, another wealthy man who can help himself. Him inna racehorses and him have a record shop and a big night club 'cross Fort Henderson, so when him come a Duke Reid and Coxsone, them give him any tape he want. One evening them a cut a dubplate – soft wax they used to call it. When them cut, it's difficult to put in the voice, and Smithy a go stop it and Ruddy say, 'No, make it run.' When it done, him say it art, and me and me and Tubbys stand up right there so, me look 'pon Tubbys and Tubbys look 'pon me. Saturday night him drop the singing cut first and the deejay name Wassy said, 'I'm going to play part two!' and the whole dancehall start to sing the song 'pon the pure rhythm – him have to play it about ten, fifteen times because it's something new. I say, 'boy Tubbs, you see the mistake whe Smithy make? A serious thing. The people a Spanish Town love it! You have to start something like that' (quoted in Katz 2004: 166).

While there is not a great deal to separate the two versions, Redwood's own recollection of events, recorded by Barrow and Dalton, seems to support Bradley's account: 'I was playin' at a dance one night and I was playin' this record [The Paragons' "On the Beach"] – it was released as a 45 before, but in those times they don't put the version on one side... So I was playin' it and it was nice for the people, so I went back to Smith – Smithy's was his name – he was cuttin' some dubs for me' (quoted in Barrow and Dalton 1997: 200). As Smith worked through the tapes of 'On the Beach', recalled Redwood, he inadvertently omitted the vocal track. Redwood liked what he heard. He continues:

> They used to call me Mister Midnight in Spanish Town. I used to come in at midnight and play fifteen or sixteen new music that nobody know about... I start playin'... I put on 'On the Beach' and I said 'I'm gonna turn this place into a studio', and I switch over from the singing part to the version part, cut down the sound and, man, you could hear the dance floor rail, man – everybody was singing. It was very happy and I get a vibe (quoted in Barrow and Dalton 1997: 200; see also Barrow 1995: 29–30).

Following this success, Redwood lost no time in cutting instrumentals of other popular Duke Reid tracks to play at his dances. Hence, whatever the precise details of this pivotal event, it is clear that, should we wish to identify a point at which the various cultural, musicological and technical developments of reggae begin to coalesce into the distinct, embryonic form of dub, it is here.

What can be understood as the second phase of the evolution of dub built on the success of the instrumental. Around the end of 1968 studio engineers began to take a greater role in the creation of what, by 1970, were termed 'versions'. It should be noted that this is rather different to other understandings of the 'version' within popular music. For example, Simon Frith has argued that a version is essentially a good cover of a song. It refers, he says, 'to a situation in which the "copy" is taken to improve on the original, to render it "bad" by revealing what it could have been'. For example, 'black covers of white originals are routinely valued positively (Ray Charles singing "I Can't Stop Loving You"), and rock arrangers are taken to make pop songs more interesting' (1996: 70). Reggae versions, on the other hand, aren't necessarily an improvement on the original and, moreover, nor do they try to be. Rather, they are understood as interpretations – texts that have been translated into a different musical language. Bunny Lee recalls what he believes to be the first use of the term 'version' in this sense: 'Tubbys just a bang on to U Roy [his deejay – Ewart Beckford]. U Roy come in an' say, "Part Two, another version" on 'Too Proud to Beg' with Slim Smith, and so the name version come in' (quoted in Katz 2004: 166). By the end of the 1960s, versions were rapidly becoming the preferred way to produce B-sides for Jamaican singles. On the one hand, they were enormously popular both with the public and also with the sound-system deejays,[24] such as U Roy, who would talk over them, and, on the other hand, they cut down on the costs that would normally be incurred when recording a separate track for the B-side of a single. The latter, of course, was an important consideration for a form of popular music that was principally developed in Jamaican ghettoes by artists with very little capital.[25] Indeed, 'riddims' were often recycled into new versions several times over. For example, one of my personal favourites, K. C. White's 'No, No, No', has been recycled numerous times. Although not strictly speaking a dub version, it was perhaps most famously reworked by Big Youth as 'Screaming Target', 'Screaming Target (Version 2)', and 'Concrete Jungle', all of which appeared on his seminal 1973 album *Screaming Target*. Another popular rendering of it, produced by Sly Dunbar, is Dawn Penn's 'You Don't Love Me (No, No, No) (Extended Remix)', on her *No, No, No* (1994). Again, a particularly creative dub version of it, 'Behind Iron Bars', was included on *African Dub All-Mighty: Chapter 4*, produced by Joe Gibbs and Errol Thompson.

In the era of dub and remix culture, it's not surprising that, eventually, whole LPs were released that were essentially compilations of versions of a single 'riddim'. The LP that began this trend, and one of the best examples of it, was produced by Rupie Edwards, namely *Yamaha Skank* – a longer version of which, including three extra tracks, was released by Trojan in 1990 as *Let There Be Version*. (Interestingly, a recent example of such an album is devoted to versions of, not a reggae 'riddim', but rather The Ruts' punk classic 'Babylon's Burning': *Babylon's Burning Reconstructed: Dub Drenched Soundscapes*).

Versions, of course, were not always instrumentals. They were often much closer to what we would now understand to be a dub remix. The core of the version was the rhythm, in that the bass and drums were brought to the fore, while the vocals and other instrumentation took a secondary role, being introduced and dropped out at the engineer's discretion. That said, it should be noted that, as Katz comments, 'rhythm tracks had already been used for more than one purpose before Ruddy and Tubby's experiments. At Studio One,[26] in 1965, for instance, Roland Alphonso blew sax on a song called "Rinky Dink", using the rhythm of Lee Perry and the Dynamites' "Hold Down" with the vocals removed' (2004: 166). However, as we will see, versions were quite distinctive in several respects, most notably for their foregrounding of the rhythm and their emphasis on the role of the engineer. For example, of particular note in the evolution of the version was 'Phantom' (1970) by Clancy Eccles, which, while an instrumental, was untypical in that it stripped the track down to the bassline. As such, it introduced the remixing technique that would become central to the development of dub.

It is now generally agreed that dub, in the contemporary sense of a fundamentally deconstructed version, first appeared in 1972 and was largely the creation of a single engineer, King Tubby (Osbourne Ruddock – 1941–1989), who is now considered by many informed commentators and musicians to be a towering influence, 'a giant of sonic history' (Prendergast 2000: 458). Taking his moniker from his mother's maiden name, Tubman, by all accounts he was a self-effacing man. Vivienne Goldman's memory of him is worth quoting:

> I met King Tubby. I went to his house with Kate Simons and remember that he was very charming and soft-spoken... He was sort of graceful, a low-key and laid-back individual. I remember that he had this filing cupboard... [and] he pulled open the bottom drawer, gets out this crown and puts it on his head for the pictures, bless him, entering into the showman role. He was obviously a very thoughtful, deep and creative sort of guy... (quoted in Colegrave and Sullivan 2001: 203 – see perhaps the most well-known photo of Tubby wearing the crown on the opposite page: 202).

Tubby's Home Town Hi-Fi, his Kingston sound system, which he formed in 1958 when he was only 17, quickly found success. Indeed, although it was termed 'Hi-Fi' because it was considerably smaller than other sound systems, nevertheless, at an event held in the Penwood district in the early 1960s, he was declared 'King of the Dancehall'. Thus he became 'King Tubby'. Bearing in mind his equipment's lack of power, it would seem that this appellation was given to him because of his creative experimentation with sound, an interest and skill which would eventually become central to the evolution of dub. Hence, successful though he was as a sound-system operator, as the 1960s progressed his creative skills came to the fore in the recording studio, having become, during the late-1960s, a noted engineer at Duke Reid's Treasure Isle. Whilst, again, using relatively basic equipment in his own studio – situated at the back of his home, 18 Dromily Avenue, Penwood, Kingston – Tubby developed the version, manipulating sounds in ways that are widely acknowledged to have been truly avant-garde (see, for example, Barrow 1995: 30–31; Barrow and Dalton 1997: 199; Bradley 2000: 314; Chang and Chen 1998: 45; Cox and Warner 2004: 113, 403; Hebdige 1987: 83; Prendergast 2000: 372; Toop 1995a: 116). By 1972 he had acquired a dub cutting machine – on which he could now make acetates for his and others' sound systems – and a two-track tape machine. He had also built his own mixer. Indeed, in a very real sense, for Tubby the art of dub impacted all stages of his work – the whole production process was dubbed. The renewing and reinventing was not simply musicological, but it was also technological, in that the very equipment used to produce the music was itself often a modification, a version of an original piece of equipment. For example, Prince (now 'King') Jammy (Lloyd James) – a friend and apprentice of Tubby who has since become one of Jamaica's most successful producers – comments that 'the reverb unit that we used to use there was a Fisher reverb, an' we change it to become a King Tubby and Fisher! The slides that we used to use, we change them from the original slides, because the mixin' console was so old you couldn't get replacement parts. We use other models to incorporate in that console' (quoted in Barrow and Dalton 1997: 205). Again, he constructed an echo delay unit 'by passing a loop of tape over the heads of an old two-track machine' (Barrow 1994). In other words, as with other early producer-engineers, such as Jammy (see Lesser 2002: 17), Tubby's background in electrical engineering enabled him to construct the equipment he needed to produce the innovative sounds he was looking for. In 1972, his creativity was given greater scope when, as a result of a deal brokered by Bunny Lee with Byron Lee's Dynamic Studios, he was able to purchase their old four-track mixing desk. Gradually, as Tubby's fame spread, his work began to grow, as producers left their tapes with him. Indeed, the increased volume of music that was being left with him seems to have encouraged him toward greater experimentation. The dub revolution had come of age.

Not only did Tubby's experiments receive an enthusiastic reception almost immediately, but his sound system, Tubby's Home Town Hi Fi, deejayed by U Roy, quickly became one of the leading sound systems in Jamaica. Part of the reason for this was undoubtedly because, from the outset, Tubby was interested in the aural experience of his audience, rather than simply producing good tunes to dance to. For example, not only was he the first to use separate tweeter boxes, but, again, his was *possibly* the first sound system to experiment with a reverb unit.[27] According to Dennis Alcapone (Dennis Smith),

> Tubby's was definitely the greatest sound ever to come out of Jamaica, in terms of the arrangements and the equipment and everything else. The technology and everything was just mind-boggling really. Them time, when you listen to King Tubby's sound, it look like it going to blow your mind. I listen to a lot of the sounds, like Duke Reid, Coxsone, and the whole of them, they was just normal sound, bringing out normal voices with normal bass and everything. Duke Reid and Coxsone, I think their tubes was 807, which is some big tubes, and their bass, it was heavy but it was not as round as the KT 88 that Tubby's came with. KT 88 was a smaller tube, and his bass was something else, it was just round like when you're kneading flour. With the 807, when the bass hit the box, you hear the box vibrate, but Tubby's now, the bass was just so solid. Then he brought in reverb, which wasn't introduced to the public before, reverb and echo… Tubbys have some steel [speakers] they used to put up in the trees, and when you listen to that sound system, especially at night when the wind is blowing the sound all over the place, it was wicked! (quoted in Katz 2000: 142; see also the similar comments made by U Roy in Katz 2004: 165).

As noted above, with the advent of Tubby's four-track studio in 1972, versions quickly evolved into what we now know as dub, which became established with a series of B-sides mixed by King Tubby released between 1972 and 1974 on the following labels: Lee Perry's Justice League and Upsetter; Glen Brown's Pantomine; Roy Cousins' Wambesi; U Roy's own Mego Ann; Augustus Pablo's Hot Stuff and Rockers; Winston Riley's Techniques; Prince Tony Robinson's High School; Bunny Lee's Jackpot; and Carlton Pattersons's Black & White (see Barrow and Dalton 1997: 204).

More significant still during this early period was the fact that, not only was Tubby working on B-sides, he was also beginning to record whole albums of dub, one of the most important of which was *Blackboard Jungle Dub* (1973) – originally entitled *Upsetters 14 Dub Blackboard Jungle* – produced by Lee 'Scratch'

Perry (Rainford Hugh Perry). Not only is this one of the first dub albums,[28] and certainly the first stereo dub album, as well as the first to include reverb, but it is still considered to be, not only one of Lee Perry's finest, but also one of the best examples of the genre *per se*. I remember the late John Peel, the veteran BBC Radio 1 deejay who, more than any other deejay, promoted dub in Britain during the late-1970s and 1980s, referring to it as one of the best albums he'd heard.[29] Similarly, David Katz has referred to it as 'nothing short of a master-piece' and 'one of the finest dub works ever recorded' (2005: 135).

While Tubby's experimental menu of dub was clearly central to his rapid rise in popularity, it has to be noted that, certainly in Jamaica, the verbal season-ing provided by his sound-system deejay consolidated that success. Although U Roy undoubtedly owed much of his own reputation to the versions Tubby provided, in turn, the sound benefited greatly from U Roy's 'toasting', which became enormously popular in the early 1970s (see Marley 2005). Basically, dub left space for the deejay to improvise. U Roy – nicknamed 'the Originator', because he was the first deejay to become famous for his toasting abilities[30] – was able to make full use of the spaces offered to him by dub, eloquently and idiosyncratically extemporizing. As Leroy Jodie Pierson comments:

> [His] thoughtful lyrics, flawless timing and totally original style, have earned him legendary status in reggae circles. His phrasing, tonal range, and keen improvisational skill bring to mind the work of jazz tenor sax greats like Coleman Hawkins and Sonny Rollins, and these same qualities have made him the most admired, influential, and imi-tated dj of them all... U Roy was the originator, the first dj to make hit records and the first dj to inspire a host of imitators and admirers to take up the microphone. His work was so pervasive, his success so profound, and his style so influential that it is hard to imagine artists like Prince Jazzbo, I Roy, Dillinger, Doctor Alimantado, and Big Youth ever even having a chance to record without U Roy's pioneering foun-dation work paving the way (Pierson 2002).

Although much of U Roy's toasting consisted of screams, shouts, rambling sen-tences and various catchphrases, it was also a medium for religious, political and social discourse – as is clearly evident on *U Roy* (1974), *Dread in a Babylon* (1975) and *Natty Rebel* (1976). Indeed, much toasting during the 1970s was politically and socially homiletic in tone. As Hebdige comments concerning I Roy's 1977 album *Crisus Time*, it was 'filled with sincere fatherly advice. And on his classic single "Black Man Time" (1974) I Roy [Roy Samuel Read] sol-emnly counsels the youth to leave the street corners and support the literacy programme which the government had just launched' (1987: 85). Indeed, it is significant that, with reference to *The Gleaner*, a Jamaican daily newspaper, the popular deejay Big Youth (Manley Augustus Buchanan) has been referred to 'the human *Gleaner*'. In other words, the deejay was explicitly understood to comment on contemporary issues and also act as spokesperson for the ghetto communities. Indeed, comment was often disseminated within days of the events. For example, Big Youth's 'Green Bay Killing' was released a few days after the notorious massacre of five Jamaican Labour Party gunmen from the Southside ghetto by Jamaica's Military Intelligence Unit in December 1977. Other, more direct criticisms of the killing and, indeed, of Michael Manley's refusal to try the soldiers responsible were voiced in Tappa Zukie's 'Murder' and Lord Sassafrass's 'Green Bay Incident'.[31] Similarly, within a week or so of the 1976 Notting Hill Carnival riots in London, Tappa Zukie provided critical comment in his 'Ten Against One' (now available on his anthology *Musical Intimidator*). 'Y'know', reflects I Roy, '[toasting is] a way of protesting against certain things, against certain physical and mental things that we Jamaican people have suffered' (quoted in Hebdige 1987: 88). As discussed above in relation to other forms of Jamaican popular music, it is the voice of resistance – a voice that has since been heard in rap, punk, and certain sub-genres of 'world music'. Hence, although overstating its difference a little, Hebdige is right to note that 'this process of feed-back – of three-way flow between artists, record producers and the audience – is what helps to make reggae different from other types of pop music. The distance between the performer and the fans is never allowed to grow too great' (1987: 88). This close relationship and the social significance of the sound system and toasting is graphically articulated in Franco Rosso's film *Babylon* (1980), which perceptively explores sound-system rivalry in London and the black community's struggle against ad-hoc and institutional racism (cf. Russell 1980). Indeed, more specifically, there are several discernible discourses that recur within reggae lyrics, some of the most important of which have been identified by Gilroy (2002). Firstly, viewed through the Afrocentric lens of Rasta, Eurocentric values allied to the concerns of the neo-colonial bourgeoisie are rejected in favour of pan-African solidarity and anti-racism. Secondly, there is a critique of the forms of waged labour offered to or withheld from African-Caribbeans, articulated through a celebration of leisure and, more particularly, a celebration of sex as symbolic of freedom from the oppression of menial or degrading labour. Thirdly, there is a questioning of the legitimacy of state authority determined by capitalist principles, articulated in terms of 'freedom', the nature of *real* 'crime', the call for equal rights, and the demand for justice. Finally, there is, as we have seen, an emphasis on the importance of historical knowledge and continuity with one's roots.

Returning to U Roy, it is a little surprising that it was not Tubby who first invited him into the studio to record his lyrical contribution on to a dubplate.

Others were quicker to capitalize on the successful meeting of the engineer and the toaster. The first to usher U Roy into the studio was another early pioneer of dub, Keith Hudson. He has since been followed by numerous influential producers and engineers, including Lee Perry, Bunny Lee (Edward O'Sullivan Lee), Lloyd Daley, Glen Brown, Joe Gibbs (Joel Gibson), Niney the Observer (Winston Holness), Tappa Zukie (David Sinclair), and, in recent years, by the UK's Mad Professor (Neil Fraser).

This brings us to the next point, in that, just as the success of U Roy paved the way for a plethora of other deejays to add their verbal contribution to dub (see Marley 2005), so in the production of the dub sound *per se*, while Tubby arguably dominated the genre in the early 1970s, there were numerous other producers and engineers emerging with new ideas that contributed to its evolution. Some of the most prominent were initially apprentice engineers working with Tubby at his studio and whose own particular styles are evident on some of Tubby's own releases, most notably 'Prince' Philip Smart, Prince Jammy and Scientist – the latter's work becoming enormously popular in Britain in the late-1970s and early 1980s (see Davis 1983b). Moreover, Tubby's small studio became a centre of activity, not only for the emerging Jamaican talent that he was fostering, but also for both long-established producers such as Bunny Lee and Winston Riley and for emerging talent on the international scene, such as Mikey Dread (Michael Campbell), who also would become enormously important in the UK. Indeed, the large amount of work Tubby was being offered led him increasingly to delegate the task to apprentices, particularly his protégé Prince Jammy, who had, in December 1976, just returned from a period working in Canada. Two years later Jammy would go on to establish his own label and, very significantly for his international reputation, to discover in 1978 and produce Black Uhuru (see Lesser 2002: 19).

Tubby's studio, however, was not the only site of dub exploration. A good example of one who was pushing at the boundaries of dub from a very early stage, almost independently of Tubby, was Errol 'T' Thompson. Working for Joe Gibbs at Randy's studio, in 1973 he produced one of the first three dub albums, namely *Java Java Java Java* (commonly referred to as *Java Java Dub*). However, perhaps the most important and influential albums produced by Thompson and Gibbs, all of which significantly helped to popularize dub during the 1970s, were the first three 'chapters' of *African Dub All-Mighty* (1975, 1976, 1978).[32] Whether it was a barking dog, a flushing toilet, or a ringing telephone, as the series progressed it seems as though few sounds were excluded from the final mix.

In the UK, especially *African Dub All-Mighty: Chapter 3*, which was particularly creative in its eclectic use of sound effects, found enthusiastic listeners amongst post-psychedelic rock fans (such as myself) weaned on Tangerine Dream, Can, Neu, Amon Düül, Gong, Hawkwind, and Brian Eno as well as like-minded punks looking for something new and challenging that was explicitly *not* progressive rock (see Letts 2007: 118). Indeed, the overall composition methods used by Jamaican producers and engineers would begin to have a significant impact on Western music during the 1970s. While the earlier recordings may have seemed a little crude to the ears of some rock fans, the advent of sixteen- and twenty-four-track studios enabled engineers to experiment with dub in complex and sophisticated ways that fascinated a growing Anglo-American audience keen to hear new avant-garde sounds. Indeed, it is worth noting here that this was a period during which there was a rapidly widening stream of experimental and ambient forms of music. Hence, because, as Erik Davis has put it, 'good dub sounds like the recording studio itself has begun to hallucinate' (2009a), it's hardly surprising that dub quickly found devotees beyond the African-Caribbean communities in Western psychedelic subcultures. What is surprising is that this is sometimes overlooked by historians of popular music. For example, Mark Prendergast's relatively comprehensive overview of ambient and atmospheric musics, 'from Mahler to trance', *The Ambient Century*, simply neglects any discussion of dub during this period – the genre is only given a couple of pages at the end of the volume (2000: 457–60). Indeed, even his discussions of contemporary artists who have not only been influenced by, but also experimented with dub, such as Bill Laswell, Massive Attack, The Orb, Tricky, and DJ Spooky, lack any substantial analysis of the significance of its techniques for their music. However, as Brian Eno recalls,

> producers and musicians discovered that tiny sounds could be made huge, and huge ones compacted. And, using echoes and reverberations, those sounds could seem to be located in a virtual space which was entirely imaginary. The act of making music becomes the art of creating new sonic locations and creating new timbres, new instruments: the most basic materials of the musical experience (2000: xi–xii; see also Doyle 2005).

This is both a good description of dub and also helps to understand why the genre was so inspirational for many musicians in the 1970s. Indeed, it's worth noting here that Eno himself, one of the most important composers for the emergence of contemporary ambient and electronica, became fascinated with the genre in the 1970s:

> The contemporary studio composer is like a painter who puts things on, puts things together, tries things out, and erases them. The condition of the reggae composer is like that of the sculptor, I think... A

> guitar will appear for two strums, then never appear again; the bass will suddenly drop out, and an interesting space is created. Reggae composers have created a sense of dimension in the music, by the very clever, unconventional use of echo, by leaving out instruments, and by the very open rhythmic structure of the music (quoted in Tamm 1995: 35–36).

Consequently, this 'sculptural' approach to composition, as Eric Tamm comments, 'influenced Eno's own way of composing' (1995: 36), as it did for many other musicians during the 1970s and 1980s.

By the 1990s the eclectic sampling described above had not only become almost de rigueur within both Jamaican and outernational dub culture, but had begun to shape the progress of dance, electronica, and digital music. Certainly many contemporary artists would agree with Rob Garza of the significantly named duo The Thievery Corporation: 'We believe that music is free for all to take and reinterpret. With samplers, musicians are able to take from the entire history of recorded music, and then create something new. The only thing you have to worry about is the lawyers' (quoted in Morley 2003: 293). That Garza and his colleague Rob Hilton are fundamentally influenced by dub is conspicuously evident throughout their work. Not only is their music permeated by dub rhythms and effects, and even samples of Rastafari elders (e.g. '2001: A Spliff Odyssey' and 'The Foundation' on *Sounds From the Thievery Hi-Fi*), but their 'kleptic' methodology can quite easily be traced to Jamaica's dub bricoleurs. 'They're such good stealers, they can nick echoes, they can nick space, they can nick holes, they can even nick different types of silence. Sometimes they don't seem to actually steal, but just sort of drain sound from one source or another. Sometimes they just plain shoplift' (Morley 2003: 292–93) – dub style (e.g. *The Richest Man in Babylon*, and the dub version, *Babylon Rewound*).

The Rise of the Upsetter: Lee 'Scratch' Perry

Alongside King Tubby, other innovative producers of dub who made an 'outernational' impact, particularly in Britain, include Lee 'Scratch' Perry, Augustus Pablo (Horace Swaby), Jesus Dread (Vivian Jackson), Glen Brown, and Keith Hudson – the last of whom produced *Pick a Dub*, the first dub album to be released in the UK. While it is always difficult and perhaps a little artificial to make such judgments, few would disagree that the most influential and culturally significant of these producers was Lee Perry, who is very often cited along with King Tubby as a father of the genre (e.g. Corbett 1994: 11; Reynolds 2000: 36; Williams 1997: 146; Kot 1997: 149).[33] Certainly Sherwood, an important British dub producer in his own right (to whom we'll turn in the final chapter), argues that 'the importance of someone like Lee Perry could not actually be measured', so significant is it (quoted in Hawkins 1996).[34] 'Utilizing low-tech studio equipment with a brilliance and panache that continues to astound record producers and music fans today, Perry earned a place along-side Phil Spector and Brian Wilson as a visionary studio wizard who transformed pop music production into an art form all of its own' (Davis 2009b). Heavily influenced, possibly more than other reggae musicians, by American blues, soul, and rock 'n' roll,[35] he became known initially during the 1960s for his work at Coxsone Dodd's Studio One. Much of his material during this early period was written for other artists, such as Delroy Wilson and Chenley Duffus, and was often explicitly 'slack'. However, following Haile Selassie's visit to Jamaica on 21 April 1966, which deeply moved him, he began increasingly to explore – both musically and personally – Rastafarian ideas (Katz 2000: 41). (That said, sexuality has continued to be, either implicitly or explicitly, a theme in Perry's work.[36]) Unfortunately, this interest in Rastafarianism exacerbated growing tensions in his relationship with Dodd. Although more open to Rasta music and ideology than Reid – who banned it from his studio throughout his entire career (a prejudice which eventually led to the demise of his Treasure Isle label) – and although he would later change his policy towards devotional Rastafarian songs when Marley and others made them lucrative, Dodd's early antipathy towards the faith and its music frustrated Perry. Moreover, as indicated, this frustration was simply one more crack in an already strained relationship. Not only did Dodd fail to credit Perry for the song writing he had done, but also he did not consider his voice mature enough to sing his own material. He also refused to pay him a fair wage for his services and, sometimes, did not pay him at all. Finally, throughout this period, Perry's own ideas were developing and, keen to experiment in the studio, he was 'angry that the musicians had to stifle themselves in their music... Dodd's sustained timidity in the musical realm was becoming increasingly bothersome' (Katz 2000: 41–42). Eventually the relationship became too difficult to sustain and Perry felt constrained to part company with Dodd. In Perry's words,

> It was what was happening between me and him that I have to leave because I wasn't getting any justice. And the songs them that I want to sing, him think them wasn't ready, that I didn't have a good voice to sing. That is what he think, so I decided that I have something that him no have, so I tell him that I'm going on a holiday. I didn't go to a holiday, I go to the studio behind him back (quoted in Katz 2000: 42).

Of course, Perry was in a strong position to go solo, in that, during his work for Dodd, he had gained not only a great deal of technical knowledge, but also many contacts within the Jamaican music industry. One such contact, who he would soon collaborate with, was Dodd's rival, Prince Buster.

Buster is an interesting man, in that, while we have seen that he was one of the key figures in the emergence of ska, he had quickly embraced the new more pedestrian and spacious sound of 'rock steady' – a short term, bridging subgenre between ska and reggae, and, as such, the next musicological step on the way to dub. In rock steady 'the regularly paced "walking" basslines that ska inherited from r&b became much more broken-up... [The] bass didn't play on every beat with equal emphasis, but rather played a repeated pattern that syncopated the rhythm. In turn, the bass and drums became much more prominent, with the horns taking on a supportive rather than lead role' (Barrow and Dalton 1997: 51). As noted above, this emphasis on a slower, bass-oriented rhythm, in which other instrumentation is secondary, would become central to the dub sound.

Before turning to look at Perry's contribution to dub, however, something needs to be said of a particular element of Jamaican society that provides the context within which he was working and to which he responded. In 1966, as well as the emergence of a new dance style for the slower music, the notorious 'rude boy' subculture rose to prominence. Rude boy criminality had been evident throughout the 1960s and condemning their activities had become 'an obsession for many Jamaican musicians between 1964 and 1967... They described a bitterly harsh urban landscape in which the rude boys were responsible for tension, violence and anguish' (Davis 1994: 51). Wearing distinctive 'short green serge trousers, leather or gangster-style suit jackets, and...eyes often hidden behind moody pairs of shades' (Hebdige 1987: 72), the rude boys were unemployed and angry. Like the punks a decade later in 1970s Britain, the rude boys challenged the established order, rejecting what they perceived to be a meaningless future of menial labour in a succession of poorly paid jobs. However, unlike many punks, and very much like British skinheads – with whom, in the UK, they joined in one of the most unlikely subcultural alliances (see Cashmore 1983: 41–44) – this anger was expressed in gang culture, violence and intimidation. Shaped by poverty and harsh conditions, gun-toting rude boys congregated on West Kingston's street corners.

> The rudies redefined Kingston street life into a phantasmagoria of insolence, mugging, trolley-hopping and purse-snatching. The rudies operated in a haze of ganga smoke and hallucinogenic white rum, and when the pressure dropped on them, the rudies got *really* crazy, indulging in haphazard, almost slapstick violence toward each other, but more likely toward anyone who happened to be in the alley and unarmed. They were ghetto poverty's shock troops and scapegoats,

whose self-image came from the lurid American gangster films to
which all rudies flocked with the same reverence that sends religious
people to church. The rudies loved the timeless moment in *Kiss of
Death* when Richard Widmark pushes an old woman in a wheelchair
down a flight of stairs, and *laughs*. They adored the early James Bond
films (the first of which, *Dr No*, was filmed in Jamaica). Later they
would revel in the brutal orgies of death depicted in... 'spaghetti westerns' like *Fistful of Dollars*... (Davis 1994: 50).

We have, of course, seen that the rude boys were not the only Jamaicans
interested in such Western films. Many musicians, including Perry, were fascinated by them, viewed them regularly, and often reflected their influence in
their music and subcultural style. However, the reason the rude boys are mentioned at this point is that a particularly notable attack on them was made by
Prince Buster in the guise of 'Judge Dread', an intimidating Ethiopian mag-
istrate.[37] His song 'Judge Dread' (1967), which was an instant and enduring
success, was recorded with Perry. It castigated the rude boys for terrorizing
African people in Jamaica and sentenced them to five hundred years' incar-
ceration and ten thousand lashes. However, whilst many, including the police
and middle-class Jamaicans, applauded the diatribe, others felt that such a
dualistic approach was too simplistic. Early songs, particularly Bob Marley's
'Rude Boy' (1965) – also known as 'Walk the Proud Land' and 'Rude Boy Ska'
– and Bunny Wailer's 'Let Him Go' (1966) – also known as 'Don Man' and
'Rudie Get Bail' – questioned Jamaican attitudes to its disadvantaged youth
and commented on their context of deprivation (both songs are available on
Bob Marley and the Wailers, *Wailing Wailers at Studio One*). Shortly after the
release of 'Judge Dread', in 1967, this same perspective was also adopted by
Perry on his 'Set Them Free' (available on *Archive*). In the guise of Barrister
Lord Defend, Perry argues that the rude boys are the product of a corrupt
system, shaped by colonialism and racist values. Similarly, 'Don't Blame the
Children' (which used the same riddim from 'Set Them Free' – which was, in
turn, taken from his 'Run For Cover') continued this defence of the rude boys,
whose education, it argued, had not prepared them for work, but had rather
sought to privilege the white, European version of history, rather than their
history – the history of the oppressed. These themes, along with a growing
commitment to Rastafari, gradually became prominent in Perry's work, and,
apart from his creative explorations in dub, account to some extent for his
subsequent appeal in the UK.

Following his contribution to Buster's rock steady success, Perry established an important and commercially successful relationship with Joe Gibbs.
As a novice in the industry, Gibbs relied heavily on Perry's expertise as a pro-

ducer and his well-known abilities as a talent spotter. The results for Gibbs were swift. Hits by such as Errol Dunkley, The Mellotones, The Pioneers, and The Versatiles ensured his position as a prime mover in the Jamaican music industry. However, again, Perry felt that his talents were not being adequately rewarded and, early in 1968, he left Gibbs, convinced again that he needed to develop his own ideas independently (see Katz 2000: 56–58). That said, continuing a working relationship with fellow engineer Lynford Anderson, he quickly established the Upset label, and then, finally, branched out on his own to establish the Upsetter label.[38] Also in 1968, in need of his own studio band, he approached The Hippy Boys: Aston 'Family Man' Barrett (bass), Aston's brother, Carlton Barrett (drums), Alva Lewis (guitar), Glen Adams (keyboards), and Max Romeo (vocals). As the band had not experienced much success with the few singles they had released, the offer from Perry seemed too good to refuse. Perry, however, immediately renamed them 'the Upsetters'. While the first few singles on the Upsetter label proved to be relatively popular, the enormous success of his 1968 release, 'People Funny Boy' (the first pressing of which sold 60,000 copies) ensured his future as an independent producer. Indeed, so successful was he at home and abroad that the British label, Trojan, which had been releasing Perry's work in the UK, launched their own version of the Upsetter label (see de Konigh and Cane-Honeysett 2003: 52–54; Katz 2000: 73–74). Apart from the considerable financial benefits – which enabled him to establish the Upsetter Record Shop on Charles Street in the heart of downtown Kingston and, indeed, import a Jaguar car from England – the deal was significant in that it was concrete evidence of his rising profile in Britain. In 1969 he achieved British chart success with 'Return of the Django' and, as a result, embarked on his first European tour. Indeed, not only was he beginning to receive international critical recognition as one of Jamaica's most influential producers (see Katz 2000: 69–101), but also it is arguable that he encouraged Bob Marley and the Wailers to produce some of their most innovative work.[39] Apart from Perry's own considerable input into their sound, it's also worth noting that Marley embarked on the road to success using Perry's studio band, who had left him to join the Wailers following the 1969 British tour – for which they claimed they had not been adequately paid, Perry having taken the lion's share of the earnings (which is surprising, to say the least, bearing in mind his own grievances against Dodd and Gibbs). That said, after an initial confrontation with Marley, Perry continued to produce the Wailers until 1973, when they left to join Chris Blackwell's Island label. (Although Marley took the Barrett brothers and the remaining Upsetters went their separate ways, Perry continued to apply the name to the various ensembles that worked for him over the next few years.)

While a great deal more could be said of Perry's career (the best study of which is unarguably Katz 2000), our principal area of interest is his work on dub, much of which was developed at the now famous Black Ark Studio, where 'Perry reckoned he would lay down the Ten Commandments of reggae' (Sleeper 1997: 160). Indeed, the Black Ark is now viewed through the mists of mythology as the inner sanctum of dub, the temple of 'Rastafarian psychedelia' (Davis 2009b), partly, I suggest, because its name is an inspired signifier, and, of course, it was terminated by a mysterious conflagration. The name was, apparently, 'conceived as an antidote to the Caucasian myth of Noah's Ark; symbolically likened by Perry to the Ark of the Covenant, it was meant to be a sanctuary for black Rastafarians' (Katz 2000: 182). Again, as we will see below, the fact that he was rumoured to be involved in Obeah and frequently spoke of dub in terms of an occult art which exposed and infiltrated the spiritual world, contributed significantly to the mythology of the Black Ark. Eshun's reflections are not untypical: 'The Black Ark switches on a technology-magic discontinuum. Operating the mixing desk demands that you explore its network of altering spaces. Perry crosses into its ghost dimension, walks through the temporal maze of aural architecture: "So me join the ghost squad longtime and them notice me as the Ghost Captain. I am the Ghost Captain"' (1998: 65; cf. Spencer 1976: 34). The idea of the ghost or 'duppie', of course, is central to both Jamaican occulture[40] and an understanding of the spiritual significance of dub. That Burning Spear's classic album *Marcus Garvey* had its dub counterpart entitled *Garvey's Ghost* is important as is the fact that, as Davis notes, 'Perry described dub as "the ghost in me coming out"' (2009a). As he says, 'dub music not only drums up the ghost in the machine, but gives the ghost room to dance' (ibid.; cf. Davis 2009b). Taking this occultural trajectory in slightly different, but no less significant direction, Perry also, as in a recent Guinness advertisement (available on YouTube[41]), refers to himself as an extraterrestrial, an alien visitor to this planet, one who appears to dispense gnosis. The point is that, with roots in West African/Jamaican folk religion and culture, Perry is not only a shamanic figure, for whom dub is an occult art, he is an occultural bricoleur. He has, as Davis comments, 'always been something of a stranger in a strange land', 'a trickster incarnate', 'a Caribbean techgnostic' (2009b), a self-constructed occultural centre of gravity.

That said, whilst the Black Ark is significant for the mythology of dub, as well as, of course, for some of its most important recordings, in retrospect, his prowess in the genre was directly forecast in early 1973 on his instrumental album *Cloak and Dagger* (recorded in 'true stereo'), two versions of which were pressed in London, one for the UK and one for Jamaica. Although the majority of the UK version comprises a collection of instrumentals, the truly avant-garde 'Caveman Skank' hints at things to come, in both Perry's work and also in remix culture generally: 'a thoroughly experimental and ironic dance number featuring toasting and vocal noises from Perry, along with running water, crashing cars, and voices lifted from an American sound effects record; the number opened with a Native American chief reading a portion of the Bible in Cherokee, and finished with the bustle of a public auction' (Katz 2000: 165). Again, decades before the imitative realism of projects such as David Holmes's *Let's Get Killed* (1997) and Thomas Brinkmann's *Tokyo* (2004) – both of which seek to replicate the noise of the contemporary city – Perry makes creative use of ambient street recordings, sound effects, and solicited comments from the general public. However, if the UK release of *Cloak and Dagger* foreshadowed the experimental nature of dub, the Jamaican version came very close to being an actual dub 'showcase' album.

> 'Retail Love', 'Creation', 'Sunshine Rock', and 'Wakey Wakey' were removed to make room for 'Sharp Razor' (a dub of 'Cloak and Dagger'), 'Side Gate' (a dub of Lloyd Parks' 'Professor Ironside'), 'Version Ironside' (a dub of 'Iron Claw'), and 'Bad Walking' (a dub of 'Rude Walking'). The Jamaican pressing of *Cloak and Dagger* thus contained another exclusive Upsetter experiment: it was the first album to have instrumentals followed immediately by dub versions of the same rhythm, in what would later be known as the 'showcase' style used for presenting vocal tracks immediately following dubs (Katz 2000: 165).

Although, strictly speaking, this is not a dub album, it is as close to dub that one can get without actually being dub, in that it introduces many of the ideas that were to be developed to great effect a few months later on *Blackboard Jungle Dub* (1973), which he recorded with King Tubby. More explicitly than *Cloak and Dagger*, *Blackboard Jungle Dub* indicated the type of sound that would evolve in the years to come at the Black Ark. As Barrow and Dalton comment,

> the Black Ark sound exemplified the Jamaican approach of making maximum demands of minimal resources. Sound textures that were unique anyway were developed further through working with four-track equipment, and the necessity of dumping completed tracks onto one track so as to free them for further overdubbing. This meant a loss of what would normally be thought of as 'sound quality' every time it occurred, but contributed to the incomparable feel of the Black Ark sound (1997: 165; see also Bradley 2000: 328 – the best introduction to the Black Ark sound is the triple album *Arkology*).

As to the origins of the Black Ark, in 1972, although Perry was at the height of his powers, frustrated by the costs and the constraints of studio time at Randy's,[42] he decided that he needed more space and time in the studio to allow his work to evolve freely. The only way he could be sure to secure the necessary time was by setting up his own studio. Fortunately, his success allowed him the funds to begin building almost immediately behind his newly purchased house at 5 Cardiff Crescent, Kingston. Perhaps more importantly, however, along with the construction of a space to create, at the end of 1972 he also began his fruitful relationship with King Tubby. However, it is clear that this was not a one-way mentor–student relationship. Indeed, it is difficult to determine the direction of the flow of influence. This confusion is not helped by Perry's own comments: '[Tubby] was brilliant. I thought he was my student. Maybe he thought I was his student. But it makes no matter. I'm not jealous' (quoted in Barrow and Dalton 1997: 204). More recently, in his wonderful advertisements for Guinness (available on YouTube), he introduces himself as 'the creator of dub'. Again, less generously, he states, 'To be fair and speak the truth, it wasn't...Tubby who brought about dub, but I alone! In those days, Tubby had a sound system and he want dubs for it from me. He'd come to Randy's studio where I worked at the time and spend days watching me messing about with the controls. As my dubs got famous and people like them, so Tubby try mixing up a few sides of his own' (from an interview with Kelly 1984: 7). (Tubby, of course, is not now alive to defend his role, having being senselessly shot outside his home by an unknown assail-ant in 1989.) However, despite Perry's stated recollection of the relationship, it has to be said that the evidence suggests the contrary, in that in the early stages it is likely that Tubby was the teacher (see Ehrlich 1983; see also King Jammy's and Bunny Lee's defence of Tubby's primacy in the film *Dub Echoes*). As Perry's biographer comments, in the early years of their relationship 'Perry began to use Tubby's skills with increasing frequency' (Katz 2000: 159). That said, Perry was an excellent student and, we have seen, quickly found ways to articulate his own sonic creativity. Indeed, some of Tubby's early work is explicitly indebted to him, one of the first discs mixed at Tubby's studio being Perry's 'French Connection' (available on *Complete UK Upsetter Singles Collection*, Vol. 4).

By the end of 1973, however, as Perry's producing skills were becoming honed, the Black Ark was operational and, with his creativity no longer cur-tailed, he began producing some of reggae's most significant and influential records – many of which found an appreciative and enthusiastic following in the UK.[43] With wiring installed by Errol Thompson, the studio was equipped with some of the best off-the-shelf equipment available in Jamaica: four-track Soundcraft board; Teac 3340 recorder for new material and 'a quarter-inch two-track Teac on which to mix down'; an Echoplex delay unit; Roland space echo; and a phaser unit (Bradley 2000: 325; Katz 2000: 180). That said, initially Perry's work was constrained a little by his silver Alice mixing desk, which he had picked up in England for, he recalls, less than £35. He also had 'an electric piano and a cheap copy of a Clavinet, a Marantz amplifier and speaker for guitar or keyboard use and a small drum kit... He also had a Grantham spring reverb and a tape-echo unit for effects...' (Katz 2000: 180–81).[44] The results were immediate, uncompromising, and successful. From 'Hurt So Good' by Susan Cadogan, which was to be an enormous success in Britain in 1975, to Max Romeo's 'War Ina Babylon' and Junior Murvin's 'Police and Thieves' – which would be particularly influential within punk and post-punk subcultures – as well as seminal reggae albums, such as The Heptones' *Party Time* and, especially, The Congos' *Heart of the Congos*, Perry produced a string of critically acclaimed international successes.

'His rhythm-building, tune deconstructing or extending of an original idea often went way past the point at which logic tells most people to stop, into a place where the instrumentation took on ethereal qualities' (Bradley 2000: 325). Unlike Tubby, he would not simply deconstruct and manipulate existing material by others, but rather began by recording his own material using his own studio band. He would then 'sculpt away at his vast stockpile of rhythms and tunes, adding, chipping bits off, echoing, distorting, and stirring in just about anything that took his fancy – his children's toys were always popular, notably the moo-cow box (turn it upside down and it moos), as were snatches of TV dialogue' (Bradley 2000: 326; see also Eshun 1998: 65). Hence, whereas Tubby made very effective use of reverb, what distinguished Perry's dub was the layers of sound he built up. Indeed, the reverb tended to be understated, being utilized simply to give the sound depth.[45] The layering, on the other hand, gave it a level of luxuriant density unusual in reggae. Indeed, the effect is striking. So much so that, as noted above of dub *per se*, it is not unusual for Perry's work to be described using semi-mystical or even alchemical or paranormal wordplay (which, it has to be said, can, at times, appear pretentious). Kodwo Eshun is not untypical in this respect:

> *Return of the Super Ape* is dub that disturbs the atmosphere until it yields poltergeists. Arriving ahead of cause, sound turns motiveless, premonitional, inexplicable... The wind of Baudelaire's wings of madness sends sound effects careering across living space... The Black Ark studio switches on a technology-magic discontinuum. Operating the mixing desk demand you explore its network of altering spaces. Perry crosses into its ghost dimension, walks through the temporal maze of aural architecture (1998: 63, 65).

However it was understood, there is little doubt concerning the impact of his dub in the 1970s. *Revolution Dub* (1975) and particularly the seminal *Super Ape* (1976) – which some consider to be 'the best dub reggae album ever made' (Bradley 2000: 328) – both produced at the Black Ark, very quickly elevated Perry to a level of international recognition that few could rival, including King Tubby.

That said, Barrow and Dalton are right to insist that the Black Ark 'never became a centre for dub in the same way that Tubby's did', for, as they go on to point out, 'the sheer number of producers who used Tubby meant that he always had more than enough rhythms to mix, and with which he could experiment endlessly' (1997: 204; cf. Spencer 1976). Hence, as indicated above, there is a sense in which Tubby's work sounded more explicitly avant-garde and experimental than Perry's. While we have noted that one of the principal reasons for Tubby's experimentation was economic – making the most of existing rhythms and sounds – as Barrow and Dalton comment, 'had the remixes not sounded completely fresh they would not have been so successful and their freshness was the result of both musical imagination and engineering ingenuity' (1997: 204). With a keener sonic curiosity than Perry (though, again, such judgments are necessarily speculative and rather artificial), Tubby was, as we have noted, continually inventing and modifying his own studio equipment, experimenting with the growing stream of tapes that came into his studio, and on the look out for new ways of manipulating and augmenting the sound. 'The sheer volume of work enabled Tubby to develop a sound in his dub mixes that is as recognizable as the Phil Spector wall of sound or the Sun Records echo chamber' (Barrow 1995: 31; see also Doyle 2005: 163–77).

Since the early 1970s, Perry has been experiencing an increasingly prominent profile within popular music, particularly within British music, beyond the African-Caribbean community. Since 1975, when he secured a lucrative deal with Island Records, many prominent white musicians were becoming interested in his work, the most famous of which were Paul and Linda McCartney who, in June 1977, employed Perry to construct some rhythm tracks for a subsequently abandoned solo album by Linda.[46] Perry and McCartney 'had met on several occasions in England, where a positive connection was established; the McCartneys thus sent Perry a demo tape of material they wanted him to re-create with his inimitable Black Ark sound' (Katz 2000: 278). Similarly, fellow Island artist, Robert Palmer, was introduced to Perry by Chris Blackwell, who wanted him to contribute to Palmer's 1978 album, *Double Fun*. Palmer was immediately impressed by the idiosyncratic producer. Although the recording sessions at the Black Ark were not without tension, and although little that Perry produced eventually made it on to the album, Palmer nevertheless considered him to be the best producer he'd worked with: 'I've been asked', said Palmer, 'who was my favourite producer and it's definitely him. He used to do amazing things that were hard to accept unless you witnessed what he did. He used to record on a Teac four track and mix as he went, occasionally cleaning the head with his T-shirt... He was just this magnet for a scene that was the real musical cutting edge' (quoted in Katz 2000: 279). (Indeed, as a result of his relationship with Blackwell and Island, we will see that he also briefly worked with the Scottish folk-blues musician John Martyn, the first white artist signed to the label.)

Far more interesting, however, was the confluence of his music with the emergence of punk. That said, one of the first white, reggae-influenced 'punk' bands to respond to Perry's music was not from the UK, but from the East Coast of America, namely The Terrorists. Formed in November 1977, Perry first met the drummer, Dro (David Ostrowe), and bassist, Gary Schiess, in the summer of that year, when they were the rhythm section for The Tribesman. As both were already very much inspired by Perry's work, when, in 1981, they were presented with the opportunity to work with him, they seized it. (That said, they collaborated far more with the Skatalite saxophonist Roland Alphonso.) As well as travelling with them and periodically fronting them during the early 1980s, Perry produced dub tracks, such as their 'Love is Better' and, using the same rhythm track, the excellent 'Guerrilla Priest' (with Perry on vocals) – both of which, unusually for the time, were nearly ten minutes long (available on *Forces 1977–1982*). Slightly later, at the beginning of the 1980s, Perry also attracted the attention of Chris Frantz and Tina Weymouth (of Talking Heads) as a possible producer for their first Tom Tom Club album (1981) – unfortunately Blackwell considered Perry's fee too high, so the collaboration was abandoned. Again, he had lengthy discussions with fellow Talking Heads member, David Byrne. This is perhaps more significant, bearing in mind Byrne's own avant-garde, dub-like creativity, particularly with Brian Eno in 1981 on the seminal album *My Life in the Bush of Ghosts* (see Hollings 2006; Toop 2006; Byrne and Eno 2006) and the Talking Heads' *Remain in Light* (1980), and also his interest in non-western music styles (see Tamm 1995: 159–63). Again, sadly, the conversations concluded unsatisfactorily, as well as a little acrimoniously.[47] However, although he was beginning to attract attention in the US, it was clearly Perry's presence in the UK during the punk era that was to be particularly fruitful. John Lydon (Johnny Rotten of the Sex Pistols) and bands such as The Clash were likewise inspired by reggae and what might be described as 'the dread culture of resistance'. As Paul Simonon, the bassist for The Clash, commented, 'I see Lee Perry as the Ennio Morricone of Jamaican music... [His] music is like the soundtrack of my childhood' (quoted in Katz 2000: 288; see also Hebdige 1979: 29). Although berating them for their inferior version of Junior Murvin's 'Police and Thieves', Perry nevertheless agreed to produce their third single, 'Complete Control' (which appears on the US version of their 1977 debut album, *The Clash*). And, of course, as we will see in subsequent chapters, he has continued to work with British and European artists and producers, from Adrian Sherwood and Dub Syndicate (perhaps their most impressive work being *Time Boom De Devil Dead*, 2001) and, after his relocation to Zurich, Dieter Meier of Yello (*Technomajikal*, 1997).

Finally, the glory years of the Black Ark were brought to an end by a conflagration in 1983. Although members of Perry's family have insisted that this was the result of an electrical fault, Perry himself has offered conflicting statements. While he has often denied his involvement, he also, just over a year after the event, admitted to incendiary activity: 'I destroyed the studio. I smashed it up and then I burnt it down. Over!' (interview with Kelly 1984: 58). Again, in an interview with Katz in 1999, he declared, 'Of course it's me who burn it...who else could burn it?... Good thing I did that' (Katz 2000: 364–65).

The Sacred Art of Dub

The heart of dub is the drum and bass rhythm. Moving away from the upbeat rhythms of ska, as noted above, to some extent dub takes the music back toward the churchical patterns of Nyabinghi drumming: 'dub means raw riddim. Dub jus' mean raw music, nuttin' water-down. Version is like your creativeness off [*sic*] the riddim, without voice' (King Jammy, quoted in Barrow and Dalton 1997: 202).[48] That said, although raw 'riddim'[49] is key, we have seen that, on this foundation producers and engineers constructed layered soundscapes through the use of echo, equalization effects, and, eventually, the introduction of novel found sounds. The aural effect of this was so stunning that early descriptions of initial exposure to it resort to metaphysical, if not spiritual terminology. (I can still remember my own initial, ethereal encounter with Augustus Pablo's important 1976 collaboration with King Tubby, *King Tubbys Meets the Rockers Uptown* in the late-1970s.) A good description of this striking aesthetic impact is provided by the British *Melody Maker* journalist Richard Williams, following his first experience of dub in 1976. He describes the slight sense of reality-shift that the genre can induce: 'One's overriding impression, on initial exposure to dub at the high volume for which it is intended, is that this is the nearest aural equivalent to a drug experience, in the sense that reality (the original material) is being manipulated and distorted' (Williams 1997: 146). Not only that, but when listened to live (which, in true dancehall style, is usually very loud), along with this intriguing manipulation of sound, one feels the somatic impact of the bass (to which we'll return in the following chapter). Again, often, particularly with the more ambient forms of dub, there is a sense in which time drifts and slows. As was noted in the previous chapter, this experiential and, for some, broadly transcendental and timeless quality of dub has been variously explained. Reynolds, for example, argues that dub invokes primal feelings of one's 'womb-time' as a foetus – 'the lost paradise before individuation and anxiety':

> ...by stimulating the way sound-waves behave under water, the effects in dub and ambient hark back to our personal prehistory in the amniotic sea of the womb. It's not for nothing that studio engineers talk of a recording being 'dry' when it's devoid of reverb. The foetus can't hear anything until the twenty-fourth week of pregnancy, but after that it reacts to external sounds and bonds with the mother's voice, which must reach its ears blurred and refracted through the fleshly prism of her body. With its submarine sonar FX and numinous reverberance, dub reggae invokes the blurry sonic intimacy of womb-time, the lost paradise before individuation and anxiety. This might also account for why dub foregrounds the bass (its frequencies are less localizable, more immersive and engulfing) and why dub reggae runs at tempos – around 70-75 bpm – that approximate the baby's heartbeat in the womb (1998: 171–72).

While this is perhaps a little too speculative, as I type this listening to dub I can sense what he means. He may have a point. Indeed, he turns to Freud for support, who, in his *Civilisation and Its Discontents*, discussed the

> long-lost selfless self, the phase of primary narcissism in which the infant does not distinguish between itself, the mother and the world. 'Originally the ego includes everything...the ego-feeling we are aware of now is...only a shrunken vestige of a far more extensive feeling – a feeling which embraced the universe and expressed an inseparable connection of the ego with the external world.' Both dub and ambient attempt a magical return to this diffuse but majestic self-without-contours, the 'royal we' of the infant/mother symbiosis, or the lost kingdom of the womb. In Rastafarian reggae, though, this lost god-self is identified with Jah, a righteous *paternal* principle; nostalgia becomes anticipation, the dream of returning to the promised land, Zion (Reynolds 1998: 172).

Again, whilst speculative, it is informed conjecture. We have seen that David Toop's short, poetic analysis evokes similar ideas: 'Dub music is like a long echo delay, looping through time. Regenerating every few years, sometimes so quiet that only a disciple could hear, sometimes shatteringly loud, dub unpicks music in the commercial sphere. Spreading out a song or a groove over a vast landscape of peaks and deep trenches, extending hooks and beats to vanishing point, dub creates new maps of time, intangible sound sculptures, sacred sites, balm and shock for mind, body and spirit' (Toop 1995a: 115). Of course, this relationship with the temporal is, as Reynolds suggests, not limited to dub. For example, similar analyses can be found in studies of experimental, ambient, and minimalist musics (see Nymen 1974: 12). Moreover, echo *per se* engenders similar experiences. This is thoughtfully articulated in Peter Doyle's analysis of echo and reverb.

> To hear one's own voice 'emanating' from the chasm, cliff or mountain, or even to hear one's footsteps bouncing off a distant wall – such phenomena have long been found intriguing, in the ancient and modern worlds, in both pre- and postindustrial societies. That which is not the self seems to talk to us with our own voice, using our own sounds. The obvious atavistic suggestion posed by the phenomenon of echo is animist: that the non-human world 'talks', that it possesses human characteristics. But other questions then arise: Does the world resemble the self or is the self simply a much lesser, relatively inconsequential emanation of the world? So where am 'I', really – here or there? And is there really an 'I' to ask the question? The phenomenon of echo is profoundly ambiguous: it suggests on the one hand an irreconcilable dualism, while simultaneously hinting at transcendent monism, that all in fact may at base be one... And this is before we get to the added degree of abstraction that recorded reverb and echo entail (2005: 39).

Furthermore, to some extent, dub is a type of music that requires what Frith refers to as 'aimless listening'. 'The listener is placed in a virtual time which has no history (no story line), no architecture (no outline), no apparent beginning, middle, or end; there is neither musical resolution nor musical expectation, nothing to help us make narrative sense of what we hear.' Quoting Wim Mertens, Frith continues, 'minimalist music is thus a "field of intensity", a "free flow of energy", less a human statement than a kind of eternal force: the music was there before we started listening and will continue after we stop' (1996: 154). Indeed, while the following reflection by Jonathon Kramer describes his experience of listening to the 'Vexations' section of Erik Satie's *Pages Mystiques*, he might easily be describing the experience of listening to dub. He recalls his perception of the music getting 'slower and slower, threatening to stop'. But then, he says,

> I found myself moving into a different listening mode. I was enter-
> ing the vertical time of the piece. My present expanded as I forgot
> about the music's past and future. I was no longer bored. And I was no
> longer frustrated because I had given up expecting. I had left behind
> my habits of teleological listening. I found myself fascinated with what
> I was hearing... True, my attention did wander and return, but during
> the periods of attending I found the composition to hold great inter-
> est. I became incredibly sensitive to even the smallest performance
> nuance... I never lost touch with myself or surroundings. Although I
> listened deeply enough to the music to accept its extended present,
> I never ceased to be aware of my mental and physical environment
> (quoted in Frith 1996: 154–55).

To develop this line of thought a little, it is, as noted above, perhaps not surprising that dub has been invested with, not only transcendental, but explicitly
religious significance. This is immediately evident in the titles of many dub
albums and tracks. For example, Winston Riley's *Meditation Dub* (1976) or,
more recently, *The Sacred Art of Dub* (1998) by the British musicians Alpha &
Omega, and *Rebirth* (1997) by The Disciples and The Rootsman. Again, tracks
such as The Hazardous Dub Company's 'Mystical Dub' and 'Spiritual Dub'
(*Dangerous Dubs Vol. 2*, 1993) and Jah Shaka's 'Immortal Dub' and 'Mystic
Dub' (*Dub Symphony*, 1990) are indicative of the ideas and feelings evoked (see
Partridge 2004a: 175–83). More specifically, in this connection, it is of some
significance that one of the principal producers of dub, Hopeton (sometimes
referred to as Overton) Brown, took the name 'Scientist', which, in Obeah,
is a designation for a spiritual healer, indicating, as Lee Perry had done, both
dub's holistic potential and, as discussed in the previous chapter, its continuity
with African indigenous spiritual practice (see Katz 2000: 64, 181–82; Beckford 2006: 71–72; Olmos and Paravisini-Gebert 2003: 131–53). While Perry
has typically denied the many rumours of his involvement in Obeah, he has
spoken of his music in terms of 'a magical process', referred to it as 'science',
named his post-Black Ark studio 'the Secret Laboratory', in 1974 named a record
label 'Black Art' (Katz 2000: 175, 182) and has produced tracks such as, most
recently, the excellent 'Voodoo' (on *Panic in Babylon*). These are all important
signifiers and, even if he has in fact consistently kept his distance from Obeah,
they indicate an understanding of dub as a spiritual practice that is holistically
therapeutic. Moreover, although Rastafarianism is, of course, the dominant
spiritual discourse within dub, the sense of it being an arcane magical art, a
'science', and its connection with African traditional religion has continued.
For example, the Dub Specialist's *Dub Store Special* (1974) includes the track
'Musical Science', and *Chapter 1 Dub Mix* (1984) by Tad's Logic Dub Band also
has a track entitled 'Science'. Again, the soundtrack to the film *Countryman*

(1982), which itself has an Obeah narrative, includes Wally Badarou's 'Obeah Man Dub'. More implicitly, Perry entitled his collaboration with Dieter Meier of Yello *Technomajikal* (1997) and several of Adrian Sherwood's productions have included African indigenous signifiers, such as Creation Rebel's *Pyschotic Jonkanoo* (1981) and African Head Charge's *Shrunken Head* (2004). Hence, there has always been a sense in which dub is evocative of African indigenous religions and cultures and in which it has been understood as an alchemical discipline that has explicit spiritual and psychological effects. Through the ordinary being made extraordinary, the everyday made strange, the listener is taken on a journey within. Hence, perhaps more than he realized, Eshun summed up 'the sacred art of dub' when, in his discussion of Perry, he referred to 'the MythScience of the mixing desk' (1998: 62).

It should be noted that the disorienting Obeah narrative, of which dub is a conspicuous musicological parallel, can be found elsewhere in Caribbean art. As Elaine Savory has commented in her discussion of the writings of Jean Rhys,[50] there are frequent references to Obeah. As with other Caribbean authors, she understood writing to be

> a sacred art, requiring absolute commitment. She gave that commitment to writing, making it more important than the love of family and friends, comfort, security, or money. She also came to refer to writing itself as coming from somewhere outside herself, as a link to the world of the spiritual... This connection to the spiritual links her directly to Caribbean writers such as [Wilson] Harris, [Edward Kamau] Brathwaite, Paule Marshall, Derek Walcott, and Dennis Scott, with whom she shares the perception that resistance to oppression can be strengthened and assisted by turning to the world of the spirit... Rhys's texts are spare, but certain codes function...as a layered pathway of meaning. One of these codes is built from reference to good and evil, God and the Devil, Obeah, ghostliness, and witchcraft (1997: 217).

It is not unusual for dub to operate with similar codes. As well as, of course, the dominant Rastafarian discourse, much of which needs to be understood in terms of resistance to the oppression of 'Babylon' – 'strengthened and assisted by turning to the world of the spirit' – there is a continual referencing of dualistic codes and an explicit articulation of African indigenous mythologies. For example, we have noted that Perry, speaking of the creation of dub, makes the following comment: 'me join the ghost squad longtime and them notice me as the Ghost Captain. I am the Ghost Captain' (quoted in Eshun 1998: 65). Hence, while the dark forces of Obeah are an ever-present danger, it is a system of belief that has continued to provide a significant reservoir of ideas that shape much Caribbean thought. It is, in other words, a significant component of dub 'occulture' (see Partridge 2004a: 66–68). Again, as Savory comments: 'The figures of Caribbean folklore Rhys had learned [as a child]... would also inform her sense of African spirituality. The "zombies, soucriants and loups-garous"... terrified and fascinated the young girl. Soucrients, Rhys explains, are women "who came at night and sucked your blood..."' (1997: 219). Hence, with these occultural referents in mind, if we think again of King Tubby's protégé Scientist, one of his most accomplished albums is particularly interesting in this respect: *Scientist Rids the World of the Evil Curse of the Vampires* (1981). Including heavily dubbed tracks such as 'The Voodoo Curse', 'Dance of the Vampires', 'The Corpse Rises', 'Your Teeth in My Neck', and 'Plague of Zombies', this is a work of art which, understood in the Jamaican context, not only references popular films of the period, but, more specifically, celebrates the dub master's myalistic power over the Obeah-like forces of evil. Again, the signification is complex. The album begins with the macabre laughter of the vampire, followed, at the beginning of the third track, with the words 'I want blood'. Throughout the album Scientist works his magic, subduing the forces of evil by means of the sacred art of dub. The immediate reference to the demonic other, therefore, is mythopoeic. However, as in Rastafarian discourse, there is also a further reference to the overcoming of vampiric earthly powers, the Babylonian forces of political oppression. Indeed, Perry even used the image of the vampire to attack Chris Blackwell, whom he considered to be an imperialist oppressor who 'wants to steal Africa' (see Corbett 1994: 130; cf. Taylor 1997: 47; Kessler 1997: 20). In 1985 he released the twelve-inch *Judgement in Babylon*, the chorus of which declared that 'Chris Blackwell is a Vampire, sucking the blood of the sufferer'. (In 2004, Blackwell is again dealt with in the lyrics of the significantly entitled 'Voodoo' on *Panic in Babylon*.) However, the point is that, while the political and the spiritual are conflated, it is clear that dub 'science' is effective in both cases.

Finally, turning again to the more general interpretation of dub as a sacred art, this is encouraged by the sense of space and depth and the stretching of time induced by the careful use of echo. 'As soon as you have echo, listening has to completely change. Your ear has to chase the sound. Instead of the beat being this one event in time, it becomes a series of retreating echoes, like a tail of sound... Echo turns the beat from a localised impact into an environment with you inside' (Eshun 1998: 64). Moreover, the emphasis on the offbeat in reggae *per se* is peculiarly conducive to states of mind that are considered mystical or indeed panenhenic ('all-in-one-ism' – Zaehner 1961: 28). Again, as Frith notes, it is no coincidence that minimal and ambient composers have been attracted by Eastern religions and monistic or panenhenic thought.

'Virtual time here describes an experience of bodilessness, an indifference to materiality' (Frith 1996: 155). Moreover, it should also be noted that the confluence of this music, a penchant for monistic spirituality, and the effects of tetrahydrocannabinol, the psychoactive chemical found in ganga, is probably not coincidental and is certainly instrumental in the production of states of mind commonly interpreted as transcendent (see Partridge 2005: 121–22). Indeed, if much roots reggae is fundamentally *religious* music, dub should perhaps be understood as its *mystical* counterpart.

Version Culture and Copyright Legislation

As will no doubt be evident, dub bricolage evolved in a culture in which issues of copyright were not a particularly pressing concern. This has given rise to various understandings of the Jamaican context.

> The wide circulation of riddims can give rise to various superficial impressions. One impression is that of a fair, orderly and well-regulated system of contracts, licensings and the like; another is the notion of a pool of riddims serving as creative commons, undergirded by an anti-materialistic Jamaican willingness to share; a third impression is that of a Hobbesian wild-west scene in which ownership and profits are determined at best by handshakes and more often at gunpoint. Each of these scenarios contains a kernel of truth, although the reality is considerably more complex (Manuel and Marshall 2006: 462).

That said, essentially, the reality is relatively simple. The music industry and culture within which dub emerged was not litigious. More particularly, we have seen that the genre emerged within a sound-system culture that relied heavily on the exclusive ownership of dub plates which were protected, not through the copyrighting of original compositions, but rather through the acquisition of rare records, the identity of which was withheld from other sound systems.

There were, however, other reasons why copyright law was not a principal concern in Jamaica. On the one hand, it was outdated – it being technically identical to the British copyright act of 1911 (Manuel and Marshall 2006: 463) – and, on the other hand, even if it had been updated and applied to music production, enforcing it was not one of the many pressing concerns of the struggling Jamaican government. Moreover, not only was the legislation inadequate, but, as has been indicated, ownership and authorship were often uncertain. As well as sound systems keeping a record's origins secret in order to maintain exclusivity, the records themselves tended to be identified less with the musicians than with the studios (who hired the musicians) or with the sound systems that acquired them. That said, questions of ownership and authorship were, as Manuel and Marshall comment, 'generally unimportant to musicians, most of whom had little knowledge of copyright, could not envision earning any royalties, and hence made records primarily for prestige, pocket money, and future opportunities' (2006: 463). Similarly, producers and sound systems did not seek to create income through royalties and licensing, but rather through revenue from live events and the direct selling of popular records.

Furthermore, since Jamaica was also not a signatory to any international copyright conventions, producers were not restricted to recording versions of homegrown tracks and riddims, but could take their pick of the international market. Of course, producers and musicians in other countries could return the compliment without fear of litigation.

Even during the late-1970s and 1980s, when international sales of Jamaican records grew significantly, copyright practice continued to be informal, with governmental efforts made to regularize it being generally unsuccessful. As Manuel and Marshall comment,

> both composers and performers on records, which were made as exclusives for sound systems – whether based in Jamaica or the UK – often remained anonymous, without any claims to royalties. As before, producers' profits derived mostly from direct sales of their own records... While DJs on riddim records were sometimes able to negotiate some royalties shared with the producer or, perhaps, with the author of the riddim, more often they accepted a flat fee as payment (2006: 463).

Indeed, although Jamaica saw the passing of a contemporary copyright act in 1993, and although the situation is beginning to change with legal battles becoming more common, the registration of copyright and the collecting of royalties continues to be irregular, it being alien to the culture for such a long period.

The point of briefly drawing attention to the issues surrounding authorship, ownership and copyright at this point is simply to indicate that, in many ways, the legislative Jamaican climate could not have been more conducive to the growth of dub. Hence, to some extent, version culture was nurtured by the Jamaican legislature.

Concluding Comments

Building on the foundational work done in the previous chapter, which sought to historically contextualize dub and reggae and critically introduce important ideological themes, the aim of this chapter has been to tighten the focus on the music and its relationship to Rastafarianism. As such, it provides a critical history of the emergence of dub – which, following ska, rocksteady and reggae, eventually evolved through three phases, namely, the instrumental, the version, and finally, dub – unpacking the continuities with Nyabinghi culture, Burru drumming, African Christian worship, West African indigenous religion, and, of course, sound-system culture (and much that contributed to the shaping of that culture, including the North American popular culture). In this sense, dub emerged, not simply as a distinct musical genre, but explicitly reflecting a particular worldview, shaped by a confluence of social, political, religious and cultural influences. In other words, the processes that shaped the evolution of dub were both sacralized and politicized.

In Part Two, we will see how dub evolved in the UK and what happened to the various meanings with which it was invested in Jamaica. Indeed, thinking of the previous section and of the various scenes that roots reggae and dub united in Britain, particularly during the 1970s and early 1980s, we will see that they provided more than simply a 'voice', but rather, as Robin Balliger says of political music generally, they reinforced solidarity, becoming 'a vehicle through which the oppressed recognize each other and become more aware of their subordination' (1999: 61). As she goes on to point out, such songs have political force, 'not because they have political lyrics, but because the music was understood in particular contexts of struggle' (1999: 61). We will see that it was the particular British *context* in which the music was produced and consumed that invested the term 'Babylon' with peculiar meanings for white punks, free festival 'post-hippies', and, later in the 1980s and 1990s, free party 'crusties'. Indeed, even if the ideas were not verbally expressed, and even if they were deconstructed and reinterpreted when they were expressed, nevertheless, some continuity was articulated through the use of reggae rhythms and dub techniques by bands as diverse as The Clash, Killing Joke, Nik Turner's Inner City Unit, and Stiff Little Fingers. As Viviene Goldman has commented, 'dub became the common vernacular for a broad swathe of artists operating in England...between 1977 and 1981' (Goldman 2003: 3).[51]

Thinking a little more closely about these issues, we have seen that competition between sound systems has been a fundamental dynamic within Jamaican popular music since the 1950s, stimulating its development from one genre and subgenre to the next. When the supply of American rhythm and blues began to dry up, as white rock 'n' roll became more popular in the US, demand led to the development of a localized, indigenous music scene. The confluence of several streams of music led, eventually, to the emergence of ska, which, for a short period at the end of the 1960s, slowed down into rock steady, which, in turn, quickly evolved into the slower bass-oriented reggae (see White 1983b: 40–41; Simon 1983: 43–44; Carr 1993: 70–81; Katz 2004: 65–95; Bennett 1999; Clayton 1999c). It was during this tumultuous and creative period at the close of the 1960s, when sound-system rivalry was fierce, when rhythm and heavy, loud bass were central to dancehall culture, that the instrumental and the version have their genesis, and from which dub was born.

Hence, a genre that would eventually have a global impact began as a relatively localized, indigenous music driven by the dynamics of Jamaican sound-system culture. Indeed, in retrospect we need to add a fourth historical 'event' to George Lamming's three events in British Caribbean history, namely the emergence of ska. In his 1960 analysis, *The Pleasures of Exile*, Lamming made the following comment (which I quote at length, as some important points are made):

> There are, for me, just three important events in British Caribbean history. I am using the term *history* in an active sense. Not a succession of episodes which can easily be given some casual connection. What I mean by historical event is the creation of a situation which offers antagonistic oppositions and a challenge of survival that had to be met by all involved... The first event is the discovery. That began, like most other discoveries, with a journey; a journey inside or a journey out and across. This was the meaning of Columbus. The original purpose of the journey may sometimes have nothing to do with the results that attend upon it. That journey took place nearly five centuries ago; and the result has been one of the world's most fascinating communities. The next event is the abolition of slavery and the arrival of the East – India and China – in the Caribbean Sea. The world met here, and it was at every level, except administration, a peasant world. In one way or another, through one upheaval after another, these people, forced to use a common language which they did not possess on arrival, have had to make something of their surroundings. What most of the world today regard as the possibility of racial harmony has always been the background of the West Indian prospect... The West Indian, though provincial, is perhaps the most cosmopolitan man in the world... The third important event in our history is the discovery of the novel by West Indians as a way of investigating and projecting the inner experiences of the West Indian community... What the West Indian writer has done has nothing to do with the English critic's assessments... As it should be, the novelist was the first to relate the West Indian experience from the inside (1992: 36–38).

As we have seen, the first two 'events' are of significance for our understanding of the roots and culture of dub. Indeed, put simplistically, the distillation of the tolerant eclecticism, the cosmopolitan nature of the culture, and make-do ethos of Jamaica have produced dub. It is difficult to imagine other histories, cultures and peoples engendering roots reggae and dub. Hence, along with Lamming's third important event in West Indian history, we must include the confluence of indigenous forms of music that led to the emergence of ska and, eventually, dub, which, we have seen, is likewise a way of investigating and projecting the inner experiences of the community. What Jamaican musicians and producers have done has 'nothing to do with the English critic's assessments'. As we will see, these various cosmopolitan, religio-political, musically eclectic streams have produced a genre of music and a way of producing music that has resonated with, influenced, and been embraced by many musicians and listening subcultures around the world. It has provided a particular identity, a particular cultural narrative with which many people imaginatively identify.

To some extent, indeed, it is helpful to think of the globalization of the genre in terms of creating a 'dub scene'. In using the term 'scene', we are thinking, not simply of the musicians, but also of the audience cultures and 'the business' in general: the labels, the sound-system events, the 'dubhead' subcultures, the informal economies, the networks, the websites, the fanzines, the worldviews encouraged, and so on. Moreover, while the malleable concept of 'scene' can refer to geographically localized cultures (such as the sound system, Rasta, and Nyabinghi cultures), it has also been used to articulate, as Sara Cohen comments,

> the fluid, loose, cosmopolitan, transitory, and geographically dispersed nature of local music activity. Rather than linking scenes with notions of a clearly defined and place-bound community or subculture with a relatively fixed population...scenes are created through heterogenous 'coalitions' and 'alliances' based on musical preferences, thus linking scene with cultural change and interaction (1999: 245; see also Straw 1991; Olson 1998; O'Connor 2002).

On the one hand, not only is a promiscuously eclectic genre like dub peculiarly conducive to musical syncretism and hybridization, but when thinking of 'dub outernational', we are thinking of a constantly shifting scene, which is the result of a confluence of scenes. Yet, on the other hand, it is predominantly a scene shaped by the ideology and music of the local Jamaican scene that birthed it. Hence, for example, we have seen that it very often explicitly references a cultural narrative that includes ganga, spirituality, Rasta style and terminology (dreadlocks, Babylon, Zion, Ital, and so on), and Rastafarian political and theological thought. This means that, although, as with the music, the receiver scenes contextualize the ideology and culture, appropriate a particular identity, emphasizing and developing the aspects of dub that are continuous with their own concerns and experiences, few 'dubheads' are unfamiliar with the basic terminology of what would otherwise be a small, obscure Jamaican millenarian new religious movement. In Britain, 'Babylon' may not have been understood by white punk bands, such as The Ruts and The Clash, in exactly the same way as it was understood by black dub artists, such as the devout Rastafarians Jah Shaka and Benjamin Zephaniah, or the politicized father of dub poetry, Linton Kwesi Johnson, but, as was indicated in the previous chapter, there are continuities of meaning. Such continuities, for example, coalesced into movements in the early 1980s, such as Rock Against Racism. Hence, as well as mapping the history of dub outernational, especially in the UK, what follows is an investigation of the significance and dynamics of such continuities – as well as an excavation of some of the discontinuities. Indeed, concerning the latter, it will be argued that, to some extent, the transition to post-punk dub led to a defusing of its ideological power, in that, although the signs remained, they eventually became detached from their original religio-political moorings.

From the perspective of spirituality, dub is a good example of popular music's involvement in what I have elsewhere referred to as 'occulture' (Partridge 2004a). Building on work done by particularly Ernst Troeltsch and Colin Campbell, I developed their theories of 'mystical religion' and 'the occult milieu' respectively. Expanding the narrow, technical definition of the term 'occult', *occulture* includes a vast spectrum of beliefs and practices sourced by, for example, Eastern spirituality, paganism, spiritualism, theosophy, alternative science and medicine, popular psychology, and a range of beliefs emanating out of a general interest in popular mythologies and the paranormal. What A. D. Duncan said of occultism *per se* is equally true of 'occulture': it 'is not so much a religion or a system as a "general heading" under which a huge variety of speculation flourishes, a good deal of it directly contradictory' (1969: 55). Going beyond what Campbell identified as 'the cultic milieu' (1972), occulture is the new spiritual atmosphere in the West; the reservoir feeding new spiritual springs; the soil in which new spiritualities are growing; the environment within which new methodologies and worldviews are passed on to an occulturally curious generation. More particularly, central to the efficacy of occulture is popular culture, in that it feeds ideas into the occultural reservoir and also develops, mixes and disseminates those ideas within particular scenes and subcultures. Like psychedelia in the 1960s and early 1970s, which significantly contributed to the process of Easternization (see Campbell 1999; Partridge 2004a: 87–118), I want to suggest that dub and some of the principal genres to which it has contributed (e.g. ambient and psychedelic trance) have been important carriers and interpreters of occultural meanings, whether explicitly Rastafarian or, when occulturally recontextualized and detraditionalized, more amorphously 'spiritual'. Indeed, concerning the spiritual signifiers, we have discussed dub occulture at some length with reference to the Obeah-Myal complex and the subsequent notion of the genre as 'science', as a powerful myalistic medium which can overcome the forces of darkness and *dis*ease and, indeed, chant/dub down Babylon. The sacred art of dub can, in other words, as Beckford puts it, 'be interpreted in and through a holistic African cosmology. In this sense dub deconstruction is always related to a deep and complex quest for freedom and wellbeing' (2006: 74). To quote Perry again, 'I don't use bad spells, I make good spells. I make evil spell good spell' (quoted in Corbett 1994: 127).

From a political and countercultural perspective, what has been discussed challenges, for example, the type of thinking exemplified in Theodor Adorno's work. Shaped by his experience of the Nazi Party's cultural policy and manipulation of the media, Adorno developed a critical variant of Marxism that was scathing of popular culture. Following the rise to power of the Nazis, in 1934 he was forced to relocate to Oxford and then, in 1938, to New York. Whilst in North America he observed the progress of popular music and, with particular reference to jazz and Tin Pan Alley compositions, argued that it is fundamentally standardized, the end product being the production of standardized reactions and an affirmation of one's current existence – opium for the people (Adorno 1990: 301–14). As Chris Barker puts it, 'This is a matter not just of overt meanings, but of the structuring of the human psyche into conformist ways' (2000: 45). Indeed, Adorno argued that 'the total effect of the culture industry is one of anti-enlightenment, in which...enlightenment, progressive technical domination, becomes mass deception and is turned into a means of fettering consciousness'. Consequently, 'it impedes the development of autonomous, independent individuals who judge and decide consciously for themselves... while obstructing the emancipation for which human beings are as ripe as the productive forces of the epoch permit' (Adorno 1991: 92). However, although Adorno was undoubtedly the most brilliant and versatile member of the Frankfurt School, his views did not persuade all his colleagues. In particular, Walter Benjamin – who, in 1933, went into exile in Paris – developed a more appreciative critique of popular culture. In his seminal 1936 essay, 'The Work of Art in the Age of Mechanical Reproduction' (reprinted in Benjamin 1992: 211–44), he argues that the reproduction of art, in particular by photography and film, can be a positive thing for society, in that, although art is thereby divested of its 'aura' – the authority and uniqueness belonging to the original

(1992: 214–17) – it is made available to the masses, and innumerable people are encouraged to think differently about the world, seeing things they might otherwise never have realized existed. Film especially captures reality in a particular way and asks its many viewers to engage with it and consider what has been captured. If this same understanding is applied to popular music, rather than stressing its potential to manipulate the audience, as Adorno had done, it suggests that the audience is put in the position of the critic – as one who contributes meaning to the artefact. Hence, as in the reader-response theories of literary meaning, which call attention to 'the active role of communities of readers in constructing what counts for them as "what the text means"' (Thiselton 1992: 515), so Benjamin's thesis foreshadows a listener-response hermeneutic, in which the participatory role of the audience is stressed. As I have noted with reference to occulture, it is not a case of individuals passively absorbing dub and the ideologies it carries, but more a case of contextualization, reinterpretation and dialogue.

Part of the problem with Adorno's analysis is that it was not sufficiently reflexive, in the sense that his methodology did take full account of the influence of his overall context on his theorizing. As Brian Longhurst has argued, his work is 'too constrained by his own historical and social location, of being a highly educated, musically literate German intellectual of the mid-twentieth century. Owing to his lack of reflection on the effects this may have, his approach has many difficulties in coping with social and historical change in music making, as he continued to value a particular and very specific form of music' (1995: 13). Nowadays, it would, for example, be difficult to argue that the music of Atomic Kitten, The Ruts, and Nusrat Fateh Ali Khan was/is received and responded to in the same way: Atomic Kitten's music is rhythmic, party-pop – and possibly productive of what Adorno referred to as 'slaves to the rhythm'; The Ruts' song 'Babylon's Burning', on the other hand, was countercultural and ideologically driven; different again is the music of Nusrat Fateh Ali Khan, one of the most well-known *qawwali* singers. This does not, of course, mean that individuals might not receive The Ruts, or indeed Mozart, in the same way that they receive Atomic Kitten, or that Nusrat Fateh Ali Khan may not inspire that which is countercultural and ideological. It is simply to say that 'some forms of music may be valued because they are exceptionally good to dance to, others may invite contemplation, and so on' (Longhurst 1995: 13). However, the point is that responses are not all as superficial as Adorno would have us believe. More specifically, I want to suggest that dub and roots reggae can be, as Jim McGuigan has argued of popular culture *per se*, a 'primary terrain of cultural struggle' (1999: 68). Hence, thinking of British reggae in the 1970s, one only has to listen to Steel

Pulse's 'Handsworth Revolution' or 'Ku Klux Klan' (on the album *Handsworth Revolution*), read the powerful dub poetry of Linton Kwesi Johnson (1991; 2002), or listen to his *Dread Beat an' Blood* and *Forces of Victory* to realize the veracity of this point. Hence, without denying that dub can be standardized and cliché-ridden, we will see that it also has the ability to 'articulate progressive possibility and disturb a prevailing sense of "reality"' (McGuigan 1999: 68).

PART TWO

Dub UK: The Arrival and Evolution of Dub in Britain

3 Sound-System Culture and Jamaican Dub in the UK

On 21 June 1948, 492 West Indians disembarked the SS *Empire Windrush* at Tilbury Docks. Thus began 'a process which has steadily and radically transformed Britain' (Wambu 1999: 20). As Ceri Peach, Vaughan Robinson, Julia Maxted and Judith Chance argue in their study of immigration and ethnicity, 'the most striking change to occur in the population of Great Britain since the turn of the century has been the growth of its...ex-colonial population from negligible proportions at the end of the Second World War to the present time when coloured ethnics account for 5 per cent of the total' (1988: 561). 'Between 1955 and 1962 there were 301,540 migrants from the entire Caribbean area, of whom 178,270 came from Jamaica alone. The numerical superiority from Jamaica points to the area whence cultural influence would emerge' (Clarke 1980: 138; see also Jones 2000: 49–51). Socially, culturally, and, to some extent, religiously, the 'official' commencement of mass migration from the Caribbean to Britain which began with *Windrush* has reshaped British life. However, while much has been written about the wider cultural and political contributions of that generation of men and women who arrived at the hub of the 'Empire' with hopeful hearts, and while there has been much discussion of the numerous fissures, problems and prejudices within British society that their arrival highlighted (e.g. Centre for Contemporary Cultural Studies 1982; Gilroy 2002; Leech 1988; Owusu 2000; Wambu 1999), comparatively little has been written about their massive influence on popular music, far less about the significance of British sound-system culture, and practically nothing on the importance of dub. Hence, while there is a history of black music in Britain prior to the 1960s (see Cowley 1990), the principal concern of this chapter is the emergence of sound-system culture in the 1970s and its relationship to dub.

'Inglan is a Bitch': Settling in the Second Babylon

During the 1940s and 1950s, inspired by the hope of employment and a better life, many Jamaican men and women saved the £28 and ten shillings necessary to purchase a one-way ticket to Britain. Many of these people were musicians. Indeed, the passenger list of the *Windrush* included not only many ex-service men and women (for whom it was initially sent to Jamaica), but also a number of professional musicians, bandleaders and singers, such as the Trinidadian vocalist Mona Baptiste (Cowley 1990: 65). Whatever their skills, however, the country into which they arrived was not the one the alluring advertisements had invited them to or the affluent, polite society they had imagined. The climate was significantly wetter and colder than the country they'd left, the people were more often than not hostile, and the government was bedevilled by racism and confused about what it should do concerning immigration. For example, it has been shown that, while the government was collecting information about black people to support a draft immigration bill prepared in 1954, it was also opposing bills such as that of Fenner Brockway, which sought to prohibit racial discrimination – despite the increasing amount of evidence that suggested it was widespread. Successive governments 'not only constructed an ideological framework in which black people were to be seen as threatening, alien, and unassimilable, but also developed policies to discourage and control black immigration' (Carter, Harris and Joshi 2000: 22). In 1950, however, the Labour government, having set up a Cabinet Committee to review the immigration of 'coloured people from the British Colonial Territories', decided against legislative control largely on the grounds of expediency. On the one hand, they felt that the current administration of immigration was sufficient to protect 'the racial character' of Britain and, on the other hand, they needed labour (see Clarke 1980: 138). Indeed, there was such a shortage of labour that a special effort was made in the early 1950s to recruit African Caribbeans. Advertisements were placed in Caribbean newspapers, principally for posts that whites were unwilling to fill. Some employers, most notably London Transport, even went so far as to send recruitment officers to the Caribbean. It is rather surprising, therefore, that, although the shortage of labour became particularly acute during the administration of the Conservative government (elected in 1951) – following the gradual demise of the European Volunteer Worker scheme – as the 1950s progressed the policy towards immigration hardened. The British government even 'went to great lengths to restrict and control *on racist grounds* black immigration...despite a demand for labour' (Carter, Harris and Joshi 2000: 22; my emphasis). That is to say, in order to control black immigration at a time when it was particularly needed, they had to construct what they felt would be a persuasive case for legislation, which they did primarily around 'a racialized reconstruction of "Britishness" in which to be "white" was to "belong" and to be "black" was to be excluded' (Carter, Harris and Joshi 2000: 22). Such an argument was persuasive because, as the theologian Kenneth Leech has shown in his thoughtful book *Struggle in Babylon* (1988), racism ran deep in British society. Indeed, to the surprise of devout Caribbean Christians, it was very often experienced in the pews on Sunday. Although numerous African Caribbeans were keen to attend a Christian place of worship, such racism led many of them to establish their own churches (see Kerridge and Sykes 1995; Beckford 2006: 38–40). And, many of their children, as young adults, simply rejected the Christian culture they had witnessed in the UK. Some abandoned religious belief altogether, whilst others turned to the black Pentecostal traditions and still others joined or identified with alternative spiritualities and lifestyles, particularly Rastafari. Hence, 'while black-led congregations have grown in the inner urban areas, often using disused buildings abandoned by the Church of England, the gulf between the black underclass and organised religion of any kind has grown to be almost as wide as that between most white working-class people and religious groups' (Leech 1988: 22; see also Hiro 1971: 26–31).

Housing was a particular issue for many of the *Windrush* generation. The growth in the British economy following the war encouraged home ownership, which, in turn, led many white, middle-class families to leave the inner cities and to purchase new houses in the suburbs. That is to say, although there was an acute housing shortage following the war, many white middle-class people were keen to move out of poorly maintained, bomb-damaged, pre-war, inner-city properties and into the new homes that were rapidly being built on greenfield sites. Hence, those arriving from the Caribbean inhabited the vacated properties, the

> bleak untended tenement lodgings or Victorian and Edwardian bay-fronted middle-class houses that had seen better days. One room per family was the norm, and the unlucky single man would find many a landlady displaying 'No coloured men' signs prominently below the cheery and welcoming 'Vacancy' notice in their window... Into these semi-derelict streets came the new immigrants, charged double for the rent of a white worker just for the privilege of being black and having nowhere else to go (de Konigh and Griffiths 2003: 12; see also Jones 2000: 54–57).

Indeed, prior to the 1968 Race Relations Act, which outlawed such discrimination, not only were 'No Coloured' and 'Europeans Only' signs so common that, as Dilip Hiro comments, 'they hardly evoked comment from coloured people', but, he continues, 'only one out of every six white landlords' who *did not* display the signs were prepared even to consider letting property to black and Asian families. Similarly 'three out of four accommodation bureaux practised racial discrimination' (1971: 69). Again, those who sought to buy houses were similarly turned away. 'If a coloured person approached an estate agent with a particular property, carrying a "For Sale" sign, in mind, he was frequently told that the house in question was "under offer"' (Hiro 1971: 70). When blacks did manage to rent or purchase property, it was almost always sub-standard or even condemned, situated in rundown areas of the inner cities, which had witnessed a steady decline in the white population.

> Inglan is a bitch
> dere's no escapin' it
> Inglan is a bitch
> you haffi know how fi survive in it
> (Linton Kwesi Johnson, 'Inglan is a Bitch', *Bass Culture*, 1980).

Within these poor, oppressed communities, within a context that often spoke of Babylon more vividly than the colonial Jamaica they had left (see Carby 1999: 187ff), the politicized, sacralized music of the Rasta found a distinctive voice of resistance and an eager audience. In this 'second Babylon',[1] the technology of the sound system was adapted 'to create a crucible in which new versions of their history and experience [could] be voiced' (Back 1988: 141).

The Emergence of Sound-System Culture

The history of black cultures in Britain is a history bound up with race, resistance, and a *bricolage* mentality. With this in mind, Paul Gilroy's short analysis of dance-floor politics is instructive and, moreover, provides a useful introduction to sound-system culture. His discussion focuses on the explicit racism levelled against black men and white women who danced together in the clubs of London during the 1940s and 1950s. Firstly, he makes the point that, 'from the beginning of post-war settlement, blacks were an ambiguous presence inside the popular culture of the "host society"' (Gilroy 2002: 211). While, on the one hand, they were welcome as producers of popular culture – as bandleaders and musicians – on the other hand, they were often not welcome as consumers of that culture in the very same places they played. Blacks performed, whites consumed.

Secondly, detached from their cultural roots, they quickly felt the need to create a unifying culture. Their efforts tended to be eclectic.

> The gradual transition from migrant to settler status involved a progression through a medley of different cultural forms. The early settlers were comparatively few in number and, beyond the British educations which were their colonial inheritance, they lacked a single

cohesive culture which could bind them together. They set about creating it from the diverse influences which were available and which
corresponded to their predicament. The dances, parties and social
functions in which students, ex-service people and workers enjoyed
themselves, reverberated to black musics drawn from the US and
Africa as well as Latin America and the Caribbean. They jived, jit-
terbugged, foxtrotted, and quickstepped, moving from one cultural
idiom to another as the music changed (Gilroy 2002: 211–12).

In other words, black cultures were syncretistic, in the sense that they were
shaped, to some extent, by both the indigenous popular cultures they travelled with and also by their white cultural contexts. Each community, in its
own way, 'combined black cultures from a variety of sources with those of
the different white communities into which the blacks were being drawn as a
replacement population' (Gilroy 2002: 212; see also 1993: 15–16).

Thirdly, this led to friction within the host culture, in that, because dancing
was a central leisure activity for many blacks, colonial ideas of fraternization
began to surface. Should whites and blacks dance together? Should they touch
when dancing? Should a black man accompany a white woman to and from
a dancehall? For example, a young Jamaican political activist, Enrico Stennett,
became famous in London for his skill and versatility on the dance-floor. After
being banned from dancing at the Lyceum, the Astoria, the Locarno, and the
Hammersmith and Wimbledon Palais, he was eventually hired to *perform*.
Because of concern about his dancing with white women as a *consumer* of
popular culture, he was *employed* to provide entertaining demonstrations of
dances to working-class, white crowds. However, as there were very few black
women to demonstrate his dances with, he had to work with white women.
This, Gilroy notes, 'provoked intense hostility from the management and
sometimes violence'. A revised contract thus required him to leave 'immediately their exemplary performances ended lest other white women asked him
to dance' (2002: 212–13).

Finally, as a result of such hostility, Stennett and other black dancers
began to meet at London's Paramount ballroom on Tottenham Court Road.
Although the Paramount became known as a dancehall primarily for black
dancers, because they were known for their expertise, many white women
used to attend. Indeed, the Paramount was frequented primarily by black
men and white women, in that very few British black women, at that time,
would attend such venues. 'Alas there were no black women', Stennett
recalls, 'but the Paramount was packed with young ladies coming in from
the stockbroker belt of Surrey, Essex and Hampshire and other small vil-
lages and towns with a 60 mile radius of London' (quoted in Gilroy 2002:

213). Although racial hostility was 'tempered by the high status that derived from the black pre-eminence on the dance-floor' (Gilroy 2002: 213), white working-class youths, fuelled by racist concerns over miscegenation, became increasingly hostile. Gangs, including police officers, would wait outside the venue to confront black men escorting white women. Hence, it would seem that, as Gilroy argues,

> long before the advent of 'rock 'n' roll', the rise of soul, disco, and reg-
> gae, the cultural institutions of the white working class were hosting
> an historic encounter between young black and white people. This
> meeting precipitated not only fear of the degeneration of the white
> 'race' in general and defilement of its womanhood in particular, but
> also the creation of a youth sub-culture in which black style and
> expertise were absolutely central (2002: 215).

In other words, as was particularly evident in later skinhead ska culture (see Hebdige 1979: 54–59), black rude boy expertise on the dance-floor (as well as its culture of violence) accrued a certain amount of subcultural capital and thus respect from those otherwise hostile to the community, thereby invert-ing typical relationships of dominance and subordination.

As well as these sites of cultural interface and resistance, Britain's new entre-preneurs were establishing spaces and outlets specifically for black workers. They had to, for many pubs and clubs refused to admit African-Caribbeans. Indeed, because few were in a position to establish their own dancehalls, and because many felt constrained to supplement their low earnings, the idea of converting a room or even a house into a make-do night club was very attrac-tive. Hence, numerous small, legal and illegal black-owned 'basement clubs' began to appear in London. 'At one time there were fifty basement clubs in South London managed and/or owned by West Indians' (Hiro 1971: 32). It is difficult to overestimate the significance of these sites of cultural expression and consumption – particularly the illegal 'blues dances' – both for the social cohesion of the African-Caribbean community and for the preservation and dissemination of Jamaican music in the UK. Indeed, Clarke has even suggested that 'the blues dance replaced the role of the preacher and the church for many Caribbeans. The new church was the blues dance itself and the preacher was the sound man' (1980: 163). While this is perhaps overstating their social significance – and certainly ignores the enormous growth in black churches, 'perhaps the largest black cultural organizations in Britain' (Harris 2000: 402), and the development of black Christian theologies (see Beckford 1998) – it does highlight the importance of the blues dance and the basement club for the African-Caribbean community in the UK.

By 1955 blues dances and basement clubs were well-established within Britain's African-Caribbean communities (see Howe 1973). However, while there will be discussion of the illegal blues dances and what were known as 'shebeens' below, it is worth noting here that by the late 1950s they had begun to attract the attention of the police and the media, which, in turn, contributed significantly to the demonization of the black community in Britain. Not only were many blues parties illegal, but they often deliberately operated quite differently to white working-class leisure venues and activities, in that, for example, they often continued throughout the night. As Jones comments, 'for blacks, the all-night entertainment of the blues party represented a suspension of the ordered time and space associated with waged labour and with the dominant culture generally. In the British context this earnest pursuit of leisure in the non-work period was all the more poignant and subversive' (1988: 35). Consequently, on the one hand, they came to be regarded as a disruptive element within an ordered society and, on the other hand, they increasingly felt the need to protect their culture and demand equality. As such, this period is widely regarded as stimulating 'a tradition of black cultural resistance spilling over into the public domain that was to become a key feature of black struggle in the decades to come' (Jones 1988: 35; see also Hall, et al. 1978; Howe 1980). The perception of black crime and vice that began to filter into wider society in the late-1950s, following the dynamics of a typical 'moral panic' (see Cohen 1972), led to media campaigns and calls for tighter regulations and prosecutions. Hence, supported by prosecuting magistrates, the police mobilized against the African-Caribbean community, interrupting and suppressing numerous cultural events, from blues dances to wedding receptions.

This increased attention on what was considered to be black deviancy also had the effect of escalating white racist militancy and incendiary activity in African-Caribbean areas. Eventually, in 1958, the increased hostility exploded in conflict on the streets of Notting Hill and Nottingham. More seriously, however, was the racist murder of Kelso Cochrane, an African-Caribbean worker. Devastated by the murder, many blacks concluded that they could not rely on the British legal system for protection, but rather needed to look after their own interests. As a consequence of this progressive polarization of the black community and the authorities, the 1960s saw the emergence of a more confident, militant, cohesive, black community – a 'colony society' within Britain.

> This winning of cultural space, in which an alternative black social life could flourish, was most noticeable in the expansion of autonomous cultural, economic and leisure institutions within black communities

throughout Britain. Black restaurants, cafes, churches, food shops and a network of night clubs and record shops emerged to cater for the cultural and recreational needs of African-Caribbean people (Jones 1988: 36–37).

That said, repressive police activity against the African-Caribbean community, particularly black youths, continued for over three decades (see Carby 1999: 229–31). State-sanctioned racism, the criminalization of many African-Caribbeans, and ad-hoc measures, such as the implementation of the notorious 'sus law',[2] had the effect of politicizing many disaffected black youths (see Letts 2007: 77–78). As we will see in Chapter Four, the dub poetry of Linton Kwesi Johnson articulated the concerns of many black Britons in the late 1970s. For example, his powerful 1979 poem 'Sonny's Lettah (Anti-Sus Poem)', released on the album *Forces of Victory* (reprinted in Johnson 2002: 27–29), is a strident critique of the sus law and an articulation of what many black Britons had experienced:

> It woz di miggle a di rush howah
> wen evrybady jus a hosel an a bosel
> fi goh home fi dem evening showah;
> mi an Jim stan-up
> waitin pan a bus
> nat cauzin no fus,
> wen all af a sudden
> a police ban pull-up.
>
> Out jump tree policeman,
> di hole a dem carryin batan.
> Dem waak straight up to mi and Jim.
>
> One o dem hol awn to Jim
> seh him tekin him in;
> Jim tell him fi let goh a him
> far him noh duh notn
> an him naw teef,
> nat even a butn.
> Jim start to wriggle
> di police start to giggle.
>
> Mama,
> mek I tell yu whe dem dhu to Jim
> Mama,
> mek I tell yu whe dem dhu to him:

dem tump him in him belly
an it turn to jelly
dem lick him pan him back
an him rib get pap
dem lick him pan him hed
but it tuff like led
dem kick him in him seed
an it started to bleed...

Mama,
more policeman come dung
an beat mi to di grung; dem charge Jim fi sus,
dem charge me fi murdah.

It is perhaps not surprising, therefore, that many increasingly identified with the religio-politics of Rastafarianism and with the sense of racial pride that the movement engendered. The point is that this is important for understanding both the African-Caribbean perception of white society as Babylon, and all that this involves, and also the white subcultural perception of black culture as authentic counterculture. That is to say, this type of information is necessary because we need to understand why this music was valued by particular subcultures. In other words, as Simon Frith has argued, 'we can only hear music as valuable when we know what to listen to and how to listen for it. Our reception of music, our expectations from it, are not inherent in the music itself – which is one reason why so much musicological analysis misses the point: its object of study, the discursive text it constructs, is not the text to which anyone else listens' (1996: 26). The text to which many dub and roots reggae fans turned was (and still is for many) the countercultural, religio-political discourse of Rastafari and the oppressed. For some it was both spiritual and political, in the broadest terms, while for others, particularly white listeners, it was more narrowly defined. For example, The Clash, The Ruts, and The Terrorists received it primarily as a political text, whereas others, such as Jah Wobble and Simon Dan (of the Manchester dub band, Nucleus Roots), read it from a more spiritual perspective (see Penman 1998: 334–35).

To return to the significance of the blues dances, however, what is clear is that they were so successful that they began to have a commercial impact on the Jamaican music industry. As Barrow and Dalton comment, 'the musical tastes of communities of Jamaican émigrés in Britain, affluent by standards back in the Caribbean, provided an important impetus for the development of Jamaica's recording industry and by the 1950s records were being produced with export principally in mind' (1997: 325). Indeed, there soon emerged an increasingly significant independent recording industry in Britain dedicated to the production of black popular music. While we will see that Planetone Records was the first black-owned record label in the UK, Melodisc Records, founded in 1946 at 48 Woburn Place, London,[3] by Emil Shallit, was already an important outlet for, primarily, jazz and blues imported from the United States. An American citizen of European-Jewish extraction, Shallit was a talented multilinguist with, apparently, little interest in music *per se* – the selling of which he likened to the selling of potatoes. With the signing of the famous calypso artist Lord Kitchener, who had arrived in Britain in 1948, from 1951 Melodisc began distributing specifically Caribbean music. Hence, long before the successful, well-received debut of ska in the 1960s (see Eddington 2004; Hebdige 1974; de Konigh and Griffiths 2003), Britain was becoming an important site for the development of black music. Following the success of Melodisc, Shallit established his important subsidiary label, Blue Beat, which would become enormously significant for the dissemination of ska in the UK – indeed, the genre became known to many white British fans as 'bluebeat'. Such were his promotional skills that several key Jamaican musicians embarked on influential tours of Britain (see Bradley 2000: 126–30). Prince Buster, for example, even appeared on popular music shows such as *Ready Steady Go!* and entered the Top 20 in 1967 with his 'Al Capone'.

It is with ska, of course, that the Jamaican music industry *initially* made its most significant inroads into British popular music (see Barrow and Dalton 1997: 325–27; Bradley 2002: 106–119; Hebdige 1987; de Konigh and Cane-Honeysett 2003; de Konigh and Griffiths 2003). In the inner-city areas where Jamaicans had settled, the reception of ska was enthusiastic.[4] This, in turn, inspired the formation of British ska bands, London becoming a particularly important centre for the development of the genre and the evolution of rock steady and reggae. Perhaps the principal pioneer of British-based ska was Sonny Roberts, who, as the founder of Planetone Records, probably established, as noted above, the first black-owned record shop and the first black-owned record label in Britain (see de Konigh and Griffiths 2003: 19). Arriving in London from Jamaica in 1953, after some years working as a joiner, in 1962 he opened the shop and set up a studio in the basement of 108 Cambridge Road, London – an address which was, by the end of 1963, to be shared by and then taken over by Chris Blackwell's Island Records (see Bradley 2000: 131–32). Some of the earliest recordings were those of important Jamaican musicians who had since moved to the UK, most notably Kingston-born Rico Rodriguez (Emmanuel Rodriguez) who, with Lovett Brown (saxophone), Mike Elliott (saxophone) and Jackie Edwards (piano), formed Roberts's studio band. Although the Planetone label was short-lived, Roberts later acquired a shop just over the road from Willesden Junction railway station, Orbitone Records, and established two new labels, Orbitone and Tackle Records, both of which released less reggae and more soul, calypso, and African indigenous music.

Another important black distributor of reggae, who arrived in England in May 1960, and who was possibly the first in Britain to establish a shop devoted solely to ska (and subsequently rock steady and reggae), rather than black music *per se*, was Daddy Peckings (George Pecking) through his Studio One shop in West London. As the name of the shop suggests, Pecking set up the London outlet primarily to distribute Coxsone Dodd's Studio One records. Pecking has a particular significance in that it was he who initially supplied the now legendary Duke Vin.

Not only was Duke Vin Tom the Great Sebastian's selector in Jamaica, but he is reputed to have inspired Coxsone Dodd to build his 'Downbeat' sound system. More significantly as far as this study is concerned, having moved to Ladbroke Grove, London in 1954, by 1955 he had taken the name Duke Vin and established the first Jamaican-style sound system in Britain. 'Other men follow about two or three years after that', he recalls.

> We used to have very good times. And all these people who used to follow the sound – if we went to Birmingham, they used to come from London. We used to play all over the country – Birmingham, Manchester, Reading, you name it. People were so glad to know there was a sound system here, because of what they were used to in Jamaica. We tried going to other people's places, but we didn't like the sort of music that we heard there. It was not our sort of music (quoted in Barrow and Dalton 1997: 12).

Although it has been claimed that Duke Vin actually first played his sound system at his brother's wedding celebrations in 1956 (Back 1992: 219), this is almost certainly incorrect. As he himself comments, 'in 1954 I came to England, and I started my own sound system the next year' (quoted in Barrow and Dalton 1997: 12). Moreover, not only was he already operating in 1956, but he was established and winning sound-system cups (one in 1956 and one in 1957).

While sound-system culture primarily catered for the Jamaican expatriate community, the emergence of ska changed all that. Particularly important for the popularization of ska in the UK was the enormous success of Millie Small's 'My Boy Lollipop'. Reworked and produced by the Jamaican expatriate guitarist Ernest Ranglin for Chris Blackwell, it was specifically designed for broad appeal (on Ranglin, see Davis 1983a). It eventually reached number two in the 'Hit Parade' and sold over seven million copies worldwide, thereby putting Jamaican-British ska on the international map. However, perhaps rather surprisingly, the white subculture initially attracted to this new Jamaican sound was the carefully dressed, manicured mods, whose favoured bands had, until then, been The Who and The Small Faces (see Hebdige 1979: 52–54; 1976a: 87–96). More bizarrely, following the decline of the mods, the most significant white, British subculture to promote the genre – which by then was beginning to be referred to as 'reggae' – was the often violent, racist, shorn-haired skinheads. As de Konigh and Cane-Honeysett comment, 'by the time The Pioneers were climbing the glittering ladder of mainstream chart success with "Long Shot Kick the Bucket" in October 1969, skinheads and reggae were inextricably intertwined' (2003: 116; see also Hebdige 1979: 54–59). Indeed, for a time the music of such as Laurel Aitken and Derrick Morgan was simply referred to as 'skinhead music' in Britain. Trojan Records were not slow to respond to this trend. Quickly becoming one of the principal suppliers of 'skinhead reggae', Trojan made the most of the opportunity with releases such as Symarip's *Skinhead Moonstomp* (April 1970), the cover of which, with its photograph of five menacing-looking skinheads, looked more like a National Front promotional poster than a ska album cover. The company also signed the white, Kentish singer Alex Hughes, who adopted the moniker 'Judge Dread' (after the famous Prince Buster song) and appealed specifically to skinheads (see de Konigh and Cane-Honeysett 2003: 107–108). Hence, while the genesis of this unlikely combination of a white, often racist subculture and reggae has been a matter of some speculation (see Cashmore 1983: 41–44; Hebdige 1979: 54–59; 1987: 92–94), what is clear is that the effect was a widespread popularization of the genre within British popular music. Ska classics, such as Desmond Dekker's 'Israelites', were successful in the British charts largely because of their popularity with skinheads.

Later, of course, as the genre evolved into reggae, the enormous success of Bob Marley's first album on Island, *Catch a Fire* (1973), would have a significant positive effect on the international reputation and appeal of reggae, not least in the UK. Indeed, several important British reggae artists were directly inspired by that album – most notably, Aswad (who signed to Island in 1975), Delroy Washington (who signed to Virgin in 1976), the Cimmarons (who eventually secured a contract with Polydor for a reported £40,000 in 1977), and Don Letts, who recalls that the album was, quite simply, 'a revelation' to him. 'Through it', he says, 'I discovered the radical and political side of reggae music' (2007: 61).

Sound Systems and Dub

While ska and reggae were beginning to have an impact on the charts and attract mainstream recognition by the beginning of the 1970s, sound-system

culture was still largely underground. That said, it was a growing phenomenon – by this time sound systems could be found in every major English
city. Places such as 007 in East London, Forest Gate's Upper Cut, North London's Club Rock Steady and the Four Aces, and Brixton's Ram Jam, as well as
numerous civic centres throughout the UK, hosted sound systems and even
sound clashes at which rival sound systems would battle for supremacy. To
some extent, for the reasons outlined above, British sound-system culture has
always been an underground affair for those 'in the know'. As Paul Bradshaw
commented in the *New Musical Express* (*NME*) in 1981, to hear a sound system 'at peak potency you need to be tapped into the wires, the handbills that
announce the upcoming sound spectaculars...underground news' (Bradshaw,
Goldman and Reel 1981: 26). Consequently, like the later rave and free-party
cultures, it was understood by some white subcultures to be authentic counterculture.

Principally instituted by the second wave of migrants, who came primarily
from the urban working-class areas of Jamaica (see Howe 1973), we have seen
that the sound-system/blues dance was an event at which the African-Caribbean community could, after a week of hard menial labour and less than ideal
living conditions, socialize and maintain some continuity with the culture they
had left behind. Jamaicans imported Jamaican records and created a familiar
environment. As Chris May comments, 'the worse the conditions the greater
the incentive, the need, to find sustenance in the culture left behind. Drink-
ing/social clubs (usually illegal) in all West Indian ghetto areas and the music
they provided came from home' (1983: 156). The common term for many
of the venues at which sound systems would play was actually an Irish one,
'shebeen'. Essentially, a shebeen was a place where illegal alcohol was sold
and consumed. The term was accurate in so far as many such venues were
unlicensed premises where alcohol and often cannabis were readily available.
Moreover, gambling was common, as well as other activities, including prosti-
tution (provided principally by white females). Still popular in 1981, the *NME*
describes a typical sound-system shebeen in London:

> It is not a glamorous room; the ground floor of a small terrace house...
> [There] are posters of reggae artists, Earth, Wind and Fire, Gladys
> Knight and, stuck incongruously over a speaker, a big poster for *The
> Great Rock & Roll Swindle*; holes peel back from the walls, showing the
> bare skeleton of wood. But it is 4:00 a.m., and we couldn't really be
> in greater luxury; it's a club that costs one pound entrance, playing
> great music; where a woman can dance on her own without being
> hassled or be sociable, as she chooses; and it's open all night from
> midnight, seven days a week... That classical sexual/economic rela-

tionship of white women supporting black men is still in evidence, but low profile. There is little racial tension. Punks come in the shebeens, bohos of every kind, earnest young white boys with thin ties and dark overcoats, hippies. There are natty dreads and youths in baseball caps, bomber jackets, kickers, khaki and dungarees... A corduroy clad dread with a weatherman hat cuts a complicated caper freezing on an off-beat, dancing a dub to the record. Out there in the hall, a man's asleep on the stairs. All the musicians of the neighbourhood pass through the shebeen, and everyone's a musician anyway, grabbing on the mike just to tell you what it's like to be fighting down in Babylon every day, when times is getting harder and harder. The shebeen is a safety valve. Sometimes a sanctuary (Bradshaw, Goldman and Reel 1981: 28).

Clearly, as these comments indicate, the shebeen and the sound system fulfilled an important social function. Whether sound systems played in shebeens or in licensed clubs, community centres or even church halls, for many West Indians in the UK they were significant social occasions. They were 'safety valves' where frustrations could be aired, discussed and left behind. They were 'sanctuaries' where, for a short period, the black person was in the majority, Jamaican Creole could be used freely, memories shared, and familiar music danced to. Moreover, it's worth noting that, later sound-system culture was continuous with the earlier recreational gatherings of the *Windrush* migrants, in that the children were simply continuing the leisure activities of many of their parents. Indeed, some were directly inspired to set up sound systems as a result of parental involvement in the scene. Dennis Rowe, for example, relates the establishment of his Saxon sound system directly to his family's involvement: 'All my family have always had sounds from when I was a boy' (quoted in Back 1992: 192). Hence, he says, from as early as the age of seven he became involved in sound-system culture (see also Henry and Back 2003: 435–36).

Sound systems, of course, were also, as they were in Jamaica, places of political and intellectual rhetoric and reflection, where the microphone would be used to 'tell you what it's like to be fighting down in Babylon every day, when times is getting harder and harder'. More particularly, sound-system culture is an expressive musical culture shaped by the concerns and experiences of both the performer and the audience. As Stephen Davis comments, 'deejaying is one of the only public positions in Jamaica [and African-Caribbean diasporic cultures] actually open to public participation in any direct sense. Thus, the tremendous national popularity of the great Jamaican deejays results from their skintight identification with the public and their ability to speak for the people. The dance halls...are the only places where the voices of the poor are clearly, consistently, and publicly heard without restraint from church and state' (1983d: 34; see also Marley 2005). In Britain during the 1970s and 1980s, for many young black people, sound-system music and 'chat'[5] is, as Back comments, 'inextricably related to coping with life in a white society... Over the past ten years or so, they have adapted its technology to create a crucible in which new versions of their history and experience can be voiced' (Back 1988: 141). The personal narratives of the poor and oppressed are often, as the deejay William 'Lez' Henry comments, 'quite uncomfortable for the people who rule... If you articulate this type of politics in a dancehall the parameters for discussion are widened. They have to be, because you can say anything you please. You can say anything you please about anyone you please.' Again, 'once you go out there and you air that to an audience, that takes on a...political dimension. It may not be political in the sense that, you know, it doesn't necessarily affect governance directly, but it does affect the political sensibilities of the people you're exposing to those knowledges' (Henry and Back 2003: 439; see also Burt and Hilliman 1978: 18). Similarly, commenting on the role of the deejay, Back helpfully draws attention to Walter Benjamin's essay 'The Storyteller: Reflections on the Work of Nikolai Leskov' (in Benjamin 1992: 83–107). Like the storyteller, he argues, the deejays' creative act is to apply their own experiences to the concerns of their audiences, who then respond to their creations (Back 1992: 195–96). This is an interesting point. 'Experience which is passed on from mouth to mouth', notes Benjamin, 'is the source from which all storytellers have drawn' (1992: 84). More particularly, he argues that 'an orientation toward the practical interests is characteristic of many born storytellers... [E]very real story...contains, openly or covertly, something useful. The usefulness may, in one case, consist in a moral; in another, in some practical advice; in a third, in a proverb or maxim. In every case the storyteller is a man who has counsel for his readers' (Benjamin 1992: 86). The point is that the deejay, likewise, has counsel for his listeners. As noted in the previous chapter, toasting or 'chatting' was often far closer to the content of Benjamin's 'real story', in that it functioned homiletically as a conduit for morals, practical advice, proverbs, education about history, and even religion. Furthermore, as we have seen, the sound-system event is one during which there is a sharing of collective experiences (see Gilroy 1991). When, for example, the London deejay Papa Levi 'chats' lyrics 'about the 35B bus ride and his experiences of growing up as a black Londoner, everyone in the dance knows what he is talking about. The physical and social reality common to the audience and the performers alike makes the music relevant and accessible' (Back 1992: 195). Consequently, the music embodied accessible and immediately relevant cultural politics.

Having noted the political significance of the deejay, it should be stressed the dancehall is a democratic space. (Prince Buster famously called his sound system 'Voice of the People'.) Hence, while the sound system affords the deejay a freedom denied in wider society, as with the preacher in African-Caribbean Pentecostal worship, s/he is not given carte blanche to say anything at all. It is a dialogic encounter. For example, Henry draws attention to the fact that, as a deejay, he was always aware that his words were being judged:

> the only thing that...can affect the story as it's being told... is whether the crowd like it or not... Because ultimately, it's what I've always said, they are your judge, jury, and executioners. So, if you chat something that they directly don't like, they will boo you off or drown you out. And, unless the sound-system owner is a complete fool, he will take you off, otherwise the next thing will be his set, especially if there's more than one set, will not be allowed to play any more (Henry and Back 2003: 442).

The music and the lyrics – certainly in later dub poetry – constituted liberationist discourse, which empowered the oppressed and challenged dominant, often racist social values. Hence, as we have seen, sound-system culture tended to be subversive. Furthermore, that many sound systems were held at shebeens immediately identified them as sites of subversion standing over against mainstream society. Consequently, during the late 1970s, partly because they were also musical cultures,[6] they became identified with countercultural discourse and popular with certain subcultures within British society, not least punks and post-hippies, such as those who attended free festivals (see Partridge 2006). Interestingly, whereas this has particularly been the case within reggae cultures, substantial evidence of such an identification can be found in other black musical cultures. For example, as Simon Jones argues,

> within the rock community...black idioms of expression provided the means through which young white musicians could articulate the collective experience of their counter-cultural audience. Black music was valued for its rebellious edge and its ability to express a particular kind of hedonistic 'freedom' unavailable in the dominant white culture... Various social groups have championed and 'borrowed' its oppositional meaning to signify their 'non-conformity' with the cultural mainstream (1988: xxiii).

This is conspicuously evident within the milieu of the sound system and the shebeen. Within these spaces of cultural consumption white youths were introduced to and absorbed the religio-political agendas and sensibilities of black culture. In this sense the sound system can be understood as an 'irenic culture'. Although, of course, such irenic encounters were bilateral – outernational sound-system cultures being inevitably shaped by their new, white,

British contexts (Gilroy 1993: 15–16) – it is significant that roots and dub in the 1970s were informed by the agendas of black performers. In other words, as Back comments, 'black styles operated as a socially cohesive force which unified young people within these alternative spaces. This was particularly profound for young white [people] who found themselves owning black cultural forms' (1992: 215). However, it is important to note that this owning of black cultural forms has a particular significance concerning African-Caribbean music in the UK. Black American popular cultural forms, for example, were, as Jones comments, 'submerged and mediated by a relative distance between their "black" point of origin and their "white" context of consumption. Black forms have tended to be consumed by white British youth and public alike as specifically *American* popular music, the conditions which have shaped them being somewhat removed from white British experience' (Jones 1988: xxiv; original emphasis). While we will see that this is true to some extent, there is a sense in which it is *not* the case for reggae and dub. It has never been received as a form of specifically *American* popular culture and thus, to some extent, distanced from its black origins. Rather, it has been mediated by 'the *presence* of a substantial section of the African-Caribbean working class in the heart of urban Britain, and by the relative familiarisation of its cultural and political traditions to British society' (Jones 1988: xxiv; original emphasis). Consequently, in Britain, the white appreciation of dub has 'been bound up with a closer relation to these traditions, and with an accompanying encounter with the contradictions of race, that has politicised the forms and conditions of white consumption in ways that Afro-American music has not' (Jones 1988: xxiv). Again, the point as far as this discussion is concerned is that the cultures of the sound system and the shebeen are excellent examples of such irenic subcultural interaction and cross-fertilization. Nevertheless, we will see in the final chapter that the transition particularly to post-punk dub included a defusion of religio-political codes within the music.

Finally, another point that is worth noting at this stage, although it will be unpacked more fully in subsequent chapters, is that as the 1970s progressed this became less of a subcultural concern. While the subcultural analysis provided by Hebdige (1974, 1976b, 1979) and others have contributed significantly to our understanding of the stylistic continuities between white and black youth subcultures, there has been a tendency to neglect the more popular, yet equally significant, forms of white interaction with black and black-derived cultural forms. The mainstreaming of Jamaican reggae in the mid-1970s and dub by the end of the decade requires that, if we are to understand its impact on white youth, we need to look beyond the subcultural periphery to the heart of British popular music culture. As Jones has commented, 'the mass availability of reggae has rendered subcultural theory's counterposition of "authentic", "underground" forms of consumption to "straight" or conventional forms, highly problematic' (1988: xxv). Although it has to be said that dub *per se* has remained closer to the subcultural periphery than the work of such as Bob Marley or UB40, by the late 1970s it had become almost *de rigueur* for white post-punks to release dub B-sides. To repeat Viviene Goldman's comment, 'dub became the common vernacular for a broad swathe of artists operating in England...between 1977 and 1981' (Goldman 2003: 3). There were few mainstream punk and post-punk bands which did not produce dub versions of their material. The Ruts, The Clash, Generation X, Basement 5, Killing Joke, The Slits, Pil, Stiff Little Fingers, Grace Jones and even Goldman herself – 'Private Armies (Dub)' – released dub versions of their music. Although, in more recent years, dub as a musical genre has become less mainstream, we have noted that its impact is still evident in popular music, particularly dance and electronica.

To return, however, to sound-system events and shebeens, while they tended to be underground, there was no shortage of them for those in the know. Indeed, a 'Directory of Sounds' compiled by the *NME* in 1981 lists 102 sound systems in London alone, as well as many others in other English cities (Bradshaw, Goldman and Reel 1981: 28–29). As Wayne Thompson, who himself ran a sound system at the time, commented to me, 'if we didn't have a party planned, we would walk the streets and simply listen for the music'. He wasn't alone. As Ari Up of the punk band The Slits recalls, 'we used to find blues parties just following the bass... We would be streets away and listen for the vibrations' (quoted in Reynolds 2005: 81). Bearing in mind the size of the speakers and the sheer power of the amplification needed to drive the bass, which is at the heart of sound-system culture, this was probably not as difficult as it sounds. A top sound system was, reported Colin McGlashan in a 1973 *Sunday Times* article, 'thirty to one hundred times as powerful as a domestic hi-fi. The point isn't the volume, but the amplification of the bass... until it becomes music you can *feel*. You feel it in your feet, in the vibrations of a Coke tin with an unlicensed shot of scotch inside, you feel it through your partner's body. The first time you hear it, it's unbelievable, unbearable, oh my God! But you get used to it' (quoted in Hebdige 1987: 90). However, the point is that sound-system culture has never been or striven to be mainstream. Even nowadays, events are promoted primarily through flyers at specialist outlets and clubs, as well as on the Internet. They are often held in West Indian community centres or in small basement clubs. Moreover, as is the case with The Mighty Operation Sound System (a prominent dub sound system based in Blackburn, Lancashire) and The Shrewsbury Dub Club (Shropshire)[7] the entry is either cheap or free. Sound-system culture has continued to do what the hippie free festivals of the 1970s and the subsequent free-party movement of the 1980s and 1990s have ceased to do (see Partridge 2006). Few dance subcultures can declare 'All Tribes Welcome' and 'Free Entry' as one recent Operation Sound System flyer does.

That said, as we have seen in the previous chapter, most sound systems do vie for popularity within their particular 'scene'. This is often done through sound-system competitions and sound clashes, at which two 'sets' will be played at the same venue. Strictly speaking there were two types of sound-system competition, 'cup dances' and 'sound clashes'. Although far less common nowadays than they used to be in the 1970s and early 1980s, the former is, as the name suggests, an event at which sound systems will compete for a cup – usually provided by a promoter. Often judged by someone involved in the music business, such competitions can take place at a single event or over a succession of heats. As we have seen, a competent selector will be able to judge the mood of the crowd and discern what music it will respond to. As Back comments, 'he has to know when to liven up the crowd and when to calm it down' (1992: 192). Hence, regardless of a person's actual ability to play an instrument, programme a sampler, or interpret a dub plate, the ability to judge the mood of an audience, to know what to play and when to play it, and, therefore, how to control a crowd is an important and valued skill – which, indeed, extends beyond sound-system culture (see Frith 1996: 53). However, success is not judged simply by the selector's skill on the decks. The criteria used include 'selection, sound quality, performance, originality of dub and counteraction, performance and presentation' (Back 1988: 144). Overall, however, a distinction can be made between technical skill and emotional engagement with the audience borne of an intuitive *feel* for the music and the context. The latter is significantly more important in sound-system culture.

A sound clash is a similar event, although it is essentially a single meeting of two rival sound systems, rather than a series of events involving up to six sets. Sound clashes are, as Back comments and as I have myself witnessed, 'exciting and spectacular; the best music is played at a volume which shakes the foundations'. He continues, 'the battles run according to a fixed order. One sound system will play two records, then the other will do the same. This can lead to problems when the DJ has more than one mix of the same music. There is a lot of banter between the sounds via the microphone' (1988: 144; see also Burt and Hilliman 1978).

Whether in a competition or not, as well as the criteria outlined above, sound systems will often be 'rated' by fans on the number of versions they have of the same record. In other words, the *recording itself* carries significant weight. Indeed, discussing sound-system culture with Back, Max of London's Mastermind sound system made the following useful comparison with the soul and dance scene in the 1970s and 1980s:

> With reggae sound-system battles, the winner is generally the one who has the most exclusive records, or just the greatest number of versions of the same music. With the soul scene, it is basically the technical skill and imagination on the turntables, with any record, whether its electro, classical, new wave, rock, or whatever. It is the way you use it, not the actual record, that is important (Back 1992: 194).

Hence, again, within sound-system culture recording technology is elevated. Consequently – and this cannot be stressed enough – the acquisition of novel dub plates becomes paramount. Therefore, as we saw in the previous chapter – and as the film *Babylon* shows – dub mixes of the same rhythms will be highly sought after, often at great financial cost. Hence, of course, smaller sound systems were simply unable to compete and tended to play reggae favourites, rather than an impressive array of new dub plates. In competition, therefore, it was important, not only to acquire new versions, but also to know what dub plates competing sound systems had acquired. Dennis Rowe of the Saxon sound system, for example, attributed his success to the fact that he had access to versions his competitors did not have and also that he always knew what his competitors were going to play. It was common, therefore, for sound systems to claim that popular rhythms or dubs had been christened on their decks.

While many 1970s and 1980s sound systems played roots and dub, many others played that peculiarly British style of reggae known as 'lovers' rock', which had an increasingly large fan base. As one fan put it in 1981, 'A party is nothing without the girls and the girls check for lovers' (quoted in Bradshaw, Goldman and Reel 1981: 26–27). The lyrics were sometimes slack and were always explicitly aimed at dancing couples. However, according to the same fan, 'You can't start a party playing lovers, so you play a little dub and a little soul.' Others, however, focused explicitly on roots and dub. Such reggae fans attended bass-heavy dub sound systems, such as that of Jah Shaka or his main rivals Lloyd Coxsone and Fatman, or, a little later in the 1980s, the famous Saxon Sound International (see Back 1992; 1988). 'That's for the Ras Tafari them, for the dub man them... They don't play lovers, 'cause they're entertaining the Rasta them. They're not entertaining the yout' them – maybe Rasta yout', but them nah entertain me' (Bradshaw, Goldman and Reel 1981: 27; cf. Letts 2007). Similarly, another fan made the following comment: 'I was chatting to this rasta guy and he was telling me how dub gives him the vibe to dance. Lovers ain't got no vibes for him. Rastaman is the kind of person who'll dance by himself and feel high' (Bradshaw, Goldman and Reel 1981: 26–27). These are important comments and highlight a key aspect of dub (to which we'll return). Whereas lovers' rock was for couples,[8] dub was more conducive to solitary appreciation and reflective, even meditative states of mind. That said, it has been noted that articulated in much toasting and, we will see, in subsequent dub poetry (which emerged in the wake of the black power movement), the genre has been used as a medium for political rhetoric and community empowerment. For these reasons, dub-oriented sound systems, such as that established by Jah Shaka, began to attract the attention of both black and white youths (see Letts 2007: 72). Indeed, concerning the latter, my impression at the time – which has subsequently been confirmed in conversations with fans – was that those coming to dub from the free festival, hippie-LSD-cannabis culture, and who were largely middle-class, tended to be impressed by its ability to promote transcendent states of mind, whilst those encountering it as punks, coming from primarily working-class cultures, fuelled by anger and an iconoclastic attitude, tended to focus on its political rhetoric. These differing approaches to dub amongst white youths will be examined in more detail in the following chapter.

We have, in the previous chapter, noted the cultural and musicological significance of the sound system. It has, we have seen, a particular importance in the history of Jamaican dub. This is no less true in the UK. While the midwives of dub are recording engineers and producers, and the cradle of the dub is the studio, its natural habitat, the environment in which it flourishes, is sound-system culture. There were, of course, numerous sound systems. Having listed several of those to emerge in the 1970s, it will be helpful at this point to examine three of them in a little more detail.

Jah Shaka, Sir Coxsone, and Fatman

One of the most well-known, widely respected and certainly influential dub sound systems in the UK is that of Lewisham's Jah Shaka (Neville Roach), who, for several reasons, can be considered the high priest of dub. Taking his name from the nineteenth-century Zulu warrior chief, Shaka (1787–1828), he is a devout Rastafarian whose music and philosophy expound a consistent Afrocentrism. Not only does he, through his work, seek to raise black consciousness and focus the minds of listeners on issues of concern for Africans around the world, but he has also established the Jah Shaka Foundation, which assists relief projects in Ethiopia, Jamaica, and particularly Ghana.[9]

Perhaps more than most, politically, Shaka is a thoroughgoing Garveyite who takes the doctrine of African repatriation seriously. Although his comments about returning to Africa need to be understood, in part, eschatologically, the belief in this-worldly, physical repatriation is explicit:

> we Rastas... [are] just passing through this place where we're living temporarily on our way home. And the knowledge which we've gained in whatever country we've been living, we'll take it back to Africa with us and use it to build up our own country there. I don't think we're asking too much to do that, and it's not a problem for anyone if we do that. People are starving there... We will not stay here and suffer brutality, with no rights to express ourselves... We don't want to fight in a country which doesn't belong to us. We Rastas are peaceful people, so we prefer to leave this place (Mosco 1984).

Repatriation is, he stated in 1981, 'a complete solution... We are not fighting to stay here. If I was to meet the head of the National Front, it would solve a lot of problems' (quoted in Bradshaw, Goldman and Reel 1981: 27).

As for his dub music, this too is unsurprisingly Afro-centric, continually referencing African music and culture. For example, he makes liberal use of drumming and drum effects, particularly the sounds of the bass drum and the *fundeh*, which he clearly intends to be evocative of African music. 'If we were recording in Africa, maybe we could get two hundred people to play drums, but until then we have to make do with other things' (Mosco 1984), such as technologies that produce similar effects. Likewise, The Disciples' Boom-Shacka-Lacka Sound System, formatively influenced by Shaka, displays a large painted board on which are written the following words: 'every sound of the drum you hear is an African beat...' Again, as in much dub, Shaka uses numerous subtle – and not so subtle – sound effects, such as the 'flying cymbal' (developed by King Tubby) and, most prominently, his trademark siren. Whereas these often appear to be random noises in the work of some artists, Shaka insists that this is not the case in his music. 'Certain sounds I use – I don't know whether people have picked this up – but they're really the sounds of the jungle, like birds and noises you would hear in the wilderness' (Mosco 1984). In other words, Shaka's music can be understood as a Pan-Africanist project which seeks to stimulate the African consciousness by evoking African environments and cultures within the minds of those living in Babylon.

While Shaka has produced some of the most carefully mixed, mature, and purely pleasurable examples of dub, it is arguable that others have been more innovative with the dub sound. Although his studio collaborations with artists such as The Disciples (e.g. *Deliverance: Commandments of Dub 6* and *The Disci-*

ples volumes 1–3) and Aswad (*Jah Shaka Meets Aswad in Addis Ababa Studio*) are more adventurous, when one thinks of the artists experimenting with digital dub since the early 1990s or even the work of Adrian Sherwood in the 1980s, Shaka's solo work is, in the final analysis, relatively conservative. Although it is extreme in its own way, being hardcore steppers dub with, more than many other sound systems, deep bass frequencies, and although he introduces powerful treble sounds, screeches and sirens that have an unnerving and yet exhilarating effect when played live, his music is faithfully articulated roots reggae. As Barrow and Dalton commented in 1997, 'the roots scene's main point of focus over the past two decades has been Jah Shaka's sound system, the only significant system that kept the faith with 1970s ideals' (1997: 352). Indeed, as we will see, he is less interested in musical innovation and novelty than he is in producing music that conveys a particular roots message, the principal content of which will be apparent to any who have seen him play or owned one of his albums. For example, most of the sleeves of his records include explicit devotional material relating to 'HIM' (His Imperial Majesty, Haile Selassie) and also biblical quotations, usually from the Psalms.

Born in Clarendon, Jamaica, he moved to England in the early 1960s. His first sound-system experience was with Freddie Cloudburst, playing 'soul records or early 78 rhythm and blues records. It was in the early days, in the sixties, people didn't have big sounds, it was very small...' (quoted in Tosi 2001). (Indeed, Shaka has maintained, from this period, a knowledge and love of soul and jazz music.) In the late-1960s he began building his own sound system in order to play the new roots reggae music coming out of Jamaica. It should be noted here that there is a little confusion as to the exact date he began doing this. In Shaka's 1984 interview with Steve Mosco (the dub artist Jah Warrior), he is clear that he began in 1970. A couple of decades later, in an interview with Pier Tosi, he suggests that he may have begun operating earlier than this. It was, he recalls, 'in the seventies or about 1968, 1969 that we start Shaka Sound and that era was the era of consciousness with sounds like Burning Spear, Abyssinians, Twinkle Brothers, Bob Marley...' (Tosi 2001). Indeed, another account, surprisingly posted on his own website, claims that his 'apprenticeship' with Freddie Cloudburst took place during the '1970s', rather than the '1960s'.[10] This is certainly erroneous. However, whatever the precise date of the Shaka sound system's genesis, what is clear is that its activity is to be located at the origins of roots reggae.

More significantly, however, he has also claimed that in 1970 he began playing 'dub' in London. Though we need not doubt this, it is a little surprising. That said, if he was, he must be speaking of the proto-dub versions or instrumentals. Indeed, in his interview with Shaka, Mosco gently questions this claim: 'There wasn't much dub around in 1970 was there? It only started happening a few years after that didn't it?' 'Well', replies Shaka, 'I had dubs at that time. I used to get a few from Jamaica, and what we couldn't get *we made ourselves*. We had a lot of musicians creating stuff for us' (Mosco 1984; emphasis added). If this is the case, it is significant, in that it is likely that, not only was his the first UK sound system to consistently play 'versions', but he may have been the first to *produce* versions in the UK.[11] While this is difficult to establish conclusively and, we will see, is challenged by Lloyd Coxsone, it does indicate his seminal importance for the early UK roots and dub scene. His versions might not have been 'dubs' in the strict sense of the term, but, as he himself refers to them as 'dubs', it is likely that they will have been very close to what we now know as dub – i.e. the deconstructed and manipulated versions pioneered by King Tubby in 1972.[12] It's perhaps worth noting that when I suggested that Shaka was first to play dub in the UK to David Katz, he was clear that it was more likely to have been Duke Vin. I wasn't convinced and, in a recent conversation with Don Letts, he confirmed to me that, as far as he was concerned, Shaka was the first to play dub in the UK. There is little doubt that Duke Vin was at the genesis of sound-system culture in the UK, but when it comes to dub, in the sense that the term is now understood, the evidence supports Shaka's primacy.

There is clearly little doubt that, whatever Shaka's overall significance in the production of UK dub, he was a faithful dub ambassador from the beginning of the genre, disseminating within the UK, Jamaican sonic developments almost as soon as they were committed to vinyl. Hence, while it is tempting to focus on the significance of the big names in Jamaican dub, there are other important figures who are too often neglected – even in discussions of the UK dub scene. Jah Shaka is undoubtedly the most important of these unsung heroes. Indeed, I have lost count of the number of times his name is mentioned when chatting to some of those involved. Much more than Perry's seminal *Blackboard Jungle Dub* is the name of Jah Shaka mentioned by UK artists and those who were fans of dub in the 1970s and 1980s.

Unlike many other sound systems, not only is Shaka's a one-man show, in that he is the owner, deejay and selector, but he has for many years eschewed that popular feature of mainstream sound-system culture, the sound clash. This may come as something of a surprise to those readers who are aware of his first album, *Dub Confrontation: Jah Shaka Versus Fatman* (1980), or those who have seen the film *Babylon*, or read Mike Russell's book based on the screenplay (1980). However, nowadays Shaka is insistent that confrontation is very much the opposite of what he wants to convey and promote. While this stance is clearly not supported by his first album, to some extent it was not his own. At this point he did not have his own label. The only album not to be released on Jah Shaka Music, it was produced by Robert Fearon (the selector for Fatman Hi-Fi), engineered by Prince Jammy, and, incidentally, included Mikey Dread on bass. Hence, it is not a typical Shaka record. It is playfully confrontational in the Jamaican style, being the meeting of two London dub sound-system giants. *Babylon*, however, is explicitly confrontational and physically aggressive. It tells the story of a sound-system competition between the fictitious Ital Lion Sound System – the deejay of which, Blue, was played by the actor and Aswad guitarist Brinsley Forde[13] – and Jah Shaka's sound system (by that time in the late-1970s, arguably the most famous in London). The description of the opening of the competition mimics that of a boxing bout – which would not have been inappropriate, bearing in mind the self-understanding of many dub sound clashes of the period:[14]

> The compere, wearing tails and white gloves, an effect made more incongruous by his scraggy dreadlocks, climbed onto the platform and stood beside a small table on which rested the winning trophy for the evening, a gleaming silver cup with twin handles, standing on a black, plastic base. He held his hands up for silence, a signal which brought forth catcalls, jeers, and booing from the rival supporters...
>
> 'Ladies an' gen'lmen...now is the moment we have been waiting for! Brothers and sisters! Tonight is de cup final *night*!'
>
> More cheering and catcalling. The compère waited for the din to subside. He gestured to one side of the dais where the Shaka team were lined up. 'On my right, I got 'ere the champion of London, champion of Great Britain – and of Europe! Is Jah Shaka! (Russell 1980: 113–14)

While *Babylon* provides a relatively accurate window on aspects of late-1970s sound-system rivalry – although there is some exaggeration for dramatic effect – Shaka is clear that it is not an accurate description of his own sound system. Hence, in his interview with Mosco, he distances himself from the film. Indeed, he makes the point that, initially, he refused to get involved when he read the script. However, eventually, he says, 'I ended up directing the scene I appeared in myself, because all the build up leading up to it, with people from my sound confronting another sound...well that just doesn't go on... I was totally against the way they portrayed the build up to the dance in that film' (Mosco 1984). Bearing these final comments in mind, one wonders why he appeared in it at all. The answer is not difficult to find. There is evidence to suggest that his attitude to the sound clash changed around 1980. Until the

1980s, it would seem that Shaka was very much involved in British sound-system competition (see his interview with Hurford 1990). He even travelled the country in order to establish his supremacy. For example, a former member of his sound crew in the 1970s remembers how he arose to prominence during this period:

> Shaka used to get his dubs from the producer Winston Edwards. He had an arrangement where any good tune being made in Jamaica, he was the first to get it, long before it was released. He also got more cuts than anyone else and better cuts than anyone else. That's how he made his name. At one time he used to sign on with twelve cuts of 'Kill Nebuchanezzar' by Fred Locks when he was playing with another sound. There was no way that anyone could match it. So that was that – he'd finished the other sound off before the dance had even begun... Eventually he'd worked his way round every sound in the country and dealt with all of them...except one, Sir Coxsone. Coxsone was regarded as the number one then and they'd heard about Shaka and they'd been avoiding playing him, until finally a dance was arranged and they played together for the first time. It was in Croydon in 1976. Well Shaka went for it that night and half way through the dance, Lloyd Coxsone took the mic and said 'Stop the dance, stop the dance! In all my years in sound system I've never heard a sound like Jah Shaka.' And that was it. That was the night Shaka took the crown as number one in England and from then on nobody could touch him for years... (quoted in Mosco 2005).

Again, as one Shaka fan comments: 'Shaka is the greatest soundman of all. I have seen sounds "string up" against Shaka and arrange to play three musics each, and by the time Shaka was in his second music the other sound was "stringing down". I rate Shaka the highest' (quoted in Back 1988: 149). However, certainly by February 1981, the *NME* was reporting that 'Shaka detests dealing in competition' (Bradshaw, Goldman and Reel 1981: 26). From this time on it is conspicuously evident that Shaka's dub is more about Rasta spirituality and politics, the promotion of peace and unity, and the chanting down of Babylon, than it is about straightforward musical entertainment, particularly when this is articulated as confrontation or rivalry.

The fact that his music does have entertainment value is, however, important for Shaka, in that it makes it all the more effective as a carrier of 'the message': 'music is the only language which everyone can understand' states Shaka. 'So, the message is being carried out, but people can also enjoy the music because of the beat – even if they can't understand the words, they get into the beat' (Mosco 1984). Music is important, but it is a means to an end, a tool for a higher purpose: 'the music is a stepping stone to get the message across' (Mosco 1984). Whereas other media can be suppressed and controlled by Babylon, the sound system can act as a subversive voice of truth, a conduit of education for the people. Hence, if taken seriously and its full potential correctly exploited, a sound-system event is not a place of verbal or physical conflict; it is a place of peace, learning and culture, where the faithful can meditate on their God, their history, and the society in which they live. Once the massive speakers are set up at the side of the hall, the lights dimmed, the photograph of Selassie I pinned up (as it always is by Shaka), and the needle comes to rest on the first dub plate, the space is sacralized – it becomes less a venue for entertainment and more a sacred space, in which the profane effects of Babylon are neutralized. Moreover, whereas Christian ritual signifies the ubiquity of the divine through the use of incense, the fragrance of which permeates the sacred space, similarly at a sound-system event, the presence and inspiration of Jah is literally felt in the primal, ubiquitous vibrations of the bass. 'God has created certain things and these things appear to you at certain times when the music is played at the right time... It's a feeling created by God himself... You can't just come out and play a certain record.' Rather, 'because God has inspired me to do what I'm doing... I just have to go with the feeling at the time. I might play one record, which then inspires me at that moment to play another to follow it, and so on' (Mosco 1984). This is part of the reason he tends to work on his own. Although he doesn't dismiss the notion of working with deejays – which, we have seen, is popular in dub sound-system culture – they would need to be in full sympathy with his Rasta spirituality and politics. Toasting which included the usual taunting of other sound systems or slack lyrics would compromise the message. (Shaka, of course, is not alone in this. Indeed, The Rootsman, a Muslim convert, made it clear to me that he found slack lyrics offensive and antithetical to what he was trying to communicate through dub.) Just as in religion generally, where issues of purity and pollution are central, there is a sense in which, for Shaka, the message that he has been entrusted with must not be corrupted or compromised: 'in the beginning was the word, and we have to put the word across' (Mosco 1984). Hence, while he has used deejays in the past, he makes the point that, 'because of our orthodox style, now there's not many deejays who would step forward and ask for the mic, knowing what our style is. It's a different set up completely from most sounds' (Mosco 1984).

Moreover, while he is aware that his commitment to 'the word' or 'the message' may impede commercial success, this does not concern him. Indeed, he is critical of commercial sound systems that simply follow trends. Whereas sound systems have become 'a gimmick now with certain people', he is committed 'to have that orthodox discipline about sound system'. Again, he doesn't 'get involved so much in the commercial side of things – it's only certain people that want to book this sound, knowing the type of music we play. I'm not playing on a commercial basis' (Mosco 1984).

Consequently, there are continuities and discontinuities with wider sound-system culture. On the one hand, the Shaka sound system does provide a conduit for news, historical and political education, and, as with earlier Rastas, spirituality. On the other hand, there is a determined move away from the aggressive sound clash culture, competition, and the felt need to demonstrate success and popularity. Shaka is, therefore, a very different sound-system operator to Duke Reid, Coxsone Dodd, Prince Buster, and even, as we will see, Lloyd Coxsone and, to a lesser extent, Fatman, for whom supremacy and commercial success were paramount. Indeed, very few, if any, early sound-system operators would have made the following statement: 'I don't know what other sounds are doing, I only know what I am doing. It's nothing to do with what kind of speakers or amps I'm building; I'm only concerned with building spirituality' (Shaka quoted in Bradshaw, Goldman and Reel 1981: 27).

It's perhaps worth noting here that, while his politics is, in many ways, straightforward Garveyite Rastafarianism, unlike some Rastas, although he is committed to the empowering of black people, he also believes that his music and message has something to offer to all peoples – particularly the disenfranchised and oppressed. 'We hope that not only black people, but also people of other countries can enjoy it and listen to what we've got to say' (Mosco 1984). Here, perhaps, we see some influence of the soul and jazz scenes with which he is familiar. During the 1970s, the soul/funk scene was just as popular as reggae, but the crowds tended to be more multi-racial. Indeed, soul became identified with black and white social integration (see Hewitt 1986). As genres began to mix in the 1980s, so sound-system culture likewise became more open. Although Shaka retained a commitment to roots reggae and dub, he welcomed the interest of white youths. Again, in his interview with Ray Hurford for the dub-zine *Boom-Shacka-Lacka*, he makes a similar point when commenting on the fact that sometimes whites outnumber blacks at his events:

> If someone was to come to our dances, they might see that 50% of the crowd is white, or even 60%. Sometimes it depends on where I'm playing. If I go to Southend there's only about ten black people... But we are not only in this for black. It's for those who believe in the truth, and who we can bring into the fold, they can do better things. They can go to work tomorrow, they might open the door for someone because they heard the record saying '...try to do good'. Just because of that they have started to become more aware, to help people,

> because that record reached their heart. We are not playing records for them just to go in peoples' ears, it's for their hearts, to help them in their lives (Hurford 1990).

For Shaka himself, the music is, we have seen, a spiritual resource. 'Some people dream mentally', he says, 'but I get my dreams through my ears, so, therefore, I expect certain things and when I hear it I know it. That's the kind of music we play – which reaches the heart – really it's a heartbeat music' (Mosco 1984). Accounts of him performing consistently draw attention to his shaman-like meditative states. Adrian Sherwood, who knows him well, comments that 'Shaka just has his own thing altogether. Playing music for ten, twelve hours without a break, until he enters a trance like state, then he's on God's plane, following God's plan' (Sherwood, in interview with Whitfield 2003). Again, Lol Bell-Brown of The Disciples – who has worked very closely with Shaka – provides an excellent description of him in action: 'Shaka is at the controls like a man possessed, his eyes rolling back into his head, body bent at the waist and rocking heavily to and fro...' (1988).

As to the style of music, as noted above, it is an assertive form of roots reggae known as 'steppers'. 'Roots' music, of course, is ideologically driven, concerned particularly with issues facing the 'sufferer' – the poor, black, oppressed person living in Babylon. And steppers rhythms, which are more pronounced, assertive and militant than other roots rhythms, such as 'rockers', seem to reflect this politically strident and spiritually devout message. Indeed, accompanied by high-stepping dance moves, it can almost be understood in terms of a powerful, bass-heavy reggae-march. As with all dub, but particularly with steppers, the emphasis is very much on the bass. Bell-Brown puts it simply: 'Bass is king' (1988). Describing one of Shaka's events, which can last many hours, he comments on the pure power of the bass, accompanied by the alchemical manipulation of treble effects. While those who have attended such events will be familiar with the sheer power unleashed, I'll quote his evocative description at length for those who have not:

> Truly, this is no place for the weak heart... The bass hits your chest. That's where you 'hear' it, rather than with your ears. They're under assault from the treble, which is threatening to take your scalp off. Your rib cage resonates alarmingly and your trousers appear to shift around your legs as if in an effort to escape the fearsome roar that is all around. 'Awesome'. Suddenly everything is still. After the fourth cut is run Shaka plucks the unidentified dubplate from his antiquated deck... 'Give thanks and praise to His Majesty, Emperor Haile I Selassie, King of Kings, Lord of Lords, Conquering Lion of Judah...and [he] drops the needle onto the next selection... ssshhhtttt-pop-crack-sshhtt, the

run-in groove plays a symphony of surface noise before the familiar intro to the beloved 'Kunte Kinte'/'Beware of Your Enemies' tune
[begins]... It's all treble at first, and everyone's holding their breath
anticipating the pressure once Shaka drops the bass. Twice he hauls
and pulls up before letting the rhythm run for about half a minute.
All the while the crowd is screaming its encouragement.... 'whip them
Shaka!' someone cries. The tune reaches its first chorus and Shaka
finally lets the weight go, BOOM! The crowd succumb to the beat and
abandon their souls to rapture... This is Jah Shaka, King of the Zulu
Tribe in session! (Bell-Brown 1988).

During the 1980s, it became increasingly apparent that the shifting sands
of popular music had led to an erosion of interest in traditional, spiritually
informed, hard steppers dub. Shaka seemed unconcerned. As we have noted,
he was not driven by market forces or influenced overmuch by changing trends
and falling audiences. Hence, he continued in the same vein, producing hardcore steppers rhythms for the faithful. Indeed, in 1980, he inaugurated his own
label, Jah Shaka Music, and released his first single, 'Jah Children Cry'/'Jah
Jah Dub' by the UK-based singer African Princess. Throughout the 1980s he
released a string of seminal dub albums, some of which were recorded by
Neil Fraser (Mad Professor),[15] the most important of which, by any standard,
was his ten-volume series, *Commandments of Dub* (1982–1991). Moreover,
during this fallow period he also collaborated with many notable roots artists, including the Twinkle Brothers, Bim Sherman, Johnny Clarke, Pablo Gad,
Vivian Jones, Gregory Isaacs, Horace Andy, and Aswad. As for the fans, some
were so inspired by what they experienced that they began to create their
own music. Indeed, during this period, seeds were sown by Shaka that significantly contributed to the revival of dub in the 1990s. In other words, he
is directly responsible for inspiring and influencing some of the key figures in
contemporary dub. This is conspicuously evident in a recent French documentary by Nathalie Valet, *Dub Stories*. In interviews with both British and French
dub producers and musicians, the name most frequently mentioned is that of
Jah Shaka. Again, the brothers Russ and Lol Bell-Brown – The Disciples – two
of most important figures in dub to emerge outside Jamaica during the 1980s,
state their indebtedness to Shaka:

We started to hear about Shaka. We knew of him before, had some of
his records, but were never amongst the sound system scene. At that
time it was very underground and mostly a black thing. Anyways, we
heard some session tapes and the power and vibe that was on them
gave us some inspiration. So I tried to emulate it in our recordings... As
we started to get more into the heavy Shaka vibes we started making

some heavier tunes, again still mostly versions of old tracks... and we tried twisting the [bass] line around to give it our own vibe... [As] time went on we started to get to know a few people, guys that worked in record shops and we played them our tracks. They said to take them to Shaka. I had got myself a dubplate cut with four different tracks... [and] took that to Shaka who had an arts and craft culture shop in New Cross. We wasn't expecting anything, just maybe some guidance or opinion. Shaka said he wanted four cuts of each and anything else we had in similar style. He didn't seem to have any prejudice about us being white and making this music. He then said come to the next dance the following week, after that we was totally hooked (Murder Tone 2005b).

Indeed, in interview with Valet, Russ Bell-Brown notes the continuing formative influence of Shaka when, in a discussion about the evolution of dub – what we might describe as trans-genre dub – he states that, in an attempt to keep his work grounded within roots and dub, he constantly asks himself, 'Can Shaka play it? If Shaka can't play it, it's not the right kind of tune' (*Dub Stories*). Similarly, Steve Mosco (Jah Warrior), another significant figure in the UK dub scene, considers him to be 'the most important figure on the dub scene today, not only in the UK, but also internationally. For without him the scene would have died a death many years ago. Every single person without exception who has produced dub music or started a roots sound system in the past ten years has been directly or indirectly influenced to do so by Shaka...' He continues:

I first heard Jah Shaka in June 1981 at The Havana Club in Derby. It was a Wednesday night and the place was packed... I'd heard a lot about Shaka so I was eagerly anticipating it. I wasn't disappointed... When [he] started playing it was like an earthquake in the place. He played one piece of plastic to sign on with and then pure dubplate the rest of the night – vintage Twinkle Brothers, Pablo, Johnny Clarke, King Tubbys, Scientist etc. I was standing a few feet away from his amp case and was transfixed by 'the little shortman' bobbing up and down in the air, eyes rolling like a man possessed, as his speakers literally shook the walls to their foundations and the sirens and syn-drums cut through your ears like piano wire. I was also amazed to see his deck vibrating up and down several inches yet not jumping on a track once – such are the tricks of soundmen. After each tune he played the crowd just stood in silent admiration – awe, even. To this day I still regret not having carried my tape machine in there. Four hours later, the dance finished and I was a confirmed Shaka follower (Mosco 2005).

Finally, it's worth noting that Adrian Sherwood, who has, even more than Shaka, been an influential force within the history of British dub, was himself inspired by his music: 'I've known Shaka for over 25 years. We are close. I've got his number, he's got mine you know. I have ultimate respect for the man Jah Shaka' (Sherwood, in interview with Whitfield 2003).

As we have seen, however, the Shaka sound system wasn't the only one working in London during the early 1970s. Indeed, as the 1970s progressed they proliferated. That said, it is arguable that, along with Shaka, there were two others that dominated sound-system culture during that period, Fatman Hi-Fi and Sir Coxsone Outernational.

'A tall, slim man whose angular features are framed by a crown of locks, Coxsone is an articulate constructive and outspoken representative of the sound-system fraternity in the UK' (Bradshaw, Goldman and Reel 1981: 29). Like Shaka, Coxsone (Lloyd Blackwood) came to England from Jamaica as a young boy. Travelling from Morant Bay, his birth place, he arrived in South West London in 1962. Originally working in London as a deejay for Barry Pierocket's sound system, he quickly established a small sound system of his own, namely Lloyd the Matador. However, following an unfortunate explosion when water got into his amplifier, he had to return to deejaying, this time for Duke Reid, who had offered him work with his successful South London sound system. Still keen to establish his own sound, his break came when he was offered a residency at one of London's premier dance clubs, the Roaring Twenties on Carnaby Street. Eventually, in 1969 he built his own sound system and, naming it after Jamaica's Coxsone Dodd, built up a committed team taken from Duke Reid's crew. He quickly established an enviable reputation in London and, indeed, was so successful that I Roy, who was the resident deejay at the Roaring Twenties, celebrated his sound system with his 1973 songs 'Coxsone Affair' (available on *Presenting I Roy*) and a special reworking of his 'Blackman Time' entitled 'Lloyd Coxsone Time' – the latter, whilst played by the sound system, was not released to the public until the following decade.

In late 1974 Coxsone established a small record shop, Intone, in Peckham Rye. Indeed, also in 1974, well before the establishment of Shaka Records, with Leonard Chin (Santic Music) he also established his own label, Ital Coxsone, the debut release of which was The Royals' 'Only For a Time' (November 1974). Although his label was short-lived, his sound system went from strength to strength during the 1970s, and in 1977 he established his Tribesman imprint, on which he re-released one of Sir Coxsone Sound's most significant and enduring records, namely his *King of the Dub Rock* (1980). Indeed, it is worth noting that this album was originally recorded and released on the Safari label in 1975, five years prior to Shaka's first dub album, two years after Lee Perry's *Upsetters 14 Dub Blackboard Jungle* (arguably the world's first dub album), and only a year after the first Jamaican dub album was released in the UK – Keith Hudson's *Pick a Dub*. Hence, Lloyd Coxsone is without doubt a cardinal figure in the history of UK dub, being one of the first British artists to record a full dub album. (An earlier dub album was recorded by Winston Edwards in 1974 on his Fay label, *Natty Locks in Dub*.) Indeed, it is not surprising that, despite the above comments concerning the supremacy of Shaka's sound system, Sir Coxsone Sound was rated the leading UK sound system in 1978 by readers of *Black Echoes* (see de Konigh and Griffiths 2003: 213) and at the beginning of the 1980s he was the holder of the 'coveted and controversial' Black Star Liner Cup for the best sound system (Bradshaw, Goldman and Reel 1981: 29). However, by this time, Coxsone was beginning to focus more on record production, his sound system – which had changed its name to Sir Coxsone Outernational – being run by his team. For example, following his earlier success, in 1982 he released *King of the Dub Rock: Part Two*.[16]

We have noted above that Shaka may have been the first person in the UK to produce and play dubs – in the sense that we now use the term. Although some I have spoken to (including Don Letts) would support this thesis, it should come as no surprise that the claim is challenged by Coxsone. Indeed, a discussion of sound systems that appeared in the *NME* in 1981 opines that, not only was Coxsone's 'sound...the first UK system to play dub', but he 'set the pace in equipment and pioneered the use of echo, reverb, [and] equiliser'. Moreover, the article explicitly states that he was instrumental in 'paving the way for a sound system such as Shaka to take sound to a new dimension, creating atmosphere out of rhythmic weight and effects' (Bradshaw, Goldman and Reel 1981: 29). However, while there was no doubt some cross-fertilization taking place, and while there is some evidence to suggest that Shaka was the first to play dub, in the final analysis, in a culture of competition and conflicting claims, it is very difficult at this distance from the original events conclusively to establish primacy.

Articulating a different philosophy to that of Shaka, Coxsone's approach was more straightforward, less interested in the volume, the weight of the bass, and the dubbed effects, and more interested in aural clarity and playing the right record at the right time. 'People can't dance to wattage', he argued in a 1981 interview. 'If a man comes to me and he deals with sound, he always deals with wattage. Listen, the more you step up weight, you lose quality, and a man must be able to hear your vocal playing... I am more interested in quality and selection of music' (quoted in Bradshaw, Goldman and Reel 1981: 29). And, as the *NME* reported,

> those who have witnessed Shaka and Coxsone in dub conference
> will know that in following Shaka's distorted swirling dubonics and
> sheer physical weight, Coxsone will operate one piece of amp less and
> maintain a sharpness and a clarity, a kind of 'round beat' and initially
> let the music do the work, before Poppa Festus – the Coxsone Hi-Fi
> controller – puts on the pressure, injecting tension into the rhythm
> and building the climax into the dub cuts (Bradshaw, Goldman and
> Reel 1981: 29).

Again, betraying a different approach to that of Shaka, central to Coxsone's thinking was the development of a sound-system team, principally made up of younger enthusiasts who could ensure that the music stayed at the cutting edge:

> To run a good sound in the UK is teamwork...a young team of men who
> are ambitious, record crazy, and have good ideas. If I get old within my
> ideas there are many young men who come up with suggestions. By
> building a team you are building your sound for a long term. In my
> time in England I have seen a lot of good sound die 'cause they didn't
> build a team to manifest the work of the sound. Teamwork and effort
> is crucial as you can't live off your name (quoted in Bradshaw, Gold-
> man and Reel 1981: 29).

Also central to his thinking – and in this he differs from Shaka – is the creation of popular entertainment. He was less, if at all, interested in nurturing spirituality than he was in getting people dancing. 'I am supposed to select music for the people to dance to, that is our job. That's what they're paying us for' (quoted in Bradshaw, Goldman and Reel 1981: 29). Hence, Coxsone was principally concerned to keep in step with the latest trends in order to maintain popularity – whether those trends be dub, lovers' rock, or ska. Shaka's philosophy and commitment to conscious sounds, on the other hand, set him apart from most sound systems, which, like Sir Coxsone Outernational and Fatman Hi-Fi, were primarily concerned with demonstrable success as musical providers.

Fatman (Ken Gordon) has a history very similar to that of Shaka and Coxsone. Having been brought up in West Kingston by his aunt, when she moved to North London, he rather reluctantly followed in 1963. Having already become a regular attendee at sound systems in Jamaica, within a month of living in Britain he was frequenting sound-system events in the Stoke Newington and Finsbury Park areas of London. It wasn't long before he was getting to know the crew of the Sir Fanso sound system, eventually becoming its principal deejay (in the style of U Roy). He stayed with Fanso for around seven years until the latter returned to Jamaica in the early 1970s, taking his sound system with him. Fatman recalls the sense of loss that he felt at the time of Fanso's departure:

> It leave me stranded, walking up an down trying to find a sound to listen to. I listen to a lot of sound them time. I couldn't find anything to please me, suit me...everything was backward! The last sound I go out and listen to before I decide to build my sound was Sir Dees sound playing out in Tottenham, and I stand up the night and listen, and... the music the man of Dees did play is music what Sir Fanso did stop play long time. I just come out and go home a my yard and I decide say I'm gonna build a sound (quoted in Bradshaw, Goldman and Reel 1981: 28).

Hence, in Hornsey in 1974, Fatman established what was to be one of London's most popular sound systems. Originally naming it the Wild Bells sound system, he soon changed it to Imperial Downbeat, largely because there was a competing sound system using the name Bells. However, he soon became affectionately known to fans as 'Fatman' and, therefore, decided to change the name of his sound system accordingly: 'The people...them named me Fatman. It was the people them did. So we just got to make the name of the sound Fatman Hi-Fi. That's how the name Fatman come about' (quoted in Bradshaw, Goldman and Reel 1981: 28).

Again, as with sound-system culture generally, Fatman's principal motivation was entertainment. However, perhaps more than Coxsone, just as Shaka was concerned to promote Rasta spirituality and ideals, so Fatman was concerned to promote reggae music. Indeed, Fatman began playing outside London, understanding his sound system more as 'mobile radio station for reggae music'. This was important for him because, he told the *NME*, 'It's the only way for the people them who really want to come and listen to reggae music. It's the only place them gonna hear it is to go and listen to a sound system, because them nah hear it upon no radio station.' The interviewer then asks, 'Would you like to see yourself playing Wembley Stadium say, and 100,000 people there?' To which he replies 'Yeah man', and his selector, Robert Fearon, comments, 'Buckingham Palace'. Fatman continues, 'We're not drawing a line from nowhere man. We want to play in all the top places. We want to see *our* reggae fans come to places like that. That's where we would really like to see reggae music. Everywhere.' He then comments, rather presciently (bearing in mind dub's current centre of gravity in France), 'Comes a time when we would really like to say we can drive our van and go and tour all the continent and just play reggae music. Comes time when we won't just be driving up to Birmingham or Manchester or Wolverhampton or wherever. We will be heading the ferry, you know. Man say, where you a go this week Fatman? We say, bwoy Paris we a go' (quoted in Bradshaw, Goldman and Reel 1981: 53).

Fatman's subsequent founding of several labels – Fatman, Boss, and Godfather – can be understood in terms of this evangelistic motivation to spread a love of reggae. One of his first releases on Boss was Michael Rose's 'Born Free' (1976).[17] As to his acquisition of records to play at his events (particularly dub), he had retained his links with the Waterhouse district of Kingston, and, more particularly, with Prince Jammy. Hence, just as Fanso had strategically ensured a steady stream of 'soft wax' from Duke Reid and the Treasure Isle studio, so Fatman, following his example, maintained a supply of exclusive dub plates from Prince Jammy (see Bradshaw, Goldman and Reel 1981: 28).

Before leaving our discussion of seminal British sound systems, Dennis Bovell's famous 'Jah Sufferer Hi Fi' Sound System should at least be noted. Established in London, in late-1969 it was, according to Bovell, 'heavier than Coxsone' (quoted in Penman 1998: 28). By the mid-1970s the bass-heavy dub of Jah Sufferer Hi Fi, as well as the fact that he travelled widely and worked continually all over London, led to his growing popularity. 'We used to play at, like, the Metro in Ladbroke Grove and get two thousand people every Friday night. All the kids used to love it...' (quoted in Penman 1998: 29). However, popular though he was, he became more widely known as a result of a notorious incident during a session at London's Carib Club in 1976.[18] The police raided the club looking for a youth on suspicion of a car theft. A fight quickly broke out and twelve people, including Bovell, were arrested. Nine were found innocent, two had no verdict recorded against them, and Bovell was wrongly convicted of causing an affray. A retrial at the Old Bailey found him guilty and sentenced him to three years' imprisonment. After six months in 'Wormwood Scrubs', an appeal court vindicated him and set him free.

> It opened my eyes to the world, I mean, in a really weird way. I'm sure, apart from maybe death, nothing as bad can ever happen to me again. There you are locked up in prison, you've done fuck all and you think to yourself...shall I go out of my head or what?... I thought I know what I'll do, just write some songs to keep me sane. That was the hottest summer I've experienced in this country and I was in the nick all through it' (quoted in Futrell 1981: 11).

Indeed, such was his experience in prison that he abandoned playing sound systems: 'I came out, and I thought, well... I've had it as far as sound systems go. I started concentrating on *making* music for sound systems, not just playing it. Even when I was playing the system, I was still making tunes; we used to go down to the studio and make tunes just for the sound system, acetates, and that was *dub-wize*, y'know?' (quoted in Penman 1998: 28–29; original emphasis).

Because, however, Bovell's significance extends beyond sound-system culture to his work with Matumbi and particularly Linton Kwesi Johnson and The Slits, it seems sensible to delay further discussion until the following chapter.

The Initial Dub LPs in Britain

While we have seen that instrumentals and proto-dub plates were being imported and possibly produced by such as Jah Shaka and Lloyd Coxsone from an early period – possibly as early as 1970 – it would be a few more years before the dub LP would make its debut in the UK. That it eventually did so, however, is important, in that it eventually contributed to the perception and reception of the genre by white rock fans as a serious form of experimental music.

As was noted in the previous chapter, so successful was Lee 'Scratch' Perry at home and abroad that the British label Trojan, which had been releasing Perry's work in the UK, launched their own version of the Upsetter label (see de Konigh and Cane-Honeysett 2003: 52–54; Katz 2000: 73–74). Apart from the considerable financial benefits for Perry himself, the deal was significant in that it bore testimony to the rising profile of one who would later be central to the emergence of dub, not only in Jamaica, but also in Britain. Indeed, we have noted that his creativity, which contributed so centrally to the emergence of dub, was forecast in early 1973 on his instrumental album *Cloak and Dagger*, two versions of which were pressed, not in Jamaica, but in London. Moreover, one of these versions was specifically crafted for the UK market. The British version (currently available on *Dub-Triptych*), which, we have noted, was daringly avant-garde – possibly his most experimental to date – makes creative use of ambient street recordings, sound effects, and solicited comments from the general public. Furthermore, as Katz comments, his 'dub' versions of tracks on the album were 'mixed in true stereo, with the lead instrument and voice overdubs in one channel and the unaltered rhythm in the other' (2000: 165). However, while the Jamaican release sold well, sales were disappointing in Britain. Perry's verdict on the relative commercial failure of the album was, firstly, the disinterest of Rhino Records in promoting it. Perry felt that they'd prejudged it to be too avant-garde for the British market. Secondly, he concluded that it was perhaps not polished enough for British tastes. For example, it lacked the strings overdubbing – which Trojan in particular had included on most of its releases in the UK – giving it a raw, sparse, slightly crude sound, which many British listeners were not used to. While the promoter Bruce

White (Commercial Entertainment) was less inclined to blame the distributor for Rhino Records/EMI, he agreed that the commercial failure of *Cloak and Dagger* in Britain was due to it being 'a bit before its time...the people weren't ready for it' (quoted in Katz 2000: 166).[19]

While Perry produced several notable hits in 1973, such as his tribute to King Tubby, 'Dub Organiser' – which used the 'Cloak and Dagger' rhythm – and another proto-dub album, *Rhythm Shower*, it was *Upsetters 14 Dub Blackboard Jungle* that proved to be his most important contribution to the genre. Becoming known simply as *Blackboard Jungle Dub* (available on *Dub-Triptych*), he originally pressed only 300 in Jamaica, 100 of which he brought to the UK the following year, selling them for the then high price of £20 each to British sound systems. As well as being a defining work of the genre, many consider it to have been the original dub album. Of course, we have noted that this is only one of three dub albums that have a claim to primacy, all of which were recorded and released at roughly the same time in 1973. The other two contenders are generally agreed to be *Java Java Java Java* (known as *Java Java Dub*), produced by Clive Chin and mixed by Errol Thompson, and *Aquarius Dub* produced and mixed by Herman Chin Loy. While Prince Buster's *The Message Dubwise* has also been suggested as a contender (Katz 2000: 177), this was actually released in 1974.[20] However, perhaps needless to say, as far as Perry is concerned it is *Blackboard Jungle Dub* that has the honour of being 'the first dub album that ever came out' (Perry, quoted in Katz 2000: 177). Whether this is true or not, as Katz comments,

> *Blackboard Jungle Dub* showed the very power of dub to transform a piece of music, to radically alter any given composition through creative mixing and spatial representation... [It] had a continuity that previous Upsetter releases lacked, and is thematically united through dub to create a sense of natural wholeness... [Whether] it was the first dub album or not, it was clearly crucial in inaugurating the genre of complete dub albums, and greatly added to the validity of the dub format in general (2000: 178).

Of course, as noted in the previous chapter, *Blackboard Jungle Dub* was not the sole creation of Perry, in that King Tubby, the engineer, possibly had more to do with the final product than the producer.

We have noted that it is generally agreed that the first dub album to be released in the UK was Keith Hudson's 1974 classic *Pick a Dub*. However, later the same year, Winston Edwards released two more significant albums on his Fay label, *Natty Locks in Dub* (arguably the UK's first indigenous dub album) and, far more significantly, *King Tubby Meets the Upsetter at the Grass Roots of*

Dub. It is this latter record more than any other that, as Barrow and Dalton have noted, 'established the dub album in UK' (1997: 218). Moreover, it is perhaps not surprising that it was Edwards who became the midwife of UK dub, since his cousin was Joe Gibbs. Gibbs introduced him both to the recording industry and also to Perry, who was, Edwards recalls, 'a friend of mine even when I was not involved in the music industry' (quoted in Katz 2000: 195). That said, he goes on to make the point that his principal musical association with Perry began when he arrived in England. Although Edwards spent much time in the early 1970s in Jamaica, he had initially moved to London with his family in the late-1960s and, by early 1974, had decided, for the sake of his education, to move permanently to Britain. However, just prior to leaving Jamaica, he decided to test his record production skills. With the assistance of Perry, he recorded Dennis Walks's 'Don't Play That Song' at the Black Ark. Then, having returned to England to study towards his 'A'-level examinations, he eventually released the song from his premises in New Cross, southeast London. (Indeed, it was in New Cross, at 29 Lewisham Way, that he later established his important record shop and distribution service for his cousin's productions, Joe Gibbs Records. And it was from here that he supplied fellow Lewisham resident, Jah Shaka, with exclusive Jamaican dub plates.) Although the song was not a strong seller, it did suggest to Edwards that the music business might be able to provide him with a much-needed income, as well as leaving him enough time to study. 'I said to myself, the easiest way to do my A levels was to continue in the music business, so I decided to get involved in the music industry proper' (quoted in Katz 2000: 196). He quickly established his own record label, Fay, named after his then partner.

Travelling to and from Jamaica throughout 1974, Edwards continued to work with Perry, eventually producing two important dub albums, *Natty Locks Dub*, from a mixture of rhythm tracks he had acquired and others produced specifically for the album at the Black Ark and at Joe Gibbs's studio – both of which studios he had virtually free use of. Although *Natty Locks Dub* demonstrated a confluence of dub and jazz, the follow-up album, *King Tubby Meets the Upsetter at the Grass Roots of Dub*, was very clearly and fundamentally dub reggae. A significant figure in the history of British dub, not only was Edwards close to Shaka, but he would later go on to work with one of the UK's leading reggae artists and producers of dub, Dennis Bovell, on their thoughtful album, *Dub Conference: Winston Edwards and Blackbeard at 10 Downing Street* (1980). However, it is for *Grass Roots of Dub* that he will principally be remembered. Apart from any other qualities (of which there were several), not only was this the album that put dub on the musical map in the UK, but it was the first purporting to be a mixing contest, with Tubby's skills displayed on side one and Perry's articulated on side two. Having said that, this was almost certainly a clever marketing gimmick – a very successful one – than a statement of the musical content. Instead of each having five tracks, says Edwards, 'maybe four tracks is Scratch and the other six were Tubby...' The name of the album simply occurred to him because 'some of the tracks were done at the Upsetter's studio, and some were done at King Tubby's studio'. Hence, he recalls thinking to himself whilst flying back to the UK from Jamaica, 'I'm going to name this album *King Tubby Meets the Upsetter*'. That was, as he says, 'the birth of...one of the best-selling dub albums in the UK' (quoted in Katz 2000: 197).

This idea of bringing mixing styles together on a single album, marketed as a dub contest, quickly became popular. Musically, it was successful in that the different styles often compliment each other – as was the case on *Confrontation Dub* by Shaka and Fatman. Katz, for example, has argued concerning *Grass Roots of Dub* that 'Tubby's side seems to have more reverb, and often features the unique equalizing of treble sounds that only his customized mixing board has been able to create, while the so-called Upsetter's side relied more on delay, occasionally isolating an electric piano in the foreground of the music' (2000: 198). That said, I would argue that there is a seamlessness of style. Indeed, not only is there a little confusion as to who contributed what to the album, but Perry's final production smooths out the distinctive traits of their respective approaches.

Perry, of course, was known to many in the UK prior to 1974, largely as a result of the output of Trojan's Upsetter label (see Letts 2007: 34, 36). However, as dub began to attract an audience, he was becoming known to an increasing number of British music fans as a truly innovative producer and a key influence in the new genre. In 1974, Perry's avant-gardism was confirmed when his creative output began to take a new, more abstract direction. He became fascinated with dub's manipulation of sound and during 1975 released four experimental albums of instrumentals and dub in the UK: *Musical Bones, Return of the Wax, Kung Fu Meets the Dragon*, and *Revolution Dub*. Perhaps nervous about their reception following the failure of *Cloak and Dagger*, not all of these were made readily available to the listening public. *Musical Bones*, for example, is said to have had only 300 copies pressed in the UK. Hence, for most fans, they were too expensive and could be heard only at sound-system events. Nevertheless, largely as a result of Perry's efforts and genius, by the emergence of punk in 1976, along with reggae generally, dub was beginning to be appreciated by a wider public than the many African-Caribbeans who attended sound-system events.

Having said that, it should be noted that, not only was 1974 an important year for dub albums in the UK, but it was arguably the first year in which a dub single entered the UK charts. Rupie Edwards's 'Ire Feelings' (on the Cactus label) sold over 250,000 copies, spent ten weeks in the charts, eventually entering the 'top ten' at number nine in November of that year. (This was followed in February 1975 by his 'Lego Skanga', which reached no. 32).

The Significance of Bass

> all tensed up
> in di bubble an di bounce
> an di leap an di weight-drop
>
> it is di beat of di heart
> this pulsing of blood
> that is a bubblin bass.
> (Excerpt from Linton Kwesi Johnson, 'Bass Culture' – 1991: 15)

At several points in the preceding discussions, attention has been drawn to an emphasis on the bass in reggae music and, particularly, its prominence within dub. This has, of course, been a conspicuous feature of sound-system culture. Indeed, it is a central feature of what Simon Frith would call its 'genre world' (1996: 88). Bass is, to a large extent, dub's stamp of authenticity. As well as being 'echo junkies', dubheads are, without exception, bass-heads. 'Our God, in a way, is bass' declares the refrain on the eponymous track by the Bass Lo-Ryders (on *Ryder Style*). Consequently, dub culture can, following Linton Kwesi Johnson's description, be understood in terms of 'bass culture'.[21]

As was noted in the previous chapter, reggae's emphasis on the drums and walking bass has some continuity with churchical patterns of Nyabinghi. However, not only have the bass and the drums become central, but there has been a growing emphasis on the sheer 'weight' of the bass, which has, in turn, been invested with a semiotic significance that elevates it above purely aural pleasure. Of course, to some extent, this is always the case with music, popular or otherwise. In aesthetic terms, to quote Frith again, 'musical sounds, ideologies, and activities, musical texts and their implied contexts, cannot be separated' (1996: 90). Sounds, styles, orchestration, emphases, and so on all convey meaning. Concerning the bass in dub, the heavier it is, the more it communicates what might be described as dread culture.[22] More broadly, bass demands that the music be taken seriously and, to this extent, regardless of whether it is instrumental or not, those subculturally in the know – genre-sensitive dubheads – recognize it as a stamp of authenticity. Consequently, the weightier it is, the more subcultural capital is accrued and, therefore, the more attractive the sound system, the artist, or the track becomes. Of course, dub does this intertextually, in that it references the meanings articulated in roots reggae and the rhetoric of Rastafari. Hence, for the most part, we are not here referring to those intrinsic qualities of sound that, for example, evoke feelings of sadness or joy, or to what Leonard Bernstein terms the 'affective' theory of musical expression[23] – 'why is the minor "sad" and the major "glad"?' (Bernstein 1976: 177) – but rather simply to the meanings and cultural codes that are invested in and associated with bass. That is to say, just as 'it is by now a deeply rooted commonsense assumption that a funk beat necessarily *means* sex' (Frith 1996: 102), so bass in dub and reggae necessarily references all that is meant by the term 'dread', often including, we will see, masculinity and notions of transcendence (see Johnson 1976a: 398).

In order to assert their subcultural value in this way, unlike discos in the 1970s, typical at sound-system events was (and still is) a large battery of speakers fed by very powerful amplifiers. For example, in 1981, Lloyd Coxsone commented that while he generally used around twenty bass speakers, 'other sounds play around 50' (Bradshaw, Goldman and Reel 1981: 29). Similarly, in 1978, London's Peoples War Sound System commented that 'some sounds have about 20 boxes of moderate sound and about 10 double boxes – as many as will fit in the hall that you are playing in' (in interview with Burt and Hilliman 1978: 17). Again, over a decade later, in 1991, The Disciples recall that they 'built up a sound powering some 5000 watts, 4000 of which were used on the bass end alone, running through to twelve 400 watt 18" Fane Colossus speakers' (Disciples 2005). (Note that the size of a speaker is directly correlated to how much bass it can produce and that, as will be explained below, the lower the bass gets, the more power is needed to make it audible.)

The term 'heavyweight', which refers primarily to the bass and is often used to describe dub, has become particularly significant. That is to say, devotees of dub (and, more recently, 'rave' sound systems[24]) are generally not interested in intricate guitar solos or catchy guitar 'licks' to the extent that the progressive rock fan might be. They are, for the reasons indicated above, far more interested in *heavyweight* bass. That this is consistently emphasized within the culture is evident in the titles of numerous tracks, album titles, and sound-system flyers. For example, the following album titles, taken from a quick perusal of my own collection, are not untypical: *Heavyweight Dub* (Inner Circle); *Heavyweight Dub Champion* (Scientist); *Forward the Bass* (Impact All Stars); *Bass Enforcement* (Power Steppers); *Bass Re-Enforcement* (Power Steppers); *Heavyweight Rib Ticklers* (Mr Scruff); and, from a techno-ambient perspective, *Set the Controls for the Heart of the Bass* (Bass-O-Matic/William Orbit).[25]

It is perhaps important at this point to restate the significance of the non-verbal qualities of dub. Although we have commented on the retention of vocal fragments in the versioning of reggae songs, by the time it was becoming established in Britain in the mid-1970s, these had begun to be omitted. Although rarely commented on, the evocative power of the music and the sonic effects employed are important for understanding the significance and the appeal of genre. As Jones writes,

> the expressive and semantic power of dub was carried by sounds, melodies and rhythms alone, sounds which had the capacity to convey emotions and express the weight of feeling without being linguistically comprehensible. The communicative power of dub in much rockers music, for example, lay in its ability to signify experiences and forms of subjectivity purely through the connotations of its drum and bass patterns, and through the use of echo and reverb (1988: 25).

Once this is understood, it is not surprising to discover that the emphasis on the bass is invested with several levels of meaning. Firstly, bass is, to some extent, gendered, being indicative of masculinity. As in many cultures, this is largely because the vocal register is gendered. As the typical male gets older, so the tone of his voice lowers and, consequently, the more masculine it is understood to be: 'singing voices become identifiably more "masculine" as they get older' (Welsh and Howard 2002: 108 – on interpretations of the high male voice, see Kopf 1995). This is certainly true of West African cultures. For example, as we saw in the previous chapter, in Burru and Nyabinghi drumming, the skin of the bass drum is, ideally, that of a ram goat – because, according to Count Ossie, 'the ram goat is less vociferous than the ewe by nature, and its bleat is of a lower tone. Hence, the skin when hit is of a desirable low pitch' (Reckford 1977: 3). Consequently, bearing in mind the theatrical displays of masculine power at sound-system events – evident in the titles adopted and the frequent references to aggression (see Cooper 2004: 145–206) – it is hardly surprising that the weight of the bass is important. However, perhaps because of this relationship, it also important because, as we will see, it is explicitly related to power *per se*.

Secondly, more subtly related to power and aggression, is the somatic impact of the bass. As has been noted several times in this chapter, descriptions of dub music rarely fail to comment on this impact, principally, I suggest, because it is a physical experience. Indeed, having been to numerous heavy metal and punk concerts over the years, I can say that, even at their volume, they don't come close to bass-oriented dub and dub-influenced events for somatic impact. As I wrote of one such event, 'along with [its] intriguing manipulation of sound, one feels the bass internally, as if being massaged within' (Partridge 2004a: 176). Indeed, at a meeting of the Bush Chemists and the Iration Steppas in Leeds, it felt as if the concrete floor had become fluid and rippled beneath my feet with the force of the bass. This, I have found, is not an unusual response. Fred D'Aguiar refers to the 'head-shaking, spine-twisting drum and bass' accompanying Linton Kwesi Johnson's poetry (2002: x). Greg Whitfield, who has been commenting on dub for several years, speaks of the 'primal underpinning' of the bass, a sound which you can 'feel in your abdomen, threatening to re-arrange and pummel your internal organs' (Whitfield 2002). McGlashan (as noted above) makes the comment that, 'the point isn't the volume, but the amplification of the bass...until it becomes music you can *feel*. You feel it in your feet, in the vibrations of a Coke tin...you feel it through your partner's body. The first time you hear it, it's unbelievable, unbearable' (quoted in Hebdige 1987: 90). Bell-Brown (also noted above) similarly comments that 'the bass hits your chest. That's where you "hear" it, rather than with your ears... Your rib cage resonates alarmingly... "Awesome"' (1988). Similarly, Julian Henriques reports that

> the first thing that strikes you in a reggae sound-system session is the sound itself. The sheer physical force, volume, weight and mass of it. Sonic dominance is hard, extreme and excessive. At the same time the sound is also soft and embracing and it makes for an enveloping, immersive and intense experience. The sound pervades, or even invades the body, like a smell. Sonic dominance is both a near overload of sound and a super saturation of sound. You're lost inside it, submerged under it... Sound at the level cannot but touch you and connect to your body. It's not just heard in the ears, but felt over the entire surface of the skin. The bass line beats on your chest, vibrating the flesh, playing on the bone, and resonating the genitals (2003: 451–52).

It is not surprising, therefore, that bass has been explicitly linked to the bodily and the sexual, the most obvious examples being Bass Erotica's dub-inspired albums *Sexual Bass* (1995), *Bass Ecstasy* (1996) and *Erotic Bass Delight* (1996). More interestingly, it is, perhaps, also not surprising that the somatic impact of the bass has been, as we will see below, invested with deeper, broader meanings relating to being and existence.

Thirdly, central to these meanings are what can be described as cardio-musicological references. These might be relational, religious or political. For example, its political significance is evident in Linton Kwesi Johnson's poem 'Bass Culture' (*Bass Culture*, 1980). The weight and depth of the bass signifies the seriousness of the black person's plight in the 'second Babylon' – Britain. Bass culture is the culture of the oppressed, the sound of the suffering: 'bass history is a moving, hurting, black history' (Gilroy 2003: 391). It is 'muzik of blood, black reared, pain rooted, heart geared'. It is also, however, 'di beat of di heart, this pulsing of blood that is a bubblin bass' (Johnson 2002: 14). In the poem this is, as so much of Johnson's early poetry was, related to racist violence, the spilling of black blood, and the pounding of the adrenaline-fuelled heart. The bass speaks of a 'dread' situation. This is also evident in his thoughtful, early essay published in *Race and Class*, 'Jamaican Rebel Music'. Reflecting particularly on the significance of the bass, he refers to reggae and dub as

> an essentially experiential music, not merely in the sense that the people *experience* the music, but also in the sense that the music is true to the historical experience of the people, that the music reflects the historical experience. It is the *spiritual expression* of the *historical experience* of the Afro-Jamaican. In making the music, the musicians themselves enter a common stream of consciousness, and what they create is an invitation to the listeners to be entered into that consciousness – which is also the consciousness of their people. The feel of the music is the feel of their common history, the burden of their history; their suffering and their woe; their endurance and their strength; their poverty and their pain... This is precisely what Leroy Sibbles of the Heptones means when he says of 'dub'... 'well... it signifies some kind of African feeling, the beat and the drum and the bass. We are all black and we have Africa deep within us. Yeah we feel it... Deep down inside from you hear it, you feel it.' You feel it because the 'bad bass bounce' is your 'blood a leap an pulse a pounce', you feel it because this 'rhythm of a tropical electrical storm', 'rhythm cutting so sharp so', it cuts at your hurt; you feel it for the 'bass history is a moving/ is a hurting black story'; you feel it because it is your pain; you feel it because it is your hunger; it is your sprout. 'Deep down inside, from you hear it, you feel it', for it is your heart-song and it touches your soul's senses. The youth sufferers who live in the ghettoes and shanty towns of Jamaica describe the music in terms of their own existence, which is basically a rebel existence... [The] music is expressive of how they 'feel' (1976a: 398–99; original emphasis).

Fourthly, from a different, more comfortable and meditative perspective, the cardio-musicological impact of the bass is sometimes related, more ontologically, existentially, and even spiritually, to the deep rhythms of life – what, I suspect, Whitfield means when he speaks of the 'primal underpinning' of the bass. An excellent example of this is Smith and Mighty's *Bass is Maternal* (1995), the cover of which has a photograph of a child standing by the sea, listening, presumably, to the heartbeat regularity of the tide. Again, the booklet accompanying the album includes four ultrasound scans of foetuses and an illustration of a small child reaching out to a bass speaker, underneath which are the words 'bass is maternal... when it's loud I feel safer'. It's worth noting here that, although, like Johnson, Rob Smith and Ray Mighty are draw-ing on the experiential dimension of the bass and its perceived relationship to the beat of the heart, they have subverted the gendered interpretation of it in terms of masculinity and aggression. It now becomes, as it is in later ambient dub, relational, maternal, feminine. A good example of this almost ontologi-cal interpretation of the *feel* of the bass is the name Steve Wilson chose for his more ambient side project, Bass Communion.[26] Indeed, his work, particularly with the dub experimentalist Bryn Jones (Muslimgauze) on the album *Bass Communion v. Muslimgauze* (1999) and the follow-up EP with the same title (2000) – both recorded just prior to Jones's death in 1999 – are good examples of both the challengingly aggressive and the maternal interpretations of bass.

Drawing on and developing these two emphases – particularly the femi-nine, the maternal, and the primal – it is not unusual for people to articulate Romanticized,[27] even spiritual interpretations of the aesthetic impact of bass in dub. Again, Whitfield is a good example of this. 'If played loud enough', he claims, the bass feels like 'a wind, literally, punctuated by eerie shards of searing guitar, and melancholy piano, which seemed to invite the mind to a deep cavernous space, a sad and lonely place of lost chances, memory, or at other times an optimistic, positive spiritual uplift, resolute and strong' (2002). Again, he relates Bunny Wailer's understanding of the significance of bass: 'this deeply dread riddim, the unifying of a dread bass and drum *physically felt* rather than heard, was a bass vibration that had been set in motion at the time of creation, and resonated onwards, like a heartbeat, primal and compelling. The vibration had echoed from source, from creation. From that time onward, it wove its mysticism, its physical, gnostic spell' (Whitfield 2002; original emphasis). Bearing in mind the use of reverb, echo, found sounds, and the deep pulse of the bass, this is a popular general perception (see Eshun 1998: 62–66). As Katz comments of Perry's 'Black Panta', it is 'liberally bathed in echo and delay, adding a surreal or ethereal quality to the rhythm, giving it a sense of timelessness or otherworldly feel' (2000: 178). It is this type of perception that is often said to be heightened by the use of ganga.[28] As Mark Kidel comments, 'whereas jazz and rock often reflect an amphetamine frenzy, reggae tunes in to the slowness of ganga' (quoted in Hebdige 1979: 30). For a spiritually-oriented dub musician such as Jah Wobble (John Wardle), the aes-thetics of dub and especially its use of bass are particularly significant. Indeed, as Peter Shapiro comments, 'Wobble treasures the bass. He protects it and caresses it even when he's just talking about it' (Shapiro 1995: 34). 'Most peo-ple', says Wobble, 'think of bass as this thing that comes out of the woofer and it's really heavy and there you go... The phrasing of it is so important as well. That's where people don't really understand the totality of the thing...

They can't really understand how the energy works' (quoted in Shapiro 1995: 34; see also Wobble 2001). Whether destructive or protective, bass is energy. More particularly for Wobble, although bass does have male characteristics, it is, again, principally a maternal, nurturing energy. In a similar way to Bunny Wailer, he argues that bass 'tends to be a feminine power, but it can be a male power as well. It's a feminine power insofar as it comes from earth and it's all-pervasive. It also has male qualities, it can penetrate and it can also be very dynamic. But the main thing for me is that it's all-supporting. It's very much the quality of the Divine Mother' (quoted in Shapiro 1995: 34). We will see that such bass-oriented interpretations of dub are important for understanding its contemporary significance and appeal.

Wobble's bass-orientation is evident in the name he chose for his record label. Following Island's refusal to release his more experimental work – because of its lack of commercial potential (which Wobble concedes) – he set up the 30 Hertz label.[29] 30 hertz is significant because it is close to the lowest frequency that humans can hear. That said, although hearing varies from person to person, with numerous factors influencing the range of frequencies that any one individual can detect, generally speaking humans can hear frequencies as low as 20 hertz and as high as 20 kilohertz. However, as we approach these frequency limits our hearing ability gradually fades. Hence, for most people, clear bass sound is limited to around 30 hertz. For example, a piano's bottom note C vibrates at roughly 33 hertz, a frequency very close to the limits of the human hearing range. However, the point is that beyond this limit lies bass infrasound, which is *felt* rather than heard. Of course, feeling is very similar to hearing, in that both are ways of detecting sonic vibration.[30] More interestingly, experiments have shown that exposure to such low frequency, infrasonic tones increase the emotional impact of the music. That is to say, studies have shown that concert-goers report higher emotional states during the times when infrasound was presented. This, some have argued, is why pipe-organ music, which produces notes as low as 16 hertz, might elicit powerful emotions, which, in Cathedral congregations, are, because of their context, subsequently invested with spiritual significance (see Amos 2003). Hence, while still a little speculative, there do seem to be good reasons for the appeal of the bass (see Todd and Cody 2000).[31] More specifically, thinking of the context in which it is heard, the layers of echo, the confluence of the familiar with the unfamiliar, and the various religio-cultural signifiers, this perhaps goes some way to explaining the interpretations of transcendence dubbed bass elicits.

Moreover, as noted above, bass and power are fundamentally linked. Consequently, a sound system's sonic emphasis on the bass requires significant amplification and, therefore, power. Indeed, 'bass extension'[32] down to lower frequencies, such as 20 hertz, requires enormous power. Because human hearing is far less sensitive in the bass range than in the midrange, to be perceptually as loud as midrange sound, bass actually needs to be substantially louder. Put simply, powerful bass requires moving lots of air. This is why, as indicated above, sound systems are preoccupied with the size of speakers – large speakers will move more air than small speakers with the same excursion (i.e. the same amount of back and forth motion). In short, because moving lots of air requires a significant level of electrical power to enable the speaker to push the air, there needs to be an allied focus on the wattage of amplification. Consequently, bass addiction necessarily includes a preoccupation with power.

This, again, goes some way to explaining, not only dub's bass-oriented, rather masculine focus on power and size, but also the very physicality of dub, the empirical sense of being sonically enveloped and handled. Such an experience, when linked to a sense of reality-shift induced by the use of found sounds, echo and reverb, as well as the related perception of space and depth engendered by reggae's off-beat, leads to a feeling of transcendence, which is often interpreted spiritually. Luke Ehrlich puts it well:

> With dub, Jamaican music spaced out completely. If reggae is Africa in the New World, then dub must be Africa on the moon; it's the psychedelic music I expected to hear in the '60s and didn't. The bass and the drums conjure up a dark, vast space, a musical portrait of outer space, with sounds suspended like glowing planets or with fragments of instruments careening by, leaving trails like comets and meteors (1983: 106).

Concluding Comments

Having introduced the Jamaican background, sound-system culture, reggae, and dub in Part One, this initial chapter in Part Two tightens the focus, concentrating explicitly on British sound-system culture. This has been important because, as noted at the end of Chapter Two and in the previous section of this chapter, just as dub had its genesis and early evolution within Jamaican sound systems, so it was within British sound-system culture that it was introduced and nurtured in the UK, prior to the punk explosion of 1976 – during and following which it experienced exponential popularity within and beyond the African-Caribbean community. Quite simply, it is in the UK that we see the nurturing of dub outernational.

Moreover, we have seen that, at this stage, within poor, oppressed, Jamaican, expatriate communities living in 'the second Babylon' much of reggae's original signification and social significance was retained and developed. However, as sites of subversion and resistance, they were beginning to be appreciated by others in Britain with countercultural sensibilities. As noted in the previous section, shebeens and sound systems appealed to disaffected white youths in that they were recognized as sites of resistance to mass culture, the sound system being understood as authentically creative and politically meaningful. Although it will be argued that there was a shift in signification, nevertheless, the feelings and ideas expressed made sense of their own experiences. In the final two chapters, we will explore the reception of dub within these subcultures and examine the religio-political continuities and discontinuities.

Focusing a little more closely on the issues raised, this chapter has identified key themes which are important for understanding the narrative context of dub, its subcultural meaning, its subsequent popularity, and the related work of the selector and the deejay. Firstly, the context in which dub evolved was, as it was in Jamaica, the poor, oppressed black community *in Babylon*. At a shebeen, listening to a sound system, a marginalized community could socialize and maintain cultural continuity with Caribbean culture. It is worth quoting some of Frith's comments concerning popular music generally:

> [M]usical identity is both fantastic – idealizing not just oneself, but also the social world it inhabits – and real: it is enacted in activity. Music making and music listening are bodily matters; they involve what one might call *social movements*. In this respect, musical pleasure is not derived from fantasy – it is not mediated by daydreams – but is experienced directly: music gives us a real experience of what the ideal could be... Whether we're talking about Finnish dance halls in Sweden, Irish pubs in London, or Indian film music in Trinidad, we're dealing not just with nostalgia for 'traditional sounds', not just with a commitment to 'different' songs, but also with experiences of alternative social interaction. Communal values can only be grasped as musical aesthetics in action. 'Authenticity' in this context is a quality not of the music as such (how it is actually made), but of the story it is heard to tell, the narrative of musical interaction in which the listeners place themselves... Music constructs our sense of identity through the experiences it offers of the body, time, and sociability, experiences which enable us to place ourselves in imaginative cultural narratives (1996: 274–75).

This, we have seen, applies in a very obvious way to African-Caribbeans in the UK and helps us to understand the significance of the sound-system culture they created.

Secondly, related to the above, the sound system is an expressive musical culture shaped by performer–audience interaction, a site of community unification, and an occasion for religio-political rhetoric. The last, the coded speech-act of the deejay, is particularly important. We have seen that, like Walter Benjamin's storyteller, the deejays' creative act is to apply their own experiences to the concerns of their audiences, even to provide counsel for their listeners. As Back comments, 'the lesson from the mike is "check yourself", don't fight among yourselves, see the "bars and chains" that confine. These messages relate to black history, black unity and struggle. This "didactic populism" is accessible to a community of listeners who come together within dancehalls. The owners, operators, and performers share a determination to speak about the issues that affect their audience' (1992: 196). Hence, there is a sharing of collective experiences and an accessible communication of cultural politics. As Letts recalls,

> the messages I heard through sound systems like Jah Shaka, Moa Ambassa and Coxsone were so compelling that my political and spiritual consciousness increased. This is what roots and culture does, it's literally musical reportage. Sound system was a way of imparting information, spiritually, politically, culturally. It raises awareness in all these departments, and as young black British guys, we were especially sensitive to these messages, these modes of communication (2007: 60).

Frith's comments about pop lyrics generally, are particularly applicable in this context: 'the use of language in pop songs has as much to do with establishing the communicative situation as with communicating' (1996: 168). Socially symbolic language establishes a context in which a particular discourse is meaningful. Moreover, as noted above, the emphasis on verbal rhetoric should not be stressed at the expense of the non-verbal, inferred meanings communicated through the music and through the samples used. Just as Jimi Hendrix's instrumental interpretation of 'The Star Spangled Banner' at Woodstock,[33] which, by means of guitar effects, immediately and powerfully articulated a counterculture's critique of the US presence in Vietnam, so a similar use of found sounds (such as barking dogs and gunshots), reverb, drums and bass likewise communicate particular meanings to a dub audience. For example, in the previous chapter, Lee Perry's imitative realism was noted. Commenting on issues that many of Jamaica's poor would have been very familiar with, he made creative use of street recordings, sound effects, and solicited comments from the general public.

Thirdly, we have seen that, because many sound systems were identified as sites of subversion there was a perceived continuity with countercultural concerns. Consequently, during the late 1970s, these musical cultures became identified with countercultural discourse and, therefore, popular with certain primarily white subcultures, not least punks and post-hippies. In other words, shebeens and sound systems, which, although organized to serve the Caribbean community as a whole (not simply the youth) became – because of their unofficial and subterranean status, as well as the particular narratives they articulated – attractive to disaffected white youths. Here was a site of black resistance to mass culture, where the sound system was seen as authentically creative and politically meaningful in a way that mainstream music and discos were not. The feelings and ideas expressed made sense of their own experiences. Hence, within these spaces of cultural consumption white youths were introduced to the religio-political agendas and sensibilities of black culture. Sound-system culture thus gradually became an 'irenic culture', a culture of reconciliation within which white youths were introduced to black culture and black-informed religio-political agendas. White youths, such as myself, found themselves owning black cultural forms. Hence, it is no coincidence, for example, that in William Gibson's classic, genre-defining 'cyberpunk' novel from the period, *Neuromancer* (1984), there are frequent positive references to Rasta culture, spirituality, and even dub: 'As they worked, Case gradually became aware of the music that pulsed constantly through the cluster. It was called dub, a sensuous mosaic cooked from the vast libraries of digitized pop; it was worship, Molly said, and a sense of community... Zion smelled of cooked vegetables, humanity, and ganga' (1995: 128).

At this point, it is perhaps worth briefly commenting on the distinction between two commonly used terms, 'community' and 'subculture'. The African-Caribbean *community* is a settled population, structured according to kinship, consisting of several generations in particular neighbourhoods. For various reasons, a central leisure activity of some members of this community became attractive to certain black and white *subcultures*. Although there is much discussion concerning the definition of 'a subculture' (see Clark, et al. 1976; Hebdige 1979; Muggleton 2000; Gelder and Thornton 1997; Bennett and Kahn-Harris 2004; Straw 2001: 67–71), essentially it is a group (usually of youths) that tends to define itself over against kin (principally parental) and always against mainstream society. The perception of deviance it engenders in outsiders is both celebrated and cultivated. Its subversive values are usually articulated through the adoption of particular symbols, dress codes, and genres of music. Punks in the 1970s, for example, were a conspicuous manifestation of most of the attributes scholars have identified as 'subcultural' (see Hebdige 1979; Sabin 1999a; Savage 2005). That this particular white subculture found dub appealing is not as odd as it may first appear when one considers the language and signs, the sense of identity, and the cultural narratives articulated within roots reggae.

Fourthly, to return to sound-system shebeens *per se* – in which, arguably, we see an embryonic form of the discotheque (see Thornton 1995: 47) – it is significant that the selector and recorded sound are primary. As Gilroy puts it, 'perhaps the most important effect of sound systems on the contemporary musical culture of black Britain is revealed in the way that it is centred not on live performances by musicians and singers, though these are certainly appreciated, but on records' (2002: 217). We have seen that the public performance of recorded music has been a central feature of Jamaican music, in that 'records become raw material for spontaneous performances of cultural creation in which the DJ and the MC or toaster who introduces each disc or sequence of discs, emerge as the principal agents in dialogic rituals of active and celebratory consumption' (Gilroy 2002: 217; see also Davis 1983d). While the idea that the creative input of the deejay is as equally important as that of the recording artist is now common in contemporary Western dance culture, its origins can be traced back to the sound system. Hence, while, in the history of recorded music, there emerged a general fetishization of the recording, and while Frith is right to note that 'to record a work is just as much to interpret it as to perform it any other way' (1996: 229), within sound-system culture the evolution of the recording took a particularly influential trajectory, in that the actual playing of the recording was invested with creative value. Indeed, as in contemporary remix culture, there is a sense in which the efforts of the selector, particularly in dub sound systems such as Shaka's, are more important than those of the recording artist. Hence, for example, when King Tubby *meets* Roots Radics (e.g. *Dangerous Dub*), or Jah Shaka *meets* Fire House Crew (e.g. *Authentic Dubwise*), or even a well-known band such as Aswad (*Jah Shaka Meets Aswad in Addis Ababa Studio*), there is little doubt who is the principal party in the encounter.

The dub reinterpretations and deconstructions of well-known songs are, at a sound-system event, live performances during which the selector and his team are responding – verbally and non-verbally – to the immediate concerns and desires of the consumer. They are skilfully reading the mood of the dancefloor and manipulating the music accordingly. This, of course, was evident in Lol Bell-Brown's evocative description of a session by Shaka (see above). Also, at a more intellectual, rather than purely emotional level, the deejay is – prompted by fractured sounds and words of the dub plate he is toasting over – speaking, almost homiletically, to the immediate concerns of his 'congregation', whether such concerns be relational, social or spiritual. On the one hand, the recorded music, which has, in dub, already been manipulated and deconstructed, becomes part of the live performance of the deejay, who is prompted by and working with the various sounds and fragments of vocal left in the mix. On the other hand, as noted above, the deejay's discourse is oriented towards the practical interests of, usually, the poor. As with Benjamin's storyteller, the narrative 'contains, openly or covertly, something useful. The usefulness may, in one case, consist in a moral; in another, in some practical advice; in a third, in a proverb or maxim. In every case the storyteller is a man who has counsel for his readers' (Benjamin 1992: 86). Moreover, as Davis comments, this is done in a context unfettered by the agendas of church and state – uninfluenced by the forces of Babylon (1983d: 34). Hence, often misunderstood, a sound-system event is rarely perceived simply as a mobile disco at which one individual plays records and another raps. It is explicitly *not* a disco; it is, as indicated above, a religio-political 'happening' at which particular values, beliefs and ideals are articulated and social cohesion is facilitated.

Related to the above, it is also worth noting here the significance of the 'pre-release'. This type of recording was understood to be more authentic, in that it was not perceived to be 'commercial'. Hence, the 'pre-release' *per se*, particularly if it was imported from Jamaica, was itself invested with ideological significance. That is to say, the very commitment to dub plates and pre-releases was a political statement, in that such records were understood to be unregulated by the Western music industry and, therefore, untainted by the values of Babylon. Moreover, an individual's commitment to *supposedly* non-commercial music set them apart from mainstream Western society, thereby affirming their subcultural credentials. Indeed, there is a sense in which, for some musicians, the pre-release is also invested with spiritual significance. That is to say, if the music industry is understood to be tainted by Babylon and the forces of darkness, then music produced apart from it is, to some extent, sacralized – non-profane. Hence, as in dub generally, it is not unusual to find subcultural statements such as 'for those who understand' (e.g. The Disciples Present the Boom Shackalacka Sound System, *For Those Who Understand*) and references to it as, for example, 'a sacred art' (Alpha & Omega, *The Sacred Art of Dub*), which implicitly suggest that this is not music for the masses. However, the main point is that, unlike discotheques, it was enormously important that the sound system played cutting-edge records, dub plates that were unavailable elsewhere. This was clearly evident in Carl Gayle's 1974 survey of black music in London:

> the youngsters of today spend more than they can afford on records, but they want the best and the rarest... 'We import our records three times a week from Jamaica' said a young guy called Michael... 'Pre-release music to me and many people like sound system men and

their followers, is like underground music. As soon as it's released it's
commercial music. So you find that for the youth of today, the ghetto
youth like myself, pre-release music is like medicine. They'll go anywhere to hear it' (quoted in Gilroy 2002: 219).

This, of course, is not unusual in subcultural aesthetics. As I have found in my
own informal discussions with music fans, the obscure, the non-mainstream,
the novel, and the avant-garde are appealing, largely, it would appear, because
they are non-commercial. Consequently, 'for those who understand', such
music carries the mark of authenticity and *feels* closer to the fan's own subcultural, non-mainstream values and ideals. It is part of a narrative with which
they identify and of which they want to be a part. Once it becomes successful
and mainstream that appeal is eroded – its subcultural capital is depleted (see
Thornton 1995: 87–115).

Bearing the above in mind, it is interesting to observe the penchant for
'white label' releases in contemporary deejay culture, in that, as we have
seen in the previous chapter, many Jamaican sound-system operators and
selectors would remove the labels from dub plates in order to reduce the
possibility of rival sound systems purchasing the same music. This, however, as Gilroy has argued, has a broader significance. 'The removal of labels
subverted the emphasis on acquisition and individual ownership which the
makers of black music cultures identified as an unacceptable feature of pop
culture. This simple act suggested alternative collective modes of consumption in which the information essential to purchase was separated from the
pleasure which the music created' (Gilroy 2002: 221). Moreover, it's worth
noting that the removal of labels also undermined the cult of celebrity,
which is so central to many popular music cultures. Although, of course,
there were and still are a surfeit of celebrities in reggae music *per se*, within
sound system and dub culture the relationship between the music and the
artist has always been played down. Indeed, there was a tendency to focus
on *the music* as celebrity, the removal of the labels declaring that anything
more than aural information is secondary. It mattered little which musicians
were involved or how the music was produced or, indeed, where it was in
any charts. Far more important was the immediate aural impact. Although,
of course, prominent figures such as King Tubby, Lee Perry, Augustus Pablo,
Scientist, King Jammy, Mad Professor, Jah Shaka, and Adrian Sherwood have
attained an elevated status within dub culture, there is no doubt that it is
the music itself that takes pride of place. Indeed, many contemporary dub
compilations will include rare or new work by obscure or unknown artists,
or even by well-known musicians using unknown pseudonyms. The point
is that, although many of the artists may not be recognized, such compila-

tions still sell well for the only word which needs to be on the cover of a CD or in the title of a track is the magic word 'dub'. Devotees of dub are more interested in hearing something new 'in dub' than they are interested in the latest release by a favourite artist.

4 Punks, Poetry, and Anti-racism

The story of reggae in the UK and, in particular, the emergence of the British dub scene, cannot be told without reference to punk rock. While some discussions of British reggae and dub treat them as if they were hermetically sealed from exogenous cultural influence, this, of course, is not the case. As Dick Hebdige has commented, 'although apparently separate and autonomous, punk and the Black British subcultures with which reggae is associated were connected at a deep structural level' (1979: 29; cf. Letts 2007). Certainly, at a relatively superficial level, there is little doubt that numerous punks and some hippies were, like the mods and skinheads before them (see Troyna 1978: 174–86; Hebdige 1979: 52–59), fascinated by Jamaican popular music. For example, in an interview with John Peel on BBC Radio 1, John Lydon ('Johnny Rotten' of the Sex Pistols) played some of his favourite records, all of which, except for one, were, to the surprise of some listeners, reggae (Colegrave and Sullivan 2001: 203). As Lydon himself comments, 'reggae was the only other radical music that was completely underground and not played on the radio' (1994: 268). Similarly, Mark E. Smith of the seminal Salford band The Fall, noting that 'roots reggae was huge when The Fall first started', makes the point that he himself was intrigued by 'dub music', especially that of 'Augustus Pablo'. (I myself can still remember the feelings evoked when I first heard Pablo's *King Tubbys Meets Rockers Uptown* – arguably his most important album – in the late-1970s.) In Smith's opinion, 'it was the only thing around worth listening to for a while' (Pouncey 2001: 51; see also Ford 2003: 14, 220). Likewise, reflecting on his youth in the 1970s, Jah Wobble (who joined Lydon in Public Image Limited) is very clear that

> the first form of music that really took me into another world was dub reggae. I was about 15 and heard it...at a party we had gatecrashed in Hackney. I was already a fan of ska, bluebeat, and early forms of reggae up to this point... However, nothing prepared me for the shock of listening to dub, especially through big custom-made 22" speaker cabs. There was the bass taking up most of the signal, resonating deep into my solar plexus, the core of my being. All the big plate reverbs and tape echoes, especially the long decaying half time ones, conveyed a sense

of inner space... Most of all I was fascinated by the bass lines... The sheer physicality of the experience set it apart from any other (Wobble 2001: 98).

The commitment of many white youths, such as Lydon and Wobble, however, not only went beyond both ska and rock steady, but also beyond the music *per se*. They embraced, with roots reggae and dub, aspects of the culture that informed them. As Vivian Goldman has commented, they identified with some of the key themes articulated within reggae and dub, 'the protesting, the inequities of society, and the injustices of the system' (quoted in Colegrave and Sullivan 2001: 203). In their own peculiarly nihilistic way, like the Rastas, they protested at what history had given them. As Greil Marcus puts it,

> there was a black hole at the heart of The Sex Pistols' music, a wilful lust for the destruction of values that no one could be comfortable with... They had begun as if in pursuit of a project: in 'Anarchy in the UK' they had damned the present, and in 'God Save the Queen' they had damned the past with a curse so hard that it took the future with it... 'No future in England's dah-rrrreeming' (1989: 10–11; cf. Christgau 1998: 229–34).

For punks such as Lydon, it was not a case of changing or challenging Babylon. Rather, the system had to be razed to the ground. Babylon must burn. But, unlike the Rastas, that was it! There was no plan and no future anticipated. In this sense, while Rastafarian thought was infused with millenarian speculation, *pure* punk tended towards visionless nihilism. Nevertheless, as Lloyd Bradley comments, 'roots reggae's revolutionary sentiments and relentless defiance of all things Babylonian were exactly what punk's scattergun-style, rebel-without-a-clue dissension needed as a focus' (2000: 449).

The aim of this chapter is to investigate the cultural confluence of punk and dub in the UK up until punk's decline in the late-1970s and also to examine the appeal of dub for white youth subcultures during that period.

Hippies, Space Cadets, and Dub

It is, of course, relatively well-known that reggae found an enthusiastic reception within the punk community (see Colegrave and Sullivan 2001: 192–203, 308–11, 351; Hebdige 1979: 67–69; Heylin 2007: 443, 518–19; Jones 1988: 87–118; Letts 2007) and that, subsequently, the effects of dub were used to provide a sense of space and depth to late- and post-punk music (a good compilation of such music is *Wild Dub: Dread Meets Punk Rocker Downtown*). Indeed, to some extent, as Miles English has noted, 'dub became the unofficial soundtrack for the era' (quoted in Colegrave and Sullivan 2001: 201). However, not only did dub appeal to a broader range of subcultures than punks, but, arguably, it was more aesthetically appealing to another group of music fans, namely those who had evolved out of, or looked back to hippie subcultures. Here was a large group of people who were not only interested in the psychedelic exploration of inner space, but who were listening to experimental musics that supported such exploration (see Partridge 2006; Southern 1995). Many punks were, of course, very familiar with this subculture themselves, even if they'd become frustrated by its increasingly insular quietism and decadence (see Lydon 1994: 64; Letts 2007: 68–69, 118). Jah Wobble, for example, relates dub very explicitly to alternative spirituality and themes that many such counterculturalists would have recognized (Wobble 2001); Lydon was following bands such as Hawkwind,[1] Can, Captain Beefheart, Miles Davis, Tangerine Dream, Curved Air, and, of course, The Stooges (Lydon 1994: 58, 79, 81; Letts 2007: 118), and Mark E. Smith was listening to the Velvet Underground, Can, Captain Beefheart, Peter Hammill, Faust, Lou Reed's *Metal Machine Music*, and even Stockhausen, as well as dub reggae (Ford 2003: 13–14; Smith 2009: 35ff.). As for those who work specifically with dub soundscapes, perhaps more than any other artist, such influences and attitudes are conspicuous in the fascinating and often difficult work of the late-dub avant-gardist Muslimgauze (Bryn Jones): 'I was first interested in Faust, Can, punk, industrial and then Arabic and Indian music. The punk explosion planted a seed which later I used to make music' (Jones 2000). Until his tragic death in 1999,[2] Muslimgauze continued to work with rock experimentalists, such as Steve Wilson (e.g. *Bass Communion v. Muslimgauze, Parts 1 & 2*) and the French psychedelic band Reverberation (e.g. *New Soul*). Indeed, interestingly, nowadays most producers of dub in France, arguably the most fertile ground for the contemporary development of the genre, were initially inspired by punk and alternative rock, including early psychedelic bands such as Pink Floyd and Tangerine Dream. These influences are made explicit in Nathalie Valet's interviews with French dub bands such as High Tone, Improvisators Dub, and Brain Damage (see *Dub Stories* – CD/DVD). However, returning to the early 1970s, the point is that dub arrived in the UK just prior to punk and at a time when, not only were many still experimenting with hallucinogenic drugs – the experiences induced by which were often invested with transcendental significance – but also at a time when many were becoming fascinated with new exploratory music. And, as Steve Severin of Siouxsie and the Banshees comments, for many in the mid-1970s, 'dub reggae...was the most experimental music going' (in Lydon 1994: 182; cf. Letts 2007: 71–72).

Thinking of its continuity with earlier forms of experimental music, although some punks, Lydon particularly, quickly distanced themselves from hippie culture, dub was a genre that connected with an appreciation of music that could be traced back to the late-1960s when many artists and musicians had sought to produce work, which, they believed, if allied to the use of cannabis and hallucinogens, would facilitate the exploration of 'inner space' and even induce mystical experience (see Bromell 2000; Lee and Shlain 1992; Partridge 2005: 82–134; Smith 2000; Stevens 1993; Dunlap 1961). As Sheila Whiteley comments of the psychedelic music of the period,

> The effect of 'psychedelic harmony' with its unpredictable patterns and textural density is intensified by complex rhythm structures. The majority of early drum machines had quantizing which effectively 'corrects' mistakes, uniforming notes into the characteristic semi-quaver structure of dance. At the same time, the layering of samples, e.g. a vocal sample over a dance rhythm, produces often a polyrhythm whilst delay machines facilitate triplet patterns over duple figures favoured by dub reggae (1997: 131).

In other words, whether one was listening to avant-garde German records, such as Can's *Tago Mago* (1972), or Brian Eno's delicate use of loops and synthesizers on *Discreet Music* (1975) and on the albums he recorded with Robert Fripp – *No Pussyfooting* (1973) and *Evening Star* (1975) – or even earlier psychedelic music, such as Pink Floyd's debut album, *Piper at the Gates of Dawn* (1967) and Tangerine Dream's groundbreaking debut, *Electronic Meditation* (1970), dub had much in common, aesthetically and musicologically, with the compositions already being appreciated by many rock fans. Hence, for those such as Smith and Lydon, who began to reject hippie lifestyles and were becoming increasingly disinterested in the accompanying music,[3] dub provided a form of musical experimentation, which not only seemed particularly avant garde at the time, but which was also politically engaged.

Seeking to strike a balance between emic subjectivity and scholarly objectivity is always difficult. Nevertheless, it is perhaps worth noting that, not only have I spoken to many who were introduced to dub in the mid- to late-1970s, but I personally remember the enormous impact dub had on me and my friends in North-West England. Although for some such as Lydon and Smith, reggae and dub were a welcome alternative, particularly to the musical doodling of a detached, white middle-class mind seeking enlightenment and escape into Tolkienesque faerie fantasies, others, such as those with whom I was familiar, seemed to move very easily from 'hippie' and experimental bands and musicians such as Gong, Here & Now, Steve Hillage, Can,

Faust, and Hawkwind into Augustus Pablo, Lee Perry, Scientist and, by the late 1970s, Creation Rebel and the New Age Steppers. Although we had all heard Bob Marley, and appreciated the new rhythms we were being exposed to, it was dub that really caught our imagination. The culture and ideals remained in place. Can, Gong, and Hawkwind would still find their way onto our turntables. We all happily attended the free festivals during the summer months and chatted about hippie utopias. But, for many of us, dub rapidly became the staple diet. It seemed to appeal to the same sensibilities as those stimulated by Gong's 'flying teapot' meanderings, Hawkwind's Moorcockesque space fantasies and enthusiasm for experimental electronica, and Here & Now's trippy anarchism – space, depth, and contemplation – but offered something new and fresh. Indeed, free festival bands such as Here & Now began to introduce dub techniques and reggae rhythms into their sets and by the early 1980s[4] it was not unusual at a free festival to hear the evocative strains of dub and its powerful, deep bass drifting, with the smell of incense and cannabis, across the site. Although hippie idealism took some time to fade, the 'conscious' music of dub quickly became *de rigueur*. Indeed, it's important to understand that this confluence of musical genres, this reception of dub within a post-hippie subculture, contributed significantly to the development of techno and trance in the late-1980s and 1990s (see Partridge 2006). Hence, for example, it is not unusual for more recent British techno, trance, and electronica artists, such as Marc Swordfish of Astralasia and David Gates of Salt Tank, to include in a list of their principal influences bands such as Hawkwind and Gong as well as reggae and dub. Gates, for example, lists 'New Order, Steve Hillage, Fripp and Eno, Gong, Hawkwind, disco, reggae, punk...' (quoted in Abrahams 2004: 205). Indeed, Gates was responsible for compiling the trance–ambient CD, *Future Reconstruction: Ritual of the Solstice* (1996), a collection of Hawkwind tracks remixed by dance and dub producers such as Zion Train ('Damnation Alley'), the Knights of the Occasional Table ('Sonic Attack') and the Utah Saints ('Silver Machine'). Other projects have also been undertaken, such as *The Bass Ritual* (due for release in 2000, but abandoned) and *The Hawkwind Remix Project* (Warlord 2000), which includes reconstructions of old tracks such 'The Golden Void' (The Future Loop Foundation), 'Brainstorm' (DJ Speedranch) and 'Master Of The Universe' (Colin Newman).

Apart from the particular attraction of dub to the post-hippie, 'space cadet' subcultures, there were other reasons why it appealed. As noted in the first chapter, because long hair had become a popular signifier of countercultural sympathies during the late-1960s, dreadlocks tended to be interpreted similarly. Moreover, for many post-hippie subcultures in the mid-1970s, along with the wearing of long hair, the use of cannabis, the articulation of counter-cultural politics, anti-authoritarianism, and alternative spirituality all carried significant subcultural capital. Although Rastas were, of course, distinctive in many respects from those Britons who had been influenced by North American hippie culture, many hippies and post-hippies who listened to space- and myth-oriented rock, as well as experimental German music and earlier British psychedelic bands, recognized areas of overlap with dub which enabled a certain level of continuity (see McKay 2000: 9–10). As Ernest Cashmore comments, 'amid the subcultural backcloth of the late 1960s and early 1970s the emergence of young blacks growing dreadlocks and adorning themselves with Ethiopian-coloured garments did not appear incongruous. The American hippie phenomenon had seared its way through Britain's white youth provoking new stances of anti-authoritarianism and corresponding symbolic gestures' (1983: 53). And as George McKay argues, 'the cringe-making neologism of *Glastafari* signals some sort of effort to claim, to relocate music, fashion, lifestyle, spirituality, ganja...of urban blacks to the Isle of Avalon' (2000: 9). Indeed, I would argue that, to some extent, dub and reggae were conciliatory genres for hippies and punks. Of course, the free festival was also irenic in this respect. As McKay comments,

> the free festival is a significant event at which, peaking in the period of subcultural transition from the mid-seventies to the mid-eighties, the hippie and the punk came together. It's a site of negotiation and transformation between radical subcultures. Their radical nature needs stressing: both hippies and punks leaned towards anarchist cultural politics, and the quarter-organized chaos of a free festival offers an easy homological fit (1996: 21–22).

However, whilst this is true, I press my point a little and suggest that one of the key factors that helped to facilitate this subcultural rapprochement was roots reggae and dub. Certainly by the late 1970s there was a meeting of taste around dub, as well as around key British bands such as Misty in Roots and Steel Pulse. Anarchist, proto-punk, hippie bands such as Nik Turner's Inner City Unit and Here & Now began to write tracks explicitly indebted to reggae and dub (e.g. 'Tele Song', on Here & Now's *Fantasy Shift*; 'Remember (Walking in the Sand)', on Inner City Unit's *Maximum Effect*). More specifically, the explicit and powerful political discourse associated with roots reggae, particularly that of Linton Kwesi Johnson, united the concerns and ideals of distinct subcultures. Hence, events at which reggae was the prominent genre, particularly Rock Against Racism, like free festivals, very clearly provided a homological fit. Consequently, by the 1980s, free festivals and protest events often included a rich mixture of subcultures, including Rastas, post-hippies, punks and post-punks. For example, at the Cannabis Law Reform Rally in Brockwell Park, Brixton, on 23 May 1982, 5000 people – including Rastas, punks and hippies – gathered to listen to Jah Shaka, King Sounds, and Coxsone sound systems along with bands from the free festival scene, including Hawkwind's Nik Turner (see Worthington 2004: 119). Again, the point is that such meetings did not happen overnight; they were the result of a gradual process, at the heart of which was, put bluntly, dub, cannabis, and radical, anti-Babylon politics. As Vivien Goldman recalls, 'We did feel like we were on the frontline of Babylon... Rasta provided this mesh of the political, the spiritual, and the apocalyptic, and it helped you to define your enemies' (quoted in Reynolds 2005: 88).

Finally, it should be noted that the hippie appreciation of dub largely happened during the transition period into punk. That is to say, just as punk was coalescing in 1975 in the UK, dub was also beginning to make itself known. As has been noted, for several reasons, in Britain dub hit the ground running. Not only did it quickly attract a large fan base within African-Caribbean sound-system culture, but we have seen that it very quickly attracted the attention of white rock fans. Certainly by 1976 it had become widely known amongst musicians and fans as an innovative new genre. In a 1976 article in *Melody Maker*, a music paper read avidly by many white rock music fans at the time, Richard Williams not only argued that 'the technique of dub may well be the most interesting new abstract concept to appear in modern music since Ornette Coleman undermined the dictatorship of Western harmony almost two decades ago', but he clearly assumed that his readers were aware of its existence and indicated that those who 'unaccountably' were not, should be! (1997: 145) Indeed, we have already noted that, since 1975, when Lee Perry signed a contract with Island Records, several prominent pop and rock musicians had become interested in his production techniques, including Paul and Linda McCartney and Robert Palmer.

A more interesting case, however, certainly as far as the hippie/rock scene was concerned, was the subtle influence dub had on the prominent, experimental folk-rock musician John Martyn. After releasing *Sunday's Child* (1974), exhausted and suffering from stress – particularly following the loss of his close friends, Nick Drake (for whom he wrote the beautiful 'Solid Air') and then Paul Kossoff (who he had struggled to release from the grip of heroin addiction) – he stopped touring and took a break from studio recording. Eventually, in the summer of 1976, at the suggestion of Chris Blackwell, he left the UK to spend some time in Jamaica in order to recoup his creative energy.

'I told Chris that I wasn't feeling very good,' Martyn remembers. 'He asked me to come over to Jamaica and relax with him. I went and crashed at his gaff in the Strawberry Hills by Spanish Town. It was cool. I just sat there. During that time, I recovered my enthusiasm for music in general. I managed to negate, at least to some extent, my hatred of the music industry.' This hatred had been cultivating for a considerable time. Aside from the recent deaths of his friends, Martyn had been growing weary of the sharp practices of the business. 'I'd been in rooms where I'd seen bands literally bought and sold,' Martyn sighs. 'With agents acting like car dealers over percentage points. When I saw that it took away the romance in my life for music.' The exact length of time Martyn spent in Jamaica is hazy ('I may have been there for seven weeks; it may have been seven months' (Easlea 2004).

While staying with the Blackwell family on their large Strawberry Hill estate outside Kingston, he was taken to meet Lee Perry at the Black Ark. Fascinated by Perry's approach to production, he sat in on some of his recording sessions, as well as those by other Jamaican artists. As Katz puts it, 'Martyn and Scratch had a certain affinity despite the vastly different spheres in which they operated; impressed by his guitar playing and genial demeanour, Perry requested that Martyn provide some fresh licks on his sessions. Martyn duly complied, structuring riffs around the loping beat supplied by Horsemouth Wallace' (Katz 2000: 264). Indeed, during the eight months he stayed in Jamaica, he contributed to several tracks and even guested on Burning Spear's classic album *Man in the Hills* (1976).

'Chris took me down to Scratch's house, the Black Ark', Martyn laughs. 'Chris had said that Scratch and I were using essentially the same recording techniques and we should meet. I was using rhythm boxes and Echoplex, and my man Scratch was into the same effect, a dub thing, man. It was the echo thing that invented dub for Scratch – and I just came across my version of it by accident. Mine was faster, mine was Bo Diddley. I loved working with Scratch and will do in the future, please God. I love him. There was always a naughty, rosy little twinkle in his eye.' This meeting led to Martyn recording at the legendary Black Ark studios, hanging out with fabled characters such as Max Romeo and Burning Spear... 'I did sessions with every motherfucker and nobody told me that I'd done them,' Martyn chortles. 'I would hear records later and then all of a sudden a fuzz solo with a touch of phased echo would come and I would think, fuck me, that's me! It was very cool – I didn't mind it at all.' Lee Perry was similarly enriched by the experience: 'Yes – John Martyn!,' Perry crackled when I spoke with him in 2003. 'Anything he'd request of me would be OK. John is full of fun, a simple guy; he's somebody very special'. 'People would steal from Perry because he's too cool,' says Martyn of the chaos at Black Ark that was to lead to Perry burning it to the ground a handful of years later. 'He's wild, very street-wise, but doesn't care much. I used to make him soup and watch his back' (Easlea 2004; see also Hillarby 2006).

Inspired and reinvigorated by his exposure to reggae and particularly to Black Ark dub, he returned to the UK and, in the summer of 1977, recorded his ethereal *One World*. Produced by Blackwell, it is not difficult to discern the subtle influence of dub. This is particularly evident on the track 'Big Muff' (co-written by Perry) and on the final track, the delicately beautiful 'Small Hours'. As Martyn indicates above, he already had a penchant for sonic manipulation. Indeed, that he had exposed rock and folk fans to dub-like experimentalism on his classic *Solid Air* (1973), and then again on *Inside Out* (1973), meant that there was an easy continuity between his early work and the understated explorations of mood on *One World*. Having used, for example, the echoplex and a phase shifter to introduce hypnotic, atmospheric musical textures, Martyn gently bridged the gap between the smoke-filled bedsits and bedrooms of Britain's suburbia and the mesmerizing soundscapes of Kingston's dub pioneers.

Hence, by 1976, whilst still not mainstream, reggae rhythms had, like the smoke of ganga that so often accompanied it, begun to drift into the minds of rock musicians with a penchant for the experimental. Peter Hammill, for example, founder member of progressive rock experimentalists Van Der Graaf Generator, introduced reggae in the latter half of the twenty-minute epic 'Meurglys III: The Songwriter's Guild' on their album *World Record* (1976). However, by 1976 things were beginning to change for both rock and reggae.

Dread Meets Punk Rockers Uptown

> I got heavily involved in the whole punk thing. Looking back punk destroyed more than it did good. But one very special thing happened, which is that white kids were introduced to dub reggae. Now, to me, that's it. If you can take the idea of dub reggae and merge it with the things I was learning about painting at college, I think that you'll find that I am still using those techniques in my writing. I mean the first dub reggae I heard wasn't even dub reggae, it was The Clash's 'Police and Thieves'. But I was amazed by the space, the emptiness that was being left there. If you're doing a dub of a story, this is the real story – I mean even just physically to look at – that's the song, this is the dub. There's only a few words there, because they're the best bits (Noon 2000a: 115; see also Noon 1999; Letts 2007).

As this quotation from the Manchester-based science-fiction author Jeff Noon illustrates, not only were white punks in the mid-1970s introduced to reggae and dub, but the music and the culture it articulated had the effect of transforming the way they viewed the world. This is evident in, for example, Noon's novel *Needle in the Groove* (2000b; see also Noon 1995). Even more explicitly, as has been noted, this influence is evident in William Gibson's genre-defining, cyberpunk classic *Neuromancer* (originally published in 1984), which references 'the bass-heavy rocksteady of Zion dub' (1995: 230), Zion being a place separate from the sad corruption of Babylon, a place populated by 'Dreads', by 'Rastas' (1995: 127), a place where hydroponic ganga is smoked, and a place where the name of Marcus Garvey (1995: 137) is celebrated: 'We have...no regard for Babylon's law. Our law is the word of Jah' (1995: 136). However, perhaps the most important influence it had on the worldviews of white youths in the 1970s was its contribution to anti-racism. Whilst it is arguable that this was little more than the commodification or detraditionalization of the politics of race, we need to begin by exploring the evidence for any antiracist influence.

We have seen that, not only would many have agreed with Chrissie Hynde (of The Pretenders) that 'before punk, only reggae was unique' (quoted in Lydon 1994: 260), but, as with hippie subcultures, central to the appeal of reggae and dub was the perception of it as countercultural, anti-establishment, subversive, and 'underground'. As Paul Simonen of The Clash has commented, when Lydon played reggae on John Peel's BBC Radio 1 show, 'it had a big effect. The radio stations wouldn't play it. You never heard Big Youth on the radio. It was *an underground thing*' (quoted in Colgrave and Sullivan 2001: 203; emphasis added). That the emergent face of anti-establishment rebellion, Johnny Rotten/Lydon, had allied himself with the genre meant that it quickly accrued significant subcultural capital. 'I remember once when Lydon said he liked reggae, and that was it – everybody liked reggae' (Paul Stahl in Lydon 1994: 214). Similarly, although, no doubt, he overstates the significance of his influence on other musicians, it's worth quoting Lydon's own recollection of the impact of an interview he gave on Capital Radio's *Tommy Vance Show* on 16 July 1977 (his first substantial broadcast interview): 'Reggae was the only other radical music that was completely underground and not played on the radio. It wasn't played on the air until I did that appearance on *The Tommy Vance Show* on Capital. Then suddenly you'd get Joe Strummer and The Clash say, "We always loved reggae." But those fucks never did. They were not brought up with it the same way I was' (Lydon 1994: 268; cf. Letts 2007: 110). Although reggae and dub were certainly not widely played and largely an underground concern, Lydon's comments are misleading. For example, Paul Simonon and Joe Strummer were both familiar with reggae prior to Lydon's evangelization. Indeed, Simonon had, from a relatively early age, been listening to reggae:

> in 1972 or 1973... I left William Penn Secondary School and I was asked to leave home and go to live with my dad in Ladbroke Grove. I went to Isaac Newton, the local school, and met a whole batch of kids and was exposed to reggae songs that were a lot more militant: Burning Spear, Big Youth and I-Roy, music more about black issues. Even though it was about the black man's situation, there were certain songs I could relate to.' Indeed, he continues, 'I learned the bass playing along to reggae records' (Simonon 2005: 3).

Likewise, Strummer had not only been brought up in an area similar to those in which Lydon and Simonon had grown up, where reggae was part of the sonic environment, but in the early 1970s he frequented The Silver Sands, an African-Caribbean reggae club in Coronation Road, Newport, the Welsh city where some of his friends were studying art (see Gilbert 2005: 21–22). Again, Mark Stewart, Bruce Smith and other members of The Pop Group grew up in Bristol where there was a large and well-established African-Caribbean community. From the early 1970s they were exposed to reggae, funk and jazz. Although The Pop Group are, chronologically and musicologically, a post-punk band (e.g. they did not release their debut single, 'She is Beyond Good and Evil', until March 1979), it is nevertheless significant that, in the early 1970s, Stewart, Smith and Simon Underwood (who would eventually play bass for the band) regularly ventured into African-Caribbean areas to go to blues parties. And, as Stewart recalls, 'Every Friday when we were, like, fourteen or fifteen, we'd go to this record store, Revolver, to check out the new reggae pre-releases that had just arrived from London by van' (Reynolds 2005: 74; see also Taylor 2004: 188–89). Indeed, thinking of Lydon's comments, not only were other punk and post-punk artists fascinated by reggae and dub from a relatively early period, but he also neglects to acknowledge that both Capitol Radio and Radio London already had their own regular reggae programmes, which were established to serve London's Jamaican population (see Boot and Salewicz 1997: 65).

Having said that, Lydon has a point. While his love of dub and reggae was not unique, it was certainly a minority concern prior to punk. It was very rarely played on national radio and few people outside the major cities knew much about it. This was principally a result of the reluctance of major labels to release and promote reggae, which, for many at the time, was not just the result of their ignorance and cultural myopia, but arguably a consequence of implicit institutional racism (Savage 2005: 570). Of course, the state of the Jamaican music industry and the relatively haphazard way in which we have seen that reggae was marketed and distributed in Britain didn't help. While the efforts of Blackwell, the Island label, and the music of Bob Marley – particularly since the release of *Catch a Fire* in the UK in 1973 and his appearance on *The Old Grey Whistle Test* on 20 May of that year – contributed significantly to the raising of reggae's profile (see Toynbee 2007: 137–52), it was still, by the mid-1970s, on the periphery of popular culture. It is interesting, therefore, that while so much popular emphasis has been placed, not entirely inappropriately, on Marley's contribution to the raising of reggae's profile in the UK, of at least equal importance were Lydon, the arrival of punk, and influential punk fans, such as the deejay John Peel (see Peel and Ravenscroft 2005: 258–59; Wall 2004: 92–93). That is to say, while the situation was gradually changing, the appreciation of reggae within white subcultures accelerated rapidly with the arrival of the punks, many of whom were quick to acknowledge authentic 'rebel music' (to use Bob Marley's term). Hence, within a short period of time, as John Savage comments, 'reggae groups became fixtures at punk clubs' (1991: 485; cf. Letts 2007).

On the other hand, of course, it is important not to overstate punk's contribution to the reception of Jamaica's 'rebel music' in the UK. While Lydon had made a significant contribution to that reception, he was only able to do so as a result of its gradual growth within the African-Caribbean communities: 'I was pleased to go to the state school... I liked the sheer variety of people, including the huge Jamaican contingent at the school. It was marvellous because I really loved reggae, and the dances were fucking brilliant. Me and my bloody long hair reggae-ing it out' (Lydon 1994: 56; see also 248). And, of course, this exposure to reggae and African-Caribbean culture is also true of other influential punk musicians. As Dave Ruffy of The Ruts comments: 'I always liked a lot of black music, and reggae was a good soundtrack. It was a music you could actually listen and chill out to' (quoted in Lydon 1994: 224). Similarly, in the early 1970s, the countercultural, politicized hippie and Captain Beefheart fan, John Graham Mellor, who would take the name 'Woody' – after Woody Guthrie – and eventually emerge as 'Joe Strummer' in the mid-1970s, was exposed to ska and reggae in his late-teens, for which he gained a deep fondness (see Gilbert 2005: 19–22). More particularly, Simonen, 'a lugubrious ex-skinhead, with many black friends' is clear that 'his music was always reggae, the sound of the urban ghettos of Jamaica and Brixton' (Topping 2004: 14–15). As Pat Gilbert comments, as a schoolboy, he and his friends would 'wander around Tavistock Road and Westbourne Grove, checking out the blues parties where reggae music and marijuana mingled pungently' (2005: 57). Hence, as Don

Letts, a former Beatles enthusiast, who is often credited with introducing reggae to the punk subculture, comments: 'Punks like Paul Simonen, Johnny Rotten, and Joe Strummer were already tuned into the reggae wavelength' (Letts 2001: 6; see also 2007: 71). Therefore, while it would be claiming too much to argue that punks were politicized by reggae, it is significant that, again, in the years immediately prior to the advent of punk, young, disenfranchised, white adolescents who were enthusiastically listening to Hawkwind, Can, and The Stooges, also enjoyed reggae and identified political and subcultural continuities with young Jamaicans and Rasta culture (see Letts 2007: 118).

Perhaps one of the first significant bridges from Jamaican popular culture into white British subcultures was the soundtrack of Perry Henzell's film *The Harder They Come* (Island, 1972) – 'the movie that brought Jamaica to Britain' (Barrow and Dalton 1997: 328; see also Hebdige 1974: 29; Letts 2007: 90–95).[5] Again, without wishing to underestimate the importance of *Catch a Fire* for the popularization of reggae in the UK, along with punk, this soundtrack was arguably more important (see Davis 1994: 111; Letts 2007: 90–95, 200–202). Not only did Jimmy Cliff become relatively well-known to white audiences following the release of the film (although his 'Vietnam' had reached 46 in the UK charts in February 1970), but other artists who contributed to the soundtrack, particularly Toots and the Maytals, achieved a level of success that had eluded other African-Caribbean artists. Indeed, while they'd had something of a hit with 'Monkey Man' in 1970, in that it reached 47 in the charts in May, after the release of the film in the UK in 1974, they secured a tour with Dr Feelgood. This is worth noting because, although Dr Feelgood had not yet released their first album, *Down By the Jetty* (1975), they were rising stars on the pub rock circuit – which would become important for the emergence of punk. Hence, for Toots and the Maytals and the music of *The Harder They Come* to be exposed to this embryonic fan base is of some significance. Indeed, particular songs from *The Harder They Come* began to find their way into the repertoires of white musicians and, from there, into the minds of a generation of white music fans.[6]

Concerning pub rock, not only were there tenuous, pre-punk connections with reggae, but its ethos had aesthetic continuities with dub culture. Pub rock began in 1972 and is a general umbrella term for bands and artists such as Ian Dury's Kilburn and the High Roads, Joe Strummer's 101ers, Ducks Deluxe, Nick Lowe, Graham Parker, Elvis Costello, and Larry Wallis (formerly of underground rockers The Pink Fairies). Eventually promoted by Stiff Records (which, in 1976, released the first punk single – 'New Rose' by The Damned),[7] pub rock focused on immediacy with its audience and a do-it-yourself mentality. Moreover, the short, choppy, even aggressive rhythm and blues songs of bands such as Dr Feelgood were a significant musical influence on several early punks, their distinctive and gifted guitarist, Wilko Johnson, often being referenced by musicians of the period (see Boot and Salewicz 1997: 27–28; see also Murray 1978). That said, as Dave Laing comments, 'punk's most important debt to pub rock lay in its opening up of a *space* for both performing and recording which lay outside the constraints of the mainstream music industry' (1985: 9; original emphasis). Moreover, the antiphonal immediacy of the relationship between the audience and the performers within pubs, such as London's Hope and Anchor, was not dissimilar to Jamaican dancehall culture. Indeed, there were significant continuities between the pub, the blues dance, and the dancehall. There was also a similar approach to making records. Because, initially, major record companies had little interest in pub bands, new labels were established to cater for the genre, most notably, Stiff and Chiswick. Hence, with the success of Stiff's first single by Nick Lowe, argues Laing, 'independent label economics had been born' (1985: 9). The first principle of this economics, he notes, 'was its refusal to heed the imperative of the hit parade' (1985: 9). There was no requirement for expensive producers, sophisticated studios, teams of promotions staff, and other overheads. Consequently, independent labels could produce music relatively cheaply and required far fewer sales to remain solvent – instead of 23,000 copies of a single to 'break-even', they only needed as little as 2000, which would then be sold at gigs and through specialist record shops. This, of course, reminds one very much of the Jamaican record industry. Hence, while one can understand Laing's comment that with the emergence of Stiff, 'independent label economics had been born', it is important to remember that, as we have seen, such economies were already alive and well in both Jamaica and the UK. Hence, overall, the point is that, pub rock, which was to have a significant formative influence on punk, not only had some interaction with reggae culture, but also had much in common with it. Hence, again, it is not surprising that, within a year or so, there would be a confluence of punk and reggae/dub cultures. White post-punk reggae and dub labels, such as Adrian Sherwood's Hitrun (1978) and On-U Sound (1980), were simply a continuation of these developments within reggae, pub rock, and punk.

By 1976 several key punks, particularly Lydon, disillusioned and infused with a distaste for, as they understood it, hippie, drug-addled hedonism and hypocrisy, had absorbed these influences and were embarking on a new subcultural trajectory. As Penny Rimbaud of the anarchist collective/band Crass put it, 'there can be no argument that punk was a kick-back against the velvet and patchouli complacency of the dope-hazed Sixties and early seventies' (Crass 2004: xx; see also O'Hara 1999: 24). While, of course, the history of the punk 'kick-back' needs to be traced not just to pub rock, but, more significantly, back across the Atlantic to The Ramones, to Patti Smith, to Johnny Thunders, to The New York Dolls, and to The Stooges (see Boot and Salewicz 1997: 10–25; Laing 1985: 22–27; McNeill and McCain 1996; Redhead 1990: 15–16; Savage 2005: 1–103; Smith and Middles 2003: 69), it is difficult to underestimate the catalytic significance of The Sex Pistols, the face of which was Lydon.[8] Although their manager, Malcolm McLaren, has famously dismissed Lydon's significance in favour of his own creative influence on the band, as Savage puts it, 'it would have been impossible for The Sex Pistols to have had the impact they did without him'. Moreover, 'it was Lydon's very interest in the quirk's of post-hippie pop – the expressionist Peter Hammill [whose own interest in reggae rhythms is noted above], the disruptive Captain Beefheart, the [dub] spaces of Keith Hudson – that gave The Sex Pistols an exit from nostalgia or lads' rock into new, uncharted territory. Lydon's interest in experimentation gave The Sex Pistols the edge to back up their increasingly extravagant demands' (Savage 2005: 122). This, of course, is also true of The Clash, The Ruts, The Slits, Alternative TV, Generation X, and other punk bands. However, again, the point is that, when one considers this central stream of influence on punk, the significance of reggae and dub is hard to avoid (see Letts 2007; Street Howe 2009).

While, however, there was a convergence of reggae and punk in the minds of influential figures such as Lydon, Strummer, Simonen, and Peel, almost equally significant was the rapprochement on the record decks of the The Roxy, a former gay disco called Chaguaramas. Located at 41-43 Neal Street, Covent Garden, it is of particular importance in the history of punk's reception of reggae and dub in the UK. Although it's often claimed that the name of the club was meant to be pronounced 'Shag-erama's' to indicate the main clientele and purpose of the club, situated, as it was, so close to Soho and London's sex district (e.g. see the notes accompanying *The Roxy London WC2* CD), in actual fact, a previous owner of the club, Tony Ashfield, worked for Trojan and had produced John Holt, with whom he had established Chaguaramas Recording Productions (probably after Chaguaramas Bay in Trinidad). The club, it would seem, was simply named after this partnership (see Marko 2007: 42). However, by 1977 the club had changed hands and Gene October, the singer of the punk band Chelsea, thought it might be a good venue to perform and rehearse. He, therefore, drew this to the attention of Chelsea's manager, Andrew Czezowski, an ex-mod who had also worked for some time as Vivienne Westwood's business advisor and accountant. As the current owner, Rene Albert, a one-armed Swiss-born barrister, was about to lose his licence,[9] Czezowski (along with Sue Carrington and Barry Jones) persuaded him to rent it out on Tuesdays and Wednesdays (when it would normally be closed). Czezowski was aware of the disco largely because it was frequented by many of the regular customers of 'Sex', the fashion outlet run by McLaren and Westwood (see Savage 2005: 3–103; Heylin 2007: 192ff.). It was soon renamed 'The Roxy' and, although it actually stayed open for just 100 days in 1977, from January to April, it was a powerhouse of punk creativity and an incubator promoting the growth of several seminal punk bands, most notably Siouxsie and the Banshees, The Clash, Generation X, The Slits, The Adverts, and Subway Sect (see Letts 2007: 82–88; listen also to CD, *The Roxy London WC2*). However, it was not only a site of innovation, it was also site of collaboration and musical syncretism, which enabled several key musicians from New York's punk scene to put down roots in the UK. Hence, those who frequented The Roxy could expect to see, along with embryonic British punk bands, The Ramones, Cherry Vanilla, Wayne County, and The Heartbreakers. However, perhaps the most interesting confluence of styles and agendas was that with which this chapter is concerned, namely that between the disaffected and rebellious cultures of Rastafari and white, urban punk. 'There were similarities between the anti-establishment ethic of punks and Rastafarian culture. Both groups were generally viewed as outsiders, and both employed contentious sloganeering as a means of promotion' (Colegrave and Sullivan 2001: 186; cf. Letts 2007: 84–85).

The catalytic figure at this interface was Don Letts, who, working as a deejay at The Roxy, is, as noted above, often credited with introducing reggae and dub to the punk scene (Letts 2007: 87–88; cf. Colegrave and Sullivan 2001: 186; listen to *Dread Meets Punk Rockers Uptown: Social Classics Vol. 2*). That said, although Letts was certainly instrumental in punk's reception of dub in London and introduced Lydon and others to the bass culture of the Sir Coxsone Sound System (Letts 2009), we have seen that he was not the only, or even the main influence, in that many influential musicians were already listening to and playing reggae. Moreover, as we saw in the previous chapter, by 1974, dub LPs were available in the UK, sound systems were playing dub, and the first dub single, Rupie Edwards's 'Ire Feelings', had sold over 250,000 copies, spent ten weeks in the charts, eventually (and rather surprisingly) entering the 'top ten' at number nine. (A good compilation of UK reggae chart hits from this period, including 'Ire Feelings', is *Ire Feelings: Reggae Chart Hits 1969–1976*.) Hence, although a select and influential few will have been introduced to reggae and dub by Letts at The Roxy, as he himself is aware (see Letts 2001: 6; 2007: 71–72), many others were already familiar with it. Nevertheless, his role was an important one. Indeed, whilst possibly exaggerating his significance a little, Colegrave and Sullivan are correct to argue that his legacy was 'to build a vibrant reggae scene beyond its ethnic roots, which would be celebrated in Bob Marley's "Punky Reggae Party"' (2001: 186). Certainly, one of the most significant punk bands to be explicitly influenced by dub, The Slits, trace their interest in the genre to 'Don Letts and his Djing stints at The Roxy' (guitarist Viv Albertine, quoted in Paytress 2000; cf. Letts 2007: 84, 86, 96–102; see Street Howe 2009: 39).

Almost as significant as Letts's residency at The Roxy was his work for Stephen Raynor and John Krevine at Acme Attractions – a rival fashion outlet to McLaren's and Westwood's shop 'Too Fast to Live, Too Young to Die' (which was soon to be renamed 'Sex'). It was here that Letts began playing dub to disaffected youth: 'The dub stuff had started... I played it very loud and that's what attracted everybody' (quoted in Savage 2005: 96). 'I... pumped dub reggae all day long, much to the chagrin of the antiques dealers who had their businesses upstairs. I came to realise that the music drew the people as much as the items we were selling' (Letts 2001: 3; see also 2007: 51–58).

It's worth noting at this point that, even before Acme Attractions had opened in Antiquarius (the antiques market in Chelsea), Bernie Rhodes – who became an important influence on the UK music scene, introducing Lydon to The Sex Pistols (Savage 2005: 71), nurturing the careers of Dexy's Midnight Runners, The Specials, and Subway Sect, and, most significantly, managing The Clash – was playing and selling reggae at his own screen-printed T-shirt stall (see Letts 2001: 4). Bearing in mind that few would disagree with Simonen that 'you can't overestimate Bernie's importance' and that he essentially 'set up the whole punk scene' (Gilbert 2005: 78), it is of some significance that he was involved in dub reggae at this early period.

That said, when it came to the dissemination of dub, Letts's contribution was clearly more significant. Dub at Acme Attractions was played to numerous young people, including many who would become key figures in popular music, including Chrissie Hynde, Patti Smith, Debbie Harry, Johnny Thunders, and 'all the major players on the London punk scene' (Letts 2001: 4).

> As I was behind the counter every day at Acme with Tappa Zukie's 'MPLA Dub' booming out of the speakers, burning spliffs and holding my corner, I started to notice the same white faces coming down to the basement... The guys were John Lydon, Paul Simonon and Joe Strummer. Initially we said nothing to each other and just observed... Eventually everyone dropped their guard and we started talking about reggae and dub whilst sharing a spliff in the basement... These guys were already into reggae and were seriously interested in the stuff I was pumping out... I was coming in with King Tubby and Lee Perry's heavy dub. I was also playing things like Keith Hudson's *Pick a Dub*,

a set of records called *African Dub: Chapters 1, 2* and *3*, the Big Youth album *Dreadlocks Dread* and Tappa Zukie's *Man Ah Warrior* album. *King Tubby Meets the Rockers Uptown* with Augustus Pablo was my theme tune (Letts 2007: 71–72).

Returning to the rise and fall of The Roxy, as well as being a business advisor to Westwood and McLaren, Czezowski was also the accountant for Acme Attractions. Familiar with the clientele of both shops, he was quick to recognize the commercial potential of an emerging subculture. The most obvious commercial opportunity that presented itself was the lack of a social focal point, in particular, the lack of a music venue. Hence, he responded quickly to Gene October's request to explore the possibility of hiring Chaguaramas as a venue for Chelsea to play in. After some negotiating with Rene Albert, he opened The Roxy and, recalls Letts, 'because of the buzz created by the music I played in the shop, he asked me to d.j.' Letts continues, 'now you gotta realise, punk was so new that none of the bands had actually released any records yet. So I played what I was into – reggae, *especially dub*. I weren't no two-deck-playing, babble-on-a-mic, request-taking d.j. No sir! Strictly one deck, two spliffs, and the gaps between tunes was crucial' (Letts 2001: 5; emphasis added). Indeed, it's interesting that, while Letts recalls playing other music that he knew proto-punks and punks appreciated, such as The Stooges, MC5, New York Dolls, and Television, and later the new punk releases, Roxy regulars insisted that he 'just keep spinning reggae' (Letts 2001: 5). 'There were no UK punk records to play as none had been made yet. So, in between the fast and furious punk sets, I played some serious dub reggae' (Letts 2007: 82). Hence, for many, dub quickly became a central genre of the subcultural soundtrack.

Again, the key feature of this subcultural exchange was, to some extent, less to do with the music, which was undoubtedly appreciated, and more to do with the style and the rhetoric. There was a collusion of signification. Again, this is indicated by Letts:

> We became closer by revelling in our differences, not by trying to be the same. They dug the bass lines, beats and *attitude* of the tunes I played, not to mention the ready rolled spliffs you could buy at the bar (the punks couldn't roll their own)... We're talking *serious cultural exchange*... It was *a culture that spoke in a currency they could identify with*... *the anti-fashion, its rebel stance* and, importantly, the fact that reggae was *a kind of musical reportage talking about things that mattered*, providing *a soundtrack for the situation*. The third world *DIY approach* to creating the reggae sound was something else that punks could relate to, as most had no formal training in music (Letts 2001: 5–6 – emphasis added; cf. Lydon 1994: 268).

Similarly, elsewhere, Letts recalls the following:

> We turned each other on through our different cultures. They liked me because I gave them access to Jamaican culture, and they turned me on to a white culture that didn't fucking exist before they came along. Punk was a focal point because there were a lot of people walking around dissatisfied, disinterested, with no hope and no future... I started taking [Lydon] to reggae clubs. We went to a place called The Four Aces in Dalston, which is the heaviest reggae club in London. No white people went in there. The only white person there was John, because I took him. Everybody left John alone. We black people had real respect for him because he came across as a real dude... It was amazing that Johnny Rotten was so acceptable to the Rastas in London. They might not have liked his music, but it was like outlaws banding together. We all felt like society's outlaws (quoted in Lydon 1994: 269–70).

Dread and Punk Meet Branson Uptown

As well as this cultural exchange and continuity, the rise of reggae and dub within white British subcultures was also indebted to the contribution of the emerging major labels. 'The news had buzzed around Kingston late in 1975 that Virgin and Island were looking to sign contracts with the top producers, and that comparatively large advances were being offered to artists, with the possibility of royalties to come later' (de Konigh and Griffiths 2003: 175). Hence, it was almost inevitable that independent British reggae labels, such as Trojan, were largely supplanted by the mid-1970s. The result, of course, was that reggae's centre of gravity shifted more towards the mainstream and, as it did, significant cross-pollination began to occur. Just as we have seen that artists on the Island label, such as Robert Palmer and John Martyn, had begun to appreciate dub techniques, so, when Richard Branson's Virgin label began to work with both punk and reggae artists, the growing interest the former had in the latter was nurtured.

As is well-known, Virgin signed The Sex Pistols and released *Never Mind the Bollocks, Here's the Sex Pistols* (1977) following the well-known debacle with EMI – shortly after signing the band, EMI panicked at their behaviour on the Thames television show *Today*, hosted by Bill Grundy on 1 December 1976 (see Savage 2005: 257–60; Marcus 1989: Heylin 2007: 173–74),[10] and immediately wanted to drop them, fearing negative publicity (the band's typically visceral response was 'EMI' on *Never Mind the Bollocks*). Branson recalls the events that led to Virgin signing The Sex Pistols:

> One day I heard this music coming through the floor from down below, and it was 'Anarchy in the UK'. I remember running all the way downstairs and saying to Simon [Draper], 'What's that? – it sounds fantastic,' and Simon saying, 'It's The Sex Pistols, they've just signed to EMI.' I then went back to my office, rang up EMI, and in those days they wouldn't actually take a call, the chairman wouldn't talk to me direct. But, he decided I could talk to his secretary. So I left a message saying that if he wants to get rid of his embarrassment, can he give me a ring. I got a curt message back saying, 'We're not embarrassed at all, very happy with The Sex Pistols. Thank you very much.' That same night, The Sex Pistols went on the Bill Grundy show, swearing left, right, and centre, and the next morning, at six a.m. I was woken up at my home by the chairman himself. He asked if I could come over right away. When I arrived he said, 'here's the contract! If you want them, you can have them!' (quoted in Southern 1995: 53)

Indeed, as far as Branson is concerned, whereas Mike Oldfield's *Tubular Bells* established the Virgin label, 'it was The Sex Pistols that put us on the map' (quoted in Southern 1995: 58). While Branson appears to have been an immediate convert to punk, he had originally spurned it as inimical to the hippie ethic he had sought to nurture at Virgin. McLaren remembers approaching Virgin prior to EMI, but 'they didn't wanna know' (quoted in Heylin 2007: 279). However, it would appear that, as the profits from *Tubular Bells* declined and the peace and love culture faded, Branson's hippie idealism was radicalized by punk nihilism and Rastafari – and his profits increased accordingly.

Not only did several punk bands follow as a result of signing The Sex Pistols, but, indirectly, so did numerous reggae artists. On 3 February 1978 Branson flew out to Jamaica to sign up new artists. As his colleague Simon Draper recalls, 'we started to get huge orders from Nigeria, so we looked into it a little bit and it became clear that something extraordinary was happening there, that reggae had suddenly become a massive new fad. So that's when Richard went off on his trip to Jamaica with suitcases stuffed full of money, to sign as many reggae artists as possible' (quoted in Southern 1995: 76). However, he did not go alone. Accompanying him were Lydon, who he employed as a consultant, Letts, Dennis Morris, and the journalist Vivienne Goldman (Salewicz 2005). That said, for Lydon, it wasn't simply the attraction of Rasta culture and reggae that took him to Jamaica, but it was also a welcome break from media scrutiny, following the demise of The Sex Pistols. For Letts, it was, quite simply, his first trip to Jamaica (see Letts 2007: 109–17).

> I got a phone call from Rotten asking me if I wanted to join him on the trip. Fuck yeah. I guess John thought that me being black and Jamaican, sort of, meant he'd be in good hands. Little did he know that the

> nearest I'd been to JA was watching *The Harder They Come* at the Classic cinema in Brixton. That trip was a trip. When the word got around the island that 'rich white man wid whole heap a money signin' up reggae artists', there was an exodus to the Sheraton hotel where Richard had taken up residence of the whole first floor... Over the next few weeks we met all our reggae heroes... Whilst we were in Jamaica we found ourselves in some surreal situations, like the time when John and I ended up at Joni Mitchell's place. We're sitting there listening to some music that definitely wasn't reggae or punk, when I exclaim, 'what is this shit, take it off', to which she replies, somewhat obviously, 'it's my latest album' (Letts 2001: 11–12; see also Letts 2007: 109–17).

To some extent, this last comment exposes the growing distance between the Woodstock generation, the hippie generation of artists that Branson had originally signed to Virgin, and the new urban rebels. Old alliances were being severed and new ones formed. The result was Virgin's influential Front Line label (see Southern 1995: 76–95), which catered specifically for the growing interest in reggae and dub, a 'cultural interaction' which, as Letts comments, 'was to leave its mark on punk'. He continues, 'Check out The Slits' (who I managed for a while – well, tried to) first album, the excellent and bass heavy *Cut*. As for The Clash, well 'nuff said and listen to Jah Wobble's bass lines on any of the PiL albums... Reggae has become part of the very fabric of popular culture, having permeated contemporary music, language, fashion, even people's attitudes' (2001: 12; see also Letts 2007: 96–102; Coon 1978: 102–14; Porter 2003: 23–29).[11]

Punks, Racists and Swastikas

The socially irenic potential of the confluence of punk and reggae would seem obvious, in that there appears to have been a subcultural rapprochement, a contribution to positive race relations, a healthy corrective to the racism that was ubiquitous within British society in the 1970s (see Cohen and Gardner 1982). However, this perception of punk has been challenged by Roger Sabin, who makes use of music papers and fanzines to show that some punks were not interested in reggae or, indeed, in left-wing, anti-racist politics (1999b). He takes issue with 'the twin ideas that punk somehow transcended the societal forces that gave birth to it, and that it can be judged as being ideologically commensurate with the "politically correct" standards of the 1980s and 90s'. In particular, he argues that punk's involvement with anti-racism 'has been exaggerated', 'its political ambiguity left ample space for right-wing interpretation', and 'its overtly racist aspects left a legacy for the fascist music scene of the post-punk era' (1999b: 199). Hence, dismissing the work of several notable scholars and journalists, such as Coon (1978), Hebdige (1979), Jones (1988), and Savage (2005 [1991]), he argues that they have been responsible for mythmaking and the construction of false orthodoxies.

Whilst, of course, there is nothing wrong with demythologizing popular orthodoxies, there needs to be good reasons for doing so. Unfortunately, Sabin's work is lacking in this respect. Perhaps the principal problem with Sabin's thesis is his implicit conception of punk as a homogenous movement with specific political goals and agendas – 'anti-racism' being a particular ideology constructed by 'the punks'. Hence, writing as if punk was a political pressure group, he makes the following comment: 'punk's biggest failure in the political sphere was its almost total neglect of the plight of Britain's Asians. For it has been forgotten over time that the focus of attention for the far right in the late 1970s was directed primarily at them, and not, as most accounts assume, at British African-Caribbeans' (1999b: 203). He then goes on to discuss the plight of British Asians and concludes by asking 'What was punk's response?', as if, again, 'punk' was an organization that could and should have made a considered political response. Sadly, he notes, 'the most striking impression was one of silence' (1999b: 203).

Sabin's comments are interesting because they raise two issues. Firstly, as noted above, he is treating punk as if it were an organized anti-racist movement with a political agenda. The problem for Sabin's thesis is that it wasn't! Rather, punks were principally disenfranchised youths gathering around some shared interests in music and fashion. It is, therefore, a mistake to look for ideological consensus. That said, although ad hoc, there were, of course, some shared and overlapping attitudes to society, to 'the establishment', and to previous music-oriented subcultures, particularly hippies and progressive rock. Nevertheless, to treat punks as an organized movement with political goals is to misrepresent what is, perhaps, better understood as a 'scene'. As already discussed in relation to dub, in using the term 'scene', we are thinking of a broad, disparate milieu, rather than an ideologically focused movement. 'Punk' refers to musicians, audience cultures, and 'the business' in general. It refers to labels, events, informal economies, networks, fanzines, the attitudes encouraged, and so on. Moreover, while the malleable concept of 'scene' can refer to geographically localized cultures, it has also been used to articulate, as Sara Cohen comments,

> the fluid, loose, cosmopolitan, transitory, and geographically dispersed nature of local music activity. Rather than linking scenes with notions of a clearly defined and place-bound community or subculture with a relatively fixed population...scenes are created through heterogenous 'coalitions' and 'alliances' based on musical preferences, thus linking scene with cultural change and interaction (1999: 245; see also Straw 1991; Olson 1998; O'Connor 2002).

Hence, thinking of punk in terms of a scene will discourage notions of homogeneity, organization, orthodoxies and orthopraxies. While we will see that *some* punks did develop political agendas – which were often the result of alliances with African-Caribbean cultures – it was not a political movement *per se*. Consequently, any attitude to Asian communities, or race in general, needs to be analysed a little more closely and cautiously.

Secondly, it is of some significance that, generally speaking, punks did not engage with Asian cultures. This was not because those attracted to punk music were inherently racist or that they purposely neglected Asians in their anti-racist rhetoric (though, of course, some may have done), but rather because the same subcultural continuities did not exist between punk and Asian cultures. On the one hand, at a fairly superficial level, tracing the genre back through rock and blues, punk had more in common with black music. Although, subsequently, post-punk, electronica, and dance music would see the growing influence of Asian culture, at this point it had little direct impact.

That said, it should be noted that any neglect of Asian communities was only partial. Many anti-racist punks were concerned about all manifestations of racism. For example, as Simon Frith and John Street comment, in Coventry, 'local musicans (led by The Specials) were able to mount an immediate, powerful, and effective outdoor concert response to a spate of "Paki-bashing" incidents (street attacks on Asian British by skinhead gangs) which had resulted in a fatal stabbing' (1992: 70).

Moreover, it is of some significance that punk itself had a positive, if minor, impact on Asian music and subcultures. For example, Aki Nawaz (Haq Qureshi) of the radical Islamic band Fun-Da-Mental (and Nation Records, which has produced a steady stream of dub-influenced projects) was significantly influenced by punk:

> I think that the only thing that I've been influenced by really is punk music; kind of the music and the attitude... To me it was more of a philosophy; to a lot of the white kids it was just a fashion; they weren't breaking away from anything because they had nothing to break away from, because they didn't have any restraints, you know, culturally or religiously. I mean punk was a massive influence on me (quoted in Hyder 2004: 161).

The punk ethic is still conspicuously evident in his music (see Bhattacharyya 2006; Wells 1995). That it was a positive influence on young Asians such as Nawaz, of course, indicates that at least some did not perceive punk discourse to be particularly hostile or racist. Rather it was liberative and, as such, it was a genre some Asians felt comfortable identifying with. Moreover, again, as

Nawaz implicitly indicates, punk had little in common with Asian cultures in the 1970s, which tended to be quieter, more conservative, more insular, and less rebellious than African-Caribbean cultures, particularly Rasta culture. It would be another decade or so before the voice of disaffected Asian youth would be heard (see Hyder 2004).

It is also important to understand that punk's neglect of Asian culture has another significance, in that the particular white subcultures explicitly rejected by many punks, principally the hippie and psychedelic subcultures, had been shaped to a large extent by Indian religion, fashion and music. Hippie subculture in particular had explicitly turned East (see Partridge 2004a: 151–56). Hence, the cultural alliances, the attitudes of peace and love, the hippie idealism, the spirituality, the cheesecloth kaftan fashion, and all that had contributed to that subculture and music, were of little interest to many punks. Indeed, Easternized hippies were very often dismissed as decadent, self-serving 'dinosaurs'. (I remember, in the late-1970s, punks wearing badges with an illustration of a dinosaur declaring precisely that.) As Lydon insists,

> The Pistols were an absolute threat to that nice little world they had all built for themselves. They came out of the ever-so-generous-and-love-everyone sixties and soon turned into fucking greedy, shifty little businessmen doing their utmost to stifle the opposition. The lot of them deserved the name *dinosaurs* – too big, too pompous, elaborate, enormous amounts of equipment, only playing very large auditoriums and open-air festivals... They bought immense houses, joined the stockbrokers' belt, and sent their kids to *public schools!* See? The system! They became it (1994: 196; cf. Letts 2007: 68–69).

Hence, to some extent, punk can be seen as a conscious reaction to hippie idealism and the process of Easternization that contributed so significantly to it. The point is that, not only was Asian culture *not* a culture with which punks could identify, but, more explicitly, Rastas provided, in a way that Asians did not, a counterculture to replace a redundant hippie idealism. Again, as one *Black Echoes* journalist commented at the time:

> The white kids have lost their heroes; Jagger has become a wealthy socialite, Dylan a mellow home-loving man, even Lennon has little to say anymore. So along comes this guy with amazing screw top hair, and he's singing about 'burning and looting' and 'brain wash education', 'loving your brothers and smoking your dope'. Their dream lives on (quoted in Jones 1988: 94).

In the final analysis, because there was no particular 'punk manifesto', it was simply a case of young people identifying with ideas, musics, and fashions that made sense of their situation, just as those involved in psychedelic culture and, before that, beat culture had done when they turned East. Therefore, to some extent, Sabin has a point when he notes that 'Asians simply didn't have the same romance as African-Caribbean youth – especially in terms of the latter's reputation for being confrontational with the police – and what was equally problematic, they had no music comparable to reggae with which punks could identify' (1999b: 204). That said, what Sabin fails to grasp is that, although we have seen that there was more to it than this, we need to understand that the lack of alliances with the Asian community were less to do with racism or selective anti-racism and more to do with subcultural continuities and discontinuities, the discontinuities being principally those with the hippie subculture, for which Asian culture, spirituality and music did possess a certain romance. Indeed, Sabin himself notes that The Clash were quick to correct and challenge perceived racist comments about Asians (1999b: 205). However, the principal point is that many punks wanted to go into the streets and 'burn down Babylon', not stay in a bed-sit and burn incense. The notion of reclining on a beanbag contemplating 'tales from topographic oceans', pondering life in a Roger Dean universe, and listening to tedious, self-absorbed ten-minute guitar and drum solos was anathema to punks. Battles needed to be fought, boredom needed to be challenged, and the mundane tedium and perceived oppression of everyday urban life had to be faced up to. The focus on African-Caribbean discourse is, therefore, entirely understandable. As Jones notes,

> There were similarities between the discourses of punk ('Crisis', 'Anarchy in the UK') and those of Rastafari ('Armaggideon Time', 'War inna Babylon'). Punks drew analogies between their position and that of Rastas on the basis that both faced discrimination as a result of their appearances and beliefs. Such connections were immortalised in the Bob Marley song 'Punky Reggae Party' which acknowledged the links between the two movements, proclaiming that while 'rejected by society' and 'treated with impunity', both were 'protected by their dignity' (1988: 95–96).

Punks tended to recognize in reggae a rebel discourse, a collective struggle for cultural and political power. Again, unlike the fantasy-oriented, stadium-based, Easternized meanderings of much progressive rock, punk identified in reggae a concern for the mundane, a closeness to its audience, a discourse focused on the lived experiences of the oppressed, and, of course, a DIY approach to music, which didn't flaunt skill. Again, as Jones notes,

> Punk's concern to expose the oppressive nature and boredom of eve-
> ryday life under capitalism resonated with reggae's antipathy to com-
> modity forms, its emphasis on 'roots' and its faithful documentation
> of topical issues and current events. That resonance was itself partly
> predicated on white youth's own developing political consciousness
> of Britain's gathering economic and social crisis, experienced increas-
> ingly in the form of unemployment (1988: 97).

Interestingly, Sabin quotes Savage out of context to support his thesis:
'punks played music that "seemed to eradicate almost every trace of pop's
black origins"' (1999b: 205). What Savage actually says is, '*To those without
a key to punk's bewildering jumble of signals*, its combination of cropped hair,
emotive symbols and brutal, harsh music that seemed to eradicate almost
every trace of pop's black origins, pointed one way', namely to racism (Savage
2005: 243; emphasis added). This, Savage suggests (correctly in my opinion),
is a superficial reading of punk style and discourse. In a racist climate, 'a song
like "White Riot" [The Clash's debut single, released on 18 March 1977] could
be taken a different way: not as an admiring shout of solidarity in sympathy
with the blacks of Notting Hill Gate [which it was], but as a racist rallying call
[which it clearly was not]' (Savage 2005: 243; see also Denselow 1989: 147–
48). It was written after the 1976 Notting Hill Carnival riot, which The Clash
witnessed 'from the first brick thrown' (see Gilbert 2005: 100–103, 134–36;
Topping 2004: 159–60). As Strummer explains, it was actually 'a black riot',
'a spontaneous expression of "We ain't taking this anymore"'. The point, he
argues, is that 'White Riot' 'was saying that white people had to become activists too or else they'd get plastered over in society' (quoted in Topping 2004:
159). Hence, he insisted that the lyrics were 'not racist at all!' (quoted in Gilbert 2005: 136; see also Bundy 2004; Coon 1978: 69). Again, in a letter to
Denselow, he wrote the following: 'For better or for worse, we felt we had a
mission. For human rights and against racism. For democracy and freedom
and against fascism. For good and against evil' (Denselow 1989: 148). Indeed,
that The Clash's lyrics were misread, deliberately or unwittingly, by those with
far-right sympathies is almost besides the point. To some extent this has also
been argued by Jimmy Pursey of Sham 69, in that, although he was actively
opposed to racism and fascism, the band did attract a far-right following from
London's East End where the National Front was prominent. (An overview
of racist politics in 1970s Britain will be provided below.) As he says, 'if kids
come from there, you're bound to get an element with those views' (quoted in
Denselow 1989: 146). Although more neutralist than the Rock Against Racism
leadership would have liked (see Laing 1985: 110–12), he did distance himself
from racism by playing at one of their events and by sharing the stage with the

reggae band Misty in Roots. Hence, for Sabin to use a photo of a stage invasion at a Sham 69 concert by a contingent of the far-right British Movement as support for his thesis is, to say the least, misleading (1999b: 211). Indeed, reports of the gig by those who were there speak of 'Pursey's well-known anti-violence and anti-fascist stance' and that 'in tears and visibly shaken, [he] led his band offstage' (Du Noyer 1979a: 11; cf. Du Noyer 1979b).

In the final analysis, the punk- and reggae-oriented gigs organized by the Anti-Nazi League and Rock Against Racism, as Paul Marko has commented, 'helped halt the rise of the [National Front]. So what if years later punk... attracted Nazi boneheads?' (2000). Of course, as has been conceded, it would be going beyond the evidence to argue that all punks thought this way, the punk milieu being a disparate and heterogeneous one.[12] However, it is significant that the most influential and widely referenced punks supported anti-racist initiatives. Indeed, it's worth noting that, although popularly accused of racism by the press at the time, even some 'skinhead bands' explicitly distanced themselves from right-wing views and supported anti-racist events. For example, in an interview with Andrew Tyler, writing for the *NME* in 1981, Infa-Riot and The Four Skins declared that they 'are not now and never have been fascists nor do they want a Nazi following' (Tyler 1981: 4).

Hence, again, it is not surprising that reggae and Rasta culture were attractive to punks and post-punks, for prior to punk, reggae 'carried the torch of protest that white rock music had in the late-1960s, but then lost' (Coon quoted in Gilbert 2005: 135).[13] As we have seen, it was always a vehicle of social and political commentary, demonstrating a dogged refusal to distinguish between recreation and politics. And punks, such as Strummer, Simonen and Lydon, were not slow to appreciate and learn from what it had to offer. As early as 1976, prior to 'White Riot', The Clash were working on versions of Junior Murvin's militant song 'Police and Thieves' and the Max Romeo and Lee Perry classic, 'War Inna Babylon' (see Topping 2004: 117–19, 153). 'Police and Thieves' was, as Caroline Coon commented at the time, 'a salutation, in a way, to the music they most respect after their own' (1978: 79).

What then are we to make of punk *bricolage*, its visual and musical hyperboles, its semiotic connotations,[14] particularly the liberal appropriation of offensive statements, such as The Sex Pistols' oft cited 'Belsen Was a Gas' (e.g. Marcus 1989: 116–23; McNeil and McCain 1996: 33), and symbols, such as the swastika? Is this not an explicit endorsement of far-right politics? Certainly this is the way it was simplistically and denotatively portrayed in the media. But how different was this use of symbols and attitudes, asks Greil Marcus, from 'the National Front campaign to purify the UK of its coloured populations, Jamaicans, Pakistanis, Indians, the backwash of Empire?' (1989: 117).

Sabin thinks there is something more sinister than simply fashion here and is particularly critical of those who limit their analysis of punk's use of Third Reich imagery to 'some kind of postmodernist triumph of style over content' (1999b: 209). The problem for Sabin's thesis is that, to a large extent, this is exactly what it was. It was intended to shock (see Laing's discussion of punk's 'shock-effect' – 1985: 76–81). For example, as Adrian Boot and Chris Salewicz comment of Mick Jones's band, London SS, 'the "London" part of the name... alluded to the "New York" in New York Dolls, whilst the "SS" initials were a conscious shock tactic, in the same way that Siouxsie's and Sid's later adoption of the swastika had more to do with the defacing of school exercise books than with approbation for fascism' (1997: 35). In other words, such imagery and language are typical examples of what Julia Kristeva (1984) has referred to as 'interruptions of disordered discourse'. More specifically, from the perspective of semiotics, such symbolism needs to be understood connotatively, rather than denotatively. It was adolescent transgressive behaviour. As Chrissie Hynde comments,

> All the bondage gear wasn't supposed to stimulate you in the sexual sense. It was more of a statement; two fingers up at the establishment. They would have T-shirts with pictures of rapists wearing rubber masks as if reflecting something from the culture back at us. They were extremely anti-establishment. When the punk kids walked around wearing swastikas and bondage gear, it was their two fingers up at the establishment. They weren't buying into or in any way associating themselves with Nazism or the National Front or sadomasochism. These were teenagers who were trying to say 'Fuck you!' (quoted in Lydon 1994: 70–71).

And as Nora Lydon (John Lydon's German partner) puts it,

> The punks didn't even know what the swastika meant. In Germany we couldn't even talk about it. Punks used it innocently just to show off. They were told that the swastika was forbidden... Siouxsie [of Siouxsie and the Banshees] wasn't particularly educated about it at that time. To them it meant that it was taboo and antisocial... Do you think Sid [Vicious] knew what the swastika stood for? Sid's idea was that it was naughty, and that was as deep as he went for it. It didn't mean anti-Semitism to Siouxsie or Sid (quoted in Lydon 1994: 168).

Lydon agrees: 'I don't think anyone knew what all the Nazi clothing really meant, and if they did know, it was perceived as a reaction to a right-wing thing. It was a reaction against mum and dad talking about World War II. It was just a look' (1994: 217). Likewise, Tony James of London SS (and, later, of

Sigue Sigue Sputnik) comments, 'we hadn't thought about the Nazi implications. It just seemed like a very anarchic, stylish thing to do' (quoted in Boot and Salewicz 1997: 35). Whilst many punks may not have been quite as naïve as this, the general point is an important one. In the final analysis, Nazi symbolism was archetypal subcultural transgressive behaviour which connotatively referenced an anti-establishment stance and, thereby, sought to undermine the dominant culture – a good example of Hebdige's 'semiotic resistance' (1979: 26, 113ff.; see also Marcus 1989: 116–23; O'Hara 1999: 49–61). It was a sartorial challenge to widely held taboos. Hence, just as the wearing of the Union Jack by punks did not indicate royalist sympathies, and nor did the use of bondage paraphernalia primarily intend to titillate, or the use of tartan express any particular Caledonian alliance, so it is a rather too simplistic and denotative reading of punk symbolism to claim that the swastika indicated the wearer's racist sympathies. As Hebdige argues,

> the punk subculture grew up partly as an antithetical response to the re-emergence of racism in the mid-70s. *We must resort, then, to the most obvious of explanations* [as we still must] – that *the swastika was worn because it was guaranteed to shock...* This represented more than a simple inversion of inflection or the ordinary meanings attached to an object. The signifier (swastika) had been wilfully detached from the concept (Nazism) it conventionally signified, and although it had been re-positioned...within an alternative subcultural context, its primary value and appeal derived precisely from its lack of meaning: from its potential for deceit. It was exploited as an empty effect. We are forced to the conclusion that the central value 'held and reflected' in the swastika was the communicated absence of any such identifiable values. Ultimately the symbol was as 'dumb' as the rage it provoked (1979: 116–17; emphasis added).

Again, while Sabin is right to note that there will have been some punks influenced by the rise of the National Front (formed in 1967) and its ubiquitous propaganda, which particularly targeted youth cultures, the overall flow of punk was in an anti-racist direction (see Marko 2000; Solomos 2003: 177–82; Troyna 1996). Moreover, it should be noted that, not only was this not a decade of conspicuous political correctness, but punks were hardly models of reflective and careful discourse. Paul Marko is certainly right to feel 'a little worried that Sabin is retrospectively applying today's standards to the past to find evidence'. Sadly, as he says, '"Nigger"... "coon"... "paki"... were, like it or not, all part of the vocabulary in 1977... [These] words were being heard on [TV] in *Love Thy Neighbour* and *The Sweeney*' (2000; cf. La Rose 1999: 123–27). Similarly, Widgery draws attention to this context:

> Racism is as British as Biggles and baked beans. You grow up with it: the golliwogs in the jam, *The Black and White Minstrel Show* on the TV and CSE History at school. It's about Jubilee mugs and Rule Britannia and how we single-handedly saved the ungrateful world in the Second World War. Gravestones, bayonets, forced starvation and the destruction of the culture of India and Africa were regrettable of course, but without our Empire the world's inhabitants would still be rolling naked in the mud (1986: 75).

The point is that, while, no doubt, some youths uncritically reflected the ambient racism of the society in which they had grown up, punk was a positive influence that led many to regret any earlier racist attitudes they may have absorbed. It was a period of transition in which punk and reggae were, overall, positive, anti-racist influences. As Sabin himself concedes: 'To be fair, many punk stars distanced themselves from any mistakes they may have made in their early career, and some, admirably, went on to do valuable work for the anti-racist cause' (1999b: 211).

That there was a confluence of punk and reggae and that retail outlets such as Rough Trade and Honest Jon's distributed both genres positively contributed to a culture of anti-racism (see Bradley 2000: 449; de Konigh and Griffiths 2003: 181). 'In these ways', as Jones has argued, 'the impact of reggae created scope for new kinds of opposition and new ways of being "political" in white youth culture which reflected the continuity of cultural expression with political action in black musical traditions' (1988: 97–98). I myself experienced the positive effects of punk in this respect: whether at concerts in which those with racist ideas were shouted down or at which bands would explicitly castigate racists. For example, my partner, Marcia, recalls attending a concert in Leeds at which Joe Strummer invited the reggae musician and producer Mikey Dread to perform with The Clash. This led to jeers from a few in the crowd, followed by a short speech from Strummer who, in no uncertain terms, denounced racism and told them to be quiet or The Clash would leave as well. The rest of the concert was a well-received mix of 'punky reggae'. (For The Clash's comments on Mikey Dread, see Millar 1980: 26–27.)

So, yes, some punks (or some of those who attended punk gigs) didn't like reggae. But, to quote the subtitle of Sabin's book, *so what?* To restate the point, punk rock was not a homogenous movement, and the questioning of and shift away from racist attitudes – which had often been simply absorbed from the society in which punks had grown up – was *a process*. Anti-racism was not a settled punk ideology. However, punk did significantly contribute to the anti-racist shift and even began that process for many youths.[15] The point here is that a central driver in this process was the ideological impact dub and reggae had on punk and, to a lesser extent, hippie subcultures. To deny this simply flies in the face of the facts.

Consequently, this was the time when dub made significant inroads into British popular culture. The Clash wore clothes stencilled with phrases like 'Dub' and 'Heavy Manners' (Hebdige 1979: 29; Jones 1988: 96) and often played against a screen-printed backdrop of the Notting Hill riots. At many punk gigs, as I myself remember, dub was played at intervals 'as the only acceptable alternative to punk' (Jones 1988: 96); artists, we have seen, declared their enthusiasm for the genre, recorded cover versions of reggae tracks, and, more significantly, dub versions of their own material on the B-sides of 12-inch singles.

'Love Music, Hate Racism': Rock Against Racism

In 1970s Britain racism was breathed in with the air and, as the decade progressed, it was exhaled increasingly vociferously. In particular, as John Solomos comments, 'one of the most important features of the politics of racism was the emergence from the early 1970s of the National Front – and other minor neo-fascist groups – as a more or less credible political force. Indeed, there was serious concern during the late 1970s that the National Front might become an established entity on the formal political scene' (2003: 177; see also Husbands 1983; Gilroy 2002; Cohen and Gardner 1982; Widgery 1986: 8–52).[16] Founded in 1967, the National Front was a union of far-right-wing groups, including the British National Party, the Racial Preservation Society, and the League of Empire Loyalists. Adopting the ideologies of these organizations, it was virulently anti-Semitic, promoted theories of racial purity, and opposed Britain's postwar decolonization. Without going into the complex reasons for the growth of popular support for racist politics in the 1970s, central to which was immigration (see Husbands 1983; Samuel 1998; Cashmore 1987; Solomos and Back 1995), it is worth noting that both the principal parties, Labour and Conservative, lost voters to the National Front. 'Throughout the 1970s the National Front's membership and level of electoral support ebbed and flowed with the tide of political debate on and public controversy over racial questions. Its membership rose from 14,000 to 20,000 between 1972 and 1974, at the height of the arrival of the Ugandan Asians' (Solomos 2003: 179). In May 1973, at a by-election in West Bromwich, the National Front candidate won 4789 votes – 16.2 per cent of the vote. In the February 1974 general election, which resulted in a minority Labour government, 54 National Front candidates gained a total of 76,865 votes. Because of his small minority, Prime Minister Harold Wilson called another general election in October 1974. Although the result was an increase in Labour's representation to just above 50 per cent, far-right sympathies in the country increased, with 90 National Front candidates obtaining a total of 113,844 votes. Consequently, by 1975, fascism was high on the political agenda. Not only did the National Front receive widespread press coverage, but so did immigration. Indeed, when Asians arrived from Malawi in 1976, they received particularly hostile coverage from several national newspapers, notably *The Sun* and *The Mirror*. This, again, stimulated support for far-right political organizations. For example, in the 1976 council elections, eight members of the far-right National Party received, on average, 40 per cent of the vote in Blackburn, Lancashire and at a local government by-election in Deptford the National Front took 44 per cent. Indeed, I remember well that 1976 was, to quote Robin Denselow, 'an unpleasant, angry year' (1989: 141). Consequently, it was apparent to most young people, if they took the time to think about it – and roots reggae and dub functioned explicitly as a politicizing catalyst – that Britain, institutionally and socially, was 'Babylon'. As we have seen in earlier chapters and as the British reggae musician and dub producer Michael Campbell put it at the time, 'Babylon is a state of mind, not geography'. Moreover, he continues, 'it is a state of mind that is prevailing on the earth right now' (quoted in Widgery 1986: 49).

1976, however, was not only 'an unpleasant, angry year', but it was also the year in which the tide began to turn and the National Front began to face significant opposition. As Lydon put it, 'anger is an energy' ('Rise': Public Image Ltd., *Album*), which in 1976 led to the rapid rise of a vociferous, anti-racist political movement. Punk, roots reggae, the voice of anti-racism, and anti-establishment attitudes began to coalesce and challenge increasing numbers of young people. Local committees were formed and counter-protests were held against fascist marches. That said, one particular racist incident can be identified as pivotal for channelling anti-racist anger and galvanizing political activism. Although several well-known rock musicians, such as David Bowie in an interview for *Playboy*, had made explicitly fascist comments (Widgery 1986: 41, 60; Gilroy 2002: 156; Denselow 1989: 141; Harris 1993: 16),[17] it was Eric Clapton's ugly outburst during a concert in Birmingham in August 1976 that proved to be the most incendiary (see Denselow 1989: 138–41). From the stage he insisted that Britain was 'overcrowded', that he wanted to 'keep Britain white', and explicitly aligned himself with the views of Enoch Powell, the Conservative MP for Wolverhampton who had become infamous for his 1968 'rivers of blood' speech opposing mass immigration (see Solomos 1992: 18–19; Gilroy 2002: 156; Frith and Street 1992: 67–68; Kirby and Jury 2004; Denselow 1989: 138–40). Scandalized that one who drew so heavily and successfully on the blues, a music of specifically black origin, could make such a statement at a time when the National Front was gaining support and race hatred was spilling out onto British streets, the photographer Red Saunders composed a blunt letter of protest and, over the phone, got the verbal signatures of six friends, including Syd Shelton, David Widgery and Roger Huddle. It was quickly published in *New Musical Express*, *Melody Maker*, *Sounds*, and the *Socialist Worker*:

> When we read about Eric Clapton's Birmingham concert when he urged support for Enoch Powell, we nearly puked. Come on Eric... you've been taking too much of that *Daily Express* stuff and you know you can't handle it. Own up. Half your music is black. You're rock music's biggest colonist. You're a good musician, but where would you be without the blues and R&B? You've got to fight the racist poison, otherwise you degenerate into the sewer with the rats and all the money men who ripped off rock culture with their cheque books and plastic crap. *We want to organise a rank and file movement against the racist poison in music. We urge support for Rock Against Racism.* P.S. Who shot the Sheriff, Eric? It sure as hell wasn't you![18] (quoted in Widgery 1986: 40, emphasis added; see also Anti-Nazi League, 2006).

Prompting 140 enthusiastically positive replies within a week and promises of support from bands, it was this letter that led directly to the formation of Rock Against Racism in August 1976, Britain's first popular-music-based political organization. The aim was simply to challenge racism through a fusion of black and white musics and, in particular, through organizing events at which black and white artists – primarily from punk and reggae – would play together (Harris 1993). Indicating the path it intended to tread, the first event was held at London's Royal College of Art in December 1976 and was headlined by Dennis Bovell's reggae band Matumbi. 'It was a wonderfully bizarre night', recalls Widgery.

> Freaks from past history and costume-drama cases from the summer of love queued up quite amiably with maximum dreadlocks and members of The Clash and The Slits. The music was extremely loud, the dancing very rowdy, and the stalls sold political and anti-racist literature, food and banners. Something was in the air: not just dope, but a serious music-politics-black-white mix-up (1986: 58).

Concerning its politics, as Simon Frith and John Street have commented, 'if Eric Clapton's mean sentiments provided the grounds for Rock Against Racism, its real political and cultural ambition was to seize the opportunity of punk and articulate a new form of proletarian cultural rebellion' (1992: 68). It explicitly and cogently politicized the links between the economic recession in Britain, racism, punk, and reggae. However, whereas Frith and Street are correct to argue that Rock Against Racism can be understood as 'the child of punk', in that it 'drew on punk's style, its rhetoric, and its music' (1992: 68), it is also important to understand that much of the rhetoric came, directly or indirectly (via punk), from Rasta culture, with bands such as Steel Pulse and Misty in Roots being principal influences (see Letts 2007: 126–27). In other words, Rock Against Racism was the child of an informal but passionate affair between black and white subcultures – between punk and reggae. As Linton Kwesi Johnson commented at the time, 'We've had a tremendous impact on the society! People said, "If the blacks can do it, so can we!" It wouldn't surprise me if the move towards socially oriented lyricism in popular songs wasn't a direct influence of reggae' (quoted in Denselow 1989: 142). Hence, to some extent, punk's explicit alliance with reggae under the aegis of Rock Against Racism led to its political maturation and a demonstration that it, not progressive rock, was the vehicle for social and cultural change.

Musically, therefore, Rock Against Racism in the UK was narrowly focused on punk and reggae, the ideal being to demonstrate cultural integration. Consequently, white bands that were influenced by reggae and dub, such as The Clash and The Ruts – or, indeed, Basement 5, a black dub band formed by Letts and influenced by punk (see Letts 2007: 125–28) – can be seen as the incarnation of the Rock Against Racism ideal. Similarly, politically engaged black British reggae artists who worked within the punk milieu and played at Rock Against Racism events, particularly Matumbi, Aswad, Misty in Roots, Steel Pulse, and Linton Kwesi Johnson, were also explicit manifestations of its cultural politics.[19] Indeed, it's worth noting that, as Frith and Street point out, just because Rock Against Racism 'did not extend to other proletarian forms (heavy metal, for example) nor into other black pop forms such as funk or disco' does not indicate 'a racist position', but rather reflects 'the punk contempt for "commercial" pop, for mainstream teenage dance music' (1992: 69). However, the point as far as we are concerned is that, here was a popular anti-racist organization explicitly encouraging cultural and political continuities between reggae and punk and, as such, between disaffected white and black subcultures. In this sense it was powerfully irenic.

Ideologically, Rock Against Racism was explicitly socialist, combining, in its magazine *Temporary Hoarding*, Jamie Reid-style cut-and-paste graphics (see Garnett 1999: 23–27) with what it referred to as 'our dubbed version of Marxism' (Widgery 1986: 61).[20] (It is of some significance, of course, that the term 'dub' quickly found its way into anti-racist argot, in that it had a particular currency directly related to the musical genre.) Working through the Anti-Nazi League (founded in November 1977), Rock Against Racism was helped to a great extent by the Socialist Workers Party, which had been keen to align itself with current trends and subcultural concerns (Hebdige 1988: 213–14).

In particular, the Socialist Workers Party loaned its premises in Shoreditch to Rock Against Racism and it was given a page in the Marxist newspaper *Socialist Worker*.[21] Hence, permeating the thought and action of Rock Against Racism was the Socialist Workers Party's Trotskyite politics, which encouraged blacks and whites to unite and fight along lines of class. Consequently, it was not simply about music, it was also very clearly a conduit for 'dubbed Marxism'. As Widgery recalls, 'the music came first and was more exciting. It provided the creative energy and the focus in what became a battle for the soul of young working class England. But the direct confrontations and the hard-headed political organization which underpinned them were decisive' (1986: 43). That said, differing from traditional leftism, it insisted on the autonomous value of youth cultures and on the radical potential of music and its subcultures. As the music paper *Sounds* put it: 'rock was and still can be a real progressive culture, not a packaged mail-order stick on nightmare of mediocre garbage. Keep the faith, black and white unite and fight' (quoted in Gilroy 2002: 156).

Many of those who, like myself, attended Rock Against Racism events, recall that they were enormously enjoyable and inspiring. Indeed, few music fans in the late 1970s could have failed to be aware of Rock Against Racism, in that, not only were its events widely reported and advertised in the music press, but the various badges produced declaring one's commitment to anti-racism were ubiquitous and, importantly, invested with significant subcultural capital. It is perhaps not surprising, therefore, that, as a confluence of punk, roots reggae, and dub, Rock Against Racism had considerable success in the struggle against racism. As Brinsley Forde of Aswad recalls, 'Racism is caused by people not being educated, being ignorant of different cultures. Before Rock Against Racism, a lot of white people would be terrified to go to a reggae show. And it was a platform for saying things that wouldn't have been said. It was the start of more bands being politically aware' (quoted in Denselow 1989: 151). That said, as noted above, this political awareness was constrained to viewing society's injustices from the perspective of *Socialist Worker*, in that the implication was that to be committed to anti-racism meant being committed to Marxist politics. Rock Against Racism worked, as Frith and Street comment, 'to confine its musicians, declaring that *this* [i.e. Marxism] is what punk or soul or reggae mean; they can stand for nothing else' (1992: 79).

Whether punks accepted Rock Against Racism's leftist propaganda – and many did – positive race relations were fostered during this period. More particularly, if many punks did not purchase reggae and dub records, for most of them, Rasta argot and symbolism represented an accepted and appreciated form of rebel culture. Gilroy is helpful here:

> Punk provided the circuitry which enabled these connections to be made...the hitherto coded and unacknowledged relationships between black and white styles an open and inescapable fact. Drawing on the language and style of roots culture in general and Rastafari in particular, punks produced not only their own critical and satirical commentary on the meaning and limits of white ethnicity but a conceptual framework for seeing and then analysing the social relations of what *Temporary Hoarding* called 'Labour Party Capitalist Britain'. The dread notion of 'Babylon System' allowed disparate and apparently contradictory expressions of the national crisis to be seen as a complex, interrelated whole, a coherent structure of which racism was a primary characteristic, exemplifying and symbolizing the unacceptable nature of the entire authoritarian capitalist edifice (2002: 159).

The point is that the politically motivated confluence of punk, reggae and Rasta led to a shift in the way black and white youths related to one another. Again, Gilroy notes that

> from now on, 'race' could no longer be dealt with as a matter for private negotiation in the shadows of the ghetto blues dance or the inner-city shebeen where a token white presence might be acceptable. The rise of an articulate British racism, often aimed squarely at the distinct experiences and preoccupations of the young, destroyed the possibility of essentially covert appropriations of black-style music and anger which had been the characteristic feature of the mod and skinhead eras (2002: 160).

At The Roxy, at Rock Against Racism events, at numerous individual gigs, racism was explicitly confronted. Signifiers such as 'British', 'empire', 'race' and 'white' were openly contested. And, of course, recasting reggae into a punk idiom and thereby appropriating its rebel discourse was a powerful way of doing this. The cover of Junior Murvin's 'Police and Thieves' by The Clash (on *The Clash*, 1977) is a good example, as is, at a more passive level, Culture's 'Two Seven's Clash' (on *Two Sevens Clash*, 1977), which became a staple punk anthem for a short time. As Gilroy comments regarding Culture's classic, this 'dread commentary on the state of Jamaica after Michael Manley's victory in 1976... masquerading as a mystical invocation of the apocalypse, was seized by punks and given a central place in their cultural cosmology' (2002: 162). Similarly, Lenny Kaye argues that *Two Sevens Clash* was one of the most influential records to arrive at 'an apex of collaboration of musical forms and subcultures and shared audience... [notably] roots reggae and punk rock' (2007: 1). As we will see in the next section, similarly irenic and political was the production of dub 'versions' of punk tracks, which powerfully signified a cultural rapprochement.

There is little doubt, therefore, that punk in general and Rock Against Racism in particular acted as powerful incubators for both the white appreciation of reggae and the appropriation of the signs and meanings produced within black culture generally and Rasta culture in particular. Of course, we have seen that, because there was already a growing appreciation of reggae and dub culture, it is likely that, as Linton Kwesi Johnson comments, 'the mix of punk and reggae would have happened anyway...because the kids grew up together. Black kids would have found an affinity with punk [and *vice versa*] because it's anti-establishment' (quoted in Denselow 1989: 152). That said, Rock Against Racism significantly accelerated and popularized that affinity. As Drummie Zeb of Aswad notes, 'Rock Against Racism was the starting point... The sound and the rhythm of reggae and dub is taken for granted now' (quoted in Denselow 1989: 152).

Punk...in Dub

As with the punk covers of classic reggae tracks, punk and post-punk music which used dub techniques, as well as, of course, the production of dub 'versions' of punk songs, constituted a set of similarly powerful, polysemic signifiers. That is to say, they provided that which was appealing because it was exotic and, therefore, as with the appropriation of the Eastern by the beat and hippie cultures, it was culturally exogenous and non-mainstream. Dub techniques connoted both anti-racist politics and, musicologically, a sense of reflective gravitas. Hence, very quickly, 'dub effectively became the code for "progressive" and "cool", and cutting a dub to your punk single was the hip thing to do' (Goldman 2003: 4). It also, of course, appealed to the do-it-yourself mentality of punk, the roots of which can, we have seen, be traced back to London's pub rock scene in the early 1970s, which had early links with reggae culture (see Boot and Salewicz 1997: 27–31; Laing 1985: 7–11).

As is well documented, punk was in search of a different aesthetic to mainstream pop and progressive rock. While this sonic revolution was rooted in anger, militancy and nihilism, as it evolved and matured, there was a desire for a new aesthetic. Indeed, this process of maturation and gradual sophistication was, in part, the result of a growing appreciation of reggae as 'the ideal of a music that seemed to embody a culture and a politics' (Laing 1985: 39). Hence, at the interface of these two music-oriented cultures, a new aesthetic began to coalesce; an aesthetic which was not a return to pop and progressive rock; an aesthetic which was informed by a rebel discourse; an aesthetic that was encouraging a more reflective appreciation of music, culture and politics; an experimental, avant-garde aesthetic; indeed, an aesthetic that was for increasing numbers of fans conducive to contemplative, even spiritual states of mind, as the political shifted towards the more religio-political stance of Rastafarianism (e.g. see Wobble 2001; cf. Penman 1998: 334–35). While we have seen that the influence of reggae was evident from an early period, these new trajectories were more clearly the result of a specific appreciation of dub.

An excellent example of this confluence of dub and punk was the first female punk band to record an album,[22] The Slits – fronted by singer Ari Up (Ariana Forster), the 14-year-old daughter of Nora Forster (heiress to the newspaper *Der Spiegel*), Lydon's partner and, therefore, eventually, his step-daughter (see Street Howe 2009: 12–14). Like Lydon, she was a reggae enthu-siast, continuing her post-Slits career in the British dub collective the New Age Steppers. Indeed, as a statement of her subcultural allegiance, Ari Up was one of the first white people to wear dreadlocks. 'In fact', she says, 'I was the first person to have a tree – I had my locks up in a tree-type shape' (quoted in Rey-nolds 2005: 81; see also Steward and Garratt 1984: 31) – a style made famous by David Hinds of Steel Pulse in the early 1980s. (She eventually relocated to Jamaica and, in 2005, following a long period of silence, released her first solo work, the dub- and ragga-inspired *Dread More Dan Dead*.)

Having said that, all The Slits were, as Reynolds puts it, 'reggae fiends' (2005: 81; see Street Howe 2009). Tessa Pollitt (bass) had been in an earlier all-female, radical feminist punk group called The Castrators (see Marko 2006). Viv Albertine (guitar) had played in the short-lived band Flowers of Romance with Sid Vicious and Keith Levene (Savage 2005: 248). Finally, Palmolive/Pal-oma Romero (drums), who eventually left to join The Raincoats, was replaced by Budgie (Pete Clarke), who would go on to join Siouxsie and the Banshees and then, with Siouxsie, to form The Creatures. Following Budgie's departure, The Pop Group's Bruce Smith joined the band and even played for both bands during a joint European tour. That they were all 'reggae fiends' is significant, in that dub was the magic dust that conjured music out of chaos. As Boot and Salewicz comment, 'The Slits were extraordinary. Creating a template for the coming deluge of female groups, their world was the infinite space suggested by dub' (1997: 81).[23] Initially, The Slits 'hadn't the slightest idea of how to do anything but climb onto stage and shout' (Marcus 1989: 37) – not that there's too much wrong with that. That they became one of the more musically inter-esting punk bands to emerge in the late-1970s has a lot to do with the fact that their debut landmark album, *Cut* (1978), was produced by the Matumbi guitarist and dub producer Dennis Bovell (who had just produced The Pop Group's seminal dub-inspired single, 'She is Beyond Good and Evil'). As Mark Paytress comments, 'the most notable influence on the album was dub reg-gae'. He continues, 'the band's motto during the making of the album was "if in doubt leave it out", a tip of the hat to the Jamaican dub pioneers' (2000). It is also extraordinarily bass-heavy. While this became important in much dub-influenced post-punk, such as Public Image Limited (PiL) and later Killing Joke, it was not usual of the punk of the period. As Simon Reynolds comments with reference to *Never Mind the Bollocks*, 'compared to the mirage-like unreality of reggae production, all glimmering reverb haze, disorienting FX and flickering ectoplasmic wisps, most punk records sounded retarded: stuck in the mid-sixties; before 24-track psychedelia; before *stereo*. The sharper bands coming out of punk knew they had some catching up to do' (2005: 5–6). Guided by Bovell, The Slits were one of those bands. They caught up quickly. Their bass-heavy, dub-influenced style continued on their second and final offering, the more reflective and, indeed, underrated *The Return of the Giant Slits* (1981) – also produced by Bovell. As those who are familiar with their music will understand, it is not easy to convey verbally their aural impact and the sonic environment they created. However, the following eloquent description of their work by Greil Marcus is worth quoting, in that it comes close to evoking, not only the force of their musical presence, but also something of its dubbed quality (without actually mentioning dub):

> Shouting and shrieking, out of guitar flailings the group finds a beat, makes a rhythm, begins to shape it; the rhythm gets away and they chase it down, overtake it, and keep going. Squeaks, squeals, snarls, and whines – unmediated female noises never before heard as pop music – course through the air as The Slits march hand in hand through a storm they themselves have created (1989: 39).

It's perhaps not surprising, therefore, that Don Letts believed them to be 'ahead of their time'.[24] He continues, 'they took reggae's emphasis on the bassline over melody and guitars. They used the mixing desk as an instrument. And they understood the rebel attitude of the music' (quoted in Paytress 2000). This is most obviously evident on their 'Typical Girls (Brink Style Dub)' (now available on the Select Cuts compilation *Wild Dub*). In many ways, one of Bovell's more delicate productions, it begins with and is held together by a heavy bass-line and the slow, persistent beat of a bass drum. Onto this sparse sonic canvas, snatches of hi-hat and snare drum are splashed and then left to evaporate, to echo into the distance. Dashes of guitar and keyboards add colour to the composition, accompanied by abstract fragments of vocal from the lips of a very untypical female repeating the words 'typical girls'. There are few more successful and striking examples of the confluence of dub and punk.

Having said that, while its difficult to overestimate the importance of The Slits in this respect, we have already suggested that they were not alone. Because the centre of musical gravity was increasingly defined by dub at the close of the 1970s, numerous bands were stepping into the echo chamber. Indeed, while we have seen in this chapter that many punks appreciated reggae as a form of protest music, a chanting down of Babylon, increasingly many were simply bewitched by dub's manipulation of sound. As Reynolds comments, several of the more experimental bands 'responded to reggae as a purely sonic revolution: an Africanized psychedelia, shape-shifting and perception-altering. During the half decade from 1977 to 1981, reggae's specialized production-yet-elemental rhythms provided *the* template for sonically radical post-punk' (2005: 6). While this is true, the notion that such bands responded to dub as a *purely* sonic revolution, without any interest in the discourses it carried, needs to be questioned. Some may have done, but others did not. Key experimentalists, such as Mark Stewart and The Pop Group, were conspicuously political. Again, there are few more striking examples of a politicized confluence of dub and punk than the outstanding 'Jah War' and 'Give Youth a Chance' by The Ruts (available on *The Crack*, 1979). To take 'Jah War', possibly the most well-known track by The Ruts after 'Babylon's Burning', it is *both* creatively washed in echo and reverb *and* a visceral critique of the actions of SPG's[25] violence in Southall, West London, in 1979, in which two black men, Blair Peach and Clarence Baker, were attacked, the former being killed and the latter severely injured. Hence, while clearly fascinated by the sonic possibilities of dub, The Ruts were also politically engaged. Indeed, as members of Southall's 'People Unite' collective, each of the band members – Malcolm Owen (vocals), Paul 'Foxy' Fox (guitar), John 'Segs' Jennings (bass) and Dave Ruffy (drums) – was actively involved in anti-racist and 'anti-Nazi' protests of the period.

Formed by Owen and Fox, who had become disillusioned with hippie idealism, having, for a time, lived in a commune on Anglesey during the early 1970s, they had, according to Fox, spent their days 'playing patience, drinking tea and growing weed' (quoted in Heylin 2007: 401). Indeed, it was here that Fox and Owen, with Paul Mattocks (all school friends from Hayes, Middlesex), first formed a band, a progressive rock group called Aslan. When the commune disbanded in 1975, first Owen, then Fox returned to London. Fox had been playing in a dance/funk band called Hit and Run with Ruffy, a well-connected record dealer (one of the first London dealers to purchase the Ramones' debut album). Finally, in 1977, having heard 'Anarchy in the UK' and inspired by the politics and music of punk and reggae, being very conscious of their roots in multi-cultural Southall, Owen and Fox teamed up with Ruffy and Jennings (Hit and Run's roadie) to form The Ruts.

It is significant that, soon after they'd formed, they began touring with another important band from Southall with a strong commitment to dub and anti-racism, Misty in Roots. Indeed, so close were they that Misty offered to finance the first Ruts' single, 'In A Rut', a powerful punk song with a creative use of echo and reverb interspersed throughout.

While the band was clearly one of the more interesting of the period, they didn't last long. In 1980, heroin claimed the life of Owen (and would, eventually, ruin the life of Fox). After much agonizing, the band added the letter 'DC'[26] to its name and continued. While this proved to be a not particularly successful venture, it was one that took them very firmly back to dub reggae. As Robbi Millar put it in his article on their comeback gig at London's Marquee, 'Ruts DC are taking their sympathetic reggae trademark to far more adventurous lengths... [They] treat dub/echo/feedback with confidence and aplomb, pulling out all the stops to complement Dave Ruffy's ceaselessly spot-on drumming' (1981: 50). Finally, in 1982, they released *Rhythm Collision* (which was a tribute to Owen), a thoughtful collaboration with the dub producer Neil Fraser/the Mad Professor, originally released on their own 'Bohemian' label and subsequently on New York's ROIR label. (Interestingly, this was one of Fraser's first albums, released shortly after his first *Dub Me Crazy* album.) Moreover, as some indication of their continued underground influence in dub culture, their work has been enthusiastically revisited by dub producers and enthusiasts. For example, not only was *Rhythm Collision* remixed in 1999 by the British dub reggae ensemble, Zion Train (*Rhythm Collision Remix*), but their punk track, 'Babylon's Burning', has been 'reconstructed' (arguably, deconstructed) by Jennings and Ruffy with the assistance of numerous artists from Don Letts to Dreadzone to Kid Loco (*Babylon's Burning Reconstructed: Dub Drenched Soundscapes*). Sadly, after involvement with several bands and a Ruts reunion gig, Paul Fox died of cancer on 21 October 2007. A talented guitarist, openly admired by numerous fellow musicians from the ska artist Lauren Aitken (with whom he recorded and performed), to Keith Richards and Ronnie Wood (who both guested on his recorded work), and Pete Townshend and Jimmy Page. Tellingly, the final album he played on was *Lockdown* by the Dubcats, a dub album produced in Jamaica by Bunny 'Striker' Lee.[27]

As well as The Slits and The Ruts, one of the most notable early examples of bands beguiled by dub was PiL, formed by John Lydon/Johnny Rotten on his return from his trip to Jamaica with Richard Branson. Indeed, if *Never Mind the Bollocks* was sonically compact and airless in comparison with reggae, it would be a mistake to think that Lydon was unaware of this; there were few people more conscious that punk had a lot to learn from Jamaican dub production techniques. Moreover, just as ethereal dub mysticism and political activism are two sides of the same coin in Jamaica, so they were for Lydon, who had been used to pressures of Babylon as the son of Irish Catholic immigrants (see Lydon

1994). As Reynolds puts it, 'Rotten's identification with the black British experience of "sufferation" and "downpression" and his passion for Jamaican riddim and bass-pressure suffused his post-Pistols music, desolating PiL's sound with eerie space and heavy dread' (2005: 6). Hence, almost as soon as he'd disembarked the plane from Jamaica, he began assembling PiL. He contacted the guitarist Keith Levene, a founding member of The Clash, who he'd met when the band had supported The Sex Pistols. He also persuaded his school friend John Wardle to play bass. Levene was a good choice, being a particularly accomplished and avant-garde guitarist, who was perfect for the experimental sound Lydon envisaged. Wardle, on the other hand, had a minimal and very recent acquaintance with the bass guitar. However, he was a fellow dub enthusiast and was keen to experiment. Indeed, as some indication of his commitment to dub and reggae culture (and his sense of humour), he had modified his name to Jah Wobble. He began learning bass quickly, which was particularly important, as Lydon's leading idea was to make music in which, like dub, bass was dominant. Indeed, he soon proved to have an aptitude for the instrument and, even after he'd left PiL, Lydon considered him 'a very, very good bass player' (Martin 1981: 30). However, the key point is that, like The Slits to some extent, although they were three very different characters, their common love of dub fused them into a viable outfit. 'The whole reason PiL worked at all', remembers Levene, 'was that we were total dub fanatics' (quoted in Reynolds 2005: 7). Jah Wobble, who has, of course, since become one of the genre's most prolific and important experimentalists, not only devoted himself to learning bass, but even went so far as to dampen the sound by using old strings. In so doing, he gradually developed a throbbing, heartbeat-like bass pulse that became central to the PiL sound. Skating over this heavy cardiac bass, Levene's guitar provided a technically brilliant, experimental eccentricity that complemented Lyden's distinctive, anarchic vocals perfectly (listen to 'Death Disco', available on *The Greatest Hits, So Far* and renamed 'Swan Lake' on *Metal Box*; 'The Flowers of Romance', on *The Flowers of Romance*; and particularly *Metal Box*). The sound was powerful, challenging and a creative interpretation of dub. Some lines from Paul Morley's review of *Race Today*'s 'Creation for Liberation' concert in Manchester 1979, which PiL headlined, are worth quoting:

> They take orthodox rock music and literally split it apart. Their noise boisterously balances between bare coherence and total chaos. Keith Levine's [sic] guitar spews out an erratic, saturating homage to white noise; Jah Wobble, disconcertingly sitting right through the entire performance, fingers a deep, droll bass... Lyden deviously pours his monstrously flexible vocals on to the very edge of the sound. His wily, consistently significant presence is remarkable (1979: 54).

When recording *The Flowers of Romance*, there was, as with Jamaican dub engineers, a clear attempt to use the studio as an instrument. Even if this was not obviously the case on earlier albums, the emphasis was still very firmly on drum and bass. Richard Dudanski, who was for a time the band's drummer, recalls that 'basically, me and Wobble would just start playing, and maybe Keith'd say something like "double-time." But it was a bass-drum thing which Keith would stick guitar on, and John would be there and then write some words and whack 'em on' (quoted in Heylin 2007: 466–67). Hence, as well as the very clear emphasis on drum and bass juxtaposed with high, flying-cymbal-like screeches (produced by Levene's guitar), Lydon essentially fulfils the role of the deejay, in that much of his lyrical output was produced following the recording of the backing track. His songs were essentially social commentary: 'All the songs I do are about people around me, just things that I know about' (quoted in Martin 1981: 32). In other words, although not toasting *per se*, Lydon's approach had the immediacy of his Jamaican heroes such as Big Youth.

As noted above, it was Jah Wobble, however, whose output would most conspicuously demonstrate an indebtedness to dub. Indeed, his commitment to his own dub side projects began to cause tensions in PiL, particularly as he, in true Jamaican style, began to recycle PiL material. Beginning in 1978, he recorded two broadly satirical dub 12"s, 'Dreadlock Don't Deal in Wedlock' (available on re-released 1990 CD, *The Legend Lives On*), followed by the EP, *Steel Leg v The Electric Dread* (1978), recorded with Levene and Don Letts ('Haile Unlikely' from the 12" is now available on the worthwhile compilation, *Death Disco: Songs From Under the Dance Floor, 1978–1984*).

PiL were, if unpredictable and uneven, unarguably a seminal band. On the one hand, they were lauded by journalists such as Paul Morley, who judged their music to be 'probably the ultimate pure rock 'n' roll sound' (1979: 53) and Gavin Martin, who declared them to be 'the most innovative and exciting noise makers in Britain' (1981: 30). On the other hand, their sound bled into and shaped the wider musical culture, shaping the sonic direction of other bands. For example, one doesn't have to listen to early Killing Joke for many minutes to identify the principal source of inspiration. Their outstanding, heavily dubbed, 1979 single 'Turn to Red' (available on *The Malicious Singles* and *Laugh? I Nearly Bought One!*) shows a clear continuity with PiL: pulsing bass; prominent, almost tribal drumming; visceral Levene-influenced guitar. However, far more than PiL allowed, 'Turn to Red' is drenched in echo and reverb and the sheer power of the pulsing bass and driving drumming far more prominent and arresting.

Killing Joke emerged out of the Matt Stagger Band, involvement in which brought Paul Ferguson (drums) and Jaz Coleman (vocals, keyboards) together.

In late-1978, they left to form Killing Joke, recruiting bassist Martin Glover (formerly of the punk group The Rage) and guitarist Kevin 'Geordie' Walker. Their dub-influenced debut EP, *Almost Red* (financed by money borrowed from Coleman's girlfriend), impressed John Peel, who promptly offered the group a session on his BBC radio show (a session which became one of the most popular shows he broadcast in the late-1970s). By the end of 1979, Killing Joke had signed with Island Records, who allowed them to set up their own label, Malicious Damage. However, following the release of their debut single, 'Wardance', on Malicious Damage in February 1980, they left Island for EG and released their eponymous debut album. Again, central to this consistently good album is, not only a sense of it being an evolution of the PiL sound, even down to Coleman's tortured and challenging vocals, but to it being, very clearly, the offspring of dub and punk, perhaps even dub and heavy metal.

Finally, as an interesting aside, it's worth noting that Martin Glover, like Jah Wobble, has become one of the principal experimentalists to develop the dub sound. Indeed, also like Wobble, he took a name that reflected his interest in dub. Originally calling himself 'Pig Youth' after 'Big Youth', it was eventually shortened to simply 'Youth'. As well as forming WAU/Mr. Modo Records, which released a range of dub styles, from industrial techno dub to more traditional sound-system dub by, for example, Jah Warrior and, most famously, the late Bim Sherman, Youth has since become a sought-after producer and musician who has played with, amongst others, The Orb, The Verve, Kate Bush, U2, Embrace, Dido, Crowded House, and Primal Scream, as well as forming the experimental ensemble The Fireman with Paul McCartney.

Of course, it's important to understand that while there was significant experimentation with echo and reverb in the UK, across the Atlantic similar developments were happening within the punk scene. As noted above, most significantly, since 1977, The Terrorists had been playing reggae, ska, dub and punk along the East Coast, particularly in New York City at clubs such as CBGB's, Max's Kansas City, Irving Plaza, and the Mudd Club. Eventually working with Roland Alphonso and Lee Perry, they developed a distinctive reggae- and dub-influenced sound which earned them a cult following. Indeed, in December 1977, prior to any collaborations with Perry and just two months after forming, they recorded some of the best examples of dub-punk creativity available, 'Anittoo' and 'Drainidge' (now available on *Forces 1977–1982*). Furthermore, as some evidence of the genre's influence on bands that played at clubs such as CBGB's, it is interesting that, while they were certainly one of the most prominent, The Terrorists were not the only band to experiment with dub. For example, the dark, slightly menacing music on the eponymous 1977 debut album of the underground New York band Suicide – who went on provide the soundtrack to Rainer Werner Fassbinder's 1978 film *In einem Jahr mit 13 Monden* – clearly betrays the influence of dub.

Whether it was played in CBGB's or The Roxy, dub reanimated punk, which, by the late-1970s, was losing its power to disrupt and challenge. Just as the influential punk magazine *Sniffin' Glue* introduced its readers to a couple of chord diagrams and then declared 'now go and form a band' (see Gilroy 2002: 158; Laing 1985: 22), so dub was now encouraging these bands to take their 'one-chord wonders' (to quote an Adverts' song title), remix them, 'forward the bass', add screams, shouts, and street noises, and introduce a sense of depth and space by means of echo and reverb. In so doing, new music was born, music which was, by its very nature, infused with the politics of anti-racism. That is to say, as dubbed punk, as white urban music conspicuously sculpted by production techniques developed in Jamaica, it contributed to anti-racist rhetoric.

As well as the conspicuous political rhetoric, there was a sense in which, for some punk musicians and listeners, dub had a certain spiritual significance, in that, referencing Rastafarianism, a sense of transcendence was introduced. Even if this was not explicit within most punk 'versions', and even rejected outright by some punks, it was there, and what Marley referred to as the 'natural mystic' has since been nurtured by dub-oriented musicians such as Youth and Jah Wobble. Commenting on this broadly spiritual trajectory, the *Sounds* features editor and reggae writer, Vivien Goldman (who, of course, has herself worked with several dub artists) puts it well: 'Jamaican creativity helped a bunch of Brits and their mates tune into their higher selves' (2003: 12).

Dread Beat an' Blood: Dub Poetry

Whether one considers the beat poets or influential texts – particularly *The Mersey Sound* (1967) by the Liverpool poets Roger McGough, Brian Patten and Adrian Henri – performance poetry, often linked with popular music, periodically emerges as an important medium within a subculture. This was no less true of punk. Not only are certain 'punk' artists poets, such as Patti Smith[28] – who herself had been introduced to reggae and dub by Letts (Letts 2007: 73) – and perhaps even Mark E. Smith of The Fall,[29] but performers, John Cooper Clarke particularly, developed the genre for the punk generation.[30] However, while Clarke became important as 'the punk poet',[31] far more politically significant[32] during this period was the work of 'the dub poet', Linton Kwesi Johnson.

Not only can there be few people with an interest in reggae in the 1970s and 1980s who have not heard of Johnson, but there can be very few with a grasp of music and protest politics *per se*, not to mention contemporary British poetry, who will not have heard of him. He dominated the political music scene in the late-1970s and early-1980s and, more recently, became the first *living* poet to have an anthology of his work published in the prestigious Penguin Classics series (2002).[33] In the late-1970s he seemed to emerge out of the blue 'as a powerful and prophetic voice' (MacKinnon 1979: 7) with a considerable breadth of appeal. For example, in 1975 fellow poet Fred D'Aguiar heard him perform at Goldsmith's College, London University:

> The audience included south-east London locals like myself, college students, academics and people who actually remember the sixties, and thus it can properly be described as varied. What struck me then and now, as I look back across a gap of more than a quarter of a century, was Linton's wide appeal. His appeared to be a poetry of inclusion, popular and broad based in the best sense of these terms, speaking a truth that cut across race and cultural differences in a form that people from a variety of backgrounds found irresistible (2002: ix).

Before turning to Johnson's work, however, something needs to be said about the genre *per se*. Originating in the reggae culture of post-independence Jamaica in the late-1960s, dub poetry is, as Christian Habekost describes,

> 'word, sound and power.' This self-proclaimed credo of the dub poets points to the double dimension of the art form: dub poetry epitomizes the antagonism between writing and orality, between *word* as text and *word* as *sound*. Dub poetry is neither a literary genre nor exclusively a musical style. Yet it is almost everything in between. Dub poetry may be presented in the form of live performances, on record or cassette, or in the medium of the printed text. Dub poets may recite their words *a cappella*, over the playback-sounds of cassette music, to the accompaniment of a percussionist, or against the amplified sounds of a fully-fledged band... On all occasions the *sound* of the spoken *word* gives rise to a musical 'riddim', the central formative aspect of the genre (1993: 1; emphasis original).

Moreover, dub poetry is arguably an irenic genre. Not only does it bring the spheres of music, literature and oral performance into a creative engagement, but it constitutes a manifestation of creolization, in that it is a confluence of African and European cultural streams. While it's important to note that the notion of Caribbean culture as an equal mix of African and European elements is passé nowadays – it being far too simplistic (see Donnell and Welsh 1996b) – when thinking of the reception of dub poetry in the UK, it is, to some extent, useful. That is to say, as indicated above, British dub poetry speaks into a countercultural context familiar with performance poetry, but does so in a distinctively Caribbean way. Furthermore, there is a sense in which it 'mirrors the whole spectrum of this continuum underlying Jamaican culture: Creole and standard language, African-derived riddim patterns, and European styled melody lines, black consciousness and socialist ideology, traditional poetic forms and call-and-response – while, in the background, reggae music encapsulates the whole continuum yet again in itself' (Habekost 1993: 2; see also Hudson 1999; Morris 1983).

As to its relationship with reggae and dub, it is what might be described as symbiotic, in that it is a form of performance poetry for which reggae rhythms are a central, defining feature. Hence, while Manuel and Marshall are not entirely incorrect to separate 'dub' *per se* from 'dub plates' and 'dub poetry' (2006: 450) – in that they refer to distinct cultural products – just as we have seen is the case with 'dub plates', so with 'dub poetry', the two are related. As is hinted at in the references to Jamaican deejays, such as Big Youth and I Roy, in Johnson's work (e.g. 'Street 66', on *Bass Culture*), dub poetry has its roots in Jamaican deejay culture.[34] Indeed, the term itself was first coined by Johnson to describe 'toasting'. While studying the sociology of reggae and also providing some textual analysis of deejay lyrics during his time at Goldsmith's College, he felt he needed a term that highlighted the *oral poetry* at the heart of Jamaican deejay culture: 'The "dub-lyricist" is the DJ turned poet. He intones his lyrics rather than sings them. Dub-lyricism is a new form of (oral) music-poetry, wherein the lyricist overdubs rhythmic phrases on to the rhythm background of a popular song. Dub-lyricists include poets like Big Youth, I Roy, U Roy, Dillinger, Shorty the President, Prince Jazzbo and others' (1976a: 398; cf. Johnson 1999: 60). Hence, at its best, dub poetry is, as Stewart Brown, Mervyn Morris and Gordon Rohlehr have argued, 'the intelligent appropriation of the manipulatory techniques of the DJ for purposes of personal and communal signification' (1989b: 18; see also Morris 1983: 189).[35] Moreover, because dub poets speak from *within* the oppressed black community and *reflect upon* that community's experiences, 'everything is political' (Stokely Carmichael[36] – quoted twice in the liner notes to Johnson's *Independent Intavenshan*). Hence, just as we have seen that toasting often provided a commentary on current events, such as Big Youth's 'Green Bay Killing' – which was released a few days after the notorious massacre of five men by Jamaica's Military Intelligence Unit – so dub poetry provides critical socio-political commentary on current events. For example, not only does Johnson explore African-Caribbean experience in Britain – some of his most powerful work being written during the Conservative government of Margaret Thatcher – but he comments on particular events, such as the killing of the teacher and anti-racist activist Blair Peach ('Reggae Fi

Peach', on *Bass Culture*). This stridently political nature of his poetry is made explicit on his first album (for which he used the moniker 'Poet and the Roots'), *Dread Beat an' Blood* (1978), the first two tracks of which, grounded in British blues party culture, speak of racist and internecine violence ('Dread Beat an' Blood' and 'Five Nights of Bleeding' are reprinted in Johnson 2002: 5–8; 1991: 9–12). Indeed, the cover chosen for the CD reissue (1989) – a black and white photograph of Johnson standing in front of two policemen on the steps of a police station addressing a crowd through a megaphone – baldly declares, not only dub poetry's socio-political intentions, but its prophetic force. In Rasta-farian terms, because it is performed in 'Babylon' from within the community of the righteous oppressed, it is, by nature, subversive.

Outside Jamaica – and particularly within white societies used to standard English – this is further emphasized by the Jamaican creole wording, which, like the use of Arabic within Islam, gives it an almost sacralized gravitas. Just by listening to the language one is encouraged to think from a different per-spective. Added to this the heavy bassline, the space between the voice and the riddim, and the muted horns, percussion, or synthesizers in the middle range, allow the prophetic voice to be heard particularly clearly and force-fully – Johnson's 'Bass Culture' and 'Street 66' being distinctive and particu-larly striking examples of this. Indeed, because dub poetry is rooted in reggae and still has a strong continuity with sound-system culture, in my experience, when one listens to a poetry reading by a dub poet such as Johnson (less so with Benjamin Zephaniah) a sense of riddim is evoked – so much so that one can almost hear the bass and the beat accompanying the reading (see Hitch-cock 1997: 163–64). As the poet Oku Onuora has argued, the dub poem is 'not merely putting a piece of poem pon a rhythm; it is a poem that has a *built-in* reggae rhythm – hence when the poem is read without any reggae rhythm (so to speak) backing, one can distinctly hear the reggae rhythm coming out of the poem' (quoted in Morris 1983: 189). In other words, *dub poetry is poetry into which musical rhythms have been dubbed.*

Moreover, although dub poetry is meant to be *heard*, and thus most effective when performed, when in print, the careful use of nonstandard, approximately phonetic transcription ('eye creole')[37] helps both to evoke a sense of rhythm (particularly if the reader has already *heard* it) and, indeed, also to engage the reader politically – in that one is conceptually trans-ported into a different frame of mind, for which 'dread beat an' blood' are core experiences.[38] As D'Aguiar puts it, 'LKJ's English language, seasoned by Jamaican creole, extends the range of the poet's palate with a certain direct-ness, viscosity and muscularity of creole verb forms and compound words' (2002: xi).

Interestingly, while Johnson is often credited as the pioneer of 'dub poetry' – and, as we have seen, also coined the term – at the same time in Jamaica in the 1970s, Onuora, a charismatic Rastafarian poet, had independently begun a similar development. Hence, although the principal focus of this section is dub poetry in the UK, Onuora is worth mentioning because of his influence on the genre and also because it is he, rather than Johnson, who popularized the term. Indeed, when Onuora began using the term to describe his own work, it was, as Habekost comments, 'picked up by the media as a convenient bag for a new wave of oral rhythm poetry using Jamaican creole'. Consequently, by the early-1980s, for many in the UK, Johnson 'had become the leading representative of *a new genre*' (1993: 16; emphasis added).

Of Chinese and African ancestry, Onuora was born Orlando Wong in Franklyn Town in 1952. Taking the name Oku Onuora, meaning 'Voice of the People' – in order to signify his African identity – he has consistently developed a Rastafari-oriented style of poetry in which reggae and dub became important components. His particular indebtedness to dub is clearly evident on his *I A Tell... Dubwise & Otherwise* (1982) and also on his more recent *Overdub: A Tribute to King Tubby* (2000). As with other dub poets, his life and work has consistently focused on the poor and disadvantaged in society.

> fi i de ghetto youth
> it kinda cute
> all day i trod earth
> a look fi work
> till i shoes sole wear down an I foot touch de groun
> wey i live fa eh?
> a nu sey i nu have faith
> but dis ya sufferation ya
> a whole heapa weight
> sufferin unda dis ya sun
> i a tell yu is nu fun
> curfew
> baton lick
> tear gas
> gun shat
> jail
> dats de lot i haffi bear...
>
> (Excerpt from Oku Onuora, 'Echo')

A practising Rastafarian, this concern for the oppressed within the Jamaican ghettoes led to his involvement in a community-based education project. That said, he was no Albert Schweitzer. His biography reads like 'a spectacular adventure story: a desperate ghetto youth who became a guerilla, prison inmate, and revolutionary poet' (Habekost 1993: 19). When the community project ended in failure, frustrated, Onuora turned to guerilla activity and armed robbery in order to raise funds for the 'ghetto youths'. Eventually, in 1970, while robbing a post office, he was arrested and was sentenced to 15 years in prison. After several attempts to escape and subsequent harsh treatment within the Jamaican penal system, he came to the conclusion that his actions were helping nobody, least of all himself, and that another approach had to be taken. He reasoned that if the system, 'Babylon', was going to be challenged, this could be done more effectively by changing peoples' minds rather than threatening their lives. Hence, always fascinated by literature, he turned to poetry, which he began to perform for his fellow prisoners. Indeed, so popular was he that the prison authorities gave him the unprecedented opportunity of performing with a live reggae band – Light of Sabba (led by the saxophonist Cedric Brooks). It was this innovation of setting poetry to music that led to the emergence of dub poetry in Jamaica. Unfortunately, however, the poetry that he performed at the event worried the prison authorities because of its subversive nature. So politically incendiary was it thought to be that his cell was searched and his first collection of poems confiscated. However, as might be expected, he refused to be silenced, and, greatly appreciated by his fellow inmates, he continued writing poems, some of which were eventually smuggled out and printed. Indeed, some even won prizes at the Jamaican Literary Festival (see Habekost 1993: 20). As his reputation grew, particularly amongst Jamaican intellectuals, so pressure to have him released grew with it. Eventually, in 1977, he was allowed out of prison to perform at the Tom Redcam Library, 'an event which had a dramatic impact on the cultural scene in Jamaica' (Habekost 1993: 20). Finally, in September of that year, after seven years in prison, he was granted his freedom.

Since his release, Onuora has continued to perform, record and write. Of particular importance was the publication of *Echo* in 1977, which is now regarded to be a key work in the history of dub poetry. A year later, Tuff Gong released his single 'Reflection in Red', the first dub poetry record released in Jamaica.[39] Moreover, having been granted a scholarship for the Jamaican School of Drama[40] following his release, he met with a small group of poets, which soon formed the embryo of the dub poetry movement in Jamaica.

As to his influence, this can be traced, not only within Jamaica, but also to Canada and Europe. For example, in 1978, Lillian Allen, having been moved by his and Michael Smith's performances at the 11th World Festival of Youth in Cuba, returned to Canada and began what would become the Canadian dub poetry movement (on dub poetry in Canada, see Habekost 1993: 33–36). Again, in 1980 he travelled to the Netherlands and to the UK, where he met

Johnson. Although Johnson was unhappy with the term 'dub poetry', Onuora persisted in using it. As Johnson recalls,

> I coined the phrase 'dub poetry' years ago in talking about reggae deejays because I was trying to argue...that what the deejays in Jamaica were actually doing is poetry, is improvised, spontaneous, oral poetry and I called it 'dub poetry'. But since then Oku Onuora and others have developed this idea of 'dub poetry' as a description of what he and Michael Smith and Muta and myself and other people do. But I think I'll be quite happy just to call it poetry' (quoted in R. Partridge 1998: 1; see also Johnson 1976a; 1999: 60; Davis 1983c: 164).

However, Onuora's development of 'dub poetry' *as a particular genre* is important, because, as Habekost argues,

> there were many people in Jamaica and in expatriate-Jamaican communities who were working instinctively in this direction, but without being aware that they were part of a developing poetic genre with a coherent core. Oku Onuora's persistence in defining and popularizing dub poetry is, therefore, *the crucial precondition for the crystallization of the art form...* Soon artists in Jamaica, Britain, and Canada who had been writing and performing in a similar style, consciously or not, came to be regarded as part of this movement' (1993: 21, emphasis added; see also Morris 1983: 189).

Of the numerous other Jamaican 'dub poets' who have had a formative impact on the genre, those that have had perhaps the most significant influence on the British scene certainly include Mutabaruka (Allan Hope) and Michael ('Mikey') Smith (see Morris 1983: 191). Indeed, the latter's influential album *Mi Cyaan Believe It* (1982) was produced by Johnson and Bovell and released on the Island label. Moreover, the first recording to be released on LKJ Records – Johnson's own label (founded in 1980) – was a 12" by Michael Smith: 'Mi Cyaan Believe It' and, on the B-side, 'Roots', an instrumental by Rico Rodriguez.

As for Mutabaruka, Johnson first encountered his work in 1974, when he read his poem 'Nursery Rhyme Lament' in the Jamaican magazine *Swing*. 'The poem wittily employs colonial nonsense rhymes to comment on post-colonial conditions of life for Jamaica's working class.' 'It made me laugh' he says. 'I was a young poet then of Muta's age, trying to find my own voice. We eventually met in the early 80s in Kingston. In 1985 we read together with other poets at a tribute for the late Mikey Smith' (Johnson 2005: 7).[41] As with Onuora, Mutabaruka became convinced that, rather than militancy, change should be brought about by encouraging people to think for themselves and to look at the world differently:

> I was doing poetry from the late sixties, early seventies, in books and
> magazines... Then a book came about, and I started to perform them
> in different literary circles. Most of what I write is what I feel and what
> I see. I learned that the pen is sometimes mightier than the sword and
> people can write things and motivate people to think; that is what my
> work is all about, to make you think. When you listen to my poems,
> when you read my poems, it must motivate you to find solutions for
> your problems. I cannot guarantee to have all the solutions to all of the
> problems, but I can make you think of these problems and be moti-
> vated towards a constructive solution (quoted in Katz 2004: 295).

It is this type of consciousness raising, borne out of critical reflection on the
poet's experience of life that gives dub poetry its cogency and force. As Brown,
Morris and Rohlehr comment, 'dub poems are heavy with testimony, warning
and prophecy' (1989b: 20). Although some poems focus on Rasta spirituality (as is the case with some of Mutabaruka's work), generally speaking, they
constitute a powerful response to oppression.

> They vividly describe underprivilege, neglect, police brutality, politi-
> cal warfare; the ghetto as a breeding ground for crime and violence.
> They expose cultural imperialism, the alien values of the schools; they
> re-enact the horrors of slavery and trace them into the present; they
> yearn to recover Africa. They distrust politicians and sometimes the
> present constitutional arrangements (Morris 1983: 190).

Whilst Mutabaruka is *the* central figure in Jamaican dub poetry, in the UK it
is Johnson who has been, as Alison Donnell and Sarah Lawson Welsh comment,
'the most enduring and maturing presence, not only in dub, but also in Black
British poetry more generally' (1996c: 367). Indeed, dub poetry has become
'almost synonymous with Linton Kwesi Johnson' (Hitchcock 1997: 164). This is,
as we will see, not only because Johnson's work is distinctive, but also because
it was the first to find its way onto, so to speak, 'a dub plate' – *Dread Beat an'*
Blood (1978), which was also the title of his second book of poems (1975a).
Moreover, although Johnson was to move to the Island label, it should not be
forgotten that *Dread Beat an' Blood* was released by Branson on Virgin,[42] who
had done so much to promote The Sex Pistols, having released *Never Mind the*
Bollocks the previous year. In other words, as has been noted above, the fact that
Virgin released both punk and reggae contributed to the growth of interest the
former had in the latter. This was, I suggest, no less true of Johnson. Moreover,
it was quickly recognized that, compared to the records released by Island and,
indeed, the rest of the Virgin/Front Line reggae catalogue, the sound was not
standard reggae and the discourse was not standard reflection on Rastafarian

themes or romantic relationships. To some extent, Johnson's poetry could be interpreted as politically articulate punk. And, with an effect not entirely unlike that of punk, its driving, powerful, Bovell-produced roots riddim demanded to be listened to; the words, the slow, insistent bass, the stabbing drums, and the sharp clash of 'flying cymbals' called the listener to action. With music specifically written around the poetry, the aural and emotional impact was double-barrelled. This was reggae to fight racism to. If any reggae was going to 'chant down Babylon', this was it![43]

Johnson was born in Jamaica on 24 August 1952, in Chapelton, in the rural parish of Clarendon. 'My mother was a domestic worker and my father did odd jobs. During the sugar harvest he would go and work on a sugar estate, but he was a baker by trade. They both belonged to that generation of Jamaicans whom the land couldn't sustain any more. They went to the town in search of a better life' (Johnson 1999: 53). Eventually, his mother emigrated to England, following which he was, for three years, raised by his grandmother on her small farm. This seems to have been a significant period for the young Johnson, in that she taught him 'belief in self, racial pride, a fierce work ethic and, most importantly, how to read the only book in the house – the Bible' (Terrell 1998: 7). 'I got most of my folk culture from my grandmother... I didn't grow up with books. The only book we had in the house was the Bible' (Johnson 1999: 52; cf. Wroe 2008). Hence, as with other dub poets, such as Benjamin Zephaniah (who can still list the books of the Bible by memory),[44] while his beliefs have evolved away from the simple Christianity of his grandmother, the biblical worldview – particularly that of the Hebrew Bible – has had a formative impact on his thinking. There is, for example, no great distance between his own rhetoric and that of the prophets who challenge injustice, rail against corrupt authorities, and champion the rights of the oppressed and the poor.

On 8 November 1963, at the age of 11, he moved to Brixton, London, to live with his mother. Beginning his British education at Tulse Hill Comprehensive school in Brixton, disillusioned by its institutional racism, although clearly intelligent (see Johnson 1999: 53–54), he terminated his education at the age of 16 and, in 1970, joined the Black Panther Youth League, a radical 'Black power' organization linked to the Black Panther Movement.[45] This, of course, was to have a profound effect on his thinking.

> The Black Panthers were a militant black organization in England that took the name from the American Panthers, but it was completely separate – there were no political ties in that sense, although we used to read the Panther papers from America, read Bobby Seale's *Seize the Time*, Eldridge Cleaver's book, we followed the teachings of Huey P.

Newton and so on. But we were an organization which was tackling racism in Britain and organizing around issues dealing with the police and the courts, because those were the burning issues of the day. That was where I first learned about Black literature and began to become interested in poetry (quoted in Katz 2004: 296–97; see also Davis 1983c; Johnson 1999: 56–58).

Consequently, this was a particularly intellectually fertile period for Johnson.

I think it was while I was in the Panthers, around the same time, that about three or four of us started something called the Black Literary Society... And what we would do is basically write our short stories and poems and have little discussions among ourselves about them. And it was around that time that I met a man called Tony Ottey who was a Jamaican Anglican priest who had just been posted to Brixton and who wanted to get to know the black youth and all that... I told him about what we were doing and he said, 'Oh, well, you should go and see a man called John La Rose. He has a bookshop in Finsbury Park.' And I went to number 2 Albert Road and I think I must have arrived about one o'clock in the afternoon and never left until about seven at night. It was a whole new world opening up to me. John introduced me to poetry by Aimé Césaire. He introduced me to other poets of negritude like Senghor, some of the black American writers like Sonia Sanchez, Gwendolyn Brooks, some people like that... It was around that time also that I discovered the Caribbean Artists Movement.[46] I think it was about the last phase of the Caribbean Artists Movement and I was invited to things they did at the Keskidee Centre and it was the perfect ambience for a young black growing up in England with literary aspirations (Johnson 1999: 56–57).

The Souls of Black Folk by W. E. B. DuBois also had a particularly strong impact on his thinking and his desire to write (see Terrell 1998: 8). 'I just felt like I wanted to write too, to express and say something about what was going on in England with young people, and how black people were treated, and so on' (quoted in Habekost 1993: 17; see also Denselow 1989: 143). Added to this, he again says, 'through John Leroux [*sic*], a Trinidadian publisher and political thinker, I was introduced to a whole range of literature and became influenced by other writers from all over the world. That stirred something within me and made me want to express the experiences of my generation of Black youth growing up in racist Britain. It was a need for self-expression' (quoted in Terrell 1998: 8). Moreover, during this early formative period, as his political mind was being shaped and his interest and skill in poetry developing, he decided to return to formal education. Having left school with six 'O' levels, he attended night classes in order to qualify for entry into Goldsmith's College, from where he graduated in 1973 with an honours degree in sociology. This is important in that it distinguishes him from many of his fellow dub poets. That is to say, while it would be crass to argue that his poetry is 'better' as a result of reading sociology at university, one cannot ignore the fact that his experiences were now filtered through a mind shaped by British higher education and the socio-logical thinking of the period. Whilst this is implicitly evident in his poetry, it is explicit in his social commentary in interviews (e.g. MacKinnon 1979) and arti-cles (e.g. Johnson 1975b; 1976a; 1976b). Whether he's speaking of Thatcher's politics (e.g. 'It Dread inna Inglan', on *Dread Beat an' Blood*), racism in the police force (e.g. 'Sonny's Lettah', on *Forces of Victory*), the Black community as 'the most revolutionary section of the working class' (in interview with MacKinnon 1979: 8), or capitalism and the music industry (e.g. Johnson 1975b; MacKinnon 1979: 52), his learning and politics are conspicuous.

As to the genesis of dub poetry proper, arguably this can be located in June 1973, when, at London's Keskidee Centre (at the invitation of the Director, Oscar Abrams), Johnson performed his poem 'Voices of the Living and the Dead' to music by Rasta Love: 'People kept on telling me my poems were rhythmic and musical. They always suggested I should put it to music and I was inspired by the idea of using words and percussion as The Last Poets[47] had done. I began to work with Rastafarian drummers called Rasta Love. We did performances and worked together in a kind of workshop situation' (quoted in Terrell 1998: 8; see also Davis 1983c: 163). Following that performance, 'I got together with Rasta Love and we had a kind of a workshop situation where we would impro-vise on different kinds of drums and I would make up words to go along with the rhythms. Some of the poems that were eventually published in *Dread Beat and Blood*, came out of that situation... We used to do a few gigs in various places like community and youth centres in Brixton and we got one gig at the Brixton Library' (Johnson 1999: 59). Hence, a year prior to Onuora's reggae-accompanied reading in prison, Johnson was already performing dub poetry proper in London. In 1977 he was awarded the Cecil Day Lewis Fellowship as a writer-in-residence for the London Borough of Lambeth:

> there was a writer's award going in Lambeth, called the C. Day Lewis Fellowship, and they would give £2000 or £3000, I can't remember how much it was, for six months... I was lucky enough to get it. And after my stint at Brixton Library as writer-in-residence, I got a job at the Keskidee Centre... [which] was to help develop the library which they were building up at the time and to organise programmes for black school children living in North London on Caribbean history and culture (Johnson 1999: 65).

Also distinctive about Johnson as a dub poet is that, although in 1973 – following the decline of the Black Panther Movement – he became interested in Rastafarianism, he quickly found its worldview unconvincing. Indeed, although his broadly spiritual interests flowered at the end of his time at Goldsmith's College, one cannot help wondering whether the type of critical thinking encouraged there and his growing socialism had a corrosive impact on his theology. However, whatever the actual reasons for his deconversion, in 1975 he came to the conclusion that he could no longer 'identify with this Selassie thing' (quoted in Habekost 1993: 17) and turned to socialist political activism, the Race Today Collective becoming his new locus of thought and activity.[48] Indeed, not only did the collective publish his first and third books of poetry, *Voices of the Living and the Dead* (1974) and *Inglan is a Bitch* (1980), but he became one of the editors of its influential magazine *Race Today*.[49] The point, however, is that, convinced by socialism, he became very critical of the otherworldly discourse of Rastafarianism, which, he argued, 'acts as a barrier to innovations in the music. Many singers are falling into the Rasta trap. You see it right here in England, y'know. One of the best reggae bands in Britain is called Aswad; they play excellent music and can sing and so on, but their lyrics don't really express any reality.' That said, he insists, 'I'm not anti-Rasta. I think there are many things within the Rasta movement which are positive... I believe it has some role to play. But I don't believe that it has any political relevance whatsoever' (in interview with Davis 1983c: 164; see also his revealing comments on politics, anti-racism, and Rastafarianism in his interview with MacKinnon 1979). Hence the reason that 'I'm a socialist, I have a socialist perspective' (in interview with MacKinnon 1979: 8). This, of course, brought Johnson far closer to the political centre of Rock Against Racism than many contemporary black musicians who were more theologically oriented.[50]

His popularity, however, as indicated above, was not principally built on his work for the Race Today Collective and his published poems, but rather it owes more to his recorded output. Following the rhetorical energy of *Dread Beat an' Blood* in 1978, he signed a contract with Island and released, arguably, his two most influential and important albums, the seminal *Forces of Victory* (1979) and *Bass Culture* (1980), followed by one of the most arresting and thoughtful examples of British dub, *LKJ in Dub* (1981).[51] As Terrell comments about *Forces of Victory*, 'the recording's galvanising impact on UK youth culture was due as much to the tight arrangements and sonic clarity of Bovell's co-production as to the poet's compellingly dramatic voice' (1998: 13). In Johnson's words,

> I'm not really a musician, but I compose the music for my albums.[52]
> I write the basslines, I decide what kind of instrumentation I want to
> use and Dennis does all the arranging and the mixing. We always go

> for a good, strong drum and bass sound and a good organ or piano sound. We have to be very careful with the equalization because my voice is very bass-y and, therefore, we have to be careful what frequencies we feed to the other instruments because otherwise there could be a serious clash. The voice always sits on top of the music, not mixed into the music (quoted in Terrell 1998: 13).

In other words, the emotive content of Johnson's message acquired, as Katz puts it, 'greater emphasis, rendering the medium accessible to audiences which might normally be turned off by politically oriented verse' (2004: 297). Indeed, as early as 1977, just after Lydon's formation of Public Image Ltd., he asked Johnson to perform with him at The Rainbow in front of 'a sea of punk rockers' (Johnson 1999: 68).

Bearing in mind the importance of his *dub* for his *poetry*, something needs to be said about the principal architect of the former, Dennis Bovell.

Blackbeard

Johnson's view of Bovell is unequivocal: 'Dennis is like the Quincy Jones of reggae music. He's one of the greatest arrangers I've ever had the pleasure to work with' (1999: 71). This is not merely the exaggerated praise of a friend, but rather an informed and accurate reflection on a truly seminal figure in the history of British reggae. Indeed, it's difficult to overestimate the debt British reggae owes to 'Blackbeard', as he was known. Not only was he the musical force behind Johnson's oeuvre, but from his days with the now legendary Jah Sufferer Sound System to the influential band Matumbi and from his seminal contribution to the popular genre of Lovers' Rock to his distinctive contributions as a producer and as the operator of several independent reggae labels, he has been a cardinal figure on the British reggae scene (see Bovell and Darwen 1998). Hence, in many ways, Bovell was as significant in Britain for the development of dub as Lee Perry was in Jamaica. Often considered to be the first to play dub live (see Bovell and Darwen 1998), he was, as Reynolds has argued, 'the only British reggae producer brilliant enough to bear any comparison with Jamaican greats like Lee Perry and King Tubby' (2005: 77). Similarly, Lloyd Bradley comments that he is 'probably UK reggae's most innovative and celebrated son'.[53] He continues:

> Dennis can look back on a three-decade international recording, writing, deejaying, playing and production history that stretches back through Matumbi, the Dub Band, Blackbeard, Sufferer HiFi, 4th Street Orchestra, the Lovers' Rock label, Linton Kwesi Johnson, Alpha Blondy and, more recently, Tokyo Ska Paradise Orchestra. Matumbi put on

one of the best live shows in Britain – dubwise or otherwise;[54] for a long time his groups were the first choice to back visiting Jamaican singers; his projects used to saturate the UK reggae charts and make regular riddim raids into the pop Top 40; while his way with the bassline was employed by a range of pop acts from Bananarama to Captain Sensible to The Slits. For years, back in the 1970s, Dennis Bovell was the hub at the centre of British reggae's wheel: very little of any worth happened that didn't have his fingerprints on it somewhere (Bradley 2000: 371).

Bovell was born in Barbados in 1953. At the age of 12, in 1965, he joined his parents in London at roughly the same time as the young Johnson. Focused on music from an early age, he had begun to play his father's guitar in Barbados at his grandmother's house, following the departure of his parents for London. Then, when in London, he learnt double bass at school and joined the school orchestra. Encouraged to play the instrument with a bow, he quickly lost interest, wanting to 'pluck it with [his] fingers. So', he says, 'I blew that out and started playing the organ in the chapel at dinnertime. The music teacher was young; he was willing to do anything; we got on really well together, and he let me go into the music hall and play the piano and stuff' (quoted in Penman 1998: 27). Also at school he formed his first band, Road Works Ahead, 'playing bubblegum and things'. This was followed by Stonehenge, a Jimi Hendrix-inspired band he formed in the late-1960s. However, having become interested in ska and rocksteady, he eventually brought together a three-part harmony section and, in 1971,[55] transformed Stonehenge into his most influential group, Matumbi – 'tipped as the biggest thing in British reggae' (Futrell 1981: 11; see also Bovell and Darwen 1998).

Prior to founding Matumbi, however, as we saw in the previous chapter, Bovell had established his sound system, Jah Sufferer Hi Fi, in late-1969, which was, he claims, 'heavier than Coxsone... I'm not just saying that, that's the truth. It was two thousand four hundred watts – can you imagine that? About forty bass bins, about forty mid-range, and about fifty or sixty treble tweeters... It was incredibly loud' (quoted in Penman 1998: 28). By the mid-1970s, the bass-heavy dub of Jah Sufferer Hi Fi, as well as the fact that he travelled widely and worked continually all over London, led to his growing popularity. 'We used to play at, like, the Metro in Ladbroke Grove and get two thousand people every Friday night. All the kids used to love it' (quoted in Penman 1998: 29). However, popular though he was, he became more widely known as a result of his arrest at London's Carib Club in 1976.[56] The police raided the club looking for a youth on suspicion of a car theft. A fight quickly broke out and 12 people, including Bovell, were arrested. Of the 12, only Bovell was convicted. A retrial at the Old Bailey found him guilty and sentenced him to three years' imprisonment. After six months in 'Wormwood Scrubs', an appeal court vindicated him and released him. However, as we noted in the previous chapter, the six months in prison had a profound effect on him. Such was his experience that, following his release, he abandoned playing sound systems: 'I came out, and I thought, well... I've had it as far as sound systems go. I started concentrating on *making* music for sound systems, not just playing it. Even when I was playing the system, I was still making tunes; we used to go down to the studio and make tunes just for the sound system, acetates, and that was *dub-wize*, y'know?' (quoted in Penman 1998: 28–29).

Whilst not wanting to underestimate the influence of Matumbi and the 4th Street Orchestra – the latter being, essentially, Matumbi in dub (see Bovell and Darwen 1998) – it was with the Dub Band and with Johnson that Bovell's peculiar talent was perhaps most conspicuously evident. Indeed, as indicated above, significant though Johnson was as a dub poet, it was the alchemical merging of his ideas with the production skills of Bovell that contributed to the peculiar potency of his work. That is to say, whilst punks and post-punks identified with the political rhetoric of Johnson, it was the aggressive distinctively dense, bass-heavy, punching beat of Bovell's dub that drove the rhetoric home to this new rebel audience. As Johnson comments, 'I think we're a good team. Certainly, he is one of the greatest arrangers in reggae music I've ever worked with and I would say that at least 50%, if not more, of my success has been due to Dennis Bovell, as a recording artist' (1999: 72).

Bovell's dub was immediately recognizable. Arguing that it is important to be able 'to identify the producer of a track as soon as you put it on', he says that 'I've always been conscious of developing my own style'. He continues:

> What I usually try to do is create a mental picture to coincide with the lyric of the track. Like, say the track is something to do with running – *'You run and you run and you run'* – well then I go: *'run-run-run-run-run'*, and then a couple of other things like that, and for me that will signify running. Then just let the dub do it from there, you just feel it, vibe it totally. You think, Oh, I'd like to hear some organ there, a little bit. Everyone's got a dub mind. If you were at a dub desk, you'd mix it differently than I would. But the thing is to mix it in a way that every time somebody hears that particular style of dubbing, the way you bring the instruments in, they'll know it's you (quoted in Penman 1998: 29–30).

That said, the chemistry between Bovell and Johnson was mutually beneficial, in that, although the distinctive sound of Bovell's dub is evident on his solo projects – particularly *Yuh Learn!* (1977), *Scientific Higher Ranking Dubb*

(1978), *Strictly Dub Wize* (1978), *I Wah Dub* (1980), and the more recent *Dub of Ages* (1997), as well as Matumbi's *Dub Planet Orbit 1* (1980) – his encounters with Johnson produced a dub sound with a particular bass force and a clinical precision that is today still unmatched and immediately recognizable.

That said, while Bovell is perhaps best known for his work with the Dub Band and particularly with Johnson, we have also noted his influential work with punk and post-punk bands, The Slits and The Pop Group particularly. He first met The Pop Group through Vivien Goldman.

> They were doing a John Peel Show and I met Viv in the corridor. She said come and have a listen... She expected me to laugh, but I thought it was good...and they were giving the bloody engineers hell... I was into that. People usually go, 'Oh, you can't do that, leave it alone, you'll blow the speakers.' From that point of view, like blowing the speakers and equipment, I wasn't into it, but playing discordant things out of tune, I was into that. Why not?' (quoted in Futrell 1981: 11).

Elsewhere he recalls his own relationship with the band: 'If I said... "You can't do that", something musically pretty distasteful, they'd say, "Right. *Why* is it distasteful? We wanna do it" – and they would do it. Mixing The Pop Group, I was saying, "We must have the levels out of the red, this is gonna distort otherwise." They'd say "Great!" – that was The Pop Group' (quoted in Penman 1998: 24).[57] While there is a certain amount of frustration evident here, to a large extent, this experimental eclecticism is typical both of his own work and of dub *per se*. Hence, although, superficially, there was little about The Pop Group that can be likened to Matumbi or, indeed, to roots reggae, and although Bovell recalls that 'it was refreshing to get away from reggae' whilst producing the band (quoted in Futrell 1981: 11), when one looks below the surface, there were substantial continuities between dub and this post-punk experimentalism. Whereas Bovell's dub-inspired natural eclecticism, particularly evident on *Brain Damage*, led him to experiment carefully and discretely with a variety of genres (see Bovell and Darwen 1998), The Pop Group's similar dub instincts led them to slam genres together and, guided by the heavy bass lines of funk, produce an orchestrated cacophony. In other words, just as, according to Goldman, 'The Pop Group had this obsession with finding a new way of doing everything' (quoted in Reynolds 2005: 76), so Bovell had a similar obsession that he was able to indulge in dub and bring to his work with the band. As Reynolds comments,

> Bovell's mix of acid-rock wildness and dub wisdom made him a perfect foil for The Pop Group. For '3-38', the B-side to 'She is Beyond Good and Evil', he took the A-side's music and ran it backwards,

psychedelia-style, then built in a new rhythm track for it with Bruce Smith. 'That really blew the band away', says Bovell. Necessity was the mother of invention here [as it was at the genesis of dub]. 'We'd almost run out of studio time. That's why I reused the A-side'… Bovell was the ideal candidate for the not hugely enviable task of giving The Pop Group's unruly sound some semblance of cohesion. Working on the debut album, *Y*, Bovell quickly grasped that the rhythm section held together the whole band. 'Simon Underwood and Bruce Smith, they were the Sly and Robbie of the post-punk period – *tight*,' says Bovell [with reference to dub's most famous drum and bass duo] (2005: 78).

Interestingly, the 1979 Animal Instincts Tour that promoted the Bovell-produced *Y*, included, along with the post-punk bands Manicured Noise and Alternative TV, Linton Kwesi Johnson, with whom the lead singer, Mark Stewart, had become friendly.

Bovell's work with The Slits, on the other hand, was more straightforward, largely because they were less eclectic and, we have seen, much more directly influenced by reggae. The main problem for Bovell was simply that they couldn't play their instruments. 'Other punk bands talked about not being able to play, but were secretly competent. Genuinely inept, The Slits really sounded cacophonous, with only the faintest subliminal skank indicating their punky-reggae intentions' (Reynolds 2005: 80). On first working with them, Bovell quickly realized that, while 'they get lots of ideas about sounds', they were not able 'to hear it at once and go straight into it, just play it' (quoted in Penman 1998: 24). 'The Slits had so much input that it was more a case of sorting out what should go… They were just bulging with material and I had the task of sorting it out… It was like an enormous jigsaw puzzle all dumped in your lap' (quoted in Reynolds 2005: 82). However, as with The Pop Group, their relationship with Bovell was inspirational, in that it gave form to their amorphous cacophony.

The point is that Bovell was the ideal producer of punk and post-punk music. Just as white youths, such as The Slits and The Pop Group, were reaching across the musical divide to understand reggae, being particularly beguiled by dub (see Paytress 2000), so Bovell was reaching back and seeking to understand punk and post-punk. Not only did he 'listen to a lot of New Wave groups', but he believed the music to be fundamentally contiguous with reggae and dub – largely, it has to be said, because he understood reggae to be a particularly inclusive genre. For example, speaking of PiL, who had just formed, he makes the following comment: 'I like Wobble's bass lines! Well, like, with New Wave bands and dub – they're certainly doing it. Why not? Reggae is capable of incorporating any style of music… They've realised it, and started doing it, which is good' (quoted in Penman 1998: 25; cf. La Rose 1999: 127). Indeed, perhaps his most important solo album, *Brain Damage* (1981), is an excellent example of musical eclecticism couched in reggae, drifting effortlessly from bass-heavy, dub-soaked landscapes of the title track and 'Aqua Dub' to funk, disco, rhythm and blues, ska, and lovers' rock. Bovell can be considered a dub universalist, in the sense that, to restate a comment quoted above, 'everyone's got a dub mind' and all sound is capable of being arranged using dub techniques.

Concluding Comments

The aim of this chapter has been both to outline the history and also to unpack the significance of the punk–dub interface and anti-racist politics in the 1970s. Whilst, of course, more could have been discussed about particular bands, artists, and their influences, little would have been added to the argument that reggae and dub has had a significant social and cultural impact. This has been just as much, if not more, to do with its relevance to the listener's socio-political context, in that, as Barry Troyna has commented, 'the black youth's attraction to reggae is not limited to its rhythmic and tonal qualities. The lyrical content functions as a vehicle for the expression of the response of many youths to their position in a racist society' (1978: 139; cf. Small 1987: 456–57). This, we have seen, has been particularly true of dub poetry, which, in the case of Johnson, articulated a strident socialist critique. Indeed, the dancehall itself, the site of live dub, toasting, and dub poetry, can be understood as a counter-hegemonic space, even, to use Michel Foucault's term, a 'heterotopia' (1986). However, the argument of this chapter is that important though this counter-hegemonic, heterotopian discourse was for the black community, its influence was not limited to that community. White youths identified continuities with their own experience. As Thomas Cushman has argued, 'because all human cultural products are essentially shared and shareable, a group's cultural codes are subject to appropriation by other groups. Such appropriation can occur through diffusion to other groups in similar existential positions' (1991: 29). This was the case with punk's appropriation of dub. While there may have been some shift in signification, in that, for example, the 'Babylon' of the punks was not quite that of Lee Perry and Burning Spear, nor indeed that of Jah Shaka and Dennis Bovell, there were significant continuities – continuities which individuals such as Don Letts, John Lydon, Joe Strummer and Paul Simonen were quick to recognize. However, if there was a distance between the original and the post/punk *version*, which there was, it was to widen significantly as post-punk evolved, in that the signifiers discussed in the first chapter increasingly become, to some extent, what Baudrillard refers to as simulacra (1994).

More broadly, we have seen that, to some extent, the hippie idealism of the early 1970s was utopian, cosseted in the prosperous society famously predicted by Harold Macmillan in 1957: 'You will see a state of prosperity such as we have never had in my lifetime – nor indeed in the history of this country... Indeed let us be frank about it – most of our people *have never had it so good*.' However, it wasn't to last, in that, as the 1970s progressed, it increasingly failed to reflect the experiences of many white youths living in the shadow of recession. If this is as good as it gets, then what sort of future is there to look forward to? Consequently, hippie idealism faded and the lifestyles and values belonging to that idealism were ridiculed and scorned. Reflecting the ideological shift and the challenge to hegemony, rock music was transformed into terse, nihilistic 'one-chord wonders'. That said, punk *bricolage* appropriated, musically and sartorially, a vast spectrum of post-war styles to articulate its contempt and frustration. Increasingly central to this interruption of hegemony were signs and discourse dominant within reggae culture. Mass unemployment, poor housing, failing social services, discrimination, alienation and boredom led to unrest and anxiety within Babylon. As Hebdige comments, 'in punk, alienation assumed an almost tangible quality. It could almost be grasped. It gave itself up to the cameras in "blankness", the removal of expression (see any photograph of any punk group), the refusal to speak and be positioned... But', he continues, 'at almost every turn the dictates of this profane aesthetic were countermanded by the righteous imperatives of another musical form: reggae' (1979: 28) – a *sacred* aesthetic. Hence, as we have seen, at a deep structural level, there were fundamental continuities between black and white British subcultures, which became particularly conspicuous in anti-racist politics. It's also worth noting that, as we will see in the next chapter, musicologically, punk *bricolage* had clear continuities with dub *bricolage* and deconstruction.

We have seen that, while those such as Johnson understood reggae and dub as a form of 'rebel music', which was simply the latest stage in a long history of protest against the colonial oppression of 'Babylon' – '*the* protest music par excellence in the modern field, a continuation of style that dates back to slavery days, with modern influences' (Johnson, quoted in Denselow 1989: 127–8) – in the case of punks, there was a process of reinterpretation in terms of a discourse against cultural hegemony *per se*. This is verbal dub in the sense that words are deconstructed and remixed in order to change their signification. As Robert Beckford comments,

> in the dub poem 'Liesense fi kill', Linton Kwesi Johnson 'plays' with the word "licence". Removing the letter 'c' and adding 's' after the first 'e' he communicates a sense of corruption and disreputable activity in

> the police. It now means to 'cover-up' – that is 'lie-sense'. Similarly, Birmingham-based dub poet Kukumo plays with the word 'diaspora', re-interpreting the word in the light of the Caribbean economic struggle in Britain to coin the term 'die-as-poor-ya' (2006: 77).

Whether punks understood the ideological significance of dub poems or not, and whether they fully appreciated the implications of Rastafarian socio-religious discourse or not, they nevertheless identified continuities and recognized a voice speaking powerfully to their own situation. Indeed, in a sense, within punk the ideology was versioned again in the white community. Lydon is an excellent example of this. For example, reggae's apocalyptic imagery and references to Babylon could easily be read in terms of the experiences of white disaffected youth – as an articulation of their frustration at a sense of there being 'no future'. It was within the context of the unnatural baking heat of the summer of 1976, the drought, the Notting Hill disturbances, and the sense of national decline, that punk began to hit the headlines. As Hebdige comments,

> apocalypse was in the air and the rhetoric of punk was drenched in apocalypse: in the stock imagery of crisis and sudden change... As the shock-haired punks began to gather in a shop called Sex on a corner of the King's Road, aptly named World's End, David Bowie's day of the *Diamond Dogs* (RCA Victor 1974) and the triumph of the 'super-alienated humanoid' was somehow made to coincide with reggae's Day of Judgment, with the overthrow of Babylon and the end of alienation altogether (1979: 27).

Again, apocalypticism was not limited to the African Caribbean community. As well as those songs which reflect an identification with African Caribbean discourse, such as The Ruts' 'Babylon's Burning', others, such as, most famously, The Sex Pistols' 'Anarchy in the UK' and 'God Save the Queen', draw on religious discourse to express a similarly oppressive and dystopian vision of the future. As we will see in the following chapter, this is, in many ways, typical of rock in a postmodern context. Punk was the response of

> a generation of children that was not only bored...and afraid, but lonely and isolated from each other and the adult world as well... They operated in a world characterized by a steady and rising rate of change... [Change] increasingly appears to be all that there is; it does not allow any appeal to a stable and predictable teleology. There is in fact no sense of progress which can provide meaning or depth and a sense of inheritance. Both the future and the past appear increasingly irrelevant; history has collapsed into the present... Rock...

> emerges from and functions within the lives of those generations
> that have grown up in the post-war, post-modern context (Gross-
> berg 1997: 479).

This is powerfully and simply articulated in 'God Save the Queen'. However, it is also essentially apocalyptic and, therefore, able to form an 'affective alliance' with Rastafarian discourse.

It is also a good example of the process of signification in dub. 'The act of deconstruction is influenced and informed by socio-political aspirations and concerns, and these concerns guide the reworking of words and their meanings... While the engineer mixes the music to create a new encoded narrative, so the dub poet reconstructs words so that they portray political realities' (Beckford 2006: 77). Similarly, dub deconstructs rock and, indeed, fascist symbolism in the service of a similar political discourse. In other words, whilst the meeting of Rastas and punks looks unlikely at first glance, in actual fact there are significant lines of continuity. This is regularly pointed out in interviews with contemporary dubheads. For example, the British dub producer Dougie Wardrop (of Centry and the Bush Chemists) makes the following point: 'I like punk; I like reggae and punk; they are my two favourite types of music because they're anti-establishment. They say "fuck off to the government". It's point-of-view music' (in interview with Nathalie Valet – *Dub Stories* [DVD]). Whether the apocalypticism is Rastafarian or secular and nihilistic, 'it's point-of-view music'.

Likewise, Neil Nehring's discussion of punk's relation to Situationist International – 'the band of artists and writers who helped in some part to fuel the events of May '68 in France' (2006: 519) – is interesting in that it is just this type of protest and activism that led to the rejection of 1970s hippie decadence and empathy with those who sought to chant down Babylon and rid society of racism. Indeed, it was just this type of activism that transformed the 'chanting' (Marley) into the 'burning' (The Ruts). This was certainly true of Johnson, who, significantly, worked with the French anarchist Jean Jacques Lebel, who was himself not only part of the 1968 revolution in Paris, but also attempted to burn down the French stock exchange (see Johnson 1999: 68). However, not only did Johnson's dub poetry appeal to French radicals and his dub music appeal to French youth, but it articulated the frustrations of many punks and oppressed minorities in the UK. Johnson was, at that time, for many, the mouthpiece for the black presence in Britain, which, he argues, influenced blacks in the rest of Europe:

> I think the reason why I've been able to find such an audience in those
> countries is that a lot of the black population in France, in Holland, in
> Germany, and all that, they look to England for leadership and I think

they're very impressed with what blacks have done and with what blacks have achieved in this country and I'm seen as a kind of person who sort of represents that through music and poetry and I suppose that would account for my popularity in those countries (1999: 70).

Musicologically, however, it's difficult to avoid the impression that dub alchemy re-enchanted punk, in the sense that, whether intentional or not, there was a return to the ethereal sensibilities engendered by the music of rock bands such as Hawkwind, Can, and Tangerine Dream. To some extent, this can be understood in terms of what Steven Feld has referred to as 'acoustemology'. As an elision of the terms 'acoustic' and 'epistemology', he is referring to the exploration of sonic sensibilities – ways in which sound is epistemologically significant. Acoustemology investigates, he says,

the primacy of sound as a modality of knowing and being in the world. Sound both emanates from and penetrates bodies; this reciprocity of reflection and absorption is a creative means of orientation – one that tunes bodies to places and times through sounding potential. Hearing and producing sound are thus embodied competencies that situate actors and their agency in particular historical worlds. These competencies contribute to their distinct and shared ways of being human; they contribute to possibilities for and realizations of authority, understanding, reflexivity, compassion, and identity (2003: 226).

Dub, I am suggesting, re-oriented punk, situating punks in Babylon, tuning them into an otherness, a heterotopia, which encouraged a certain reflexivity and a sense of real or imagined transcendence. Hence, as we will see in the next chapter, along with the nihilistic 'one-chord wonders', there was, to some extent, a re-introduction of certain aesthetic elements that softened punk's directness and aggression, giving it depth and space, which has often been described using religious metaphors or, in the case of some, such as Jah Wobble and Youth, interpreted in explicitly spiritual or esoteric terms. Goldman, for example, has spoken of the 1970s as a time when 'reggae was our religion and dub our sacred sacrament' (Goldman 2003: 2). As we will see in the following chapter, this became particularly apparent as the 1970s drew to a close and the 1980s dawned.

5 Psychotic Jonkanoo: Theorizing Post-punk Dub

Once the musical, historical and social contexts of dub are understood – the history of reggae, Jamaican subcultures, the religio-politics of Rastafarianism, African indigenous belief, and the emergence of distinctive discourses of resistance – it is not difficult to understand the various homological relations and the ideological and musicological continuities with other musics and subcultures. To a large extent, this is what the previous chapters have been concerned to expose. That said, we have seen that, perhaps inevitably, the project became more complex when dub was traced to Britain and to its reception within quite distinct cultures and scenes – such as post/punk or localized sound-system scenes, such as that in South-East London (see Back 1988) or, indeed, the sound-system rivalry explored by Franco Rosso in the film *Babylon* (1980). This final chapter can be understood in terms of a development of this analysis. Theorizing post-punk dub in relation to discussions of post/modernity, it will focus on some particular developments of the genre during the early-1980s, at which point dub's sun began to set. That said, although its light shone dimly throughout the 1980s, reflected in the continued work of particularly Adrian Sherwood, the Mad Professor (Neil Fraser), and Jah Shaka, and although it would rise again at the beginning of the 1990s, when sound systems such as that of Nick Manasseh and hip hop artists and producers such as Michael West (Congo Natty/Conquering Lion/ Rebel MC) began to attract crowds – drawn, to some extent, from the growing urban and rave scenes (see Partridge 2006) – the early-1980s provides a good point at which to bring this particular analysis of the early history of British dub to a close. (Bearing in mind the history of dub discussed in Part Two of this book and with an awareness of the more occluded progress of dub during the 1980s, it is odd to read discussions of dub arguing that its influence outside Jamaica was 'just beginning' in the mid-1980s [e.g. Veal 2007: 221].[1] This is clearly wrong.)

Furthermore, while the work of numerous post-punk and dub artists could have been analysed, from Cabaret Voltaire to the Mad Professor, this final chapter focuses on the work of Adrian Sherwood and key

On-U Sound artists. This is largely because Sherwood's On-U Sound was the principal site of dub experimentalism during the 1980s and it has fairly clear musicological and cultural continuities with post-punk.[2] As such, it provides an interesting case study.

Having said all that, it does feel like it should be a criminal offence not to mention the Mad Professor in a book on dub, especially British dub. He was, of course, central to the emergence of British dub during the 1980s. Inspired by Prince Buster's classic early contribution to the genre, *The Message Dubwise*, he put his skills as an electronic technician to good use and set up the Ariwa[3] studio and label in 1979 in Thornton Heath, London – moving to larger premises in Peckham in 1980 and, finally, to his current studio in Whitehorse Lane, South Norwood. Throughout the 1980s, he was involved in several important dub collaborations, arguably the most significant in the 1980s being with Jah Shaka – *Jah Shaka Meets the Mad Professor at Ariwa Sounds* (1984) – and in the 1990s with Massive Attack – *No Protection* (1995). He has also, particularly during the 1990s, been one of Lee Perry's most consistent collaborators. More recently, he collaborated with the Turkish folk band Babazula to produce, arguably, one of his most thoughtful and accomplished works, *Ruhani Oyun Havalari* (2003).[4] However, whilst his work, particularly his justly famous *Dub Me Crazy* series (1982–1993),[5] is important within the evolution of British dub, he remained (during the period with which this thesis is concerned), as did Jah Shaka, very much within the Jamaican tradition of dub. (The obvious exception to this was his 1982 collaboration with Ruts DC, *Rhythm Collision*, discussed in the previous chapter.) Sherwood/On-U Sound, on the other hand, provided a conspicuously British and, indeed, distinctively post-punk interpretation of the genre, which would go on to influence a generation of producers and artists.

African Space in an Age of Plunder: Some Comments on Dub and Postmodernism

Dub problematizes attempts to locate it within postmodernism or modernism – not that anyone has systematically attempted to do this[6] and not that there is a consensus as to the meaning of the terms. Indeed, there is some discussion as to whether postmodern theory is useful at all in seeking to understand popular music (e.g. Redhead 1990; Goodwin 1991). As Fredric Jameson has pointed out, 'the concept of postmodernism is not widely accepted or even understood today. Some of the resistance to it may come from the unfamiliarity of the work it covers, which can be found in all the arts'. This is undoubtedly true, but, nevertheless, concerning music he notes that the postmodern can be observed in 'the moment of John Cage but also the later synthesis of classical and "popular" styles found in composers like Philip Glass and Terry Riley, and also punk and new-wave rock with such groups as The Clash, Talking Heads and Gang of Four' (1997: 192). These observations are interesting, in that, while we might not concur with Jameson's identification of some of this music as 'postmodern' (for a good critique, see Goodwin 1991: 177–78), I want to argue that it is precisely within post-punk and its milieu of style-synthesis that we can locate dub as postmodern. Having said that, as will be apparent by now, there were already intimations of postmodernity within the genre, prior to its confluence with post/punk.

Why then might Jamaican dub be understood to be *potentially*, if not *actually*, postmodern? At a relatively basic level, discussions of postmodernism have generally focused on two trends, the first being the shift towards intertextuality, pastiche, and the penchant for eclecticism, and the second being the blurring of previously established distinctions between cultural categories (see Stratton 1989). To begin with the latter, if we think of the collapsing of distinctions between art and the everyday, we have seen that, particularly in the case of Lee Perry's and Errol Thompson's playful development of the genre (e.g. Thompson's seminal *African Dub Almighty: Chapter 3*), there was an explicit attempt to incorporate everyday found sounds – à la *musique concrète*.[7] To take an early example, Perry's 'Caveman Skank' (on *Cloak and Dagger*) presciently hints at (if not actually manifesting) postmodern developments within contemporary remix culture: 'a thoroughly experimental and ironic dance number featuring toasting and vocal noises from Perry, along with running water, crashing cars, and voices lifted from an American sound effects record; the number opened with a Native American chief reading a portion of the Bible in Cherokee, and finished with the bustle of a public auction' (Katz 2000: 165). Again, in the post-punk period, we will see that Sherwood, inspired by Perry – with whom he later recorded *Time Boom X De Devil Dead* (2002) – has made similar use of everyday, ambient sounds. As he comments of African Head Charge's *Environmental Studies* (1982), 'woven into the mix, you can hear car crashes, water flowing, bottles breaking. We used a lot of "found sounds" and many "environmental sounds" from the studio down at Berry Street where it was recorded... I think we may have even used water sounds from the toilets and humming vibrations from the boiler room' (quoted in Whitfield 2003). Hence, we have noted that, decades before the imitative realism of projects such as David Holmes's *Let's Get Killed* (1997) and Thomas Brinkmann's *Tokyo* (2004) – both of which seek to evoke the sonic environment of the contemporary city – some dub producers, such as Perry and Thompson, were making creative use of ambient street recordings, sound effects, and solicited comments from the general public. This breaching of the boundary between art and the everyday is a characteristic feature that has become increasingly conspicuous as the genre has evolved since the late-1970s. Whether one thinks of flushing toilets, barking dogs, football crowds chanting, missiles being launched, the voices of William Burroughs and Albert Einstein, or the sampled rhetoric of a range of religious and political figures, including Malcolm X, Margaret Thatcher, Lenny Bruce, Desmond Tutu, and Martin Luther King (e.g. Barmy Army's *The English Disease* and Leblanc and Simenon's *Stop the Confusion*), the boundaries between art and the everyday have been significantly eroded in dub. Social history has been sampled and versioned.

While in Jamaican dub, this sampling could be understood as social critique of ghetto life/Babylon, this is less the case in post-punk dub. Here the sounds are, generally speaking, detached from their contexts and incorporated as part of an essentially meaningless montage. I say 'generally speaking' because, of course, this was not always the case. For example, Retribution's 'Repetitive Beats' (on the compilation *Dubitamin*), which samples a speech by Margaret Thatcher, is a specific attack on the Criminal Justice and Public Order Act. Again, Fun-da-mental's 'Dog Tribe' (on *Seize the Time*), which samples an ugly and disturbing threat made by a far-right activist over the phone, is a powerful critique of British racism.

More specifically, the argument is that, while the marriage of dub and punk may seem an unlikely union at first – the one being extended, ethereal, sophisticated, and rooted in Jamaican popular music; the other being brief, aggressive, purposively amateur, and rooted in white, urban, Anglo-American rock music – there are conspicuous continuities. Bearing in mind what Hebdige refers to as punk's 'self-consciously subversive *bricolage*' – by which he meant the 'hints of disorder, of breakdown and category confusion: a desire not only to erode racial and gender boundaries, but also to confuse chronological sequence by mixing up details from different periods' (1979: 123) – it is not difficult to see why there was a natural confluence of the two genres. As we have seen, as in punk style, so in dub music there is an improvised juxtaposition of heterogeneous fragments. Dismantling music, stripping it down to the bare rhythm, and then rebuilding it using an eclectic range of musics, sounds and effects – reverb, fragments of vocal, found sounds – constitutes a playfulness and mixing of codes that is both typically 'punk' and typically postmodern. Indeed, this deconstruction certainly has poststructural potential, in that it functions as a challenge to and a decentring of dominant narratives. It takes discourses, well-known tracks and popular sounds, makes them strange, and produces a new sonic montage.

For Jameson, of course, postmodernism emerges as a specific reaction to established forms of high modernism.

Those formerly subversive and embattled styles – Abstract Expressionism; the great modernist poetry of Pound, Eliot or Wallace Stevens; the International Style (Le Corbusier, Frank Lloyd Wright, Mies); Stravinsky; Joyce, Proust and Mann – felt to be scandalous or shocking by our grandparents are, for the generation which arrives at the gate in the 1960s, felt to be the establishment and the enemy – dead, stifling, canonical, the reified monuments *one has to destroy to do anything new*' (1997: 192; emphasis added).

This last sentence can be read in terms of punk rhetoric, particularly the rhetoric of The Sex Pistols. Dub too, we have seen, is essentially iconoclastic, in that it takes the reified, the canonical, destroys it and reworks it into something fresh, new and subversive: 'by adjusting the controls at the mixing desk, a tune as bright and breezy (some might say cheesy) as "Kingston Town" can be reinvented as something so edgy and surprising as "Tribesman Rockers"'[8] (Bradley 2000: 309).

Having said that, it should be noted that, in much Jamaican dub, the deconstruction of the canonical and, arguably, the reified in reggae,[9] was less a subversion of musical hegemony and more of a celebration of it. Dub producers and musicians were all roots reggae enthusiasts. As we have discussed in detail, for various reasons the version emerged as simply another way of reading reggae, another interpretation of an accepted musical canon. This is distinct from punk's relationship to rock and from post-punk's development of dub. That is to say, the signification shifted in the process of its reception by punks. We have seen that, not only was roots reggae *per se* received as an essentially subversive genre by punks, but dub was received as a more ethereal and exotic reading of reggae and, subsequently, of punk. Whereas, for example, in the face of widespread and institutional racism, reggae provided a reaction and a subversive discourse, in the context of post-punk, dub provided a musical technique by which the established musical order could be torn down and re-imagined. In post-punk's articulation of dub – the use of repetition, pastiche, irony, and play – its innate postmodern potential was made manifest. Tunes were 'destroyed', reconstructed and enhanced by the apparently random introduction of found sounds. Indeed, in a Baudrillardian sense (1994), post-punk dub provides a good example of floating signifiers that refer to little but themselves.

Again, unlike much modernist music, such as traditional classical compositions – and, arguably, progressive rock (see Goodwin 1991: 180ff.) – and like punk's celebration of the 'one-chord wonder', dub can be understood as not being particularly concerned with the demonstration of technical genius and the foregrounding of the musicians' abilities.[10] That said, as some indication of the fluid and subjective nature of post/modern classification in general and the problematic nature of such categorization in popular music studies in particular, there is a lack of consensus. It is arguable, for example, that rock *per se* has always been postmodern, it being fundamentally eclectic, predicated on the dissolution of the conceptual boundary between 'high' and 'low' culture and its birth also being coincidental with 'the historical moment of postmodernism... Pop songs are the soundtrack of postmodern daily life' (Frith and Horne 1987: 5; cf. Goodwin 1991). One only has to think of the work of 'rock' bands such as Soft Machine, Neu, Can, Faust, and Henry Cow and their continuities with post-punk, industrial or dub-oriented bands such as Test Department, The Pop Group, Missing Brazillians, Creation Rebel, African Head Charge, Throbbing Gristle, and Einstürzende Neubauten to realize that post/modern classification can be problematic. More specifically, Brian Longhurst has briefly argued that dub actually encapsulates the modernist movement in reggae, in that the producer becomes the musical expert.

> In the dub style there is play with the sound itself. Rather than being smooth and developing in a similar fashion the music became disjointed and 'difficult' in ways that parallel similar developments in art forms like the novel and 'classical' music. Attention is directed to the form itself. The familiarity of the reggae sound is made strange, and the role of the producer in the production of such strangeness is called attention to (1995: 148).

That is to say, while the musicians may recede into the background, the producer as an expert in sound manipulation is foregrounded (see Goodwin 1990). As we have seen, Longhurst has a point. Although some musicians associated with dub, Sly and Robbie particularly, are foregrounded, we have seen that, generally speaking, it is the producers, such as King Tubby, Lee Perry, Errol Thompson, Scientist, Augustus Pablo, and Prince Jammy who become more prominent. Consequently, more than any other genre, dub is responsible for the shift towards the understanding of the producer as the principal musician, whose expertise in the studio (understood in terms of an instrument) is celebrated. That is to say, whereas modernist authorship and authenticity in rock largely reside in the ability to play – principally demonstrated at live performances – the notion of authenticity in dub and 'plunder culture' generally lies in the competence of the engineer and producer to manipulate sound in new and exciting ways. The focus is on the producer as auteur. However, whilst this is certainly true of Jamaican reggae, I'm not convinced that this fact alone is enough to support a modernist thesis concerning post-punk dub. As we will see, other factors need to be taken into account.

Again, while the explicit foregounding of the producer was the case in Jamaican communities and is still evident in sound-system culture, in post-punk Britain dub is not received in the same way as typically modernist music. Whilst fans prefer certain styles of production and trust certain producers (such as Sherwood), the reception of dub was (and still is in Europe) often less about an appreciation of the expertise of the producer and more about the sonic environment that the music creates. While I realize that I may be on thin ice in distinguishing dub in this way – although the same would be true of the various forms of ambient and much electronic dance/trance music – there would appear to be a difference in the way the musics are received. Steven Feld's concept of 'acoustemology' is instructive in this respect, in that it enables an explication of the epistemology of dub and, more specifically, its primacy 'as a modality of knowing and being in the world' (2003: 226). Feld's ethnographic work in the dense rainforests of Papua New Guinea with the Kaluli found that they used sound very much as a visual cue to locate themselves spatiotemporally (see Feld 1982; 2003). Thinking of the reception of dub in the post-punk period (and previously in the progressive rock period), as with ambient, it was appreciated because it located the listener in a particular sonic environment – an imagined space. It's worth quoting Brian Eno at this point:

> Until recently music was inseparable from the space in which it was performed – including social space. One very strong movement in the late-nineteenth and twentieth centuries was towards music as an immersive, environmental experience... But it was recording which really liberated music from the moment of performance and from the performers themselves... Recording and electronics also allowed performers to work with impossible perspectives and relationships. Producers and musicians discovered that tiny sounds could be made huge, and huge ones compacted. And, using echoes and reverberations, those sounds could seem to be located in a virtual space which was entirely imaginary. The act of making music becomes the art of creating new sonic locations... Perhaps the strangest surprise was watching these threads weaving together in the popular music of the 1980s and 1990s (2000: xi–xii; see also Schütze 1995).

It was these virtual environments that punks, post-punks and hippies imagined themselves into. Moreover, these were spaces which could, of course, be more easily imagined under the influence of cannabis, to which, furthermore, was attached a significant level of subcultural capital. Indeed, many seem to have been attracted, not only to a sense of squatting in another culture's space, but also to this particular space within which cannabis use was, as we have seen, positively encouraged and, indeed, sacralized. Cannabis and dub, therefore, are not just 'drugs and music', but rather – as with earlier interpretations within psychedelic culture (see Partridge 2005: 82–134) – understood in terms of 'a modality of knowing and being in the world'. They provided a particular environment, which was, of course, pure simulation – the simulacrum (see Baudrillard 1994). Indeed, the title of the second track on Creation Rebel's classic *Psychotic Jonkanoo* (1981), 'African Space', sums up the effects of post-punk dub. This is British dub creating the simulacrum of an African space in the minds of its listeners. Few fans I have spoken to had any real understanding of the title *Psychotic Jonkanoo*, but it seemed to summon up notions of the psyche, psychedelic experimentation, along with the African and the exotic. 'Psych-', for example, which has been ubiquitous in drug-oriented cultures since the 1960s – and, arguably, has a lot to do with Aldous Huxley's coining of the term 'psychedelic' and the subsequent cultures that adopted that term in the 1960s (see Partridge 2005: 90ff.) – references notions of 'journeying within' and 'inner space'. Of course, for many, music and the arts generally have been central to this journeying, which for many within the dub community has been interpreted in terms of a journey to an African space. Indeed, the title of Creation Rebel's *Starship Africa* (1980) signified the post-punk's journey within – it was the psychonaut's Black Star Liner travelling to an imagined African space. The point is that, to quote Baudrillard, 'simulation is no longer that of a territory, a referential being, or a substance. It is the generation by models of a real without origin or reality: a hyperreal. The territory no longer precedes the map, nor does it survive it. It is nevertheless the map that precedes the territory... that engenders the territory' (1994: 1). The African space mapped by dub precedes Africa in the post-punk mind. It's an imaginary, almost psychedelic, hyperreality. Hence, to return to the earlier acoustemological point, dub is often appreciated more for the environment it creates than for the musicianship of its creators. Indeed, David Toop's typically emic descriptions of dub, which provide an appreciation of the *sonic effects* of the music, rather than an analysis of particular musicians and producers, serve to highlight this principal aspect of its reception:

> drop-out, extreme equalisation, long delay, short delay, space echo, reverb, flange, phase, noise gates, echo feedback, shotgun snare drums, rubber bass, zipping highs, cavernous lows. The effects are there for enhancement, but for a dubmaster they can displace time, shift the beat, heighten a mood, suspend a moment. No coincidence that the nearest approximation to dub is the sonar transmit pulses, reverberations and echoes of underwater echo ranging and bioacoustics (1995a: 116; cf. Davis 2009a).

Again, as in contemporary remix culture, dubheads are generally not interested in whether or not the sound took a great deal of skill to produce; they are principally interested in its affective impact, its function 'as a modality of knowing and being in the world'.

To push some of these points a little further, there is a typically postmodern celebration of repetition, reproduction and eclecticism in dub. While dub has evolved somewhat from the days of the 'version', it is nevertheless a 'kleptic' genre that pilfers and circulates tracks, narratives, and everyday found sounds.[11] While this is, on the one hand, an example of sampling technology's 'Age of Plunder' (Goodwin 1990: 271), it is also, on the other hand, simply an example of Jamaican resourcefulness. Lloyd Bradley makes the point well:

> This is a Caribbean island that probably hasn't seen snow since the ice age, yet sent a creditable bobsleigh team to a Winter Olympics. So there's nothing Jamaicans can't do with whatever they happen to have to hand. Take the roadside barbecue pit just off Slipe Road that cooks on half an oil drum, where the customer tables are eight foot electrical-cable spools laid on their sides and the seats are cut from a tree trunk... Dub is part of this astonishing capacity for recycling (2000: 310).

That said, as it has evolved within British culture, like the art of Jamie Reid, it has become increasingly postmodern.

It is worth breaking off at this point to think for a moment about the significance of Jamie Reid. Reid is a British artist, an anarchist with a background in Situationism, who, in 1970, co-founded the radical Suburban Press. He also contributed significantly to forming the image of punk in Britain. His ransom note lettering, for which he used text cut from newspaper headlines, became immediately recognizable following his designs for the cover of The Sex Pistols' album *Never Mind the Bollocks*, as well as the covers for the singles 'Anarchy in the UK', 'God Save the Queen', 'Pretty Vacant' and 'Holidays in the Sun'. However, the key point is the relationship of the art on the cover to the music in the cover. Robert Garnett makes this point well: If the Pistols are the first band that springs to mind at the mention of the word punk, then the first images that would spring to mind would be the visuals created for the Pistols by Jamie Reid. Reid's work is important not just because it amounts to the greatest single contribution to punk's visual identity, but because it also articulated 'the most vital aspects of the Pistols' critique of pop.' He continues (and this point is important):

> Reid's work became even more than the visual equivalent of the music; his visuals inflected the experience of listening to the music to the extent that they became part of it... The most direct way in which

Reid's visuals relate to the Pistol's music is in terms of their montage form, their decentered pillaging of fragments from pop-cultural detritus. The Pistols pilfered their riffs from a repository of stock rock 'n' roll prototypes and, in so doing, literally trashed them, along with any last vestiges of 'authenticity', 'competence', 'originality', 'meaning', 'artiness' and 'significance'. Reid appropriated his materials from the trash populism of tabloid culture and downmarket advertising, and he added to this a vital element in the form of his appropriation of the language of the 'alternative'...'agit-prop' political press (see Garnett 1999: 23).

This kleptic confluence of the visual, the aural, and the ideological helps us to understand the post/punk appreciation of dub. Indeed, thinking of the cover art on reggae albums, the visual and aural are likewise closely related in dub.[12] In post-punk dub, particularly the covers of On-U Sound and, most brilliantly, the cover of *Psychotic Jonkanoo* (which will be discussed below), there is clearly a 'decentered pillaging of fragments', but in this case, the fragments are from an imagined continent in which Obeah men weave powerful, psychedelic spells over those who understand. The cover, therefore, becomes a gateway into an African space.

Following Jameson, Stephen Connor's discussion of rock music as a form of cultural postmodernism helps us towards understanding. He makes the point that, 'along with the fashion industry, the rock industry is the best example of the elastic saleability of the cultural past, with its regular recyclings of its own history in the form of revivals and remakes, comebacks and cover-versions'. He continues, 'in recent years the development of new forms of technology has accelerated and to some degree democratized this process, to the point where the cultural evidence of rock music can be physically dismantled and reassembled in the form of pastiche and collage, much more quickly and uncontrollably than ever before' (1997: 206–207). Unsurprisingly, he notes that sampling technology provides 'the clearest exemplification of the postmodernist aesthetic of the fragment, as well as showing rock music's willingness to live off its own history and forms' (Connor 1997: 207; cf. Goodwin 1990). Again, this takes us to the heart of dub. The point is that most accounts of the postmodern in popular music celebrate the principles of parody, pastiche, and stylistic multiplicity (see Connor 1997: 207; Redhead 1990: 8; Shusterman 1991). And, of course, the endless versioning of rhythms can be understood in poststructuralist terms as an explicit celebration of 'the death of the author' (Barthes 1977: 142–48; see also Partridge 2009c: 512–14).[13] *Bricolage*, the eclectic reappropriation of previous forms, intertextuality, and pastiche represent a shift from modernism's referent of the real. There is no 'real' or authentic version.[14]

This postmodern turn makes possible postmodern politics, in that, as Frith and Horne have commented, 'their very involvement in the pop process gives artists new opportunities for cultural intervention' (1987: 8). To return again to Jamie Reid, his aim was, he argues, 'very much to create images for the street, for newspapers, for TV, which said something complicated quite simply. I mean, you could take an image like the safety-pin through the Queen or the Anarchy flag, which to me were expressing the experiences I'd had throughout the previous sixteen years. And I was coming out of the period of alternative politics, remember that' (quoted in Frith and Horne 1987: 8; see also Garnett 1999). Again, the point is that much post-punk dub, through its montage of sounds – evidenced in the music of The Slits or The Pop Group – put a safety pin through a popular or well-known musical nose and made a political state-ment about music, as well as evoking a particular sonic space – an African space.

Hence, again, we should question Longhurst's assumption that dub is an example of modernism within reggae. The Jamaican producer may have been foregrounded as an artist, an auteur, but the genre itself evolved and the way it came to be received, certainly within post-punk, was fundamentally post-modern.

A Journey of their Own: The Emergence of On-U Sound

The first person that comes to mind when thinking of post-punk dub is undoubtedly the creative force behind the On-U Sound label, Adrian Sher-wood. Indeed, as Gregory Whitfield comments,

> the man hardly needs an introduction... To anyone who has followed roots and culture music closely, it is generally acknowledged that he has produced truly innovative, ground-breaking UK roots music of the highest order since the late-'70s. He had uncompromisingly worked with roots and dub, even when roots music was at its lowest ebb in the early '80s and many people had moved on to early digital dance-hall and slackness.[15] A lot of people considered roots music a spent force, but Adrian had persevered with the form, working with artists he respected, and artists who still had a lot of originality to offer the reggae world, even though they were no longer considered 'fashion-able' (2003).

Sherwood is particularly interesting in that, while there were others produc-ing innovative dub, such as the Mad Professor, it was he who developed the peculiar form of often visceral, hybrid dub that is now so closely identified with the post-punk period. Sherwood epitomizes the dub *bricoleur*, able to move easily between the worlds of post-punk, blues, funk, reggae and rock. Indeed, thinking in terms of the postmodern turn within popular music, I find David Stubbs's reflection on his 'exceptional individual touch' interesting:

> like the legendary dub creators, he's not afraid of getting his fingers on the music, to mess with it, morph and stretch it into something bigger and better. He has a horror of purism, of music as sacred and untouchable. This is why his forays into what might spuriously be described as world music – his collaboration with Talvin Singh on Bim Sherman's *Miracle* and African Head Charge, with whom he broke taboos about 'dubbing up' African music – have worked, informed as they are by love rather than reverence (2007: 39).

The 'horror of purism', of course, to some extent, runs throughout dub, but in post-punk dub, and particularly in Sherwood's work, there seems to be no boundaries. In this sense he provides a thoughtful example of intertextuality and deconstruction in music. There is no reverence for the purity of a genre or a piece of music, but rather simply a collection of sounds and styles to be pillaged and manipulated. Hence, again, it can be understood in terms of Baudrillardian simulation, the penchant of the cultural and sonic nomad, who visits and revisits numerous musical cultures and sources of sound.

Born in London in 1958, Sherwood spent much of his adolescence listening firstly to soul music and then, increasingly, to reggae and, eventually, to punk: 'When I was pretty young', he says, 'I was heavily into soul music. I loved that, but I was really carried away by early reggae music and ska tunes. Those were pretty eccentric, freaky tunes... I was soaking up all that energy, even when I was at school, and when I heard reggae music at the local black clubs I went to. That was when I really got into it' (quoted in Whitfield 2003; see also his interview on *Dub Stories* [DVD]). Again, he recalls the following: 'I started to deejay when I was thirteen, at school, with another friend for fun. We set up a discotheque in the science laboratory...at lunchtime and then we became popular and started to deejay in a club in [High Wycombe], a reggae club... [We] played pop music, soul and reggae at wedding parties' (quoted in Tosi 1998). As well as a growing interest in reggae *per se*, he particularly remembers the impact of the first dub album he listened to, the seminal *King Tubby Meets the Upsetter at the Grass Roots of Dub* (1974). Fascinated by the dub sound, he quickly sought ways to become more involved in the burgeoning London reggae scene. During his school holidays he would work for Soundville, Jet Star's record shop, and then for the Pama and Vulcan labels. After leaving school, driven by an entrepreneurial spirit and, following the demise of a friend's club, he came up with the idea of buying Jamaican records on minor labels and distributing them to independent retailers. As he says, after college, 'when I was seventeen, the owner of that club...a Jamaican... [went] out of business. So we started a distribution company buying and selling reggae records' (quoted in Tosi 1998). As Ari Up of The Slits recalls, 'Adrian was a hustler in a true sense... He managed various reggae artists and toasters, distributed reggae records and sold them out of the back of his van, taught himself how to do studio engineering' (quoted in Reynolds 2005: 90). Such activities, along with a growing involvement in reggae roadshows, not only significantly increased his exposure to reggae culture, but also gave him access to numerous Jamaican artists, many of whom he established close friendships and working relationships with. Hence, when he decided to set up his own label in 1975, Carib Gems, even as a teenager he was able to gather together some significant musicians. For example, the first music he recorded drew on the talents of the calypso bass player Clinton Jack whom he met in a club whilst deejaying, along with the drummer Eric 'Fish' Clarke (who had recently come to England with Prince Far I) and the guitarist 'Crucial' Tony Philips. Similarly, his new label attracted 'Black Uhuru, Dillinger, Trinity, Twinkle Brothers [and] Prince Far I... [The] records were produced by Jamaican producers and we had distribution with the Carib Gems label' (quoted in Tosi 1998).

More importantly, by 1978, just as dub was putting down roots into the emerging post-punk scene, he founded the Hitrun label, which released some of the most creative and important British dub albums of the 1970s. For example, during his work with Carib Gems he had become friendly with the Jamaican deejay Prince Far I, who was recording his album *Message From the King* (1977) on the label. Following the final cut of the album, several rhythm tracks were left over. Sherwood asked Prince Far I if he could work on them himself. The rhythms weren't anything special in themselves and were even, he thought, rather 'boring' (*Dub Stories* [DVD], 2007). However, keen to develop his own sound, this was just the raw material he needed. As Stubbs has commented, 'unencumbered by any musical or technical skills whatsoever, Sherwood showed no signs of intimidation. Though young, he'd already got many miles on the clock, and, egged on and abetted by friends such as Dennis Bovell...he seized his chance to mess on the mixing desk with the gleeful alacrity of a fan let loose in the studio and the natural fearlessness of youth' (2007: 39). Moreover, it's important to understand that, while he might have simply produced dub in the style of his heroes, notably King Tubby and Lee Perry, he was very conscious of the fact that, as we have seen, Jamaican producers sought to create a signature style. In other words, he didn't want to simply produce something that mimicked the Jamaican producers. Rather, he wanted to continue within the sound-system tradition by articulating his own ideas and, thereby, developing a distinctively Sherwoodian sound. 'It's not a matter of whether I'm black or white. It's just that I hear things that someone in England would hear, someone who had experiences that were different from the experiences of a first generation black child.' He continues, 'the fact that I'm white is only relevant to the fact that I have different references in my childhood than, perhaps, the first generation black [children] that I grew up with' (Sherwood, in interview with Tosi 1998). This is important to understand about the punk and post-punk attitude to dub and reggae. For example, Paul Simonon of The Clash recalls that when they famously covered Junior Murvin's 'Police and Thieves', 'instead of mimicking it, we used it to create something different: our own punk rock style. Lee Perry, the producer of the original "Police and Thieves", said we ruined it! To his ears, yeah, we probably did. But people would go and check out the original song, which would take them on a journey of their own' (2005: 3). A journey of their own! This is exactly what was being sought within British dub. They were seeking to recreate, from Jamaican raw materials, an authentically local *version* – the outernational sound, London style! Hence, overdubbing found sounds and noises on the leftover rhythms from *Message From the King*, and Sherwood produced what was actually his second dub album, *Cry Tuff Encounter: Chapter 1* (1978), a truly outernational contribution to dub – a truly British *version*. His first dub album, which the 19-year-old Sherwood worked on at the same time, was the seminal *Dub From Creation* (1978), performed by his newly formed studio collective, Creation Rebel, and mixed by Dennis Bovell and Sid Bucknor. (Released at virtually the same time as *Cry Tuff Encounter: Chapter 1*, I can still remember the excitement with which this album was received by dubheads in the UK – or, at least, in Lancashire.) These albums were closely followed by Creation Rebel's *Close Encounters of the Third World* (1978) and *Rebel Vibrations* (1979). Also in 1978, with Tony Henry, the bass player from Misty in Roots, he recorded Creation Rebel's seminal *Starship Africa*, which was eventually released on another of Sherwood's labels, 4D Rhythms – indeed, it was the only album to be released on the label, which, in 1980, evolved into On-U Sound Recordings.

Creation Rebel was primarily a studio band, created by Sherwood to undertake experimental, studio-based projects. That said, between 1978 and 1983 it became one of the world's first live dub bands. Nevertheless, there were no fixed members of Creation Rebel as such. It was always essentially fluid and experimental. Like The Fall's constantly changing membership, the only identifiably continuous feature being Mark E. Smith, so Creation Rebel was oriented around the creativity and distinctive production skills of Sherwood. Having said that, it included some of the most important figures in dub at that

time, several of whom would become Roots Radics, one of the most impor-
tant dub session bands of the 1980s. Indeed, the original band was made up
of The Arabs, another studio outfit who had done backing work for Prince Far
I and who are now primarily remembered for their work on Sherwood's *Cry
Tuff Encounter: Chapter 1*. Over the years the band evolved and included key
figures in the late-1970s and early-1980s dub and post-punk scenes, including
Fish Clarke (drums), Clinton Jack (bass), Crucial Tony (guitar), Clifton 'Bigga'
Morrison (keyboards), Dr. Pablo/Peter Stroud (Melodica), Lincoln Valentine
'Style' Scott (drums),[16] Keith Levene (guitar), 'Lizard' Logan (bass), John Lydon
(vocals), and Jah Wobble (bass).

Released in March 1978, Creation Rebel's first album, *Dub from Creation*,
began life as rhythm tracks recorded in Jamaica. These were then brought to
Gooseberry Studios in London, where Sherwood added overdubs. On com-
pletion, Clarke returned to Jamaica and the rest of the group reformed as
The Arabs for Prince Far I's European tour. The next incarnation of Creation
Rebel produced the seminal and ethereal *Starship Africa* in late-1978. Surprisingly unacknowledged by Stubbs in his 'Primer' on Sherwood (Stubbs 2007),
Starship Africa stands alone in the world of dub as a carefully crafted piece of
spacious sonic art, becoming for many in the early 1980s *the* album for those
wanting to explore inner space, African space. Like much psychedelic, progressive rock, its layered, expansive soundscape, textured with intricate and
delicate fragments of sound, and washed over with lush ambient electronic
orchestration, seemed particularly conducive to the effects of cannabis. As
Steve Barker has put it, 'it has no cerebral equivalent. *Starship Africa* can be
interpreted critically as forming the third point of a sonic triangle equilaterally
occupied by the disparate output of The Grateful Dead and Tangerine Dream'
(2007a). However, although completed in 1978, the album was not released
until 1980 and then only on the obscure 4D Rhythms label. Barker relates the
history of the album:

> Just after the completion of the *Dub from Creation* LP, the young Sher-
> wood found himself with the basic Creation Rebel cutting a bunch
> of rhythms in the studio for a character with the wonderful name of
> 'DJ Superstar'... Most of these tunes had bass lines from Tony Henry
> of Misty In Roots. Sherwood had hummed the bass lines and Tony has
> re-created them – hence the melodic quality of the bass lines on the
> finished tracks. What happened to these original tracks, who knows.
> But two years later Sherwood and Chris Garland, a friend from Chel-
> tenham, were starting up a record company/agency in London's Soho
> with the strange name of 4D Rhythms. The agency side of the busi-
> ness was to run acts like Dexy's and Medium Medium, but they were
> also desperate to get some vinyl out on the street. In fact, so desper-

ate that Sherwood turned to the bunch of rhythms he had created a couple of years earlier, which up to that time he had considered quite 'lame'. They were up for transformation! Style Scott, in from Jamaica, did not so much overdub, but rather played live over the original drum tracks from Charlie 'Eskimo' Fox. Freed from the stylistic requirements of the Roots Radics, 'Scotty' was encouraged to loosen-up and lay rolls and splashes all over the tracks in his now inimitable style. Six percussionists, that is the rest of the musicians and engineers and whoever was around the studio appeared phasing in and out of one channel, creating a trippy treble effect – which hid the fact that they were all out of time. Amongst these players was Sucker, a friend of Del from Osibisa, who occasionally gives the percussion mix a rich calypso feel. When the album was being mixed Chris was urging Adrian to get madder, 'more reverb, more delay...' But nothing could be so mad as the idea to mix the tracks blind. That is, turn over the quarter inch tape on the deck and feed in the effects and run the mix backwards, turn it back over for the finished product. Somehow, it made a crazy kind of sense. So much so that the mix was finished in one day! On the original vinyl, there was just one track listed for each side. The title track was credited as 'A Soundtrack from a Forthcoming Motion Picture' (Barker 2007a).

This approach to music could hardly be more different from a carefully crafted modernist composition.

Moreover, it is interesting that the sonic ambience created by *Starship Africa* influenced William Gibson's writing of the postmodern, cyberpunk classic, *Neuromancer* (1984). The strange, alien otherness of the music finds its literary equivalent in the postmodern dystopia of cyberpunk. As we have already commented, Gibson makes conspicuous reference to Rastafarian and post-punk themes and, more particularly, to 'the bass-heavy rock-steady of Zion dub' (1995: 230). He is describing Creation Rebel. Reading *Neuromancer* now, as Barker observes, 'one can only hear Creation Rebel's *Starship Africa* pounding out of the in-flight sound system on board the dread-crewed space-tug Marcus Garvey' (2007a). Again, as noted above, the listener is acoustemologically transported by *Starship Africa* to an inner African space.

Two further experimental Creation Rebel albums, recorded and released in the late-1970s, *Close Encounters of the Third World* (1978) – mixed by Prince Jammy – and *Rebel Vibrations* (1979), have been described by Sherwood, rather enigmatically, as exploring 'the unique possibilities of space in sound within the disciplined structures of rhythm, using bass line melodies and relying as much on the understated side of the overall result as on the overstated' (quoted in Barker 2007a). By the turn of the 1980s, members of Creation Rebel were beginning to spend most of their time working as the backing band for various Jamaican artists, notably Prince Far I, Jah Woosh, Prince Hammer, and Bim Sherman. Indeed, as a relatively loose collective with numerous other demands on their time as session musicians needing to earn a living, the band was beginning to drift apart. As well as working for visiting Jamaican artists, most of the musicians were also contributing to a range of other On-U Sound post-punk dub projects, such as Mark Stewart and the Maffia, New Age Steppers, Singers and Players, African Head Charge, Playgroup, Noah House of Dread, Undivided Roots, The Mothmen, London Underground, and Dub Syndicate. That said, the early 1980s saw Creation Rebel return with three albums, *Psychotic Jonkanoo* (1981), *Lows and Highs* (1982), and, with New Age Steppers, *Threat to Creation* (1981).

As his career and that of On-U Sound evolved, so intertextuality became more pronounced. Although rooted in reggae, Sherwood and the growing On-U Sound collective increasingly worked with (and dismantled) a range of genres, drawing particularly from punk and post-punk. The New Age Steppers, for example, included Ari Up of The Slits, and 'Mother Don't Cry' on *Psychotic Jonkanoo* featured, rather unusually, John Lydon on vocal harmony. Indeed, Sherwood even produced tracks for *Slates* by The Fall at the Berry Street studio[17] and frequently worked with post-punk musicians such as Mark Stewart, Keith Levene and Jah Wobble. Hence, as well as being deeply involved in the reggae community, he was a respected and sought-after producer within post-punk circles. As Sherwood recalls:

> I knew John Lydon well and it was through John that I got to know Keith Levene and Jah Wobble... Ari Up, Neneh Cherry, Junior and I, we all lived in a squat down Battersea way, and John Lydon was living with Nora...round the corner. John Lydon used to visit us, and we all hung out together... John really knew his reggae; he loved his reggae. I can tell you that John really helped the progress of roots and culture in Britain at that time... You should realize that it was John Lydon who suggested that I work with Keith Levene, who I was really impressed by, and then through him I linked up with Jah Wobble, which was great for me at the time. I was so happy to work with Keith, because Keith just had such an original sound, and I knew I could translate that originality he had into a dub context, and it worked totally if you listen to those Creation Rebel and Singers and Players records. He also played guitar on some of those New Age Steppers sessions... (quoted in Whitfield 2003; see also Street Howe 2009: 175).

Again, as post-punk evolved, Sherwood found himself increasingly at its creative and political heart. As Stubbs comments:

[he] found himself bumping into, hanging out and sharing squats with a range of new characters and adventurers the scene had thrown up, including Mark Stewart, The Slits, and Judy Nylon. Sherwood acted as a sort of social conduit, a person who made meetings of minds happen. Sherwood...found himself breathing in the new clouds of eclectic energy in the air, with the political (such as Rock Against Racism, Misty in Roots's 'People Unite', the Legalise Cannabis Campaign) fusing quite logically with the groundbreaking experimentalism of the new music coming out of West London and Bristol, in which unheard-of alliances were being struck between black and white music. This unruly cross-fertilisation got in among Sherwood's creative bloodstream (2007: 39).

Bearing the above in mind, arguably Sherwood's most significant contribution to British dub – although his contributions are so extensive and varied that to single out individual examples is a little artificial – was the founding of On-U Sound in 1980. Founded with his partner at the time, the photographer and musician Kishi Yamamoto, On-U Sound became an important catalyst for the flowering of a new wave of British dub. In particular, while Creation Rebel had marked Sherwood out as an idiosyncratic and creative producer, On-U Sound seemed to encourage the proliferation of numerous innovative studio-based projects. Indeed, as Barrow and Dalton point out, 'what is clear is that it laid the foundation for much of the modern UK dub scene, with its emphasis on layered percussion and sound effects' (1997: 353). Whether producing the hard-edged, eclectic funk-oriented, post-punk dub of Tackhead's *Friendly as a Hand Grenade* (1989), or the abstract, disorienting noise of the Missing Brazilians' *Warzone* (1984), or combining acoustic reggae with strings from an Indian movie playback orchestra or, indeed, seamlessly blending blues and dub as on the Little Axe albums, Sherwoodian pastiche has consistently sought to efface genre boundaries and challenge the notion of a musical norm. To a large extent, Sherwood's work can be understood in terms of a 'psychotic Jonkanoo', to quote the title of one of his best albums. Jonkanoo (Junkanool/ Jonkunnu) is a festival involving street parades that take place in Jamaica and other islands of the Caribbean (particularly Nassau in the Bahamas) during the Christmas holidays. While the origins of the festival are debatable, it is an eclectic, vibrant celebration drawing on a range of traditions, with little sense that anything is taboo, and with close links to African and Caribbean indigenous spiritualities. The focus of the festival is the mythical 'John Canoe' (John Koonah/John Kooner), represented by the leader or chief dancer in the parade. His name is significant in that, as Carolyn Cooper comments (quoting John Rashford), '"objects named 'John' are often associated in Jamaica with the world of spirits", thus underscoring the African genesis of what now appears to be secularized religious practices transformed into entertainment in the annual Jonkunnu ritual celebration' (2004: 174). Similarly, Stephen Nissenbaum has described the ritual as it was performed in nineteenth-century North Carolina:

> Essentially, it involved a band of black men – generally young – who dressed themselves in ornate and often bizarre costumes. Each band was led by a man who was variously dressed in animal horns, elaborate rags, female disguise, whiteface (and wearing a gentleman's wig!), or simply his 'Sunday-go-to-meeting-suit'. Accompanied by music, the band marched along the roads from plantation to plantation, town to town, accosting whites along the way and sometimes even entering their houses. In the process, the men performed elaborate and (to white observers) grotesque dances that were probably of African origin' (Nissenbaum 1997: 285; see also Dunn 1999).

Indeed, Nissenbaum, not inappropriately, draws parallels with the wassailing tradition of medieval Britain, in that both can be understood as ritualized inversions of established social hierarchies. However, the point is that central to Sherwood's oeuvre there is, as is clearly evident on Creation Rebel's *Psychotic Jonkanoo*, a sense in which this music is conspicuously rooted in and intended to evoke 'African space'. Indeed, the collage on the cover of *Psychotic Jonkanoo*, which combines Rastas, dreadlocks, and what appears to be a headless man feeling his way through the disorienting montage, introduces the listener into the sonic experience prior to the vinyl reaching the turntable. Designed by Sherwood's partner, Kishi Yamamoto, it can be described as a psychedelic African interpretation of Jamie Reid's work. This also describes the music, the first two tracks, 'The Dope' and 'African Space', being, in themselves, excellent introductions to the whole of Sherwood's work. Hence, while he is an unapologetic Englishman seeking to articulate his own particular experiences through dub, *Pyschotic Wassailing* would not have been a good title for the album. Sherwood's is a psychedelic, post-punk vision of Africa.

Added to this, there is an eclectic and vibrant mix of genres and sounds that transcend the ordinary, subvert authorities, transgress boundaries, and invert established ways of making music. Indeed, going beyond Jonkanoo – which is a particular cultural tradition – to add the adjective 'psychotic', indicates a further development in Sherwood's work, in that it suggests that, as in psychoses, contact with reality may become highly distorted. The On-U sound is a radical inversion and transgression of the norm. Musical signifiers and everyday noises float free, to be understood only in their relation to each other. Deconstruction is *de rigueur*; questions seem to be continually raised about the nature of the music; there is a denial that any particular musical 'text' is settled and stable. Disparate genres and sounds are weaved together into a new musical fabric, instruments are stripped out, noises added, soundtracks speeded up, slowed down or played in reverse. Sonic collage, the postmodern style, is the epitome of the On-U sound – psychotic Jonkanoo.

One of Sherwood's most interesting projects was African Head Charge,[18] the creative centre of which was the percussionist Bonjo Iyabinghi Noah. A loose collective of musicians formed in the wake of Creation Rebel, it was initially inspired by an enigmatic comment of Brian Eno's that Sherwood had read concerning his 'vision of a psychedelic Africa'. As might be expected, the idea of an African 'head charge' was enormously appealing to Sherwood. As with many dub experimentalists, there was, if not, strictly speaking, a psychedelic interest, then certainly an interest in the reception of sound whilst being, to quote the title track of another of Sherwood's albums, 'stoned immaculate' – which, significantly, references and samples Jim Morrison[19] (whose band, The Doors, took its name, of course, from Aldous Huxley's psychedelic classic *The Doors of Perception*).[20] 'The idea', remarked Sherwood, 'was to make a psychedelic, but serious, African dub record' (quoted in Toop 1995a: 121).

African Head Charge's debut album, *My Life in a Hole in the Ground* (1981) – still one of the most interesting pieces of work to emerge from the On-U Sound studio – was similarly inspired, not only by Eno's 'vision of a psychedelic Africa', but, more specifically, by the seminal album Eno created with David Byrne of the Talking Heads, *My Life in the Bush of Ghosts* (1981) – arguably, one of the most important albums of the 1980s.[21] It's also worth noting that this latter album was, in turn, inspired by Amos Tutuola's 1952 novel of the same name. The book itself is a strange text, an esoteric African confluence of the exotic, the spiritual and the paranormal. Indeed, to the Western mind, it can, quite accurately, be understood in terms of dubbed reality; reality made strange and ghostly; reality interpreted from another, distinctively African perspective; reality filtered through the prism of the psychotic Jonkanoo. That is to say, the novel is, in many ways, the African literary equivalent of Sherwood's music. Writing about, for example, the 'television-handed ghostess', his work, as David Toop argues,

> anticipates the musical Afro-futurism exemplified in the 1960s and '70s by Sun Ra, Funkadelic, Fela Anikulapo-Kuti, Sly Stone, Lee Perry, and Miles Davis. Dylan Thomas described his writing as 'thronged, grisly and bewitching'. The book is a visceral accumulation of disgust, fear, torment, and humiliation, but its narrative, the tribulations of a young boy who finds himself in a parallel world of weird, frightening ghosts, contains echoes of such familiar stories as *Alice in Wonderland* or *The Wizard of Oz* (2006: 5; see also Toop 1995a: 121–23).

Of course, the narratives of both the book and the recording by Eno and Byrne, not to mention African Head Charge's homage, breach boundaries. For example, as with reggae and dub, the distance between Africa and the West is contracted. Tutuola was writing in a colonial context within which African indigenous ideas mixed freely with European thought, and Eno and Byrne were working in a situation in which specifically West African, African-diasporic and Arabic music were stimulating new understandings about composition. As Eric Tamm observes, 'both Eno and Byrne had, for a number of years, been interested in non-Western musical styles, particularly those of sub-Saharan Africa and of the Arabic cultural sphere: in the Talking Heads/ Eno records, such influences function implicitly, but on *My Life in the Bush of Ghosts* they become explicit' (1995: 161). Indeed, Eno's own understanding of what he was aiming at is very similar to Sherwood's approach to dub, in that he wanted to create 'music...done in sympathy with and with consciousness of music of the rest of the world, rather than just with Western music or just with rock music. It's almost collage music, like grafting one piece of culture onto a piece of another...and trying to make them work as a coherent music idea, and also trying to make something you can dance to' (quoted in Tamm 1995: 161). Again, as Toop comments, 'there were signs that dub aesthetics and funk beats were subverting whitebred fantasies of musical sophistication. Punk's embrace of roots reggae and dub, and the punk-funk of James Chance, heard on the Eno-produced *No New York* album of 1978, were two indications of growing inclusiveness' (2006: 9; see also Schaeffer 1990: 113–50). Furthermore, in both works, the spiritual and the material merge. In the book, Tutuola introduces the reader to an eight-year-old boy who, abandoned during a slave raid, flees into 'the bush' – 'a place of ghosts and spirits' – and on the recording, Eno and Byrne take the listener into the sonic bush. Apart from the carefully crafted otherness of the music itself, the ghostly and the spiritual are made explicit in the samples of, for example, Dunya Yusin, a Lebanese mountain singer – lifted from the album *The Human Voice in the World of Islam* – the fragments of a sermon broadcast by Rev. Paul Morton in New Orleans on 'Help Me Somebody', and, of course, most famously, the sampled rhetoric of an exorcist struggling to dispense with a malevolent spirit on 'The Jezebel Spirit'. As Eno said at the time, 'It satisfies a lot of interesting ideas for me. One is making the ordinary interesting... The other is finding music where music wasn't supposed to have been. And another is finding a pre-delivered message, which you put in a context so that the meaning is changed, or the context amplifies certain aspects of the meaning' (quoted in Toop 2006: 6). Again, the point is that this is, to a large extent, an articulation of the rationale informing Sherwood's various projects. Hence, for example, on *My Life in a*

Hole in the Ground this intertextuality and pastiche is replicated *in dub*. The 'hole in the ground' was Berry Street Studios in London and the music, rejecting the notion of a norm, was an experimental work, 'a search for a fresh musical template... At the time it was made... it was a case of "What next?" "How about trying this?" "Will this work?" (Barker 1998a). Less coherent than *My Life in the Bush of Ghosts*, it is nevertheless an impressive and important work of British dub created at a time when, as Barker says, 'samplers, even in their most rudimentary form, had not yet arrived in commercial studios'. Consequently, 'the introduction of pre-captured sound had to be managed by the use of precious channels or the mind-numbingly tedious process of multi-edits' (Barker 1998a).

As some indication of the bewildering, sometimes disturbing, otherness of the dub created by Sherwood on *My Life in a Hole in the Ground*, David Lynch originally used 'Far Away Chant' off the album as the soundtrack to the torture scene in *Wild at Heart* (1990). As Sherwood recalls:

> it came out of the same sessions we had been working on with Prince Far I and the Dub Syndicate for the *Cry Tuff* album. There was a slow and hard track, 'Plant Up', with a classic, growling Far I chant about the herb... Anyway, I wanted something even slower, more threatening, heavier, so I took a similar sounding rhythm track, and slowed it right down, right down, making it ridiculously slow and heavy, and laid Far I's anti-nuclear chant over the top... David Lynch took that track, and slowed it down even further, which made it even more threatening, and used it in *Wild at Heart* as part of his soundtrack which really pleased me. The mood of the scene he chose it for was pretty dark... (quoted in Whitfield 2003).

It added, as Toop comments,

> further dimensions of hoodoo otherness to Lynch's trademark shade-world of sexual violence, Prince Far I's warping soundblast vocals rising up from the catacombs...in this unholy place a steady throb of Rastafarian repeater and funde drums somehow twisted in the unconscious to draw on archaic fears, fear of voodoo, fear of the primeval occult, the old unhealthy fear of Rastas as 'menacing devils with snake nests for hair (1995a: 120–21).

Similarly experimental is African Head Charge's second album *Environmental Studies* (1982). While we have seen that some of Sherwood's album titles are significant or peculiarly apposite, reflecting again something of a postmodern attitude, others were chosen fairly arbitrarily, having little reference to the actual music.[22] In this case, 'Environmental Studies' just happened to be a subject at school that Sherwood had been interested in. As for the music, seeking a truly avant-garde dub sound, Sherwood recalls talking to Geoff Travis of Rough Trade and Pere Ubu's avant-garde front man David Thomas about 'water noises and other ambient sounds playing "louder" than the band' (Barker 1997). Indeed, according to Barker, the particular sound Sherwood produced on *Environmental Studies* was greatly indebted to the rather basic studio at Berry Street. 'They had an old style reverb plate just waiting to be used and abused...a mainly stone-built toilet where Adrian stacked big speakers with an auxiliary microphone to obtain the sound of distant drums' (Barker 1997). It's perhaps not surprising therefore that the On-U sound changed when Sherwood moved to Southern Studios and started using state-of-the-art digital studio equipment. This is evident on African Head Charge's third album, *The Drastic Season* (1983), which is a disorienting album clearly not intended to attract commercial airplay. As Sherwood himself comments, it's a series of 'experiments in active frequencies, out of time noises, rhythms within rhythms, and endless tape edits (edits on edits) resulting in the ultimate cut-up and paste job' (quoted in Barker and Parker 2007a).

In 1984, whilst in New York working on a remix of Akabu's 'Watch Yourself' for Tommy Boy Records, Sherwood met Keith Leblanc. For various reasons, this meeting was a pivotal event in the history of On-U Sound, in that it marked the beginning of some of the most creative and important collaborative projects in Anglo-American dub. While Leblanc had released solo work on Tommy Boy, mixing DMX drumbeats[23] with his own distinctive drum sound, it was Malcolm X's *No Sell Out* (1983), on which he sampled the rhetoric of the civil rights activist, that caught the attention of Sherwood. The meeting was also significant, in that it was Leblanc who introduced Sherwood to the guitarist Skip McDonald and the bassist Doug Wimbish, who had been working together since the mid-1970s on various disco and funk projects and who had met Leblanc in 1979 at Sugarhill Records. Indeed, together the three of them became Sugarhill's house rhythm section, providing backing for such important rap records as 'Rapper's Delight' by the Sugarhill Gang, Grandmaster Flash's 'The Message', and 'White Lines (Don't Do It)'. While they continued to work together, their meeting with Sherwood brought them into the mainstream of British dub. Perhaps the most conspicuous of these projects was the funk-oriented Tackhead (to which we'll return below). However, the point here is that, by 1986, African Head Charge's style had changed. Under the influence of McDonald, Wimbish and Leblanc, *Off the Beaten Track* (1986), while, to some extent, it was less avant-garde and experimental, it was more funk-oriented and disciplined than earlier African Head Charge material. That said, as Eno and Byrne had done, also evident was a desire to experiment more formally with a range of genres drawn from world music. Consequently, *Off the Beaten Track*

> sounded like nothing else around at the time... [It was a] combination of fat [*sic*] beats and ethnic chants [that provided] the template which many lesser lights would attempt to emulate over the ensuing years... The title *Off The Beaten Track* was not just an example of a great piece of wordplay, but also incredibly apt, as the music was not only a departure for On-U Sound, but also a landmark album for what was to become the whole new ethno-beat strand within the commercial category of what we now know as 'world music' (Barker and Parker 2007a).

The 1990s, however, saw African Head Charge turn back to the Jamaican roots of dub with the development of explicitly churchical rhythms and chants. This is conspicuous on two of their best albums, *In Pursuit of Shashamane Land* (1993) and especially the slightly earlier *Songs of Praise* (1990), the latter being, arguably, their most accomplished work.

While African Head Charge was always central to Sherwood's creativity, he is quick to point out that he is also 'very proud of the period with Dub Syndicate' (quoted in Tosi 1998). Arguably the backbone of the On-U Sound label, the collective quickly became oriented around the talents of the drummer Style Scott, who had become well-known for his work with Roots Radics and Prince Far I and who had already worked with Sherwood on Creation Rebel projects. As he recalls,

> after Creation Rebel got broken up... I was still coming back up with rhythms and these were much stronger than the ones I was coming up with in the past. So we just decide that 'boy we had better start to do something, you know; do some funny mix and put it out ourselves. Dubs and funny noises that's how it went you know, really and truly... Some of those years I would be just bringing up those rhythms, but other times I would stay maybe a month or two and then go back to Jamaica while I leave [Adrian Sherwood] here with these rhythms working on them and doing whatever he wanted to do with them. Then I would be getting a call in Jamaica going 'Scotty-boy we've done an album irie, irie'... Adrian is a man who likes the acoustic sound. Myself love the acoustic more as well, so it started there. As things started to get much stronger we decided to name the thing 'Dub Syndicate'... (Free Radical Sounds, 2007).

Arguably, Dub Syndicate was Britain's most influential dub collective during the 1980s and 1990s and is, as Greg Kot has commented, 'in many ways... the starting point for the current underground scene' (1997: 150). Albums such as *The Pounding System* (1982), *Tunes From the Missing Channel* (1985), *Stoned Immaculate* (1992) and *Ital Breakfast* (1996) quickly became classics and formative standard bearers for dub in the UK. The name Dub Syndicate first appeared in the credits to Prince Far I's *Cry Tuff Dub Encounter: Chapter 3* (1980). Indeed, as Sherwood himself has noted, 'the "original Dub Syndicate" predates both Creation Rebel (which formed in late 1977) and Roots Radics (1979)' (Sherwood 1996). Moreover, for all three bands – Dub Syndicate, Creation Rebel and Roots Radics – the catalyst in their formation was Prince Far I. Sherwood continues, 'Dr Pablo, Clifton "Bigga" Morrison... Sucker (Osibisa) and Crucial Tony...were all responsible for the final overdubs on the now legendary Prince Far I and the Arabs *Cry Tuff Dub Encounter* series. The early albums were credited as mixed by Dub Syndicate. At this stage the Dub Syndicate was literally that and had not evolved into a conventional band' (Sherwood 1996). Although Scott contributed to the early albums – *Pounding System* (1982), *One Way System* (1983), *North of the River Thames* (1984) – along with the drummer Charlie 'Eskimo' Fox,[24] it was not until 1985 and *Tunes from the Missing Channel* that he became the creative force behind the band. Moreover, this is a pivotal album, in that, as Barker and David Parker argue, 'what we now know today as "new roots" can track its modern development back to this album as its source. What was different about *Tunes* though was the discovery of some new technology' (2007b).

Developing his links with avant-garde rock and, thereby, going beyond the experimentalism of many Jamaican producers at the time, Sherwood worked in Switzerland with Marc Hollander of Aksak Maboul.[25] It was during this period that, with Kishi Yamamoto, he discovered the 'Emulator'.[26]

> Hence the delight in pulling the sitar sound from the keyboard which resulted in the almost prosaically titled 'Ravi Shankar Pt.1'. Also, before sampling had a name, Sherwood stumbled upon the technique of what he called 'captured sound' by utilizing the locking function in the AMS digital harmoniser. No need to bleed all over the tape deck à la Double D and Steinski as a result of razored edits. Instead, you just invoke Emperor Rosko via machine triggers to appear in 'The Show Is Coming'. And so in *Tunes* we have the earliest manifestation of the use of the kind of technology which is today commonplace in the production of the new roots reggae/dub all over the world' (Barker and Parker 2007b).

Moreover, this collaboration brought together (with members of African Head Charge and Creation Rebel) Bim Sherman, Jah Wobble, Keith Levene and the creative genius of Steve Beresford. The result was *Tunes from the Missing Channel*, 'one of the best-selling albums in the entire On-U catalogue' (Barker and Parker 2007b).

Finally, although it strays a little outside the principal period covered in this thesis, it is worth noting that in the late-1980s, On-U Sound became identified with Tackhead,[27] a funk-oriented project that combined the talents of Sherwood, Leblanc, McDonald and Wimbish. Critically acclaimed and with numerous admirers, including Mick Jagger, formed in 1986, Tackhead began life as Fats Comet, a typically Sherwoodian studio-based collective committed to the development of experimental dub-funk. That said, while the music is clearly dub-oriented, it is bewilderingly eclectic and has been described by one French journalist as, not inappropriately, 'outlaw-hardcore-dub-ska-punk-funk-industrial-jazz-rap' (Plantenga 1997: 172). Beginning with a number of 12"s, their first album, *Tackhead Tape Time*, was released under the name Gary Clail's Tackhead Sound System after its confrontational and idiosyncratic 'MC'/'chanter'/'rapper'. Described as 'Billy Bragg in dub' (Plantenga 1997: 173), Clail was a scaffolder and used-car salesman from Bristol who had been introduced to Sherwood by Mark Stewart. Indeed, throughout the late-1980s, he became the regular support for a range of On-U Sound events, and the musicians on his first 12", *Half Cut for Confidence*, although credited as 'TOTP—The Occult Technology of Power', were essentially the future members of Tackhead.[28] That said, we have seen that this was by no means unusual. For example, the various musicians that made up Tackhead were also working as the Maffia, backing Mark Stewart – 'a collaboration which resulted in probably some of the most deranged Hip-Mutant-Funk-Metal-Dub-Hop records ever to be made' (Barker 2007b; see also Fisher 2008). While much of Tackhead's work is, as Barker indicates, experimental and postmodern in approach, arguably their most important and certainly most accessible work emerged out of Bernard Fowler's modernizing influence on the band. Introduced to the band by Mick Jagger, Fowler – an accomplished musician and singer who has worked with, among others, Ryuchi Sakamoto, Gill Scott-Heron, Sly & Robbie, Material, Bootsy Collins, Philip Glass, Duran Duran, Herb Alpert, Paul Carrack, Yoko Ono and The Rolling Stones, as well as his own project The Peach Boys – gave, as Parker comments, 'a soulful edge to their beats…making them more accessible to a wider audience' (2007b). Arguably, he also ensured that their album *Friendly as a Hand Grenade* established Tackhead as 'a vast monumental influence on the music of the eighties and nineties' (Parker 2007; see also Plantenga 1997).

Concluding Comments

As post-punk dub evolved, the notion of a culture of resistance, as discussed in the previous chapter, retreated before an increased emphasis on the affective. While some of the terminology continues and while artists such as Bim Sherman and Prince Far I were seeking to communicate something of their deep Rastafarian spirituality, overall there was decreasing religio-political significance being attached to the music. Even some of the titles of the tracks and albums began to have a fundamentally postmodern feel. Little Axe's *The Wolf That House Built* (1994) is a salient example of this. It vaguely reminds one of well-known themes in children's stories and, as such, conjures up images that have little to do with the actual music. However, in the final analysis, it's a collection of words that mean nothing. The point is that, as we have seen, as dub evolved in the post-punk period, particularly within the On-U Sound studios, it became a cognitive and symbolic veneer. As I have suggested, dub became increasingly carnivalesque, a Jonkanoo of signs with few stable or fixed meanings attached. Signifiers such as 'Africa' and 'Babylon', in post-punk dub, became loosened from their Rastafarian and countercultural moorings and began to float free, whereas in punk, there was still something of the original signification.

Having said that, thinking of popular music *per se*, Goodwin has argued that 'while it is possible to discover categories of postmodern music and perhaps practices of postmodern consumption, the grand claims of postmodern theory remain insubstantial as an account of the current state of popular music' (1991: 174–75). He is particularly critical of what he understands to be a superficial understanding of pastiche that is often applied to 'postmodern rock' and particularly music videos and television. Likewise, he is critical of theorists, such as Angela McRobbie and Deena Weinstein, who argue that rock music is 'postmodern by virtue of its eclecticism, through its foundations in interracial, intercultural and intertextual practices' (1991: 176). Essentially, such theses that focus on eclecticism as the cardinal motif of postmodernism argue that (a) rock can be understood in terms of eclecticism and intertextuality, (b) eclecticism and intertextuality are central to postmodernism, therefore (c) rock is postmodern. The problem is, Goodwin argues (a little unfairly), this *explains* little about the music itself – or, indeed, about postmodernism. Bearing in mind that popular music *per se* (including reggae) has roots in a range of genres, most notably blues and gospel, arguably eclecticism and intertextuality have always been a feature. Hence, according to this line of argument, all popular music is, to some extent, postmodern. Consequently, 'postmodernism might as well be a parasite *description* of post-war pop, rather than an explanatory paradigm' (Goodwin 1991: 176; original emphasis). This, of course, is a persuasive argument with which I do not fundamentally disagree. Certainly, it's important for postmodernism to be an explanatory theory, rather than little more than a label. However, Goodwin's conclusions are a little too sweeping.

There are, of course, some forms of popular music that *can* be considered postmodern and, I have argued, post-punk dub is one of them. Indeed, I would argue that postmodern theory is a useful explanatory tool because it helps us to distinguish between dub, as it emerged out of reggae within Jamaican sound-system culture, and dub as it was developed within the very different milieu of post-punk Britain. It also helps us to identify the continuities between both forms of dub. For example, Richard Middleton has commented that 'a blurring of the high/low boundary can be seen, symptom of a broader emergent postmodern formation, marked by acceptance of commodity form, valorization of local, fragmented identities, celebration of ironic surface. Such blurring is certainly apparent on the aesthetic level: compare minimalism and rave, for example; or try to categorise Brian Eno, Orbital, Psychic TV or Glenn Branca' (2001: 224). We have seen that some far more cogent examples might be added to the list, such as the various experimental projects developed within the On-U Sound studios.

This, however, raises further questions relating to post-punk dub and cultural appropriation. To understand the principal point here, we need to begin by reminding ourselves that not only is post-punk dub a fundamentally postmodern genre, but dub *per se* has postmodern potential in that it decentres and redistributes cultural power through what we would now understand to be an essentially intertextual methodology. For example, we have demonstrated that, whereas official, mainstream, 'modern' culture values originality, identity and uniqueness, dub elevates repetition and plural identity. As Hebdige has argued, 'the cut 'n' mix attitude was that no one owns a rhythm or a sound. You just borrow it, use it and give it back to the people in a slightly different form. To use the language of Jamaican reggae and dub, you just *version* it. And anyone can do a "version"' (1987: 141). Again, versioning is 'a democratic principle because it implies that no one has the final say. Everybody has a chance to make a contribution. And no one's version is treated as Holy Writ' (Hebdige 1987: 14). Having said that, thinking of a Gramscian understanding of the process of cultural hegemony (see Grossberg 1992: 244–55), is there a sense in which the dominant British rock/post-punk culture has negotiated and maintained hegemony by transforming and diffusing the countercultural potential of Rastafarian religio-political discourse in reggae and dub? Through the work of those who are not as/not at all persuaded by the Rastafarian convictions that inspired earlier producers such as Augustus Pablo and Lee Perry, there is a sense in which 'Babylon' has absorbed, diluted, and even emptied dub of its religio-political content. In other words, dub's democratizing, post-modern strengths have, perhaps more than any other form of popular music, undermined its religio-political potency. The point is that, while we have seen that punks identified with and, in their own way, were able to continue the countercultural discourse, generally speaking, the transition to post-punk has all but transformed the original signification. Of course, even punks filtered the discourse. As Don Letts recalls, 'a lot of young people during the mid-seventies were taking what they needed from Rastafari and left what they didn't' (2007: 65). Hence, by the post-punk period, 'Africa', 'the herb', 'Babylon', 'Jah', 'dread', and even Alexander Bedward became largely floating signifiers. Bedward is a good example of this, for, as discussed in Chapter 1, he is an important religio-political figure in Jamaican history. However, while celebrated in dub by the Jamaican deejay Prince Far I – 'Bedward the Flying Preacher', on Singers and Players, *Staggering Heights* – the dub remix of that track by the British dub collective Zion Train (1996) retains little of Prince Far I's thoughtful reflection. The name 'Bedward' is detached from Jamaican history and functions simply as an element in a sound montage, which, while excellent dub, actually empties Far I's original of its religio-political power (Zion Train, 'Bedward', on Dub Syndicate, *Research and Development*). As Thomas Cushman has argued, 'the appropriation of cultural codes merely on aesthetic grounds is integral to defusing their operation *qua* revolutionary cultural forms' (1991: 29).

Conscious dub in the Jamaican tradition, of course, such as that of Jah Shaka, was significant in that it afforded an opportunity for the affirmation of cultural identity to subordinated and oppressed social groups in Britain and Jamaica. As we have seen, reggae is a good example of music functioning as a form of communication that creates and articulates socially shared meanings. Again, Cushman comments that, 'historically, groups and classes have developed styles of music which reflect their histories, their present structural circumstances and the collective consciousness of their members. Drawing on their cultural repertoire of available musical forms, such groups relate their perceptions about society and their places as individuals within it.' He continues, following basic Durkheimian insights, 'while music can be viewed as the product of individual genius, or simply as an organized syntax of sounds, it can also be read sociologically as an expression or reflection of the existential and social situation of social classes and groups to which individuals who make it belong' (1991: 23). Cushman is here conspicuously influenced by Basil Bernstein's work on codes and the sociology of language (Bernstein 1975). Bernstein had argued that language functions as a code that contributes to identity formation and social solidarity within the English working class. Jamaican cre-

ole/patois, for example, functions in this way because it has limited accessibil-
ity to outside groups. Because such 'restrictive codes' distinguish insiders from
outsiders, emic knowledge contributes to social cohesion and communicates
tradition and community knowledge. In other words, for an individual to use
a restricted code reinforces the community structure of which one is a part
and is, consequently, formative of one's identity as a member of that community. However, in addition to restricted codes, there are also, Bernstein argued,
'elaborated codes', which are diffuse, not context dependent and, therefore,
more flexible in the construction of speech acts. As Cushman argues, 'when
using elaborated codes, speakers select from a more extensive range of linguistic alternatives and, thus, elaborated codes are more diffuse, "unpredictable", and reflective of the self-expressive qualities of the speaker. Restrictive
codes are "closed", the language of the group, while elaborated codes are
"open", the language of the self' (1991: 24). The point is, as far as we are concerned, this thesis can be applied to dub and reggae, in that music can likewise
be understood in terms of a cultural code that has meanings for the members
of particular communities. For example, drawing on Albert Bergesen's work,
Cushman argues that 'groups who use restrictive codes have higher degrees of
social solidarity, whereas those who use elaborated codes have lower degrees
of social solidarity' (1991: 24). This type of thinking is not new of course. For
example, within theology similar points have been made about gospel music
by James Cone (1991), in that it functioned as a restricted code within black
communities during the period of North American slavery. However, again,
the point is that while most, if not all musical codes, certainly in their initial
phases, tend to be restricted, over time they become increasingly elaborated.
What was once significant to a particular group, such as Rastas and Jamaicans in Britain, becomes, we have seen, increasingly elaborated. This happens
through a process of cultural diffusion and appropriation.

Reggae articulated the particular identity of African diaspora groups at the
margins of society – it had particular 'subcultural capital' (Thornton 1995:
11–14). However, like other forms of capital, musical codes are alienable,
in that they are capable of being transferred beyond the boundaries of the
group. This was the case with punk, in that many felt they could identify with
the genres and cultures. Although there was a process of filtering and selection, nevertheless, we have seen that there was continuity 'at a deep structural
level' (Hebdige 1979: 29; see also Letts 2007).

In the case of much post-punk dub, however, whilst versioning the signifiers and codes within Jamaican dub and, thereby, providing opportunities
for the expression of heterogenous cultural experience, it tended to further
undermine its particular force. Similarly, as discussed in the first chapter, in

the late-1980s dreadlocks were appropriated by white subcultures and then by the fashion industry, the result being that the style was divested of its Rastafarian religio-political significance (see Mercer 1994: 104–105). In other words, as with most subcultural challenges to dominant culture, contemporary capitalist culture has appropriated the dissident energies of Rastafarian style and music, codifying and simplifying them for the market, thereby draining their religio-political energy. While Sherwood and the post-punk dub of someone like Mark Stewart can hardly be considered part of the contemporary capitalist mainstream, and while their cultural appropriation has a quite different dynamic, the effect is similar. They may have been socialist, anti-establishment and countercultural, but they nevertheless diluted the dominant discourse within reggae and dub.

This process has become particularly conspicuous since the late-1980s. As dub/ambient dub became popular and central to the growing rave scene and, latterly, to club culture, it became detached from its cultural roots. Take, for example, the following comment by Laurent Diouf:

> After a long inertia, dub is coming back in force, like a phoenix from the flames. Techno and its musical byproducts, including ambient, have incorporated dub's creative strength, thus contributing to its rediscovery and renewal. The rebirth was inevitable... It would take too long to make a list, group by group and title by title, of all the sounds copied from the dub masters, which often go unnoticed by an audience lacking in reggae culture (1997: 176–77; see also Partridge 2004a: 166–84).

This is the point. Dub, since the post-punk period and certainly in later rave and club contexts – which tend to be predominantly white[29] – lacks 'reggae culture'. It appropriates the music and undermines the discourse.

For Gramsci, as is well known, dominant classes attempt to establish hegemony by naturalizing systems of class relations in order that those with a subordinate or oppressed status come to accept the status quo. Understood from this perspective, cultural appropriation is a process whereby the cultural practices of the oppressed, particularly if they (as in reggae culture) threaten to disrupt the status quo, are transformed through the diffusion and, thereby, defusion of their social power. Again, while the powerful political and even incendiary rhetoric of some post-punk dub, such as that of Mark Stewart, can hardly be considered benign regarding the status quo, it does, nevertheless, alter and thereby weaken the particular liberationist religo-political discourse developed within Jamaica, the central themes of which were discussed at the beginning of this thesis. Again, Cushman's work is useful in helping to unpack this process: 'the authenticity of the original code as a cultural articulation of dissent is compromised and so too is the power of the original code to serve as the cultural bulwark for more general social transformation' (Cushman 1991: 29). The journey from 1960s JA to 1980s UK gave the latter a peculiarly influential genre that has since reshaped much contemporary popular music, but, at the same time, it also gradually defused the liberationist discourse discussed in the first chapter. Indeed, following Baudrillard's influential hypothesis (and perhaps exaggerating the point a little) the signs dub articulates, which once, within Jamaican sound-system culture, reflected a basic reality, now have little verifiable contact with that world. Just as Marcus Garvey has become the space-tug in Gibson's postmodern novel *Neuromancer* and 'Zion dub' has become its sonic environment – having only the most tenuous connection to 'the days of slavery' and Jamaican liberationist discourse – dub is not only a key methodology and, even, philosophy within the world of simulacra, but is itself a simulacrum.

Endnotes

Chapter 1

1. Interestingly, since his death, Bob Marley has become a significant political and cultural icon across Africa. As Nigel Williamson comments, 'in Africa, his music continues to reign supreme. Indeed, in death his reputation has continued to grow to the point where today he is probably the continent's number one political, cultural, and even quasi-religious icon' (2005: 36). Moreover, not only was his 60th birthday posthumously celebrated in Addis Ababa on 6 February 2005, but his family are, at the time of writing, seeking to have his remains reburied in Shashamene, Ethiopia.

2. For example, the British theologian, Robert Beckford, has argued that Bob Marley needs to be understood in terms of a liberation theologian (1998: 115–29).

3. A few days after writing this, I was interested to hear it explicitly quoted by the Bristol (UK) musician Armagideon on his 'Grow More Dub' (*Through the Haze*, 1998).

4. Linton Kwesi Johnson has argued that, 'more than anybody else, Burning Spear captures very naturally the whole folk traditions of Jamaica, all of the sentiments and all of the feelings of the common people... [His] work is very rural, and it involves the Church as well' (Johnson in interview with MacKinnon 1979: 52; see also Johnson 1976a: 403).

5. In Jamaica, the principal Christian denominations at this time were Methodist and Baptist. Of the latter, there were two traditions, the London Baptist Mission, whose clergy were principally white missionaries, and an older Native Baptist Church, founded by George Liele, an American Baptist slave-preacher, transported to Jamaica following the American Revolution. (Liele actually named the denomination he founded, the Ethiopian Baptist Church.) While there is some debate as to which tradition Sharpe belonged to, Barrett shows that there is good evidence to suggest that he was probably Native Baptist (1997: 40–45). Concerning the Native Baptist Church *per se*, he notes that it 'grafted Christianity to the African ethos of the slaves and took on a messianic-millenarian fervour'. Moreover, it was this spiritual combination that 'became the energizing force behind the slaves in their demand for freedom as a command from God' (Barrett 1997: 40).

6. This type of syncretism is, of course, not unusual in African-Caribbean culture. One only has to think of relatively syncretistic movements such as Umbanda, Candomblé, and Santería (La Regla de Ocha), which, broadly speaking, combine Roman Catholicism and indigenous religion, often of West African origin (see Olmos and Paravisini-Gebert 2003; Clarke 1998; Dawson 2004a; 2004b; York 2004).

7. References to Christian worship, hymnology, and terminology are not unusual. An excellent example of this is African Head Charge's *Songs of Praise* (1981),

which has frequent theological and musicological references to the Christian tradition. Again, just as we have noted a referencing of the preacher Alexander Bedward in British dub, so Bim Sherman's 1982 song 'Sit and Wonder' (Singers and Players featuring Bim Sherman, *War of Words*) references 'When the Roll is Called Up Yonder' (1893), a popular nineteenth-century eschatological hymn by James Black.

8. Concerning the notion of diaspora, William Safran's understanding is helpful: 'diaspora' can be applied to 'expatriate minority communities whose members share several of the following characteristics: (1) they, or their ancestors, have been dispersed from a specific original "center" to two or more "peripheral", or foreign, regions; (2) they retain a collective memory, vision, or myth about their original homeland... (3) they believe that they are not – and perhaps cannot be – fully accepted by their host society and therefore feel partly alienated and insulated from it; (4) they regard their ancestral homeland as their true, ideal home and as the place to which they or their descendants would (or should) eventually return... (5) they believe that they should, collectively, be committed to the maintenance or restoration of their original homeland and to its safety and prosperity; and (6) they continue to relate...to that homeland in one way or another, and their ethnocommunal consciousness and solidarity are importantly defined by the existence of such a relationship' (quoted in Daynes 2004, 30).

9. Founded by a group of Presbyterian ministers in Washington, DC, on 28 December 1916, as the American Society for the Colonizing of Free People of Color in the United States, the American Colonization Society promoted the emigration and colonization of free African Americans to West Africa. Essentially, the organization understood their *raison d'être* missiologically. African Americans should take this opportunity to return to their homeland in order to encourage education and Christianity. To southern whites, concerned that the growing number of freed Africans would destabilize their system of slavery, the plan was portrayed as a solution to the problem. Consequently, many blacks believed it to be a proslavery, racist organization. That said, many black leaders, while rejecting the American Colonization Society, did support the notion of a return to Africa. As the society grew, so did the number of influential supporters, including Abraham Lincoln, James Madison, James Monroe, and the United States Supreme Court Justice, Bushrod Washington, the society's first president.

10. Pan-Africanism is complex, but at a fundamental level, is a political movement dedicated to the unification of all Africans to a single African state to which those in the African diaspora can return. More broadly and amorphously, Pan-Africanism seeks culturally to unite Africans in Africa and in the diaspora through literary and artistic projects.

11. The dub-dance outfit Black Star Liner (Choque Hosein, Chris Harrop, Tom Salmon) are, of course, referencing this company and what it stood for, as does Fred Locks with his *Black Star Liner* (1975). Indeed, reproductions of Black Star Liner posters can be purchased on reggae sites: e.g. <http://www.reggaewales.com/shop/catalog/index.php?cPath=22&osCsid=c007bceec60532fa97494c42227161cf> (accessed 24 May 2005).

12. Some Garveyites dispute the claim that Garvey intended the company to provide transportation to Africa. It was simply there 'to link the colored peoples of the world in commercial and industrial discourse' (Davis 1994: 5).

13. While the Garvey scholar Robert Hill argues that 'no evidence has so far been found or cited to show that Garvey ever made this assertion', he does draw attention to a comment made in September 1924 by James Morris Webb, a black clergyman, concerning the advent of a 'universal black king' as the fulfilment of biblical prophecy (Hill 1983: 25). Others have argued a similar thesis to Edmonds, namely that, although no documentation has been found, 'it is likely that Garvey made some oral declaration...and that it was kept alive in the memory of people steeped in oral tradition' (Edmonds 2003: 147 n. 34).

14. The Twelve Tribes of Israel sect, for example, seem not to insist on the doctrine of the divinity of Haile Selassie, though many do accept it (Rubenstein and Suarez 1994: 3–4). For example, when I raised this belief with Simon Dan, a committed member of the Twelve Tribes of Israel in Manchester, UK, and the lead singer of the dub band Nucleus Roots, he was adamant that, while Haile Selassie is enormously important in salvation history, he is not literally divine. Indeed, apart from the obvious Rastafarian elements, Simon's beliefs, which we discussed at some length, have much in common with those of orthodox Evangelical Christianity. He even describes himself as 'a born again Christian'.

15. The Ashanti had, for some years, been popular in Jamaica, the Maroons having 'a special affinity for Ashanti slaves liberated by the British navy and domiciled in Sierra Leone. One author has written: "when a group of Ashanti was liberated the Maroons welcomed them as countrymen, took them into their homes, and taught them trades. Eventually, they were given lots in the Maroon town."... Ashanti...cultural influence was very strong among the Leeward Maroons during their eighty-five years of rebellion against the British in Jamaica' (Schafer 1981: 208).

16. The full text of *The Holy Piby* is available online: <http://www.sacred-texts.com/afr/piby/> (accessed 6 April 2005).

17. This, it would appear, was the pseudonym he used for *The Promised Key* – i.e. G. G. Maragh.

18. This interpretation of 'Gangungu Maragh' accords well with similar terms used in Indian religion and culture: 'Mahãrãja', meaning great king, and sometimes guru; 'guru', meaning religious guide or teacher.

19. 'Semiotic promiscuity' is a recent term coined to refer to an obsession with reading history in terms of signs indicating events leading to, usually, the end of the world and/or to conspiracy theories (see Partridge 2005: 279–327; Landes 2004).

20. As discussed in Chapter Four, Linton Kwesi Johnson became a Rasta for a brief period in the early 1970s, but soon found the worldview unconvincing and left the movement. Indeed, even in 1976, he was much more supportive of Rasta notions of physical repatriation. For example, in *Race and Class* he argued that 'the Rastafarians' demand of repatriation back to Africa...is *not unreasonable or unrealistic, but quite legitimate. And it is the historical experience that legitimizes this demand.* In fact, it was the same hopelessness and despair which substantiates the Rastafarians' demand that led to mass emigration since the turn of the century to places like Cuba, Panama, North America, and the UK' (1976a: 403; emphasis added).

21. A small area of land in the South of Ethiopia given to Rastafarians by Haile Selassie. It is the particular focus of the Twelve Tribes of Israel sect, who, unlike some Rastas,

encourage ideas of self-repatriation, rather than waiting for the supernatural intervention of Jah.

22. The Twelve Tribes of Israel sect was founded in 1968, in Jamaica, by Vernon Carrington (known to members as 'Prophet Gad' or simply 'Gadman'). Carrington's principal message was straightforward and simple: read a chapter of the Bible everyday. Indeed, apart from the photographs and sayings of Haile Selassie on the wall, the first thing I noticed when I first visited the house of a member was a well-thumbed Bible on the table. And one of the first points made clear to me was the importance of reading a chapter a day. Also central to our discussions and to the work of the Twelve Tribes of Israel generally is the collection of money for physical repatriation. Indeed, Haile Selassie gave Rastafarians a small area of land in the South of Ethiopia called Shashamane, which the Rastafarian I spoke to has, with his partner, visited, their aim being to set up a project to help youths in the small Rastafarian community that lives there. However, as Hannah Rubenstein and Chris Suarez comment, 'members do not wish to pack their belongings and leave immediately. They stress the importance of getting prepared and organising before they go. Only in this way and by living the word of Jah do they believe that they will reach the Promised Land' (1994: 4).

23. Both singles can be found on their 1979 album *The Crack*. 'Give Youth a Chance' was the B-side of the single 'Something I Said' and is reproduced on the reissued CD of *The Crack*. An interesting dub-techno 'repetitive beats mix' of 'Babylon's Burning' was produced by Zion Train on *Grow Together* (1996). More recently, a limited edition album of dub versions of 'Babylon's Burning' has been released: *Babylon's Burning Reconstructed: Dub Drenched Soundscapes* (2006).

24. I mention the literary genre 'cyberpunk' simply because of the use William Gibson makes of Rastafarian symbolism and ideology in his important and influential 1984 novel *Neuromancer* (1995).

25. The screenplay by Martin Stellman and Franco Rosso was also developed into a successful novel with same title by Mike Russell (1980).

26. The term 'groundings' was originally coined by Walter Rodney and used for the political and educational workshops he ran in Jamaican communities during the 1960s (see Rodney 1969; Campbell 1997: 128–33).

27. 'Bag A Wire Dub' is a dub of Johnny Clarke's version of the Mighty Diamonds' 'Them Never Love Poor Marcus', which, very appropriately, expresses the outcaste status of Marcus Garvey, who, we have seen, is a seminal figure in Rasta thinking.

28. A Nazirite is one who has been 'separated' or 'consecrated' to carry out the work of God. The most famous Nazirite, of course, was Samson, the legendary hero of the Tribe of Dan and the last of Israel's 'judges' (i.e. tribal leaders) prior to Samuel and the establishment of the monarchy under Saul. The story, which Rastas know well, tells of a man with supernatural strength who, when his locks were cut by Delilah (thereby breaking the Nazirite vow), lost his energy.

29. The idea of 'earthforce' would seem to be similar to that of *ch'i* in Chinese thought, in that it is a universal, primordial energy that can be accessed and manipulated.

30. While many Rastafarians do smoke ganga sacramentally some explicitly do not. For example, Benjamin Zephaniah made the following comment to me about a photograph accompanying an encyclopaedia article I had written on Rastafarianism (Partridge 2004c: 63): 'As soon as I looked at the piece...the photo stood out. I was having

a conversation recently with some brothers and we were talking about the experiences we've had trying to tell police officers that we didn't smoke – they wouldn't have it. An officer once told me that in training they are told that it is a fact that all Rastafarians smoke, which makes life hard for people like me. And I remember that, somehow, it was worked out that there were more non-smoking Rastas than smoking ones' (9 January 2004).

31. It's worth noting at this point that, although sometimes treated as synonymous, there is a distinction between the two. Peter Doyle describes the difference well: 'Both reverberation and echo are reflected sound. Echo occurs when a sound is reflected in such a way that the source of sound is distinctly reproduced, as when a shout bounces off a distant, relatively flat wall, for instance. Echo might be single or multiple, depending on how many times the sound bounces. Reverberation, on the other hand, occurs when sound is reflected either so many times that no single, discontinuous repeat of the source sound is heard, or when the reflective surfaces are too near the listener to allow subjective aural separation' (2005: 38). Technically, of course, echo is a particular type of reverberation.

Chapter 2

1. See Cowley 1990: 'British music from that of the social "elite" to that of the "folk" had considerable influence, including the "mother country's" military repertoire, represented by black membership in the bands of armed forces and the police' (59).

2. The term has various spellings: Nyabinghi; Nyabinghi; Nyabingi; Niabingi.

3. There have been several conflicting explanations concerning the origins and use of this term. For example, whereas Campbell links it to the anti-colonial movement in Kigezi, Uganda, which called for 'death to black and white oppressors' (1997: 72), Chevannes relates it to a myth, circulated in an article published in *The Jamaica Times* in 1935, claiming the existence of a secret *Nya-binghi* ('death to whites') order, founded by a Congolese king in the 1920s. The leadership of this order, claimed 'Philos' (the author), had now passed to Haile Selassie 'whom its members revered as God and on whose behalf death was a sure admission to heaven' (1994: 43).

4. Good introductions to this complex, West African-influenced drumming include: *Drums of Defiance: Maroon Music from the Earliest Free Black Communities of Jamaica* (Smithsonian Folkways, 1992); *Churchical Chants of the Nyabingi* (Heartbeat, 1997); *Trojan Nyahbinghi Box Set* (Trojan 2003).

5. Kumina (also spelled Cumina) is an African-derived Jamaican religion that emerged among the freed slaves working as contract labourers in Jamaica during the late nineteenth century. Kumina ceremonies, which are usually associated with burials and wakes – but can also be performed at births, anniversaries and thanksgivings – focus on the summoning of and possession by ancestral spirits. Central to Kumina worship is dance and music, drumming being particularly important during rituals. Nowadays, Kumina is practised primarily in the Jamaican parish of St. Thomas and, to a lesser extent, in the parishes of St. Mary and St. Catherine (see Ryman 1984).

6. For a discussion of the Jamaican Christian (particularly Pentecostal/'charismatic')

absorption of African musical and spiritual components, see Dianna Austin-Broos's analysis (1997; see also Stewart 2005).

7. Similar types of drums are, of course, central to much African indigenous music. In Ethiopian music, for example, there are three broad types, the negarit, the kabaro, and the atamo. The negarit is a type of kettle drum, with a body of wood (although the Emperor's are silver and gold) and the skin is usually that of an ox. Entirely ceremonial, 'one of the distinctive emblems of authority', it is always played with a stick and never with the hands. The kabaro is usually tall and slender made of the hollowed-out section of a tree trunk, with the hide of an ox stretched over each end. Usually reserved for religious ceremonies, it is played with the hands (rarely with a stick). Finally, the atamo is a largely secular instrument – although it sometimes played during indigenous healing practices. A small drum that is held under the arm or between the knees, it is played with the fingers or the palm of the hand (see Powne 1980: 13–21).

8. 'Riddim' is a distinctive feature of Jamaican music. Essentially, it is 'an autonomous accompanimental track, typically based on an ostinato (which often includes melodic instrumentation as well as percussion)' (Manuel and Marshall 2006: 447).

9. The term 'churchical' is interesting, in that it betrays the influence of Christianity, particularly non-conformist Christianity in Jamaican culture. (This influence has been discussed at length in the previous chapter.) As Linton Kwesi Johnson comments concerning the work of one of reggae's most significant influences, Winston Rodney/Burning Spear, 'a lot of his songs are like Baptist hymns or Bible songs. All those influences are very strong' (Johnson, in interview with MacKinnon 1979: 52). Again, Christian spirituality is evident in contemporary Nyabinghi music. Listen particularly to Wingless Angels, *Wingless Angels* (1997), which even includes Wesleyan hymns. (Interestingly, this is the first release on Rolling Stone Keith Richards' label, Mindless Records. A 'hardcore reggae fan' (Kaye 1983: 170; see also Fitzgerald 1995: 57), he even chose the name of the band and plays and sings on several tracks.)

10. This isn't quite true, in that similar African drumming had been used several years earlier on Laurel Aitken's 'Ghana Independence (They Got It)' and 'Nebuchadnezzar' (both of which are now available on Aitken, *Pioneer of Jamaican Music*, Vol. 1).

11. In Jamaican culture, the term 'slack' has, as Cooper comments, 'almost exclusively sexual overtones and is synonymous with licentiousness' (2004: 2). That said, she also argues that, in reggae, it is 'not mere sexual looseness, though it is certainly that. Slackness is a contestation of conventional definitions of law and order; an undermining of consensual standards of decency. At large, slackness is the antithesis of restrictive uppercase Culture. It thus challenges the rigid status quo of social exclusivity and one-sided moral authority valorized by the Jamaican elite. Slackness demarcates a space for definitions of "culture"' (2004: 3–4; see also 73–97; Stolzoff 2000: 204–5, 228–32, 237–46).

12. Blake runs Merritone, Jamaica's longest-running sound system.

13. This type of musical competition was, of course, not unique to Jamaica. For example, in turn-of-the-century New Orleans there were frequent 'bucking contests' between bands, each of them seeking the approval of the crowd (see Frith 1996: 17).

14. The title, of course, references the popular 1961 film *The Guns of Navarone*, an adaptation of the successful Alistair MacLean novel with the same title.

15. Interestingly, the force of the rhetoric extended beyond the African-Caribbean community, in that reggae- and dub-influenced punk and post-punk outfits such as The Clash and Big Audio Dynamite played with similar codes and signifiers (see, for example, the covers of The Clash, *Sandinista* and Big Audio Dynamite, *This is Big Audio Dynamite*). Indeed, Paul Simonen, the member of The Clash most influenced by reggae culture and the one who was principally responsible for their martial image, was, like many Jamaican musicians, fascinated by filmic violence, particularly spaghetti westerns and Clint Eastwood (see Gilbert 2005: 52–54). That said, because of the quite distinct context, there was a shift in signification and an inevitable defusion of the power of the original rhetoric. In other words, wearing 'pop star army fatigues' specifically designed for The Clash by Sebastian Conran, Terence Conran's son (Gilbert 2005: 169), it was more a case of punk fashion than, as in Jamaican culture, a reflection of any experiences of living in poor, oppressed circumstances in black, ghetto societies. That said, they had a socialist, anti-racist, anti-fascist message, which sought to challenge the status quo, identify with ethnic minorities and champion their cause. Like the Nicaraguan Sandinista revolutionaries and the storylines of 1960s and 1970s Westerns they were inspired by the ideals of justice, heroism, sacrifice and victory.

16. Tom moved to a safer suburban venue, the Silver Slipper Club at Cross Roads. However, his glory days were clearly over and, it is said, he committed suicide sometime in the early 1960s (see Katz 2000: 13).

17. Whilst this is true, we must not forget the significance of mento, which, as discussed above, is the genre that can, to some extent, be credited with the birth of Jamaica's recording industry – even though the manufacturing was done outside Jamaica.

18. Some had originally been inspired to enter the music business after seeing African Americans earning money organizing rhythm and blues dances while working on American farms. Clement Dodd, for example, seems to have come into the business 'almost accidentally, after he met a man on a farm in America [where he had gone to work] who had been buying rhythm and blues records to bring back to Jamaica... Dodd decided to bring back the records himself, and promptly delivered them to Duke Reid, who was an old friend of the family' (Katz 2000: 13). Eventually, Dodd would set up an enormously successful rival sound system, many of the records for which he purchased from Harlem's Rainbow Records.

19. Conflicting explanations have been given for the etymology of the term 'ska'. However, perhaps the most popular explanation links it to Clue J, who had become famous for addressing his fellow musicians with the greeting 'Skavoovie'. This is certainly how Tommy McCook remembers the emergence of the term: 'Skavoovie is a greeting. That's the way he used to greet you, even long before the ska came in' (quoted in Katz 2004: 31).

20. Listen to *El Buya* (1991) and especially *Shabeesation* (1993), which was produced by Bill Laswell.

21. This term, which is shorthand for music released on *independent* record labels, refers, more generally, to 'alternative' (i.e. not mainstream) music.

22. Listen particularly to the creative use of dub on *Vanishing Point* (1997) and then to the versions of the album on *Echo Dek* (1997), mixed by dub producer Adrian Sherwood.

23. The term, of course, quickly found its way into dub culture: e.g. Stamper Doctor, *Dub Zone* (1979).

24. It should be noted that, a little confusingly, the term 'deejay' came to refer to a vocalist in Jamaican music, an artist who voices over riddims, rather than the 'selector', who selects and spins the records. Moreover, a deejay 'toasts', 'chats', 'chants' or 'voices' over riddims, rather than sings ('a singer') or sings and toasts ('a singjay').

25. It should be noted that, while the standard explanation for the production of 'versions' often focuses on poverty and necessity being the mother of invention, as I have sought to show in this chapter and as Peter Manuel and Wayne Marshall have argued, the reality is rather more complex than this. 'The reliance on riddims is better seen as being conditioned by and constituting part of the entire evolution of modern Jamaican music culture, including its special emphasis on sound systems and studio production, rather than live bands' (2006: 448–49).

26. The Jamaica Recording and Publishing Studio, known as Studio One, founded by Coxsone Dodd in October 1963, was enormously important for the evolution of Jamaican popular music. Although some have claimed that this was the first studio owned by an African Jamaican, in actual fact Linden Pottinger had already set up his Gay Disc recording studio on Molynes Road in 1961. Studio One's significance relates to its fundamental role in popularization and development of ska. It was also the home of one of Jamaica's finest recording engineers and producers of dub, Sylvan Morris. Indeed, it was Morris who was largely responsible for moulding the Studio One sound. For his distinctive dub-style, listen particularly to his *Morris on Dub* (1975) and (with Harry J) *Cultural Dub* (1978).

27. According to Lloyd the Matador, Tubby heard the reverb 'sometime in 1960' at one of his dances in the yard at Brown's Funeral Parlour: 'King Tubby came to the dance as an admirer of my sound. He asked if I could give him a circuit diagram for the reverb my sound was using, so I sat on one of the coffins that was in the yard, draw the circuit, and gave Tubbys. That was the reverb that Tubbs built from my circuit diagram and used on his sound system for a long time' (quoted in Katz 2004: 165).

28. There are actually four dub albums that have a claim to primacy, all of which were recorded and released at roughly the same time in 1973: *Blackboard Jungle Dub* produced by Perry and mixed by Tubby; *Java Java Java Java*, produced by Clive Chin and mixed by Errol Thompson; *Aquarius Dub* produced and mixed by Herman Chin Loy; and Prince Buster's *The Message Dubwise*. All three, whilst subdued compared to later dub, are outstanding pieces of work that bear strong testimony to the creativity of this period of Jamaican popular music history. However, it should perhaps be noted that these were not one-rhythm dub albums. As noted above, the LP that began this trend of releasing whole albums of versions of a single rhythm track was actually produced the following year by Rupie Edwards, namely *Yamaha Skank*.

29. Although, rather oddly, preferring to list other of Perry's contributions in their *Reggae: 100 Essential CDs* (1999), nevertheless, Barrow and Dalton elsewhere claim that this dub album is his 'strongest to date' and 'one of the half-dozen dub albums that should be in any reggae collection' (1997: 206).

30. It should be noted that King Stitt (Winston Spark) was, although not as influential as U Roy, the first deejay to make records (see Barrow and Dalton 1997: 113–15). Furthermore, it should be noted that the roots of toasting over riddims can, perhaps, be traced back to Clement Dodd's Studio One. Although distinct from deejay toasting, Dodd would record the likes of Larry Marshall singing over imported records.

31. 'Green Bay Killing' has, like many reggae songs, been released numerous times. Big Youth's version was subsequently released on *Progress* (1979) and *Some Great Big Youth* (1981). A dub version can be found on Lee Perry's *Megaton Dub Vols I & II* (1978). Kojak also released 'Green Bay Killing' on *Joe Gibbs Original DJ Classics* (1979), as did Johnny Ringo on the Glen Brown produced compilation *Green Bay Killing* (1978). Also on the latter compilation is Tappa Zukie's 'Murder'. Listen also to The Revolutionaries, *Green Bay Dub* (1979), produced by Linval Thompson. Lord Sassafrass, 'Green Bay Incident', can be found on Lee Perry's *Build the Ark* (1990) and the compilation *Producer Series: Trojan Box Set* (1999). Finally, 'Green Bay Incident' has also been recorded by Jah Lloyd on *Black Moses* (1979).

32. Two further chapters were also released in 1979 and 1984, but it was the first three that were particularly influential.

33. Personally speaking, it was the work of Augustus Pablo that first drew me to the genre, especially his seminal *King Tubbys Meets the Rockers Uptown* (1977) – still one of my favourite dub albums. While it is difficult to be sure about such things, it is sometimes claimed that Augustus Pablo was the first to use the term 'rockers' in relation to the new heavier riddims used in dub (see Spencer 1976: 37).

34. It is indicative of his significance that discussions of his work often resort to hyperbole: 'In truth, the felling of all the forests of Scandinavia couldn't produce enough pages to do justice to the wondrous art of Lee Perry' (Kelly 1984: 6).

35. This is, for example, evident in John Corbett's interview with him: 'I asked him what music he was listening to at the time, and his answer was unequivocal: "American music! What do you think I am, stupid?! Blues, soul. And I'm a rock man, can't change that"' (1994: 128).

36. Of course, sex and spirituality are by no means necessarily antipodal to each other. They certainly weren't for Perry: 'God is sex! If there was no sex, we would die, and with us would die truth and religion. God loves sex' (Perry, in an interview with Kelly 1984: 7).

37. Alex Hughes, a white nightclub bouncer from Snodland in Kent, UK, borrowed the appellative 'Judge Dread' and became relatively successful in Britain in the 1970s with his unimaginatively entitled ska songs, 'Big Six', which reached no. 11 in the charts in August 1972, 'Big Seven', which reached no. 8 in December the same year, and 'Big Eight', which reached no. 14 in April 1973. Much of this success was indebted to his skinhead following.

38. Just as his moniker 'Scratch' had been taken from a record he released with Dodd, 'Chicken Scratch' (1961), so the name 'Upsetter' was another enduring nickname from one of his releases with Gibbs, 'The Upsetter' (1968).

39. Perry and Marley did some of their best work together whilst Marley was temporarily lodging with Perry and, subsequently with Perry's mother (for an account of his work with the Wailers during this period, see Katz 2000: 102–36).

40. For a discussion of 'occulture' see Partridge 2009c: 500–502; 2004a: 62–86.

41. 'Lee Perry Guinness', YouTube <http://www.youtube.com/watch?v=ENnFjxHzdIw> (accessed 25 April 2010)

42. The principal rival to Dodd's Studio One, Randy's was a four-track studio situated above Randy's Record Mart, 17 North Parade, downtown Kingston. It was established by Vincent Chin in late 1968, at the same time that reggae emerged and quickly

became the studio of choice for reggae musicians. Indeed, it is arguable that reggae *per se* started in Randy's studio (see Bradley 2000: 202; Katz 2004: 126–27).

43. All of the singles released in the UK on Trojan's Upsetter label are now available as the four-volume *Complete UK Upsetter Singles Collection*.

44. Katz continues by making the significant point that 'perhaps the most vital piece of equipment' at the Black Ark 'was a copy of the Bible, which not only served to consecrate the studio as a holy place, but could also be a source of inspiration for song lyrics' (2000: 181).

45. As Doyle comments of reverb *per se*, it 'does much to define what we perceive as timbre, volume and sound colouration, and largely determines our perception of how particular sounds are located, whether they are near or far. If all real-world sounds were to be somehow stripped of their cloaking of reverberation, it would be a wholly disorienting, dead, almost spaceless and depthless world' (2005: 38).

46. Two reggae tracks from the project, 'Mr. Sandman' and 'Sugartime', were eventually released posthumously in 1998 on a collection of her recordings, *Wide Prairie*.

47. As is well known, the relationship between Perry and Blackwell, who owned Island Records, became very acrimonious. Consequently, in the early 1980s, Perry would not work with any who had been involved with Island. This included Tom Tom Club and Byrne, who was using Blackwell's Compass Point studio – Perry also erroneously thought Byrne was signed up to Island.

48. While it is now a distinct genre in its own right, it was Tubby who coined the phrase 'drum 'n' bass' to describe a particular type of music (see Prendergast 2000: 372).

49. 'Riddim' is a distinctive feature of Jamaican music. Essentially, it is 'an autonomous accompanimental track, typically based on an ostinato (which often includes melodic instrumentation as well as percussion)' (Manuel and Marshall 2006: 447).

50. The daughter of a Welsh physician and a white Creole mother, Jean Rhys was born Ella Gwendolen Rees Williams at Roseau, Dominica, in 1890. While she wrote several important books, she is now primarily remembered for her novel *Wide Sargasso Sea* (1966), which won the W. H. Smith Literary Award in 1967. She was made a Fellow of the Royal Society of Literature in 1966, a CBE in 1978, and died in 1979.

51. Goldman was a musician and prominent popular music journalist during the punk era, writing a weekly column for *Sounds*.

Chapter 3

1. Bearing in mind that Jamaica was itself understood as Babylon, Britain was sometimes referred to as the 'second Babylon' (see, for example, Back 1988: 150).

2. 'Sus' is an abbreviation of 'suspicion'. Repealed in 2000, the infamous 'sus law', which polarized the black community and the police, was actually the enforcement of the 1824 Vagrancy Act, which was passed to stop begging on the streets by soldiers returning from the Napoleonic wars. Essentially, an individual could be convicted on the sole testimony of the arresting officer for being 'a suspected person loitering with intent to steal'. Since the 1970s, up until its repeal, sus law led to disproportionate arrests of black youths.

3. It should be noted that he seems to have already founded the Melodisc label in the USA – perhaps in 1945.

4. In Brixton, London, at the beginning of the 1970s, 80 per cent of the black population had travelled from Jamaica. Consequently, as Hebdige comments, 'the record shops in the area soon began to specialise in bluebeat and ska' (1974: 22).

5. 'In DJ culture we "chat" mic. This is not to be confused with idle "chit chat" as "chatting" generally denotes profound social commentary...' (Henry and Back 2003: 449).

6. As Thornton argues, 'youth subcultures tend to be music subcultures' and 'youth leisure and identity often revolve around music' (1995: 19). While there is some debate concerning the significance of music for subcultural affiliation (e.g. see Muggleton 2000: 69ff.), and while there are exceptions and other formative factors involved, Thornton's general point is difficult to disagree with.

7. See the following websites: Shrewsbury Dub Club <http://www.dubclub.tv/> (accessed 24 March 2007); Operation Sound System <http://www.operation-soundsystem.co.uk/> (accessed 24 March 2007).

8. The term 'lovers' rock' was taken from the name of a South East London record label. From his Dip Studio, Dennis Harris, along with Dennis Bovell and other musicians, produced a distinctively British form of reggae that, as the name suggests, slowed down the riddim, fostered a mellow sound, and lyrically focused on romance. Originating in the early 1970s within the sound-system culture of South London, it presented an alternative to the religio-political content of much reggae of the period. As Barrow and Dalton comment, 'the early years of lovers' rock have two main resonances, London blues parties and discs by girl singers who sounded as if they were still worrying about their school reports' (1997: 337). Indeed, Matumbi were the backing group for the first single of the genre, Louisa Marks's 'Caught You in a Lie', which was produced by the London sound-system operator Lloyd Coxsone. However, perhaps Britain's lovers' rock's most successful artist in the 1970s was London's Janet Kay, whose Dennis Bovell-produced 'Silly Games' reached number two in the UK charts (now available on Janet Kay, *Ultimate Collection* – see Penman 1998: 22; Barrow and Dalton 1997: 339; Henry 2002; Bradley 2002: 118–19). Incidentally, the B-side of 'Silly Games', 'Dangerous (Version)', is a superb example of Bovell's brand of British dub.

9. While it is a small-scale charitable foundation, it has purchased seven acres of land in Agri, thirty miles south of Ghana's capital, Accra, where it has established links with local communities and helps in the provision of materials for local projects, as well as contributing to the distribution of medical and educational supplies.

10. See <http://www.jahshakasoundsystem.com/3024.html> (accessed 11 October 2005).

11. It should be noted that the terminology is important here, in that these were not 'dubs' in the contemporary sense of the term. The first person in the UK to play pre-release, 'soft wax' records, which became known as 'dubs', was almost certainly Duke Vin.

12. The question of what is and what is not 'dub' is a matter of some debate. For example, the British dub producer and reggae musician, Dennis Bovell, considers the first dub track to have been produced, not in Jamaica by King Tubby or Lee Perry, but in America by Jimi Hendrix – namely his atmospheric 'Third Stone From the Sun' (see Reynolds 2005: 77). However, if we are to broaden the term 'dub' to include such

tracks (which do, of course, have many similarities with the genre as it was developed in Jamaica), then there are other pieces of early experimental music that will need to be drawn into the discussion. Hence, there is much to be said for limiting the definition to those forms of music that can be directly traced to 'dub reggae'.

13. A common face to many British children in the 1970s, Forde (1952–) is a talented actor who had previously appeared in the television series *The Magnificent Six and a Half* (1968), *Here Come the Double Deckers* (1970) and *The Georgian House* (1976), as well as popular films such as *Please Sir!* (1971), *To Sir, With Love* (1974), and even, uncredited, in the James Bond film *Diamonds Are Forever* (1971).

14. We have noted the narrative of confrontation common at the time. Indeed, *Scientist Heavyweight Dub Champion* (1980) and *Scientist v. Prince Jammy* (1980) both draw explicitly on boxing imagery.

15. In interview with Zion Train, for a booklet accompanying a compilation of his work, he is asked, 'How much of the early Shaka stuff was recorded by yourself?' He replies, 'Most of it. Say up to '84. The last ones we did were, maybe, *Commandments of Dub: Chapter IV, Brimstone and Fire, Revelation Songs*' (Zion Train 1999: 11).

16. It should be noted that, not only was *King of the Dub Rock: Part Two* released on both the Regal and Tribesman labels, but that these were actually two different mixes. The original and arguably superior Regal pressing includes numerous early video-game-style sound effects, while the Tribesman pressing had these effects edited out.

17. Michael (also Mykal) Rose, of course, was subsequently spotted and enlisted by Derrick 'Duckie' Simpson to replace Don Carlos as a singer in Black Uhuru.

18. In his interview with Penman he wrongly remembers the year as 1974 (Penman 1998: 28).

19. That said, White and his partner, Tony Cousins, did recognize that a company such as EMI was perhaps not going to do as much for experimental music, which attracted very little airplay. Hence, they decided to establish their own label, Cactus, which would cater for less commercial Jamaican music, such as dub.

20. It is interesting that *The Message Dubwise*, Prince Buster's only dub album, was released first in the UK.

21. The dub poem 'Bass Culture' (Johnson 2002: 14–16) can be heard on his album *Bass Culture* (1980). Listen also to the excellent dub version, 'Cultural Dub', on *LKJ in Dub* (1980).

22. The concept of dread has been described in Chapter 1 (above).

23. For Bernstein's critique of affective theorizing, see 1976: 177ff. 'whatever darkness, or sadness, or passion you feel when you hear music in the minor mode is perfectly explainable in purely phonological terms' (177).

24. A good contemporary example of this dub-influenced commitment to bass is the Miami bass scene, one of the principal outfits of which being the Bass Lo-Ryders, whose album covers include subculturally appealing statements such as, 'Warning! This album contains mega low bass – may damage speakers' (Bass Lo-Ryders, *Lo Bouncing Bass*). Other Miami bass titles include: *Bass Hit*; *Bass Killaz*; *Ultimate Bass Challenge*; *Strictly for Da Bassheadz*.

25. Orbit is, of course, referencing Pink Floyd's 1968 psychedelic classic 'Set the Controls for the Heart of the Sun' (*A Saucerful of Secrets*, 1968).

26. Steve Wilson is the guitarist and founder of the post-psychedelic, Manchester band Porcupine Tree.

27. I am, of course, here referring to the sensibilities of Romanticism, which are common in contemporary alternative spiritual cultures (see Partridge 2004a).

28. It is interesting to note that, when Raphael Mechoulam – the Israeli chemist who isolated tetrahydrocannabinol (the active ingredient in ganga) – discovered the neurochemical to which cannabinoids are related, he called it 'anandamide', a term taken from the Sanskrit meaning 'bliss' (see Plant 1999: 195ff.). Moreover, bearing in mind that 'most people who have used cannabis report a higher sensitivity to sound' and even synesthesia (Hughes 1999: 166), it is not surprising that its use with dub (which is common) leads to states of awareness which are interpreted transcendentally and often explicitly spiritually (see also Devereux 1997; Partridge 2005: 121ff.).

29. 30 Hertz website: <http://www.30hertzrecords.com/> (accessed 30 October 2005).

30. This is why deaf people, who are more sensitive to changes in vibration frequency, are able to enjoy music. Indeed, research has shown that congenitally deaf people process sound vibrations in the auditory cortex – i.e. the same part of the brain in which hearing people process sound (e.g. see Phillips 1998; Klarreich 2001).

31. It should be noted, of course, that, although bass is a particularly powerful example, the same can be said of all sound. This somatic reception was, for example, essentially what Steven Feld was referring to when he coined the term 'acoustemology': 'the primacy of sound as a modality of knowing and being in the world' (2003: 226). Again, Bruce Smith makes the point that 'sound is at once the most forceful stimulus that human beings experience, and the most evanescent. Periodic waves of air molecules strike against the listener's ear drums and set up vibrations inside the body. If the waves are strong enough [as in loud bass], the vibrations can be felt in the viscera of the gut as well as in the ears' (2003: 128).

32. 'Bass extension' is the enabling of bass to be heard at low levels.

33. See particularly Michael Wadleigh's film *Woodstock* (1970). A less aggressive version of the 'Star Spangled Banner' also appears on *Rainbow Bridge* (1971).

Chapter 4

1. It's interesting that many British punks appreciated the work of Hawkwind, including Lydon, Pete Shelley, and Joe Strummer. Indeed, there was a mutual appreciation in that, for example, Hawkwind saxophonist Nik Turner formed Inner City Unit to develop a particular brand of psychedelic punk ('punkadelic'), with some reggae overtones. Listen to particularly *Passout* (1980), *Maximum Effect* (1981), and, of course, *Punkadelic* (1982).

2. Sadly, on 30 December 1998, Bryn Jones was admitted to hospital with a rare blood infection. His condition deteriorated and he died on 14 January 1999.

3. For example, commenting on his life during this period, Smith writes, 'I started going out with Una Baines... [and] moved in with her soon after... It was hell for me. It was like a semi-commune... [Martin] Bramah meditating, somebody giving a lecture on vegetarianism, and Baines, my supposed girlfriend, in bed with some hippy...

Playing... Pink Floyd and all that. It's where my dislike of hippies came from, I think' (Smith 2009: 35–36).

4. Compare, for example, Here & Now's 1978 album *Give and Take* with their 1983 album *Fantasy Shift*.

5. Having said that, the film was also enormously significant for many within the black community as well. As Don Letts recalls, 'I had seen *The Harder They Come* and it had a big effect on me... It was *The Harder They Come* that gave me a true feeling of empowerment. It gave blacks in Britain a sense of identity that was much more relevant than *Shaft* or *Superfly*. *The Harder they Come* taught me a lot about my culture, much of which I'd been unaware of up until that point. I had already grasped the musical element of life in Jamaica, but it was this film that gave me the visual element' (2007: 90–91).

6. The influence of Toots and the Maytals on British rock continued throughout the 1970s and into the 1980s. The Clash, for example, covered the hit from the film, 'Pressure Drop', on their May 1977 White Riot Tour (now available on *Super Black Market Clash*) and John Martyn started playing his own version of 'Johnny Too Bad' in the 1970s, eventually releasing it on *Grace and Danger* in 1980.

7. Established in 1976 by Dave Robinson and Andrew Jakeman with a £400 loan from Dr. Feelgood's Lee Brilleaux, Stiff was ostensibly a pub rock label.

8. It should be noted that some punks, particularly Penny Rimbaud and Crass, have been very critical of punk for what they perceive to be superficiality and a lack of political credibility. 'Whereas Rotten's call for "Anarchy in the UK" had been little more than a hollow nihilistic groan (and where's my percentage?), to us it represented a battlecry. For over a decade the various members of what became known as Crass had been involved in exactly the free-thinking anti-commercial ideology the McLaren clique were now attempting to exploit as a commodity. We believe that you could no more be a socialist and signed to CBS (The Clash) than you could be an anarchist singed to EMI (The Sex Pistols) and we set out to prove the point' (Crass 2004: xxiv).

9. 'Following a petition by local residents, a closing order had been served on the premises in September 1976, but an appeal had been lodged which gave the club a 90 day stay of execution' (Marko 2007: 43).

10. The interview with Grundy, which lasted three minutes, is now recognized as an important moment in the history of popular music. Hence, *The Guardian* newspaper published the transcript as a booklet in their series 'Great Interviews of the 20th Century' (Guardian News and Media, 2007).

11. It is of some interest that, not only were several of the key journalists writing about the confluence of punk and reggae women (e.g. Goldman and Coon), but also mixed or female-only bands, such as The Slits, The Mistakes, The Au Pairs, The Mo-Dettes, and The Raincoats, were particularly quick to utilize reggae rhythms (see Steward and Garratt 1984: 126).

12. While it isn't clear whether they were punks or not, John Peel received several threats during the period because he played black music, particularly reggae (see Peel and Ravenscroft 2005: 258–59).

13. Even if bands didn't reference reggae *per se*, they did reference blues and other music of black origin. Lydon, Strummer, Simonen, The Slits, The Ruts, and The Fall have all explicitly mentioned these influences. Mark E. Smith, for example, explicitly men-

tions Bo Diddley, rockabilly, and reggae (Smith and Middles 2003: 66) and, as is well documented, The Fall were only one of many such bands involved in widespread and explicit anti-racist politics (e.g. Ford 2003: 24–28; Jones 1988: 94–104). And, again, to some extent, as well as the appeal of the music, this was because of its rhetoric.

14. Following Dave Laing (1985), who contrasts helpfully 'denotation' with 'connotation', the latter is used here to refer to 'extra-musical fields of association'. While denotation refers to direct correspondence, such as a 'dictionary definition', the level of connotation, as Laing puts it, 'is that of the culturally-defined web of associations a word or sound has acquired. Thus, while "red" denotatively stands for a certain colour, a band of the spectrum, its connotations include "danger", "passion", and "the Left"' (1985: x).

15. It is perhaps worth noting that the same processes are evident elsewhere in the world. For example, inspired by punk, especially The Clash, in South Africa there has been a reaction to Afrikaner nationalism. As in Britain in the 1960s and 1970s many white youths simply regurgitate racist attitudes prevalent in South African society. 'The vision of a lawless black-ruled country, seeking revenge for the atrocities of apartheid and obliterating Afrikaans culture has driven Afrikaners back into the laager of self-preservation where language is the main weapon' (De Vries 2006: 16). In response to a rise in racist sloganeering at some gigs, notorious and influential bands such as Fokofpolisiekar and Rokkeloos have challenged such attitudes. Consequently, as in Britain in the 1970s, a process of anti-racism was initiated. More specifically, for many years, prior to the work of South African artists such as the late Lucky Dube, reggae was considered protest music. 'The mystique surrounding it, the tone of contestation of certain lyrics met the frustration of a young audience from whom censorship had amputated rebellious music... Even without direct musical references to South Africa, reggae was able to offer an incontestable pertinence to the ears of township youth' (Martin 1992: 202).

16. 1979 witnessed the decline of the National Front, which was largely the result of the election of a reinvigorated Conservative Party. Under Margaret Thatcher, Conservatism adopted a tough right-wing stance on immigration and law and order, which led to a haemorrhaging of support for the National Front. (For a good overview of race, politics and society in Britain during this period, see Solomos and Back 1995.)

17. It should be noted that Bowie's comments were possibly, as in punk, more to do with style than conviction. He has since spoken out against far-right and racist groups and actively supports anti-fascist causes. For example, in a letter to the *New Musical Express* he writes: 'My wife is black, as is my step-daughter, and my best friend is Jewish... We are all brothers and sisters, united by one heartbeat... One has to stand up and make one's position absolutely clear, through music and articles such as this one...' He concludes by exhorting the music community to stand against the rise of fascism (quoted in George 1993: 3).

18. This final comment, of course, refers to Clapton's popular cover of Bob Marley's classic song, 'I Shot the Sheriff', from the album *461 Ocean Boulevard* (1974). The song revived his own career, as well as contributing to the popularization of reggae, in that it became his first top ten single in the UK and his first number one in the US.

19. While reggae was central to Rock Against Racism, it has been pointed out that reggae bands 'were often marginalised' (Wood 2002: 265), in that white punk acts usually

headlined the events. To some extent, perhaps, this was understandable, in that the focus of activism tended to be on the mitigation of racism within white urban youth cultures. That said, the statement is unfair, in that reggae artists were, for the most part, central to Rock Against Racism events. Reggae bands always played and it was not unusual for bands such as Aswad to headline (see the copies of flyers in Widgery 1986, e.g. 57, 63, 95).

20. By 1979, *Temporary Hoarding* was selling 12,000 copies. It was 'a brilliant agitator in the campaign against racism and fascism in Britain and against the National Front's efforts to mobilise youth support' (Guy Brett, quoted in Widgery 1986: 62).

21. The Socialist Workers Party is an anti-capitalist Marxist organization based in the UK. Its roots lie in the Revolutionary Communist Party (formed in 1944) and particularly the Socialist Review Group (formed in 1950), which became the International Socialism Group in 1962 and, finally, the Socialist Workers Party in January 1977. The *Socialist Worker*, on the other hand, is a Marxist newspaper launched in 1968 and published by the International Socialist Organization.

22. Their importance as a female band is often commented on. For example, Letts argues that, 'although they were never commercially successful, through sheer emotion and desire, The Slits created some great music and remain not only one of the most significant female punk rock bands of the late-1970s, but had the potential to be one of the greatest female rock bands ever. Madonna bow down, Courtney Love step back and, as for the Spice Girls – don't make me laugh. Whatever you think they've done, The Slits did it before' (2007: 102).

23. Indeed, Alex Murray-Leslie of Chicks on Speed has recently commented that *Cut* was 'so utterly important to us Chix and all other knowing and unknowing women of the world' (Chicks on Speed 2006: 77).

24 Adrian Sherwood makes a similar comment. Comparing The Slits to Siouxsie and the Banshees, he insists that, while the Banshees may have been more popular at the time, 'I tell you what, you play a Banshees record from that period, it doesn't stand up. Not slagging Siouxsie Sioux, respect to Budgie and all that, but the Slits' stuff shines out like a beacon' (quoted in Street Howe 2009: 174).

25. As part of Greater London's Metropolitan Police Service, the Special Patrol Group (SPG) was a centrally organized unit responsible for policing serious public disorder that could not be dealt with by local police divisions. It was active from 1961 to 1986, and anyone engaged in politics or with any awareness of popular culture in the late-1970s will remember the acronym, such was the outrage its actions caused. Most notoriously, in 1979, the policing of a protest by the Anti-Nazi League in South-all involved a running battle, during which a black demonstrator, Blair Peach, was allegedly beaten to death by the SPG. Indeed, the unit was later found to have been carrying a range of unauthorized weapons, including sledgehammers, baseball bats and crowbars. Although, shockingly, nobody was convicted of killing Blair Peach, the Metropolitan Police paid an out-of-court settlement to his family. For a powerful dub response to the murder of Blair Peach, listen to Linton Kwesi Johnson's 'Reggae Fi Peach' (available on *Bass Culture*).

26. 'DC' is the acronym for 'Da Capo', which refers to 'going back to' or 'repeating from the beginning'.

27. Dubcats began life as Dub Honey. After a jam session with them, Fox, who had

been impressed by their 'hypnotic, mesmeric bass lines', suggested a dub reggae ensemble.

28. Patti Smith has, for many years, written poetry. Of particular note is her collection of early work (1995) and her recent *Auguries of Innocence* (2006). The title of the latter references one of her principal influences, William Blake. Indeed, on 28 November 2006, she delivered the annual William Blake Memorial Lecture at St. James Church Hall, Piccadilly, London.

29. Mark E. Smith has released two spoken word albums, *The Post Nearly Man* (1998) and *Pander! Panda! Panzer!* (2002). He has also published a collection of his work (1985).

30. Of particular note are his first two albums from 1978, *Où est la Maison de Fromage?* and *Disguise in Love*.

31. The title was applied to Clarke by the Manchester deejay and promoter Anthony Wilson.

32. This, of course, is not to say that John Cooper Clarke was apolitical. He was not. His social commentary, although very humorous and idiosyncratic, is also intelligent, incisive and sharply political. A good example is his critique of the then Conservative government minister Michael Heseltine, bluntly entitled 'Twat' – available on *Walking Back to Happiness* (1979).

33. This honour is still shared with only one other poet, the Nobel Polish Laureate Czeslaw Milosz.

34. 'I was very influenced', says Johnson in 1983, 'by what the dub lyricists were doing, people like Big Youth and I Roy, and earlier on U Roy' (in interview with Davis 1983c).

35. Having said that, unlike the extemporised 'chat' of the dancehall deejay, dub poets will write their poems first and then compose the music – or have music composed – to accompany the poem.

36. Stokely Carmichael (1941–1998) – a name he changed to Kwame Ture in 1978 – was a Trinidadian-American Black activist, a leader of the Student Nonviolent Coordinating Committee and honorary 'Prime Minister' of the Black Panther Party (an African-American civil rights and self-defense organization, active within the United States in the late 1960s). A significant influence on African-American civil rights and anti-racist thinking, he popularized the concept of 'Black power' to encourage black pride and independence and is credited with coining the phrase 'institutional racism'.

37. It should be noted that, while 'eye creole' is most often used, some dub poets will occasionally write in standard English. A good example is Johnson's 'Jamaica Lullaby' (1991: 23–24).

38. Many dub poets are indebted to the work of Louise Bennett-Coverley (1919–2006), popularly known as 'Miss Lou'. Through her poems, since the 1940s she popularized Jamaican patois and demonstrated its beauty as a medium of verbal art.

39. Johnson, of course, had, by this time, already released *Dread Beat an' Blood* (1978) in the UK.

40. The School of Drama was part of the Cultural Training Centre, the establishment of which was central to the cultural policy of Manley's government. The aim of the Centre was to direct 'the creative subcultural energy of the ghettoes into official channels. Scholarships were granted to talented young people from underprivileged sections of society who could not otherwise have afforded regular visits to the school'

(Habekost 1993: 22–23). It was one of these scholarships that Onuora benefited from. Indeed, the Drama School became central to the new dub poetry movement. 'The only Jamaican dub poet of importance who did not start his career from the springboard of the Drama School [was] Mutabaruka' (1993: 25).

41. It's worth noting that the light of inspiration shone both ways, in that Johnson's work has also influenced Mutaburaka, as well as other dub poets and, indeed, politically articulate musicians generally, such as Michael Franti. Indeed, Franti's list of 'Top Ten Protest Songs' includes both Johnson's 'Sonny's Lettah (Anti-Sus Poem)' and Mutabaruka's 'De System' (see Bower 2006).

42. 'I met a guy, a teacher in Brixton, called John Varnum. John Varnum was working for Virgin Records because Virgin Records had just gotten involved in exploiting reggae music. He used to read my poetry with the kids at school and he thought I would be the right person to help him with the marketing of it... So one day I said to John... "Listen man, I've got these poems that I do and people tell me that they are very musical and very rhythmic, you know, why don't I make a record?" And he said, all right then, I'll ask Richard Branson... So, he said "yes" and they gave me £300 and I went to the little recording 4-track studio in Wimbledon and did a demo and brought it back and they liked it. And I made my first album *Dread Beat An' Blood* in 1977' (Johnson 1999: 62–63).

43. In 1978 it was voted 'Album of the Year' by *Melody Maker* (see Johnson 1999: 63) and its 30th anniversary was celebrated on 9 March 2008 at the Barbican in London (Wroe 2008).

44. For a thoughtful and revealing interview with Zephaniah, see Jones and Zephaniah 2005.

45. The Black Panther Party was founded in October 1966 in Oakland, California by Huey P. Newton and Bobby Seale.

46. The Caribbean Artists Movement, based in London, was founded in 1966 by John La Rose, Andrew Salkey and Edward Kamau Brathwaite. 'Through CAM, artists, musicians and poets got an opportunity to exchange ideas and arrange performances of poetry and play readings which filled a need in the artistic development of our community' (Connor-Mogotsi 1999: 13).

47. The Last Poets were formed by Felipe Luciano, Gylan Kain and David Nelson on 19 May 1968 (Malcolm X's birthday) at Marcus Garvey Park in East Harlem, New York City. As the collective evolved, the principal members included Jalal Mansur Nuriddin, Umar Bin Hassan and Abiodun Oyewole, along with the percussionist Nilaja. Although their work is not 'dub poetry' as such, they have had a significant influence on dub poets, most notably on Johnson. Musically, although much of their early work was accompanied by relatively sparse percussion, their 1972 album *Chastisement* introduced a sound they referred to as 'Jazzoetry' (the title of the second track on the album) – the merging of poetry with jazz and funk instrumentation. Although they declined in popularity during the 1970s, the 1980s witnessed a resurgence of interest in their work. This was, to some extent, the result of the rise of dub poetry, but also because of the emergence of rap – upon which, along with Gil Scott-Heron, they had a formative influence. Indeed, interestingly, they collaborated with the dub-influenced, Bristol-based post-punk band The Pop Group. (A selection of their poems and a history of the group can be found in Oyewole, Bin Hassan and Green 1996).

48. His poem 'Man Free' was specifically written for the *Race Today* leader, Darcus Howe, who had been imprisoned – hence the refrain 'Darcus outta jail' (on *Dread Beat an' Blood*).

49. '*Race Today* was a combative journal that not only reported on the struggles and burning issues of the day, as far as the Black community was concerned, but was also involved in helping to build organizations, working in close alignment with the Black Panthers movement and other organizations like the Northern Collectives in Bradford and Leeds... We were involved in several important campaigns that helped to transform both the political and the cultural lives of Black people in Britain' (Johnson, quoted in Katz 2004: 297).

50. An excellent analysis of the significance of *Dread Beat an' Blood* was provided by Benjamin Zephaniah on BBC Radio 4 (22 July 2008).

51. Johnson has since released, on his own label, two further dub compilations, *LKJ in Dub: Volume Two* (1992) and *LKJ in Dub: Volume Three* (2002). However, whilst they included some excellent versions, they lack the creativity and slow energy of the initial 1981 album.

52. When questioned by Stephen Davis about whether he considered himself to be 'a professional musician', he responded curtly: 'Definitely not. I'm a poet. Period' (1983c: 164).

53. It should be noted, of course, that such comparisons can only be approximate. Moreover, the groundbreaking work of dub pioneers, particularly Adrian Sherwood (to whom we'll turn in the next chapter), has been equally influential and, arguably, more creative.

54. The Rootsman related to me that his own interest in dub was, in part, stimulated by seeing Bovell and Matumbi live.

55. Interestingly, there has been some confusion over the year Matumbi was formed. For example, whereas LKJ Records claims that the band was formed in 1970 (see <http://www.lintonkwesijohnson.com/lkj-records-artists/dennis-bovell/>), both de Konigh and Griffiths (2003: 134) and Barrow and Dalton (1997) state that the year was 1971, and Chris May (1983: 158) and Reggae Reviews.com (<http://www.reggae-reviews.com/matumbi.html>) suggest that it was in 1972. Bovell himself, rather unhelpfully, remembers that it was either 1970 or 1971 (see Penman 1998: 27).

56. In his interview with Penman he wrongly remembers the year as 1974 (1998: 28).

57. It's interesting to compare his recollection of his own early career, which almost mirrors his experience of The Pop Group: 'when we went into the studios, I wouldn't put up with the engineer going, "Oh, you can't touch that, man, you can't go over the red." I'd go, "Well, I want it all in the red, so put it there..." Can you imagine telling Led Zeppelin [they] couldn't have a bit of distortion? So, I took that out on them – Right, I'm at the controls now and started finding frequencies that were what we wanted to hear' (Bovell and Darwen 1998).

Chapter 5

1. Michael Veal's recent analysis of dub, while insightful in many respects, is also a little uneven. For example, he confuses Mark Stewart of The Pop Group with Massive

Attack (2007: 227) – presumably because both emerged out of the Bristol dub scene and Stewart, at one point, was a mentor to Tricky who had close links with The Wild Bunch sound system, which eventually evolved into Massive Attack (on whose first album he rapped). He also tends to conflate styles, such as 'jungle' and 'drum 'n' bass' (2007: 233), which are technically distinct.

2. Mark Stewart, for example, went on to become an On-U Sound stalwart for many years. For an excellent overview of his career, see Eden 2009.

3. 'Ariwa' is, apparently, a reworking of the word *ariwo*, a Yoruba term meaning 'noise'.

4. This work is reminiscent of the classic Twinkle Brothers collaboration with the Polish folk band, the Trebunia-Tutka Family, *Dub with Strings* (1992).

5. *Dub Me Crazy* (1982); *Beyond the Realms of Dub: Dub Me Crazy, Part 2* (1982); *The African Connection: Dub Me Crazy, Part 3* (1983); *Escape to the Asylum of Dub: Dub Me Crazy, Part 4* (1983); *Who Knows the Secret of the Master Tape: Dub Me Crazy, Part 5* (1985); *Schizophrenic Dub: Dub Me Crazy, Part 6* (1986); *Adventures of a Dub Sampler: Dub Me Crazy, Part 7* (1987); *Experiments of the Aural Kind: Dub Me Crazy, Part 8* (1988); *Science and the Witchdoctor: Dub Me Crazy, Part 9* (1989); *Psychedelic Dub: Dub Me Crazy, Part 10* (1990); *Hijacked to Jamaica: Dub Me Crazy, Part 11* (1992); *Dub Maniacs on the Rampage: Dub Me Crazy, Part 12* (1993).

6. Beckford touches on it in a short analysis of what he refers to as 'dub hermeneutics' (2006: 83–84). Having said that, when he is discussing dub as 'deconstruction', which might naturally lend itself to an analysis of the genre as postmodern, he explicitly states that he is 'in no way aligning it to the post-modern, post-structural critique in Western scholarship', for, he says, not unreasonably, 'the philosophy of deconstructionism is a complex tradition of thought and action and is too multifaceted to review in its entirety here' (2006: 72).

7. My point here is simply that found sounds and montage in electronic music have a distinguished history, beginning with the invention of magnetic tape and the *musique concrète* compositions of Luciano Berio, Karlheinz Stockhausen, Luc Ferrari, Pierre Schaeffer and Pierre Henry between the 1940s and 1960s. Also in this tradition was the work of the BBC Radiophonic Workshop, which, founded on 1 April 1958, produced some particularly creative found sound compositions for radio and television drama, perhaps the most memorable being the theme tune for the children's television series *Dr. Who* – composed in collaboration with Ron Grainer (see Briscoe and Curtis-Bramwell 1983). While the influence on Jamaican dub producers cannot be established, *musique concrète* has had an interesting influence on experimental popular music in the UK. For example, perhaps Henry's most avant-garde and haunting project was *Ceremony* (1970), a collaboration with the British rock band Spooky Tooth (see Partridge 2005: 254), the drummer of which, Mike Kellie, went on to work with the seminal post-punk-era band The Only Ones. (I say 'post-punk-era' because The Only Ones are not a typical post-punk band.) Again, the work of the BBC Radiophonic Workshop has been explicitly referenced by dub-influenced experimentalists such as Adrian Utley (of Portishead) and The Mount Vernon Arts Lab. Listen particularly to *Warminster* (1999) by Utley and The Mount Vernon Arts Lab, the cover of which references the Radiophonic Workshop. Similar collaborations can be found on *Gummy Twinkle* (1998) by The Mount Vernon Arts Lab.

8. 'Tribesman Rockers' can be found on the seminal *African Dub All-Mighty: Chapter 3* (1978) produced and mixed by Joe Gibbs and Errol Thompson.

9. For example, dub was essentially a capitalist concern in that, in a poor economy, there was a strong tendency for the music to become formulaic and to be endlessly repeated, simply to make money and supply demand. In this sense, some Jamaican reggae and dub became commodified and reified.

10. Similarly in punk, post-punk and rave, there was, unlike disco, a shift in the way fans understood themselves, particularly as dancers. No expertise was required and there was an almost contemplative or even trance-like turning in, rather than an exhibitionism which was conscious of the gaze of the other.

11. In urban culture, the term 'kleptic' is a useful abbreviation of 'kleptomaniac', meaning the recurrent urge to collect or steal, usually without any concern to profit from the action. This is, I think, a helpful way to understand core aspects of 'plunder culture'.

12. For example, as I've discussed elsewhere, the millenarian discourse of Rastafari is explicitly articulated in reggae cover art (see Partridge 2009b). Lee Perry's *Rastafari Liveth Itinually*, the cover of which is typically millenarian, depicting Selassie in royal garb travelling in a chariot pulled by a lion (symbolizing his status as the Lion of the Tribe of Judah). The background is one of dark clouds and volcanic fire and the songs on the album include 'Ethiopian Land' and 'Judgment Day'. In short, the overall message of the record is first revealed on the cover: Selassie is the divine deliverer who will, in the last days, come to judge the living and the dead. As Chris Morrow argues in his overview of reggae album cover art, 'Haile Selassie is shown on album covers mainly as a powerful deity or...king. On illustrated sleeves like *African Museum All Star* and *Rockers Almighty Dub*, he assumes supernatural powers, showering the earth with lightning and using his dreadlocks to destroy the structures of Babylon' (1999: 24).

13. 'The removal of the Author...is not merely an historical fact or an act of writing; it utterly transforms the modern text (or – which is the same thing – the text is henceforth made and read in such a way that at all its levels the author is absent). The temporality is different. The Author, when believed in, is always conceived as the past of his own book' (Barthes 1977: 145). There are continuities between this understanding and that of music within dub.

14. On the difference between parody and pastiche, see Jameson's analysis: 'One of the most significant features or practices of postmodernism today is pastiche... [Parody produces] an imitation which mocks the original... [The] general effect of parody is – whether in sympathy or with malice – to cast ridicule on the private nature of... stylistic mannerisms and their excessiveness and eccentricity with respect to the way people normally write and speak. So there remains somewhere behind all parody the feeling that there is a linguistic norm in contrast to which the styles of the great modernists can be mocked... But what would happen if one no longer believed in the existence of normal language, of ordinary speech, of the linguistic norm...? That is the moment at which pastiche appears and parody has become impossible' (1997: 194–95).

15. 'Digital dancehall' is actually not an early-1980s phenomenon. It has its roots in a packed venue on Waltham Park Road, Kingston, on 13 February 1985. Although in the early-1980s Sly Dunbar and Robbie Shakespeare had introduced synth drums and

a cheap keyboard sound to their dancehall productions, the immediate origins of digital dancehall can be traced to King Jammy's Super Power Soundsystem, which played Wayne Smith's groundbreaking 'Under Mi Sleng Teng', an anti-drugs record that included no traditional instrumentation. As David Stelfox comments, 'constructed around a stripped down Casio keyboard loop, its gut-punching electronic bassline was quite unlike anything that had ever been heard before' (2008: 34). Consequently, 'Under Me Sleng Teng', as well as becoming the founding anthem of ragga, inspiring literally hundreds of imitations, more significantly, shifted the focus of Jamaican music from the drums and the bass to the synthesizer. In so doing it made the modulating synth bassline the ubiquitous sound of Jamaican and, eventually, global urban music. Indeed, some would argue that it was easily as influential as Kraftwerk and Giorgio Moroder in the history of electronic music (e.g. Shapiro 2000b: 51). (Listen to Wayne Smith & Prince Jammy, *Sleng Teng/Prince Jammy's Computerised Dub*.)

16. Although Creation Rebel had several drummers, the most influential was undoubtedly 'Style' Scott. Having just finished service in the Jamaican army, he had been introduced to Sherwood by Prince Far I, who had brought him to London to play for him and to contribute to Creation Rebel. However, as well as working with Creation Rebel, he went on to be the key creative force behind Dub Syndicate and also a founding member of Roots Radics. Indeed, his distinctive rhythms dominated the scene during the 1980s and 1990s (see Free Radical Sounds 2007).

17. Smith invited Sherwood back in 1990 to produce 'The Littlest Rebel' on *Extricate* (1990).

18. 'African Head Charge were the best. I never sold a lot of records. Our biggest selling was thirty-, perhaps forty-thousand copies... So it's always been underground' (Sherwood, in Tosi 1998).

19. 'Wandering, wandering in hopeless night/ Out here in the perimeter there are no stars/ Out here we is stoned/ Immaculate' (words by Jim Morrison – sampled on 'Stoned Immaculate', on Dub Syndicate, *Stoned Immaculate*).

20. I fully realize that the tracing of such connections can be artificial and irritating, like much of the convoluted reasoning of conspiracy narratives, but, in this case, it seemed worth mentioning.

21. Interestingly, the album is also referenced by Don Letts in his discussion of Big Audio Dynamite's music (2007: 158).

22. Barker exposes the arbitrary nature of naming albums at On-U Sound, in his comments on Dub Syndicate's *Strike the Balance* (1989): 'I fully confess to giving the album its rather prosaic title. As was usually the case at On-U HQ, an album had been finished and it was time to get down to the boring routine of manufacture, distribution, promotion and sale – a process traditionally never approached with any great enthusiasm by On-U staffers through the years. Question: "So, what are we going to call this one?" Answer: "Ask Steve if he can think of anything!" Not quite up to the standard of 2 Bad Card's *Hustling Ability* or Little Axe's *The Wolf that House Built*, but *Strike the Balance* was at least a combination of studio language, political word-play, in-joke that removed the unacceptable obstacle of an album without a title' (Barker 1998b).

23. The DMX was, at that time, a sophisticated drum machine that used sampled recordings of actual instruments. Easy to operate, it had eight separate outputs for individ-

ual processing, a hundred sequences, and fifty songs. Indeed, not only was the DMX the original drum machine of hip-hop and rap, but it was used by such diverse artists as Stevie Nicks, Mike Oldfield, the Thompson Twins, Run DMC, Prince, Roni Size, and, perhaps most famously, by New Order on 'Blue Monday' (1983).

24. Born Vernal R. O. Kelly in St. Thomas, Jamaica, like so many of Jamaica's significant musicians, Charlie Eskimo Fox attended the Alpha Boys School in Kingston. Following the musical inspiration he received at school, after he left he began to develop his drumming skills. Eventually he travelled to England and settled in North West London. In the mid-1970s, as the drummer in The Davrocks, he got the opportunity to work with some of the most important singers and deejays from Jamaica. By the late-1970s he had founded The Freedom Fighters, joined Creation Rebel, and drummed for numerous Jamaican musicians, such as Gregory Isaacs, Dennis Brown, Delroy Wilson, Dillinger, Tappa Zukie and Prince Far-I. As far as On-U Sound is concerned, as well as drumming for Creation Rebel and Dub Syndicate, he has been a member of New Age Steppers, Singers and Players, African Head Charge and even Mark Stewart's Maffia (on the first album, *Learning to Cope with Cowardice*).

25. Founded in Belgium in 1977 by Marc Hollander and Vincent Kenis, Aksak Maboul/ Aqsak Maboul recorded two studio albums, *Onze Danses Pour Combattre la Migraine* (1977) and *Un Peu de l'Ame des Bandits* (1979), the latter including former members of Henry Cow, Chris Cutler and Fred Frith. It is not difficult to imagine the appeal of the band to Sherwood when one listens to *Onze Danses Pour Combattre la Migraine*. While not dub, it is an eclectic mix of genres, including, for example, basic drum machine beats, improvised jazz, Turkish music, and classical music. Indeed, parts of the album, particularly the initial track, 'Mercredi Matin', does include slight reverb and delay that produce a distinct dub feel. Reflecting the influence of Cutler and Frith, their second album, *Un Peu de l'Ame des Bandits*, is more complex and experimental. As well as including improvised ambient compositions, as with Sherwood's work, it is a good early example of the use of 'captured sound'/sampling.

26. On the use of the Emulator and the Synclaviar in sampling, see Goodwin's discussion (1990: 261–62).

27. Supplied by Doug Wimbish, the name 'Tackhead' is New Jersey slang for 'homeboy'.

28. In 1991 Gary Clail reached ten in the UK charts with his 'Human Nature' (on Paul Oakenfold's Perfecto label), which originally included a sample of Billy Graham (removed under threat of legal action). The single is now available on Gary Clail and On-U Sound System, *Emotional Hooligan* (1991).

29. This is suggested in, for example, recent studies, such as that by Gordon Lynch and Emily Badger, which reports that all of the participants in their study of 'mainstream post-rave events' were 'white, and most were in full-time education or full-time employment' (2006: 32). This is quite different from the cultures within which dub had its genesis.

Bibliography

Abrahams, I. 2004. *Hawkwind: Sonic Assassins*. London: SAF Publishing.

Abrahams, R. D. 1976. *Talking Black*. Rowley: Newbury House.

Adorno, T. 1990. 'On Popular Music'. In Frith and Goodwin, *On Record*, 301–14.

— 1991. *The Culture Industry: Selected Essays on Mass Culture*, ed. J. Bernstein. London: Routledge.

Alleyne, M. C. 1988. *Roots of Jamaican Culture*. London: Pluto Press.

Amos, J. 2003. 'Organ Music "Instils Religious Feelings"'. *BBC News* (8 September): <http://news.bbc.co.uk/1/hi/sci/tech/3087674.stm> (accessed 12 November 2005).

Anti-Nazi League. 2006. 'Rock Against Racism': <http://www.anl.org.uk/04-rar.htm> (accessed 9 October 2006).

Appiah, K. A., and H. L. Gates (eds). 1999. *Africana: An Encyclopedia of the African and African American Experience*. New York: Basic Civitas Books.

Assembly of Jamaica. 1970 [1796]. *The Proceedings of the Governor of Jamaica, in Regard to Maroon Negroes*. Westport, CN: Negro Universities Press.

Austin-Broos, D. J. 1997. *Jamaica Genesis: Religion and the Politics of Moral Orders*. Chicago: Chicago University Press.

Back, L. 1988. 'Coughing Up Fire: Soundsystems in South-East London'. *New Formations* 5 (Summer): 141–52.

— 1992. 'Youth, Racism, and Ethnicity in South London: An Ethnographic Study of Adolescent Inter-Ethnic Relations'. Unpublished doctoral thesis, University of London.

Balliger, R. 1999. 'Politics'. In Horner and Swiss, *Key Terms*, 57–70.

Barker, C. 2000. *Cultural Studies: Theory and Practice*. London: Sage.

Barker, S. 1997. 'African Head Charge: *Environmental Studies*': liner notes to African Head Charge, *Environmental Studies*.

— 1998a. 'African Head Charge: *My Life in a Hole in the Ground*': liner notes to African Head Charge, *My Life in a Hole in the Ground*.

— 1998b. 'Dub Syndicate: *Strike the Balance*': liner notes to Dub Syndicate: *Strike the Balance*.

— 2007a. 'Creation Rebel'. Available at: <http://www.skysaw.org/onu/artists/creationrebel.html> (accessed 24 February 2007).

— 2007b. 'Gary Clail'. Available at: http://www.skysaw.org/onu/artists/garyclail.html (accessed 1 March 2007).

Barker, S., and D. Parker. 2007a. 'African Head Charge'. Available at <http://www.skysaw.org/onu/artists/africanheadcharge.html> (accessed 22 February 2007).

Barker, S., and D. Parker. 2007b. 'Dub Syndicate'. Available at <http://www.skysaw.org/onu/artists/dubsyndicate.html> (accessed 26 February 2007).

Barrett, L. E. 1978. 'African Roots in Jamaican Indigenous Religion'. *Journal of Religious Thought* 35: 7–26.

— 1997 [1988]. *The Rastafarians*. Boston: Beacon Press.

Barrow, S. 1994. 'Dub Gone Crazy': liner notes to King Tubby, *Dub Gone Crazy*.

— 1995. 'Version Therapy'. *The Wire* 132 (February): 28–32.

Barrow, S., and P. Coote. 2004. 'Mento Madness': liner notes to *Mento Madness: Motta's Jamaican Mento: 1951–1956* (V2 Music).

Barrow, S., and P. Dalton. 1997. *Reggae: The Rough Guide*. London: Rough Guides.

— 1999. *Reggae: 100 Essential CDs*. London: Rough Guides.

Barthes, R. 1977. *Image – Music – Text*. Translated by S. Heath. London: Fontana.

Baudrillard, J. 1994 [1981]. *Simulacra and Simulation*. Translated by S. F. Glaser. Ann Arbor: University of Michigan Press.

Beckford, R. 1998. *Jesus is Dread: Black Theology and Black Culture in Britain*. London: Darton, Longman & Todd.

— 2006. *Jesus Dub: Theology, Music and Social Change*. London: Routledge.

Bell-Brown, L. 1988. 'King of the Zulu Tribe ina Roots and Culture Style'. *Boom-Shcka-Lacka* 1. Available at <http://www.disciplesbslbm.co.uk/shak1.html> (accessed 12 October 2005).

Benjamin, W. 1992. *Illuminations*, ed. H. Arendt. Translated by H. Zorn. London: Fontana.

Bennett, A., and K. Kahn-Harris. 2004. *After Subculture: Critical Studies in Contemporary Youth Culture*. Houndmills: Palgrave Macmillan.

Bennett, E. 1999. 'Reggae'. In Appiah and Gates, *Africana*, 1600–1.

Bernstein, B. 1975. *Class Codes and Social Control: Theoretical Studies Towards a Sociology of Language*. New York: Schocken Books.

Bernstein, L. 1976. *The Unanswered Question: Six Talks at Harvard*. Cambridge: Harvard University Press.

Beyer, M. 1996. 'Fifteen Years of On-U Sound': liner notes to Various artists, *Roots of Innovation: 15 and X Years On-U Sound*.

Bhattacharyya, A. 2006. 'Aki Nawaz from Fun-Da-Mental Talks About Imperialism and His Album *All Is War*'. *Socialist Worker* 2012 (August): <http://www.socialistworker.co.uk/article.php?article_id=9369> (accessed 4 October, 2006).

Bilby, K. 1985. 'The Holy Herb: Notes on the Background of Cannabis in Jamaica'. In Nettleford, *Caribbean Quarterly Monograph: Rastafari*, 82–95.

Bilby, K., and E. Leib. 1986. 'Kumina, the Howellite Church and the Emergence of Rastafarian Traditional Music'. *Jamaica Journal* 19.3: 22–28.

Bishton, D. 1986. *Blackheart Man: A Journey Into Rasta*. London: Chatto & Windus.

Blyden, E. W. 1967 [1887]. *Christianity, Islam, and the Negro Race*. Edinburgh: Edinburgh University Press.

Boot, A., and C. Salewicz. 1997. *Punk: The Illustrated History of a Music Revolution*. New York: Penguin.

Bourdieu, P. 1984. *Distinction: A Social Critique of the Judgement of Taste*. Translated by R. Nice. Cambridge: Harvard University Press.

— 1990. *In Other Words*. Cambridge: Polity Press.

Bourdieu, P., and L. J. D. Wacquant. 1992. *An Invitation to Reflexive Sociology*. Cambridge: Polity Press.

Bovell, D., and N. Darwen. 1998. 'Dennis Bovell: The Interview': <http://www.jovemusic.cwc.net/british/dbovell.htm> (accessed 17 November 2006).

Bower, C. S. 2006. 'Michael Franti's Top Ten Protest Songs'. *Blender* (October): <http://www.blender.com/guide/articles.aspx?id=2157> (accessed 27 November 2006).

Boyne, I. 2005. 'Waltzing with Wolves: Dancehall's Link to Violence'. *Sunday Gleaner* (5 June):

<http://www.jamaica-gleaner.com/gleaner/20050605/focus/focus1.html> (accessed 1 August 2005).

Bradley, L. 2000. *This is Reggae Music: The Story of Jamaica's Music*. New York: Grove Press; published in the UK as *Bass Culture: When Reggae Was King*. London: Viking.

— 2002. *Reggae: The Story of Jamaican Music*. London: BBC.

— 2006a. 'Brain Damage'. Liner notes for Dennis Bovell, *Brain Damage* (EMI): 2–4.

— 2006b. 'Brain Damage'. Liner notes for Dennis Bovell and the Dub Band, *Audio Active* (EMI): 2–5.

— 2006c. 'Brain Damage'. Liner notes for Dennis Bovell and the 4th Street Orchestra, *Scientific Higher Ranking Dubb* and *Yuh Learn!* (EMI): 3–6.

Bradshaw, P., V. Goldman and P. Reel. 1981. 'A Big, Big, Sound System Splashdown'. *New Musical Express* (21 February): 26–29, 53.

Braham, P., A. Rattansi and R. Skellington (eds). 1992. *Racism and Antiracism: Inequalities, Opportunities and Policies*. London: Sage.

Breiner, L. A. 1985–86. 'The English Bible in Jamaican Rastafarianism'. *Journal of Religious Thought* 42.2: 30–43.

Briscoe, D., and R. Curtis-Bramwell. 1983. *The BBC Radiophonic Workshop: The First 25 Years*. London: BBC.

Bromell, N. 2000. *Tomorrow Never Knows: Rock and Psychedelics in the 1960s*. Chicago: University of Chicago Press.

Brown, S., M. Morris and G. Rohlehr (eds). 1989a. *Voice Print: An Anthology of Oral and Related Poetry from the Caribbean*. Harlow: Longman.

— 1989b. 'Introduction'. In Brown, Morris and Rohlehr, *Voice Print*, 1–23.

Bundy, J. 2004. 'From Westway to the World'. *Socialist Worker* 1917 (4 September): <http://www.socialistworker.co.uk/article.php?article_id=2167> (accessed 24 July 2005).

Burt, L., and C. Hilliman. 1978. 'The Birth of a Sound System'. *Race Today* 10.1 (1978): 17–18.

Burton, R. D. E. 1997. *Afro-Creole: Power, Opposition, and Play in the Caribbean*. Ithaca: Cornell University Press.

Byrne, D., with B. Eno. 2006. 'The Making of *My Life in the Bush of Ghosts*': liner notes to Brian Eno and David Byrne, *My Life in the Bush of Ghosts* (remastered version).

Campbell, C. 1972. 'The Cult, the Cultic Milieu and Secularization'. In Hill, *Sociological Yearbook of Religion in Britain 5*, 119–36.

— 1999. 'The Easternization of the West'. In Wilson and Cresswell, *New Religious Movements*, 35–48.

Campbell, H. 1980. 'Rastafari: Culture of Resistance'. *Race and Class* 22.1: 1–22.

— 1997 [1985]. *Rasta and Resistance: From Marcus Garvey to Walter Rodney*. St John's, Antigua: Hansib Caribbean.

Campbell, M. C. 1988. *The Maroons of Jamaica, 1655–1796: A History of Resistance, Collaboration and Betrayal*. Granby: Bergin and Garvey.

Carby, H. V. 1999. *Cultures in Babylon: Black Britain and African America*. London: Verso.

Carr, C. 1993. 'The History and Development of Jamaican Reggae with Particular Reference to the Music of Bob Marley'. Unpublished MPhil thesis, University of Sheffield.

Carter, B., C. Harris and S. Joshi. 2000. 'The 1951–1955 Conservative Government and the Racialization of Black Immigration'. In Owusu, *British Black Culture and Society*, 21–36.

Cartledge, F. 1999. 'Distress to Impress? Local Punk Fashion and Commodity Exchange'. In Sabin, *Punk Rock*, 143–53.

Cashmore, E. 1983 [1979]. *Rastaman: The Rastafarian Movement in England*. London: Unwin Paperbacks.

— 1987. *The Logic of Racism*. London: Allen & Unwin.

Cashmore, E. (ed.). 1996 [1984]. *Dictionary of Race and Ethnic Relations*, 4th edn. London: Routledge.

Centre for Contemporary Cultural Studies. 1982. *The Empire Strikes Back*. London: Hutchinson.

Chang, K. O., and W. Chen. 1998. *Reggae Routes: The Story of Jamaican Music*. Philadelphia: Temple University Press.

Chevannes, B. 1979. *The Social Origins of Rastafari*. Kingston: Institute of Social and Economic Research, University of the West Indies, 1979.

— 1994. *Rastafari: Roots and Ideology*. Syracuse: Syracuse University Press.

Chevannes, B. (ed.). 1995a. *Rastafari and Other African-Caribbean Worldviews*. New Brunswick: Rutgers University Press.

— 1995b. 'The Origin of the Dreadlocks'. In Chevannes, *Rastafari and Other African-Caribbean Worldviews*, 77–95.

— 1995c. 'The Phallus and the Outcast: The Symbolism of the Dreadlocks in Jamaica'. In Chevannes, *Rastafari and Other African-Caribbean Worldviews*, 97–126.

Chicks on Speed. 2006. 'The Inner Sleeve: The Slits, *Cut*'. *The Wire* 275 (January 2007): 77.

Christgau, R. 1998. *Grown Up All Wrong: 75 Great Rock and Pop Artists From Vaudeville to Techno*. Cambridge: Harvard University Press.

Clarke, J., S. Hall, T. Jefferson and B. Roberts. 1976. 'Subcultures, Cultures, and Class: A Theoretical Overview'. In Hall and Jefferson, *Resistance Through Rituals*, 9–74.

Clarke, L. C. 2000. 'Music Politics, and Violence: Calypso and Steel Band from Trinidad, Reggae from Jamaica, and the Impact of These on the People of North East London at the End of the Twentieth Century'. Unpublished doctoral thesis, University of London.

Clarke, P. B. 1994 [1986]. *Black Paradise: The Rastafarian Movement*. Black Political Studies 5. San Bernardino: Borgo Press.

Clarke, P. B. (ed.). 1998. *New Trends and Developments in African Religions*. Westport, CN: Greenwood Press.

Clarke, S. 1980. *Jah Music: The Evolution of Popular Jamaican Song*. London: Heinemann Educational Books.

Clayton, J. 1999a. 'Dub'. In Appiah and Gates, *Africana*, 634–35.

— 1999b. 'Mento'. In Appiah and Gates, *Africana*, 1289.

— 1999c. 'Rocksteady'. In Appiah and Gates, *Africana*, 1630–31.

Cohen, Sara. 1999. 'Scenes'. In Horner and Swiss, *Key Terms*, 239–50.

Cohen, Stanley. 1972. *Folk Devils and Moral Panics*. London: MacGibbon & Kee.

Cohen, Phil, and C. Gardner. 1982. *It Ain't Half Racist Mum*. London: Comedia.

Colegrave, S., and C. Sullivan. 2001. *Punk: A Life Apart*. London: Cassell.

Collingwood, J. 2005. *Bob Marley: His Musical Legacy*. London: Cassell Illustrated.

Cone, J. 1991. *The Spirituals and the Blues*. Maryknoll, NY: Orbis Books.

Connor, S. 1997 [1989]. *Postmodernist Culture*, 2nd edn. Oxford: Blackwell.

Connor-Mogotsi, P. 1999. 'First Talk in the *Life Experience with Britain* Series at the George Padmore Institute, London (20.1.97)'. In Harris and White, *Changing Britannia*, 1–18.

Conrad, J. 1994 [1902]. *Heart of Darkness*. Harmondsworth: Penguin.

Coon, C. 1978. *1988: The New Wave Punk Rock Explosion*. London: Ominbus.

Cooper, C. 2004. *Sound Clash: Jamaican Dancehall Culture at Large*. New York: Palgrave Macmillan.

Corbett, J. 1994. *Extended Play: Sounding Off from John Cage to Dr. Funkenstein*. Durham: Duke University Press.

Cowley, J. 1990. 'London is the Place: Caribbean Music in the Context of Empire 1900–60'. In Oliver, *Black Music in Britain*, 58–76.

Cox, C., and D. Warner (eds). 2004. *Audio Culture: Readings in Modern Music*. New York: Continuum.

Crass. 2004. *Love Songs*. Hebden Bridge: Pomona.

Craton, M. 1978. *Searching for the Invisible Man: Slaves and Plantation Life in Jamaica*. Cambridge: Harvard University Press.

Curtin, P. D. 1968. *Two Jamaicas: The Role of Ideas in a Tropical Colony 1830–1865*. New York: Greenwood Press.

Cushman, T. 1991. 'Rich Rastas and Communist Rockers: A Comparative Study of the Origin, Diffusion and Defusion of Revolutionary Musical Codes'. *Journal of Popular Culture* 25: 17–61.

D'Aguiar, F. 2002. 'Introduction: Chanting Down Babylon'. In Johnson, *Mi Revalueshanary Fren*, ix–xiv.

Darwen, N. 1998. 'Dennis Bovell: The Interview': <http://www.jovemusic.cwc.net/british/dbovell.htm> (accessed 17 November 2006).

Davidson, S. V. 2006. 'Babylon in Rastafarian Discourse: Garvey, Rastafari, and Marley'. *Society for Biblical Literature Forum*: <http://www.sbl-site.org/Article.aspx?ArticleId=496> (accessed 24 March, 2006).

Davis, E. 2009a. 'Roots and Wires: Polyrhythmic Cyberspace and the Black Electronic'. Available at: http://www.techgnosis.com/chunkshow-single.php?chunk=chunkfrom-2005-02-21-1551-0.txt (accessed 26 May, 2009).

— 2009b. 'Dub, Scratch, and the Black Star: Lee Perry on the Mix'. Available at: http://www.techgnosis.com/dub.html (accessed 10 June, 2009).

Davis, J. D. 1997. 'Children of the Ras'. In Potash, *Reggae, Rasta, Revolution*, 253–54.

Davis, S. 1983a. 'Ernest Ranglin on Ska'. In Davis and Simon, *Reggae International*, 43.

— 1983b. 'Scientist'. In Davis and Simon, *Reggae International*, 110.

— 1983c. 'Linton in London'. In Davis and Simon, *Reggae International*, 163–64.

— 1983d. 'Talking Drums, Sound Systems, and Reggae'. In Davis and Simon, *Reggae International*, 33–34.

— 1994. *Bob Marley: Conquering Lion of Reggae*. London: Plexus.

Davis, S., and P. Simon (eds). 1983. *Reggae International*. London: Thames & Hudson.

Dawson, A. 2004a. 'Candomblé'. In Partridge, *Encyclopedia of New Religions*, 287–88.

— 2004b. 'Umbanda'. In Partridge, *Encyclopedia of New Religions*, 294.

Daynes, S. 2004. 'The Musical Construction of the Diaspora: The Case of Reggae and Rastafari'. In Whiteley, Bennet and Hawkins, *Music, Space and Place*, 25–41.

de Konigh, M., and L. Cane-Honeysett. 2003. *Young, Gifted and Black: The Story of Trojan Records*. London: Sanctuary.

de Konigh, M., and M. Griffiths. 2003. *Tighten Up: The History of Reggae in the UK*. London: Sanctuary.

Denselow, R. 1989. *When the Music's Over: The Story of Political Pop*. London: Faber & Faber.

Devereux, P. 1997. *The Long Trip: A Prehistory of Psychedelia*. Harmondsworth: Penguin/Arkana.

De Vries, F. 2006. 'Global Ear: Pretoria'. *The Wire* 272 (October): 16.

Diouf, L. 1997. 'Dub Power: The New Connections'. In Potash, *Reggae, Rasta, Revolution,* 176–79.

Disciples, The. 2005. 'BSL Sound System': <http://www.disciplesbslbm.co.uk/bslp6.html> (accessed 25 October 2005).

Donnell, A. (ed.). 2002. *Companion to Contemporary Black British Culture.* London: Routledge.

Donnell, A., and S. L. Welsh (eds). 1996a. *The Routledge Reader in Caribbean Literature.* London: Routledge.

— 1996b. 'General Introduction'. In Donnell and Welsh, *Routledge Reader in Caribbean Literature*, 1–26.

— 1996c. '1980–89: Introduction'. In Donnell and Welsh, *Routledge Reader in Caribbean Literature*, 361–73.

Doyle, P. 2005. *Echo and Reverb: Fabricating Space in Popular Music Recording 1900–1960.* Middletown: Wesleyan University Press.

Duncan, A. D. 1969. *The Christ, Psychotherapy and Magic: A Christian Appreciation of Occultism.* London: George Allen & Unwin.

Dunlap, J. 1961. *Exploring Inner Space: Personal Experiences Under LSD 25.* London: Scientific Book Club.

Dunn, C. 1999. 'Carnivals in Latin America and the Caribbean'. In Appiah and Gates, *Africana*, 376–81.

Du Noyer, P. 1979a. 'Sham 69 Riot'. *New Musical Express* (3 February): 11.

— 1979b. 'If This Doesn't Make Him Think Twice, Nothing Will'. *New Musical Express* (3 February): 39.

Easlea, D. 2004. 'One World'. Liner notes for John Martyn, *One World. Deluxe Edition* (Island). Available at <http://www.mindbrix.ltd.uk/johnmartyn/?location=/web/Liner%20Notes%20-%20One%20World> (accessed 1 December 2006).

Eddington, R. 2004. *Sent From Coventry: The Chequered Past of Two Tone.* London: Independent Music Press.

Eden, J. 2009. 'The First taste of Hope is Fear: A Bluffer's Guide to Mark Stewart and the Mafia': <http://www.uncarved.org/music/maffia/maffia.html > (accessed 20 July 2009).

Edmonds, E. B. 1998. 'Dread "I" In-a-Babylon: Ideological Resistance and Cultural Revitalization'. In Murrell, Spencer and McFarlane, *Chanting Down Babylon*, 23–35.

— 2003. *Rastafari: From Outcasts to Culture Bearers.* New York: Oxford University Press.

Edwards, R. 1999. 'Early Rastafarian Leaders'. In Appiah and Gates, *Africana*, 645.

Ehrlich, L. 1983. 'X-Ray Music: The Volatile History of Dub'. In Davis and Simon, *Reggae International*, 105–109.

Eno, B. 2000. 'Foreword'. In Prendergast, *Ambient Century*, xi–xii.

Erskine, N. L. 2003. 'Rap, Reggae, and Religion: Sounds of Cultural Dissonance'. In Pinn, *Noise and Spirit*, 71–84.

Eshun, K. 1998. *More Brilliant Than the Sun: Adventures in Sonic Fiction.* London: Quartet.

EWF, Local 111. 2005. 'History of the EWF Inc Local 111': <http://www.ewflocal111.com/about.htm> (accessed 8 April 2005).

Feld, S. 1982. *Sound and Sentiment: Birds, Weeping, Poetics, and Song in Kaluli Expression.* Philadelphia: University of Pennsylvania Press.

— 2003. 'A Rainforest Acoustemology'. In Bull and Back, *The Auditory Culture Reader*, 223–39.

Fisher, M. 2008. 'Prometheus Unbound: Mark Stewart'. *The Wire* 293 (July): 28–33.

Fitzgerald, B. 1995. 'Sympathy for the Old Devil'. *New Musical Express* (8 July): 32–34, 57.

Flood, G. 1999. *Beyond Phenomenology: Rethinking the Study of Religion*. London: Cassell.

Foehr, S. 2000. *Jamaican Warriors: Reggae, Roots and Culture*. London: Sanctuary.

Ford, S. 2003. *Hip Priest: The Story of Mark E Smith and The Fall*. London: Quartet Books.

Foucault, M. 1986. 'Of Other Spaces'. *Diacritics* 16 (Spring): 22–27.

Free Radical Sounds. 2007. 'Interview with Style Scott (Dub Syndicate/Roots Radics): <http://freeradicalsounds.com/style.htm> (accessed 1 March 2007).

Frith, S. 1996. *Performing Rites: Evaluating Popular Music*. Oxford: Oxford University Press.

Frith, S., and A. Goodwin (eds). 1990. *On Record: Rock, Pop and the Written Word*. London: Routledge.

Frith, S., and H. Horne. 1987. *Art Into Pop*. London: Methuen.

Frith, S., and J. Street. 1992. 'Rock Against Racism and Red Wedge: From Music to Politics, From Politics to Music'. In Garofalo, *Rockin' the Boat*, 67–80.

Frith, S., W. Straw and J. Street (eds). 2001. *Cambridge Companion to Pop and Rock*. Cambridge: Cambridge University Press.

Futrell, J. 1981. 'He's Got Sammy Davis Eyes. A Doctor Recommends: Brain Damage'. *Black Echoes* (27 June): 10–11.

Garofalo, R. (ed.). 1992. *Rockin' the Boat: Mass Music and Mass Movements* (Boston: South End Press).

Garnett, R. 1999. 'Too Low To Be Low: Art Pop and The Sex Pistols'. In Sabin, *Punk Rock*, 17–30.

Garvey, M. 1983. *The Marcus Garvey and Universal Negro Improvement Association Papers: Volume 1, 1826–August 1919*, ed. R. Hill. Berkeley: University of California Press.

— 1986. *The Philosophy and Opinions of Marcus Garvey*, ed. A. J. Garvey. Dover: Majority Press.

Gelder, K., and S. Thornton (eds). 1997. *The Subcultures Reader*. London: Routledge.

George, I. 1993. 'Fascists, Turn to the Left!' *New Musical Express* (16 October): 3.

Gibson, W. 1995 [1984]. *Neuromancer*. London: HarperCollins.

Gilbert, P. 2005 [2004]. *Passion is a Fashion: The Real Story of The Clash*. London: Aurum Press.

Gilroy, P. 1991. 'It Ain't Where You're From, It's Where You're At... The Dialectics of Diasporic Identification'. *Third Text* 13 (Winter): 3–17.

— 1993. *The Black Atlantic: Modernity and Double Consciousness*. London: Verso.

— 2002 [1987]. *There Ain't No Black in the Union Jack*. London: Routledge.

— 2003. 'Between the Blues and the Blues Dance: Some Soundscapes of the Black Atlantic'. In Bull and Back, *The Auditory Culture Reader*, 381–95.

Goldman, V. 1989. 'Dread Beat an' Blood': Liner notes for Linton Kwesi Johnson, *Dread Beat an' Blood*. Heartbeat, 1998.

— 2003. 'Dread Meet Punk Rocker Downtown'. Liner notes for *Wild Dub: Dread Meet Punk Rocker Downtown* (Select Cuts): 2–5, 8–12.

Goodwin, A. 1990 [1988]. 'Sample and Hold: Pop Music in the Digital Age of Reproduction'. In Frith and Goodwin, *On Record*, 258–73.

— 1991. 'Popular Music and Postmodern Theory'. *Cultural Studies* 5: 174–90.

Gray, A., and J. McGuigan (eds). 1997. *Studying Culture: An Introductory Reader*, 2nd edn. London: Arnold.

Green, J. 1998 [1988]. *Days in the Life: Voices from the English Underground 1961–1971*. London: Pimlico.

— 2007. 'It's a Mad, Mad, Mad, Mad Professor: Take a Lesson from the Genius of Nineties Dub'. Available at: <http://www.ariwa.com/> (accessed 22 February 2007).

Grossberg, L. 1992. *We Gotta Get Out of This Place: Popular Conservatism and Postmodern Culture*. New York: Routledge.

— 1997 [1984]. 'Another Boring Day in Paradise: Rock and Roll and the Empowerment of Everyday Life'. In Gelder and Thornton, *The Subcultures Reader*, 477–93.

Guardian News and Media. 2007. *Sex Pistols – Bill Grundy, 1976: Great Interviews of the 20th Century*. London: Guardian News and Media.

Habekost, C. 1993. *Verbal Riddim: The Politics and Aesthetics of African-Caribbean Dub Poetry*. Amsterdam: Rodopi.

Hall, S., C. Critcher, T. Jefferson and B. Roberts. 1978. *Policing the Crisis: Mugging, the State, and Law and Order*. London: Hutchinson.

Hall, S., and T. Jefferson (eds). 1976. *Resistance Through Rituals: Youth Sub-Cultures in Post-War Britain*. London: Hutchinson.

Harris, J. 1993. 'RAR! RAR! Disputin'! The History of Rock Against Racism'. *New Musical Express* (16 October): 16–17.

Harris, R. 2000. 'Openings, Absences and Omissions: Aspects of the Treatment of "Race", Culture and Ethnicity in British Cultural Studies'. In Owusu, *British Black Culture and Society*, 395–404.

Harris, R., and S. White (eds.). 1999. *Changing Britannia: Life Experience with Britain*. London: New Beacon Books/George Padmore Institute.

Hawkins, E. 1996. 'The Secret History of Dub: Reggae Historians Delve Into the Dub Chamber'. *Eye Weekly* (18 April). Available at: <http://www.eye.net/eye/issue/issue_04.18.96/MUSIC/mf0418a.htm> (accessed 8 August 2005).

Hebdige, D. 1974. *Reggae, Rastas, and Rudies: Style and the Subversion of Form*, CCCS occasional paper. Birmingham: Centre for Contemporary Cultural Studies, University of Birmingham.

— 1976a. 'The Meaning of Mod'. In Hall and Jefferson, *Resistance Through Rituals*, 87–96.

— 1976b. 'Reggae, Rastas, and Rudies'. In Hall and Jefferson, *Resistance Through Rituals*, 135–55.

— 1979. *Subculture: The Meaning of Style*. London: Methuen.

— 1987. *Cut 'N' Mix: Culture, Identity, and Caribbean Music*. London: Routledge.

— 1988. *Hiding in the Light: On Images and Things*. London: Comedia.

Heelas, P. 1996. *The New Age Movement: The Celebration of the Self and the Sacralization of Modernity*. Oxford: Blackwell.

Heelas, P., S. Lash and P. Morris. 1996. *Detraditionalization: Critical Reflections on Authority and Identity*. Oxford: Blackwell.

Henriques, J. 2003. 'Sonic Dominance and the Reggae Sound System Session'. In Bull and Back, *The Auditory Culture Reader*, 451–80.

Henry, W. 2002. 'Lovers' Rock'. In Donnell, *Companion to Contemporary Black British Culture*, 185.

Henry, W., and L. Back. 2003. '"Chatting" for Change! Interview with William (Lez) Henry'. In Bull and Back, *The Auditory Culture Reader*, 435–49.

Hetherington, K. 2000. *New Age Travellers: Vanloads of Uproarious Humanity*. London: Cassell.

Hewitt, R. 1986. *White Talk, Black Talk: Inter-Racial Friendship and Communication Amongst Adolescents*. Cambridge: Cambridge University Press.

Heylin, C. 2007. *Babylon's Burning: From Punk to Grunge*. London: Viking/Penguin Books.

Hill, R. 1983. 'Leonard P. Howell and the Millenarian Visions in Early Rastafari'. *Jamaica Journal* 16.1: 24–39.

Hillarby, J. 2006. 'Live at the BBC'. Liner notes to John Martyn, *Live at the BBC*. Available at <http://www.mindbrix.ltd.uk/johnmartyn/?location=/web/Liner%20Notes%20-%20 Live%20At%20The%20BBC> (accessed 1 December 2006).

Hiro, D. 1971. *Black British White British*. London: Eyre & Spottiswood.

Hitchcock, P. 1997. '"It Dread Inna Inglan": Linton Kwesi Johnson, Dread, and Dub Identity'. In Potash, *Reggae, Rasta, Revolution*, 163–67.

Hollings, K. 2006. 'Brian Eno & David Byrne, *My Life in the Bush of Ghosts*'. *The Wire* 266 (April): 56.

Homiak, J. P. 1995. 'Dub History: Soundings on Rastafari Livity and Language'. In Chevannes, *Rastafari and Other African-Caribbean Worldviews*, 127–81.

Horner, B., and T. Swiss (eds). 1999. *Key Terms in Popular Music and Culture*. Oxford: Blackwell.

Howe, D. 1973. 'Fighting Back: West Indian Youth and Police in Notting Hill'. *Race Today* 5.11: 333–37.

— 1980. 'From Bobby to Babylon: Blacks and the British Police. Part 1'. *Race Today* 12.1: 8–14.

Hudson, P. 1999. 'Dub Poetry'. In Appiah and Gates, *Africana*, 636–37.

Hughes, J. 1999. *Altered States: Creativity Under the Influence*. New York: Watson-Guptill Publications.

Hurford, R. 1990. 'Jah Shaka: The Indomitable Lion'. *Boom-Shacka-Lacka* 6. Available at <http://www.disciplesbslbm.co.uk/shak2.html> (accessed 12 October 2005).

Hurwitz, S. J., and E. F. Hurwitz. 1971. *Jamaica: A Historical Portrait*. London: Pall Mall Press.

Husbands, C. 1983. *Racial Exclusion and the City*. London: Allen & Unwin.

Hutton, C., and N. S. Murrell. 1998. 'Rastas' Psychology of Blackness, Resistance, and Somebodiness'. In Murrell, Spencer and McFarlane, *Chanting Down Babylon*, 36–54.

Hyder, R. 2004. *Brimful of Asia: Negotiating Ethnicity on the UK Music Scene*. Aldershot: Ashgate.

Jameson, F. 1997. 'Postmodernism and Consumer Society'. In Gray and McGuigan, *Studying Culture*, 192–205.

Johnson, L. K. 1974. *Voices of the Living and the Dead*. London: Race Today.

— 1975a. *Dread Beat an' Blood*. London: Bogle-L'Ouverture.

— 1975b. 'Roots and Rock'. *Race Today* 7: 237–38.

— 1976a. 'Jamaican Rebel Music'. *Race and Class* 17.4: 397–412.

— 1976b. 'The Reggae Rebellion'. *New Society* 36:714 (10 June): 589.

— 1980. *Inglan is a Bitch*. London: Race Today.

— 1991. *Tings an Times*. Newcastle-upon-Tyne: Bloodaxe Books.

— 1998. 'Notes on Poems'. Liner notes for Linton Kwesi Johnson, *More Time* (LKJ Records).

— 1999. 'Linton Kwesi Johnson in Conversation with John La Rose (17.3.97)'. In Harris and White, *Changing Britannia*, 50–79.

— 2002. *Mi Revalueshanary Fren: Selected Poems* (London: Penguin).

— 2005. 'Cutting Edge of Dub'. *The Guardian: Review* (27 August): 7.

Johnson-Hill, J. A. 1995. *I-Sight: The World of Rastafari. An Interpretive Sociological Account of Rastafarian Ethics*. Lanham: The Scarecrow Press.

Jones, B. 2000. 'Interviews with Bryn Jones': Liner notes for Muslimgauze, *The Inspirational Sounds of Muslimgauze* (Universal Egg).

Jones, C. 2000. 'The Caribbean Community in Britain'. In Owusu, *Black British Culture and Society*, 49–57.

Jones, S. 1988. *Black Culture, White Youth: The Reggae Tradition from JA to UK*. London: Macmillan Education.

Jones, S., and B. Zephaniah. 2005. 'Dread Right?' *Third Way* 28.5: 16–20.

Junique, K. 2004. *Rastafari? Rastafari For You: Rastafarianism Explained*. London: Athena Press.

Katz, D. 2000. *People Funny Boy: The Genius of Lee 'Scratch' Perry*. Edinburgh: Payback Press.

— 2004. *Solid Foundation: An Oral History of Reggae*. London: Bloomsbury.

— 2005. 'Upsetters: 14 Dub Blackboard Jungle'. *Q/Mojo Bob Marley and Reggae Special Edition – Q Classic* 1.6: 135.

Kaye, L. 1983. 'White Reggae: On Guard Babylon'. In Davis and Stephen, *Reggae International*, 167–70.

— 2007. 'Two Sevens Clash: Lenny Kaye Version', from the booklet in the CD Culture, *Two Sevens Clash: The 30th Anniversary Edition* (Shanachie): 1–4.

Kelly, D. 1984. 'Lee Perry'. *New Musical Express* (17 November): 6–7, 58. Also available at: <http://www.uncarved.org/dub/scratch.html> (accessed 11 August 2005).

Kennedy, M. 2005. *Dictionary of Music*. Hoo: Grange Books.

Kerridge, R., and H. Sykes. 1995. *The Storm is Passing Over: A Look at Black Churches in Britain*. London: Thames & Hudson.

Kessler, T. 1997. 'The Kook Report: Lee "Scratch" Perry'. *New Musical Express* (26 July): 20–21.

King, S. A. 2002. *Reggae, Rastafari, and the Rhetoric of Social Control*. Jackson: University Press of Mississippi.

Kirby, T., and L. Jury. 2004. 'Why They're Rocking Against Racism Again'. *The Independent* (22 March): <http://enjoyment.independent.co.uk/music/news/article65430.ece> (accessed 9 October 2006).

Klarreich, E. 2001. 'Feel the Music'. *Nature Science Update* (27 November): <http://www.nature.com/news/2001/011129/pf/011129-10_pf.html> (accessed 30 October 2005).

Kopf, B. 1995. 'Unnatural Highs'. *The Wire* 140 (October): 26–30.

Kot, G. 1997. 'Instrument of Expression'. In Potash, *Reggae, Rasta, Revolution*, 149–51. Originally published in *Chicago Tribune* (13 February 1996).

Kristeva, J. 1984. *Revolution in Poetic Language*. Translated by M. Waller. New York: Columbia University Press.

Laing, D. 1985. *One Chord Wonders: Power and Meaning in Punk Rock*. Milton Keynes: Open University Press.

Lamming, G. 1992. *The Pleasures of Exile*. Ann Arbor: University of Michigan Press.

Landes, R. 2004. 'Millennialism'. In Lewis, *New Religious Movements*, 333–58.

La Rose, M. 1999. 'Michael La Rose with Roxy Harris in the Chair (12.5.97)'. In Harris and White, *Changing Britannia*, 120–48.

Lee, M. A., and B. Shlain. 1992. *Acid Dreams: The Complete Social History of LSD. The CIA, The Sixties, and Beyond.* New York: Grove Books.

Leech, K. 1988. *Struggle in Babylon: Racism in the Cities and Churches of Britain.* London: Sheldon Press.

Lesser, B. 2002. *King Jammy's.* Toronto: ECW Press.

Letts, D. 2001. 'Dread Meets Punk Rockers Uptown'. Booklet with the CD, Various artists, *Dread Meets Punk Rockers Uptown,* Social Classics, Vol. 2 (EMI/Heavenly, 2001).

— 2007. *Culture Clash: Dread Meets Punk Rockers.* London: SAF Publishing.

— 2009, 'Lament for Bass Culture', on 'Broadcasting House'. BBC Radio 4 (19 April).

Lewis, I. M. 2003 [1971]. *Ecstatic Religion: A Study of Shamanism and Spirit Possession,* 3rd edn. London: Routledge.

Lewis, J. R. (ed.). 2004. *The Oxford Handbook of New Religious Movements.* New York: Oxford University Press.

Lewis, R. 1998. 'Marcus Garvey and the Early Rastafarians: Continuity and Discontinuity'. In Murrell, Spencer and McFarlane, *Chanting Down Babylon,* 145–58.

Longhurst, B. 1995. *Popular Music and Society.* Oxford: Polity.

Lydon, J. 1994. *Rotten: No Irish, No Blacks, No Dogs.* New York: Picador.

Lynch, G., and E. Badger. 2006. 'The Mainstream Post-Rave Club Scene as a Secondary Institution: A British Perspective'. *Culture and Religion* 7: 27–40.

Lynch, H. 1967. *Edward Wilmott Blyden: Pan Negro Patriot 1832–1912.* Oxford: Oxford University Press.

Mack, D. R. A. 1999. *From Babylon to Rastafari: Origin and History of the Rastafarian Movement.* Chicago: Research Associates School Times Publications and Frontline Distribution International.

MacKinnon, A. 1979. 'Forces of Reality'. *New Musical Express* (21 April): 7–8, 52.

Mansingh, A., and L. Mansingh. 1985. 'Hindu Influences on Rastafarianism'. In Nettleford, *Caribbean Quarterly Monograph: Rastafari,* 96–115.

Manuel, P., and W. Marshall. 2006. 'The Riddim Method: Aesthetics, Practice, and Ownership in Jamaican Dancehall'. *Popular Music* 25: 447–70.

Marcus, G. 1989. *Lipstick Traces: A Secret History of the Twentieth Century.* Cambridge: Harvard University Press.

Marko, P. 2000. 'Punk and Racism': <http://www.punk77.co.uk/groups/sabinmyreply.htm> (accessed 9 October 2006).

— 2006. 'The Castrators and Early Slits': <http://www.punk77.co.uk/groups/slitscastrator-searlyslits.htm> (accessed 2 November 2006).

— 2007. *The Roxy London WC2: A Punk History.* London: Punk 77 Books.

Marley, Brian. 2005. 'The Primer: Jamaican Deejays'. *The Wire* 262 (December): 42–49.

Martin, D. 1992. 'Music Beyond Apartheid?' In Garofalo, *Rockin' the Boat,* 195–208.

Martin, G. 1981. 'Company Lore and Public Disorder'. *New Musical Express* (14 March): 30–33.

May, C. 1983. 'A History of British Reggae'. In Davis and Simon, *Reggae International,* 155–58.

McGough, R., B. Patten and A. Henri. 1967. *The Mersey Beat.* Harmondsworth: Penguin.

McGuigan, J. 1999. *Modernity and Postmodern Culture.* Buckingham: Open University Press.

McKay, G. 1996. *Senseless Acts of Beauty: Cultures of Resistance Since the Sixties.* London: Verso.

— 2000. *Glastonbury: A Very English Fair.* London: Victor Gollancz.

McIntyre, P. 1995. 'Muslimgauze'. *The Wire* 136 (June): 12.

McNeill, L., and G. McCain. 1996. *Please Kill Me: The Uncensored Oral History of Punk.* New York: Grove Books.

Melechi, A. (ed.). 1997. *Psychedelia Britannica: Hallucinogenic Drugs in Britain.* London: Turnaround.

Mercer, K. 1994. *Welcome to the Jungle: New Positions in Black Cultural Studies.* New York: Routledge.

Middleton, R. 2001. 'Pop, Rock and Interpretation'. In Frith, Straw and Street, *Cambridge Companion to Pop and Rock*, 213–25.

Millar, G. 1980. 'Armagideon Time: On the Road with The Clash'. *Sounds* (2 February): 25–27.

— 1981. 'Ruts DC: Marquee'. *Sounds* (7 March): 50.

Millar, R. 1981. 'Ruts DC: Marquee'. *Sounds* (7 March): 50.

Morley, P. 1979. 'Public Image Ltd: Manchester'. *New Musical Express* (3 March): 53–54.

— 2003. *Words and Music.* London: Bloomsbury.

Morris, M. 1983. 'People Speech'. In Davis and Simon, *Reggae International*, 189–91.

Morrow, C. 1999. *Stir It Up: Reggae Album Cover Art.* San Francisco: Chronicle Books.

Mosco, S. 1984. 'Interview with Jah Shaka': <http://www.jahwarrior.freeuk.com/ivshaka.htm> (accessed 6 October 2005).

— 2005. 'Profile of the Legendary Jah Shaka': <http://www.jahwarrior.com/> (accessed 12 October 2005).

Muggleton, D. 2000. *Inside Subculture: The Postmodern Meaning of Style.* Oxford: Berg.

Mulvaney, R. M. 1990. *Rastafari and Reggae: A Dictionary and Sourcebook.* Westport, CN: Greenwood Press.

Murder Tone, P. 2005a. 'Disciples Interview (Part One): <http://articles.dubroom.org/pmt/part01.htm> (accessed 12 October 2005).

— 2005b. 'Disciples Interview (Part Two): <http://articles.dubroom.org/pmt/part02.htm> (accessed 12 October 2005).

Murray, C. S. 1978. 'Wilko – To Hell and Back via the M1 Caff'. *New Musical Express* (3 June): 6–7.

Murrell, N. S., W. D. Spencer and A. A. McFarlane (eds). 1998. *Chanting Down Babylon: The Rastafari Reader.* Philadelpia: Temple University Press.

Nagashima, Y. S. 1984. *Rastafarian Music in Contemporary Jamaica: A Study of Socioreligious Music of the Rastafarian Movement in Jamaica.* Tokyo: Institute for the Study of Languages and Cultures of Asia and Africa.

Nehring, N. 2006. 'The Situationist International in American Hardcore Punk, 1982–2002'. *Popular Music and Society* 29: 519–30.

Nettleford, R. (ed.). 1985. *Caribbean Quarterly Monograph: Rastafari.* Kingston: University of the West Indies.

New Musical Express. 1981. 'Directory of Sounds'. *New Musical Express* (21 February): 28–29.

— 1993. 'Fascists, Turn to the Left!' *New Musical Express* (16 October): 3.

Nissenbaum, S. 1997. *The Battle for Christmas.* New York: Vintage Books.

Noon, J. 1995. 'Artificially Induced Dub Syndrome'. In Palmer, *Technopagan*, 87–101.

— 1999. 'Dub Til It Bleeds'. *Spike Magazine*: <http://www.spikemagazine.com/0800jeffnooninterzone.php> (accessed 20 September 2006).

— 2000a. 'Dub Fiction'. In Redhead, *Repetitive Beat Generation*, 111–18.

— 2000b. *Needle in the Groove*. London: Transworld.

Nymen, M. 1974. *Experimental Music: Cage and Beyond*. London: Studio Vista.

O'Connor, A. 2002. 'Local Scenes and Dangerous Crossroads: Punk and Theories of Cultural Hybridity'. *Popular Music* 21: 225–36.

O'Hara, C. 1999. *The Philosophy of Punk: More Than Noise*. London: AK Press.

Oliver, P. (ed.). 1990. *Black Music in Britain: Essays on the Afro-Asian Contribution to Popular Music*. Milton Keynes: Open University Press.

Olmos, M. F., and L. Paravisini-Gebert. 2003. *Creole Religions of the Caribbean: An Introduction from Vodou and Santeria to Obeah and Espiritismo*. New York: New York University Press.

Olson, M. J. V. 1998. '"Everybody Loves Our Town": Scenes, Spatiality, Migrancy'. In Swiss, Sloop, and Herman, *Mapping the Beat*, 269–90.

Onuora, O. 1977. *Echo*. Kingston, Jamaica: Sangsters.

Owens, J. 1979. *Dread: The Rastafarians of Jamaica*. London: Heinemann Educational Books.

— 'The I-Words'. In Davis and Simon, *Reggae International*, 62.

Owusu, K. (ed.). 2000. *Black British Culture and Society: A Text Reader*. London: Routledge.

Oyewole, A., U. Bin Hassan and K. Green. 1996. *Last Poets on a Mission: Selected Poetry and a History of the Last Poets*. New York: Henry Holt & Co.

Parker, D. 2007. 'Tackhead/Fats Comet'. Available at: <http://www.skysaw.org/onu/artists/tackheadfatscomet.html> (accessed 1 March 2007).

Partridge, C. 2003. 'Sacred Chemicals: Psychedelic Drugs and Mystical Experience'. In Partridge and Gabriel, *Mysticisms East and West*, 96–131.

— 2004a. *The Re-Enchantment of the West: Alternative Spiritualities, Sacralization, Popular Culture, and Occulture*, Vol. 1. London: Continuum.

— (ed.). 2004b. *Encyclopedia of New Religions: New Religions, Sects, and Alternative Spiritualities*. Oxford: Lion; New York: Oxford University Press.

— 2004c. 'Rastafarianism'. In Partridge, *Encyclopedia of New Religions*, 62–64.

— 2005. *The Re-Enchantment of the West: Alternative Spiritualities, Sacralization, Popular Culture, and Occulture*, Vol. 2. London: Continuum.

— 2006. 'The Spiritual and the Revolutionary: Alternative Spirituality, British Free Festivals, and the Emergence of Rave Culture'. *Culture and Religion* 7: 41–60.

— 2009a. 'Schism in Babylon: Colonialism, Afro-Christianity and Rastafari'. In J. R. Lewis and S. M. Lewis (eds), *Sacred Schisms: How Religions Divide*, 306–31. Cambridge: Cambridge University Press.

— 2009b. 'Babylon's Burning: Reggae, Rastafari, and Millenarianism'. In J. Wallis and K. G. C. Newport (eds), *The End All Around Us: Apocalyptic Texts and Popular Culture*, 43–70. London: Equinox.

— 2009c. 'Religion and Popular Culture'. In L. Woodhead, H. Kawanami and C. Partridge (eds), *Religions in the Modern World: Traditions and Transformations*, 2nd edn, 489–522. London: Routledge.

Partridge, R. 1998. 'Reggae Greats: Linton Kwesi Johnson': Liner notes for Linton Kwesi Johnson, *Reggae Greats* (Island).

Patterson, S. 1967. *Dark Strangers*. London: Tavistock.

Paytress, M. 2000. 'The Slits': Liner notes for The Slits, *Cut* (Island, 1979).

Peach, C.. V. Robinson, J. Maxted and J. Chance. 1988. 'Immigration and Ethnicity'. In Halsey, *British Social Trends Since 1900*, 561–615.

Peel, J., and S. Ravenscroft. 2005. *John Peel: Margrave of the Marshes*. London: Transworld Publishers.

Penman, I. 1998. *Vital Signs: Music, Movies, and Other Manias*. London: Serpent's Tail.

Phillips, H. 1998. 'Hearing the Vibrations'. *Nature Science Update* (13 August): http://www.nature.com/news/1998/980813/pf/980813-3_pf.html (accessed 30 October 2005).

Pierson, L. J. 2002. Liner notes for *U-Roy: The Lost Album – Right Time Rockers* (Heart Beat).

Pinn, A. (ed.). 2003. *Noise and Spirit: The Religious and Spiritual Sensibilities of Rap Music*. New York: New York University Press.

Plant, S. 1999. *Writing on Drugs*. New York: Farrar, Straus, and Giroux.

Plantenga, B. 1997. 'Tackhead's Heady Tacktics'. In Potash, *Reggae, Rasta, Revolution*, 172–75.

Pollard, V. 1982. 'The Social History of Dread Talk'. *Caribbean Quarterly* 28.2: 17–40.

— 1985. 'Dread Talk – The Speech of the Rastafarian in Jamaica'. In Nettleford, *Caribbean Quarterly Monograph: Rastafari*, 32–41.

Porter, D. 2003. *Rapcore: The Nu-metal Rap Fusion*. London: Plexus.

Potash, C. (ed.). 1997. *Reggae, Rasta, Revolution: Jamaican Music from Ska to Dub*. London: Books With Attitude.

Pouncey, E. 2001. 'Invisible Jukebox: Mark E Smith'. *The Wire* 203 (January): 50–53.

Powne, M. 1980. *Ethiopian Music: An Introduction. A Survey of Ecclesiastical and Secular Ethiopian Music and Instruments*. Westport: Greenwood Press.

Prendergast, M. 2000. *The Ambient Century: From Mahler to Trance – The Evolution of Sound in the Electronic Age*. London: Bloomsbury.

Reckford, V. 1977. 'Rastafarian Music: An Introductory Study'. *Jamaica Journal* 11: 1–13.

— 1982. 'Reggae, Rastafarianism and Cultural Identity'. *Jamaica Journal* 16: 70–79. Also reprinted in Potash, *Reggae, Rasta, Revolution*, 3–13.

— 1998. 'From Burru Drums to Reggae Ridims: The Evolution of Rasta Music'. In Murrell, Spencer and McFarlane, *Chanting Down Babylon*, 231–52.

Redhead, S. 1990. *The End-of-the-Century Party: Youth and Pop Towards 2000*. Manchester: Manchester University Press.

Redhead, S. (ed.). 2000. *Repetitive Beat Generation*. Edinburgh: Rebel Inc./Canongate.

Reel, P. 2000. *Deep Down with Dennis Brown: Cool Runnings and the Crown Prince of Reggae*. London: Drake Bros.

Reynolds, S. 1998. *Energy Flash: A Journey Through Rave Music and Dance Culture*. London: Picador.

— 2000. 'Back to the Roots'. *The Wire* 199 (September): 34–39.

— 2005. *Rip It Up and Start Again: Postpunk 1978–1984*. London: Faber & Faber.

Rhys, J. 1966. *Wide Sargasso Sea*. London: Andre Deutsch.

Robinson, A. J. 1999. 'Jamaica'. In Appiah and Gates, *Africana*, 1024–32.

Rodney, W. 1969. *The Groundings with My Brothers*. London: Bogle-L'Overture Publications.

Rogers, R. A. 2000 [1924]. *The Holy Piby*. Kingston: Headstart; Chicago: Research Associates School Times Publication. <http://www.sacred-texts.com/afr/piby/> (accessed 6 April 2005).

Rowe, M. 1998. 'Gender and Family Relations in Rastafari: A Personal Perspective'. In Murrell, Spencer and McFarlane, *Chanting Down Babylon*, 72–88.

Rubenstein, H., and C. Suarez. 1994. 'The Twelve Tribes of Israel: An Explorative Field Study'. *Religion Today* 9.2: 1–6.

Rubin, V. (ed.). 1957. *Caribbean Studies: A Symposium*. Seattle: University of Washington Press.

Russell, M. 1980. *Babylon*. London: New English Library.

Ryman, C. 1984. 'Kumina – Stability and Change'. *African Caribbean Institute of Jamaica Research Review* 1: 81–128.

Sabin, R. (ed.). 1999a. *Punk Rock: So What?* London: Routledge.

— 1999b. '"I Won't Let that Dago By": Rethinking Punk and Racism'. In Sabin, *Punk Rock*, 199–218.

Sakolsky, R. 1997. 'Dub Diaspora: Off the Page and Into the Streets'. In Potash, *Reggae, Rasta, Revolution*, 168–71.

Salewicz, C. 2005. 'A Cheap Holiday in Other People's Misery?' *Q/Mojo Bob Marley and Reggae Special Edition – Q Classic* 1.6: 108–11.

Samuel, R. 1988. *Island Stories: Unravelling Britain*. London: Verso.

Savage, J. 2005 [1991]. *England's Dreaming: Sex Pistols and Punk Rock*. London: Faber and Faber.

Savishinsky, N. 1998. 'African Dimensions of the Jamaican Rastafarian Movement'. In Murrell, Spencer and McFarlane, *Chanting Down Babylon*, 125–44.

Savory, E. 1997. '"Another Poor Devil of a Human Being..." Jean Rhys and the Novel as Obeah'. In Olmos and Paravisini-Gebert, *Sacred Possessions*, 216–30.

Schaeffer, J. 1990. *New Sounds: The Virgin Guide to New Music*. London: Virgin.

Schafer, D. L. 1981. *The Maroons of Jamaica: African Slave Rebels in the Caribbean*. Ann Arbor: University Microfilms International.

Schütze, P. 1995. 'Strategies for Making Sense'. *The Wire* 139 (September): 34–38.

Shapiro, H. 2003. *Waiting for the Man: The Story of Drugs and Popular Music*. London: Helter Skelter.

Shapiro, P. 1995. 'Bass Invader: Jah Wobble'. *The Wire* 140 (October): 32–35.

— (ed.). 2000a. *Modulations: A History of Electronic Music. Throbbing Words on Sound*. New York: Caipirinha Productions/Distributed Art Publishers.

— 2000b. 'Dub'. In Shapiro (ed.), *Modulations: A History of Electronic Music. Throbbing Words on Sound*, 50–51. New York: Caipirinha Productions/Distributed Art Publishers.

— 2005. *The Rough Guide to Hip-Hop*. London: Rough Guides.

Sherman, C., and A. Smith. 1999. *Highlights*. Berkeley: Ten Speed Press.

Sherwood, A. 1996. 'Dub Syndicate: *Research and Development*'. Liner notes for Dub Syndicate, *Research and Development*.

Shusterman, R. 1991. 'The Fine Art of Rap'. *New Literary History* 22: 613–32.

Simon, P. 1983. 'Talking Rock Steady'. In Davis and Simon, *Reggae International*, 43–44.

Simonon, P. 2005. 'I'm in the Mood for Ska'. *Q/Mojo Bob Marley and Reggae Special Edition – Q Classic* 1.6: 3.

Sleeper, M. 1997. 'Shocks of the Mighty'. In Potash, *Reggae, Rasta, Revolution*, 157–62. Originally published at: <http://www.oanet.com/homepage/sleeper/scratch.htm> (accessed July 1996).

Small, C. 1987. *Music of the Common Tongue: Survival and Celebration in Afro-American Music*. London: Calder Publications.

Smith, B. R. 2003. 'Tuning into London *c.* 1600'. In Bull and Back, *The Auditory Culture Reader*, 127–35.

Smith, H. 2000. *Cleansing the Doors of Perception: The Religious Significance of Entheogenic Plants and Chemicals*. New York: Jeremy P. Tarcher/Putnam.

Smith, M. E. 1985. *The Fall: Lyrics*. Berlin: Lough Press.

Smith, M. E. (with A. Collings). 2009. *Renegade: The Lives and Tales of Mark E. Smith*. London: Penguin Books.

Smith, M. E., and M. Middles. 2003. *The Fall*. London: Omnibus Press.

Smith, M. G., R. Augier and R. Nettleford. 1960. *The Rastafari Movement in Kingston, Jamaica*. Mona: Institute for Social and Economic Research, University College of the West Indies.

Smith, P. 1995. *Early Work: 1970–1979*. New York: Norton & Co.

— 2006. *Augeries of Innocence*. London: Virago.

Solomos, J. 1992. 'The Politics of Immigration Since 1945'. In Braham, Rattansi and Skellington, *Racism and Antiracism*, 7–29.

— 2003. *Race and Racism in Britain*, 3rd edn. Houndmills: Palgave Macmillan.

Solomos, J., and L. Back. 1995. *Race, Politics and Social Change*. London: Routledge.

Southern, T. 1995. *Virgin: A History of Virgin Records*. Axminster: A Publishing Company.

Spencer, N. 1976. 'The Rockers Uptown'. *Musical Express* (23 October): 30–31, 34, 36–37.

Spencer, W. D. 1998. 'The First Chant: Leonard Howell's *The Promised Key*'. In Murrell, Spencer and McFarlane, *Chanting Down Babylon*, 361–89.

Stelfox, D. 2008. 'Digital Dancehall'. *The Wire* 294 (August): 34–39.

Stevens, J. 1993. *Storming Heaven: LSD and the American Dream*. London: Flamingo.

Stewart, D. M. 2005. *Three Eyes for the Journey: African Dimensions of the Jamaican Religious Experience*. Oxford: Oxford University Press.

Steward, S., and S. Garratt. 1984. *Signed, Sealed and Delivered: True Life Stories of Women in Pop*. London: Pluto Press.

Stolzoff, N. C. 2000. *Wake the Town and Tell the People: Dancehall Culture in Jamaica*. Durham: Duke University Press.

Stratton, J. 1989. 'Beyond Art: Postmodernism and the Case of Popular Music'. *Theory, Culture and Society* 6: 31–57.

Straw, W. 1991. 'Systems of Articulation, Logics of Change: Communities and Scenes in Popular Music'. *Cultural Studies* 5: 368–88.

— 2001. 'Consumption'. In Frith, Straw and Street, *Cambridge Companion to Pop and Rock*, 54–73.

Street Howe, Z. 2009. *Typical Girls: The Story of The Slits* (London: Omnibus).

Stubbs, D. 2007. 'The Primer: Adrian Sherwood'. *The Wire* 276 (February): 36–43.

Swiss, T., J. Sloop and A. Herman (eds). 1998. *Mapping the Beat: Popular Music and Contemporary Theory*. Oxford: Blackwell.

Tamm, E. 1995. *Brian Eno: His Music and the Vertical Colour of Sound*. New York: Da Capo.

Taylor, C. 1997. 'Lee Scratch Perry: Return to the Ark'. *Straight No Chaser* 40: 38–47.

Taylor, P. 1990. 'Perspectives on History in Rastafari Thought'. *Studies in Religion* 19: 191–205.

— 1991. 'Rastafari, the Other, and Exodus Politics: EATUP'. *Journal of Religious Thought* 17: 1–2, 95–107.

Taylor, S. 2004. *The A to X of Alternative Music*. London: Continuum.

Terrell, T. 1998. 'Everything is Political'. Liner notes for Linton Kwesi Johnson, *Independent Intavenshan: The Island Anthology* (Island): 6–15.

Thiselton, A. C. 1992. *New Horizons in Hermeneutics*. Grand Rapids: Zondervan.

Thornton, S. 1995. *Club Cultures: Music, Media and Subcultural Capital*. Cambridge: Polity Press.

Todd, N. P. M., and F. W. Cody. 2000. 'Vestibular Responses to Loud Dance Music: A Physiological Basis of the "Rock and Roll Threshold"?' *Journal of the Acoustical Society of America* 107.1 (January): 496–500.

Toop, D. 1994. 'A to Z of Dub'. *The Wire* 123 (May): 20. Available at: <http://www.thewire.co.uk/archive/essays/a_z_dub.html> (accessed 20 July 2005).

— 1995a. *Ocean of Sound: Aether Talk, Ambient Sound and Imaginary Worlds*. London: Serpent's Tail.

— 1995b. 'David Toop Turns up the Heat on the Sampling Debate'. *The Wire* 139 (September): 74.

— 2006. 'My Life in the Bush of Ghosts': Liner notes to Brian Eno and David Byrne, *My Life in the Bush of Ghosts* (remastered version): 5–12.

Topping, K. 2004 [2003]. *The Complete Clash*. London: Reynolds & Hearn.

Toynbee, J. 2007. *Bob Marley: Herald of a Postcolonial World?* Cambridge: Polity.

Tosi, P. 1998. 'Interview with Adrian Sherwood': <http://www.vibesonline.net/news/interv/i-adrian.html> (accessed 10 October 2005).

— 2001. 'Interview with Jah Shaka': <http://www.vibesonline.net/news/interv/i-jahsha.html> (accessed 10 October 2005).

Troyna, B. 1978. 'The Significance of Reggae Music in the Lives of Black Adolescent Boys in Britain: An Exploratory Study'. Unpublished MPhil thesis, University of Leicester.

— 1996. 'National Front'. In Cashmore, *Dictionary of Race and Ethnic Relations*, 252–53.

Tutuola, A. 1978 [1952]. *My Life in the Bush of Ghosts*. London: Faber.

Tyler, A. 1981. 'Skinhead Bands Disown the Sieg Heilers'. *New Musical Express* (14 March): 4–5.

Veal, M. E. 2007. *Dub: Soundscapes and Shattered Songs in Jamaican Reggae*. Middletown: Wesleyan University Press.

Wagley, C. 1957. 'Plantation–America: A Cultural Sphere'. In Rubin, *Caribbean Studies*, 3–13.

Wall, M. 2004. *John Peel: A Tribute to the Much-loved DJ and Broadcaster*. London: Orion.

Wambu, O. (ed.). 1999. *Empire Windrush: Fifty Years of Writing about Black Britain*. London: Phoenix.

Waters, A. M. 1985. *Race, Class, and Political Symbols: Rastafari and Reggae in Jamaican Politics*. New Brunswick: Transaction Publishers.

Waugh, E. 2005. *The Coronation of Haile Selassie*. London: Penguin.

Weidenbaum, M. 1997. 'Dub, American Style'. In Potash, *Reggae, Rasta, Revolution*, 180–84.

Wells, S. 1995. 'Bummer Holiday'. *New Musical Express* (8 July): 28–31.

Welsh, G. F., and D. M. Howard. 2002. 'Gendered Voice in the Cathedral Choir'. *Psychology of Music* 30: 102–20.

White, G. 1983a. 'Music in Jamaica – 1494–1957'. In Davis and Simon, *Reggae International*, 25–32.

— 1983b. 'Mento to Ska: The Sound of the City'. In Davis and Simon, *Reggae International*, 37–42.

— 1984. 'The Development of Jamaican Popular Music: Part 2'. *African Caribbean Institute of Jamaica Research Review* 1: 47–80.

Whiteley, S. 1997. 'Altered Sounds'. In Melechi, *Psychedelia Britannica*, 120–42.

Whiteley, S., A. Bennet and S. Hawkins (eds). 2004. *Music, Space and Place: Popular Music and Cultural Identity* (Aldershot: Ashgate).

Whitfield, G. M. 2002. 'Bass Cultural Vibrations: Visionaries, Outlaws, Mystics, and Chanters'. *3 a.m. Magazine*: <http://www.3ammagazine.com/musicarchives/2002_oct/bass_cultural_vibrations.html> (accessed 25 October 2005).

— 2003. 'The Adrian Sherwood Interview: The On-U Sound Experience, the On-U Sound Family': <http://www.uncarved.org/dub/onu/onu.html> (accessed 12 October 2005).

Widgery, D. 1986. *Beating Time*. London: Chatto & Windus.

Williams, R. 1997. 'The Sound Surprise'. In Potash, *Reggae, Rasta, Revolution*, 145–48. Originally published in *Melody Maker* 1976 (21 August 1976).

Williamson, N. 2005. 'Uprising'. *Songlines: The World Music Magazine* 30 (May–June): 36–37.

Wint, E. (in consultation with members of the Nyabinghi Order). 1998. 'Who is Haile Selassie? His Imperial Majesty in Rasta Voices'. In Murrell, Spencer and McFarlane, *Chanting Down Babylon*, 159–65.

Wobble, Jah, 2001. 'Epiphanies'. *The Wire* 203 (January): 98.

Wood, A. 2002. 'Rock Against Racism'. In Donnell, *Companion to Cotemporary Black British Culture*, 265.

Worthington, A. 2004. *Stonehenge: Celebration and Subversion*. Loughborough: Alternative Albion.

Wroe, N. 2008. 'A Life in Writing: I Did My Own Thing'. *Saturday Guardian: Review* (8 March): 11.

Yawney, C. D. 1978. 'Dread Wasteland: Rastafarian Ritual in West Kingston, Jamaica'. In Crumrine, *Ritual, Symbolism and Ceremonialism*, 154–74.

York, M. 2004. 'Santería (La Regla de Ocha)'. In Partridge, *Encyclopedia of New Religions*, 280, 87.

Zaehner, R. C. 1961. *Mysticism, Sacred and Profane*. Oxford: Oxford University Press.

Zephaniah, B. 2005. 'I am a Rastafarian'. In Partridge, *World's Religions*, 447.

— 2008. 'Dread, Beat an' Blood'. BBC Radio 4 (22 July).

Zion Train. 1999. 'Conversation with Neil "Mad Professor" Fraser': liner notes to Mad Professor, *The Inspirational Sounds of Mad Professor*.

Zips, W. 1999. *Black Rebels: African Caribbean Freedom Fighters in Jamaica*. Princeton: Marcus Wiener.

Correspondence cited

Zephaniah, Benjamin: 9 January 2004.

Discography

African Head Charge, *My Life in a Hole in the Ground*. On-U Sound, 1998 (1981).
African Head Charge, *Environmental Studies*. On-U Sound, 1997 (1982).
African Head Charge, *The Drastic Season*. On-U Sound, 1983.
African Head Charge, *Off the Beaten Track*. On-U Sound, 1986.
African Head Charge, *Songs of Praise*. On-U Sound, 1990.
African Head Charge, *In Pursuit Of Shashamane Land*. On-U Sound, 1993.
African Head Charge, *Shrunken Head*. On-U Sound, 2004.
Aggravators & the Revolutionaries, *Aggravators Meets the Revolutionaries*. Third World, 1987.
Aisha Kandisha's Jarring Effects, *El Buya*. Barraka el Farnatshi, 1991.
Aisha Kandisha's Jarring Effects, *Shabeesation*. Barraka el Farnatshi, 1993.
Laurel Aitken, *Pioneer of Jamaican Music*, Vol. 1. Reggae Retro, 2000.
Aksak Maboul, *Onze Danses Pour Combattre la Migraine*. Crammed Discs, 1977.
Aksak Maboul, *Un Peu de l'Ame des Bandits*. Crammed Discs, 1979.
Alpha & Omega, *The Sacred Art of Dub*. A&O Records, 1998.
Ambient Meditations. Return to the Source, 1998.
Anhrefn, *BWRW CWRW: The Ariwa Sound and Studio One Sessions*. Workers Playtime, 1989.
Ari Up, *More Dread Dan Dead*. Collision, 2005.
Armagideon, *Through the Haze*. Dubhead, 1998.
Babazula & The Mad Professor, *Ruhani Oyun Havalari*. Double Moon, 2003.
Barmy Army, *The English Disease*. On-U Sound, 1989.
Basement 5, *1965–1980*. Island, 1980.
Basement 5, *Basement 5 in Dub*. Island, 1980.
Basement 5, *1965–1980/Basement 5 in Dub*. Universal, 2004.
Bass Communion and Muslimgauze, *Bass Communion v. Muslimgauze* – Part 1. Soleil-moon, 1999.
Bass Communion and Muslimgauze, *Bass Communion v. Muslimgauze* – Part 2. Soleil-moon, 2000.
Bass Erotica, *Sexual Bass*. Neurodisc, 1995.
Bass Erotica, *Bass Ecstasy*. Neurodisc, 1996.
Bass Erotica, *Erotic Bass Delight*. Neurodisc, 1996.
Bass Lo-Ryders, *Strictly for Da Bassheadz*. Neurodisc, 1999.
Bass Lo-Ryders, *Lo Bouncing Bass*. Neurodisc, 2000.
Bass Lo-Ryders, *Ryder Style*. Neurodisc, 2004.
Bass-O-Matic, *Set the Controls for the Heart of the Bass*. Virgin, 1990.
Big Audio Dynamite, *The is Big Audio Dynamite*. CBS, 1985.
Big Youth, *Screaming Target*. Trojan, 1973.
Big Youth, *Progress*. Nichola Delita, 1979.
Big Youth, *Some Great Big Youth*. Heartbeat, 1981.
Dennis Bovell/Blackbeard, *Strictly Dub Wize*. Moving Target, 1978/1987.
Dennis Bovell/Blackbeard, *I Wah Dub*. EMI, 1981/LKJ Records, 2000.
Dennis Bovell, *Brain Damage*. EMI, 2006/1981.

Dennis Bovell, *Dub of Ages*. LKJ Records, 1997.

Dennis Bovell and the Dub Band, *Audio Active*. EMI, 2006/Moving Target, 1986.

Dennis Bovell and the 4th Street Orchestra, *Scientific Higher Ranking Dubb* and *Yuh Learn!* EMI, 2006 – *Scientific Higher Ranking Dubb* was originally released on RAMA, 1977; *Yuh Learn!* was originally released on RAMA, 1978.

David Bowie, *Diamond Dogs*. RCA Victor, 1974.

Thomas Brinkmann, *Tokyo*. max.E, 2004.

Burning Spear, *Man in the Hills*. Island, 1976.

Burning Spear, *Hail H.I.M*. EMI, 1980.

The Bush Chemists, *Strictly Dubwise*. Universal Egg, 1994.

The Bush Chemists, *Light Up Your Spliff*. Conscious Sounds, 1996.

The Bush Chemists, *Light Up Your Chalice*. Dubhead, 1999.

Can, *Tago Mago*. United Artists, 1972.

Clive Chin, *Java Java Java Java*. Impact, 1973.

Gary Clail's Tackhead Sound System, *Tackhead Tape Time*. Funf und Vierzig, 1988.

Gary Clail & On-U Sound System, *Emotional Hooligan*. BMG Records, 1991.

Eric Clapton, *461 Ocean Boulevard*. Polydor, 1974.

The Clash, *The Clash* – UK version. CBS, 1977.

The Clash, *The Clash* – US version. Epic, 1977.

The Clash, *Sandinista!* CBS, 1980.

The Clash, *Super Black Market Clash*. Columbia, 1993.

The Congos, *The Heart of the Congos*. Black Ark, 1977.

John Cooper Clarke, *Où est la Maison de Fromage?* Epic, 1978.

John Cooper Clarke, *Disguise in Love*. CBS, 1978.

John Cooper Clarke, *Walking Back to Happiness*. Epic, 1979.

Count Ossie & The Mystic Revelation of Rastafari, *Grounation*. Ashanti, 1974.

Lloyd Coxsone/Sir Coxsone Sound, *King of the Dub Rock*. Safari, 1975.

Lloyd Coxsone/Sir Coxsone Sound, *King of the Dub Rock: Part Two*. Regal, 1982.

Creation Rebel, *Dub From Creation*. Hitrun Records, 1978.

Creation Rebel, *Close Encounters of the Third World*. Hitrun Records, 1978.

Creation Rebel, *Rebel Vibrations*. Hitrun Records, 1979.

Creation Rebel, *Starship Africa*. Hitrun Records, 1980.

Creation Rebel, *Psychotic Jonkanoo*. Statik Records, 1981.

Creation Rebel, *Lows and Highs*. Cherry Red Records, 1982.

Creation Rebel, *Return From Space*. Ruff Cutt Records, 1984.

Creation Rebel, *Historic Moments: Vol. 1*. On-U Sound, 1994.

Creation Rebel, *Historic Moments: Vol. 2*. On-U Sound, 1994.

Creation Rebel/New Age Steppers, *Threat to Creation*. Cherry Red Records, 1981.

Sidney Crooks, *Bag-O-Wire*. Klik, 1975.

Culture, *Two Sevens Clash*. Joe Gibbs, 1977.

Culture, *Two Sevens Clash: The 30th Anniversary Edition*. Shanachie, 2007.

Dayjah & The Disciples, *Storm Clouds*. Third Eye Music, 1994.

Death in Vegas, *Dead Elvis*. Concrete, 1997.

The Disciples present the Boom Shackalacka Sound System, *For Those Who Understand*. Boom-Shacka-Lacka, 1995.

The Disciples, *Infinite Density of Dub*. Dubhead, 1996.

The Disciples Meet the Rootsman, *Rebirth*. Third Eye Music, 1997.

Dreadzone, *Second Light*. Virgin, 1995.

Dr Pablo and The Dub Syndicate, *North of the River Thames*. On-U Sound, 1984.

Dubblestandart, *Streets of Dub*. Select Cuts/Eco Beach, 2002.

Dubcats, *Lockdown*: http://versionist.com/members/55/ (accessed 17 July 2009).

Dub Specialist, *Dub Store Special*. Studio One, 1974.

Dub Specialist, *Better Dub*. Studio One, 1974.

Dub Specialist, *Ital Dub*. Studio One, 1974.

Dub Specialist, *Mellow Dub*. Studio One, 1974.

Dub Syndicate, *Pounding System*. On-U Sound, 1982.

Dub Syndicate, *One Way System*. On-U Sound, 1983.

Dub Syndicate, *Tunes From the Missing Channel*. On-U Sound, 1985.

Dub Syndicate, *Strike the Balance*. On-U Sound, 1989.

Dub Syndicate, *Classic Selection: Vol. 1*. On-U Sound, 1989.

Dub Syndicate, *Classic Selection: Vol. 2*. On-U Sound, 1991.

Dub Syndicate, *Stoned Immaculate*. On-U Sound, 1992.

Dub Syndicate, *Echomania*. On-U Sound, 1993.

Dub Syndicate, *Classic Selection: Vol. 3*. On-U Sound, 1994.

Dub Syndicate, *Ital Breakfast*. On-U Sound, 1996.

Dub Syndicate, *Research and Development: A Selection of Dub Syndicate Remixes*. On-U Sound, 1996.

Dub Syndicate, *Fear of a Green Planet*. On-U Sound, 1998.

Dub Syndicate & Lee Perry, *Time Boon X De Devil Dead*. EMI, 1987.

Sly Dunbar & Robbie Shakespeare, *Raiders of the Lost Dub*. Mango, 1981.

Clancy Eccles, *Joshua's Rod of Correction*. Jamaican Gold, 1996.

Rupie Edwards, *Ire Feelings*. Cactus, 1975.

Rupie Edwards All Stars, *Dub Basket*. Cactus, 1975.

Rupie Edwards and Friends, *Yamaha Skank* (Success, 1974); a longer version was later released as *Let There Be Version*. Trojan, 1990.

Rupie Edwards and Friends, *Ire Feelings: Chapter and Version*. Trojan, 1990.

Winston Edwards, *Natty Locks Dub*. Fay, 1974.

Winston Edwards and Dennis Bovell, *Dub Conference: Winston Edwards and Blackbeard at 10 Downing Street*. Studio, 1980.

Brian Eno, *Discreet Music*. Editions E.G., 1975.

Brian Eno and David Byrne, *My Life in the Bush of Ghosts*. EG/Sire, 1981; remastered: Virgin, 2006.

Ethnic Fight Band, *Musical Explosion*. Ethnic Fight, 1975.

Ethnic Fight Band, *Out Of One Man Comes Many Dubs*. Ethnic Fight, 1975.

EZ3kiel, *Handle with Care*. Jarring Effects, 2001.

The Fall, *Slates*. Rough Trade, 1981.

The Fall, *Extricate*. Cog Sinister/Fontana, 1990.

Robert Fripp and Brian Eno, *No Pussyfooting*. Editions E.G., 1973.

Robert Fripp and Brian Eno, *Evening Star*. Editions E.G., 1975.

Fun-da-mental, *Seize the Time*. Beggars Banquet, 1994.

Joe Gibbs and Errol Thompson, *African Dub All-Mighty*. Lightning, 1975.

Joe Gibbs and Errol Thompson, *African Dub All-Mighty: Chapter 2*. Joe Gibbs, 1976.

Joe Gibbs and Errol Thompson, *African Dub All-Mighty: Chapter 3*. Lightning, 1978.

Joe Gibbs and Errol Thompson, *African Dub All-Mighty: Chapter 4*. Joe Gibbs, 1979.

Joe Gibbs and Errol Thompson, *African Dub All-Mighty: Chapter 5*. Joe Gibbs, 1984.

Joe Gibbs and Errol Thompson, *African Dub All-Mighty: Chapters 1 & 2*. Joe Gibbs Enterprises, 1999.

Joe Gibbs and Errol Thompson, *African Dub All-Mighty: Chapters 3 & 4*. Crazy Joe Records, 2005.

Derrick Harriott, *Scrub A Dub*. Crystal, 1974.

Derrick Harriott, *More Scrubbling Dub*. Crystal, 1975.

Hawkwind, *Future Reconstructions: Ritual of the Solstice*. Emergency Broadcast System/4 Real Communications, 1996.

Hawkwind, *The Hawkwind Remix Project*. Warlord, 2000 – no actual label is identified, only the catalogue no.: warlord777CD.

Hazardous Dub Company, *Dangerous Dubs*, Vol. 1. Acid Jazz, 1992.

Hazardous Dub Company, *Dangerous Dubs*, Vol. 2. Acid Jazz, 1993.

Jimi Hendrix, *Rainbow Bridge: Original Motion Picture Soundtrack*. Reprise, 1971.

The Heptones, *Party Time*. Island, 1977.

Here & Now, *Give and Take*. Charly Records, 1978.

Here & Now, *Fantasy Shift*. Chic Records, 1983.

High Tone, *Opus Incertum*. Jarring Effects, 2000.

David Holmes, *Let's Get Killed*. Go! Beat, 1997.

Keith Hudson, *Pick A Dub*. Atra Records, 1974; Blood & Fire, 1994.

Impact All Stars, *Forward the Bass: Dub from Randy's 1972–1975*. Blood & Fire, 1998.

Inner Circle, *Heavyweight Dub*. Top Ranking Sounds, 1978 – also available on Inner Circle & The Fatman Riddim Section, *Heavyweight Dub/Killer Dub*. Blood & Fire, 1999.

Inner Circle, *Killer Dub*. Top Ranking Sounds, 1978 – also available on Inner Circle & The Fatman Riddim Section, *Heavyweight Dub/Killer Dub*. Blood & Fire, 1999.

Inner City Unit, *Passout*. Riddle Records, 1980.

Inner City Unit, *Maximum Effect*. Flicknife, 1981.

Inner City Unit, *Punkadelic*. Avatar, 1982.

I Roy, *Presenting I Roy*. Trojan, 1973.

Jah Lloyd, *Herbs of Dub*. Dip, 1974.

Jah Lloyd, *Black Moses*. Virgin, 1979.

Jah Power Band vs. Sly & the Revolutionaries, *Sensi Dub*, Vol. 7/1. Original Music, n.d.

Jah Shaka, *Commandments of Dub*. Jah Shaka Music, 1982.

Jah Shaka, *Commandments of Dub 2*. Jah Shaka Music, 1984.

Jah Shaka, *Commandments of Dub 3: Lion's Share of Dub*. Jah Shaka Music, 1984.

Jah Shaka, *Commandments of Dub 4: Dub Almighty*. Jah Shaka Music, 1985.

Jah Shaka, *Commandments of Dub 5: Jah Dub Creator*. Jah Shaka Music, 1985.

Jah Shaka, *Commandments of Dub 6: Deliverance*. Jah Shaka Music, 1987.

Jah Shaka, *Commandments of Dub 7: Warrior*. Jah Shaka Music, 1987.

Jah Shaka, *Commandments of Dub 8: Imperial Dub*. Jah Shaka Music, 1988.

Jah Shaka, *Commandments of Dub 9: Coronation Dub*. Jah Shaka Music, 1989.

Jah Shaka, *Commandments of Dub 10: African Drum Beats*. Jah Shaka Music, 1991.

Jah Shaka, *Revelation Songs*. Jah Shaka Music, 1983.

Jah Shaka, *The Disciples*. Jah Shaka Music, 1989.

Jah Shaka, *The Disciples 2: Addis Ababa*. Jah Shaka Music, 1992.

Jah Shaka, *The Disciples 3: The Lion*. Jah Shaka Music, 1993.

Jah Shaka, *Dub Symphony*. Island, 1990.

Jah Shaka, *New Testaments of Dub 1*. Jah Shaka Music, 1992.

Jah Shaka, *New Testaments of Dub 2*. Jah Shaka Music, 1993.

Jah Shaka, *Dub Salute 1*. Jah Shaka Music, 1994.

Jah Shaka, *Dub Salute 2*. Jah Shaka Music, 1994.

Jah Shaka, *Dub Salute 3*. Jah Shaka Music, 1994.

Jah Shaka, *Dub Salute 4*. Jah Shaka Music, 1995.

Jah Shaka, *Dub Salute 5*. Jah Shaka Music, 1996.

Jah Shaka & Aswad, *Jah Shaka Meets Aswad in Addis Ababa Studio*. Jah Shaka Music, 1985.

Jah Shaka & Fatman, *Dub Confrontation: Jah Shaka Versus Fatman*. Live & Love, 1980.

Jah Shaka & Fire House Crew, *Jah Shaka Meets Fire House Crew: Authentic Dubwise*. Blow Recordings, 2002.

Jah Shaka & Mad Professor, *Jah Shaka Meets the Mad Professor at Ariwa Sounds*. Ariwa, 1984.

Jah Warrior, *Great Kings of Israel in Dub*. Jah Warrior Records, 1996.

Jah Warrior, *African Tribes Dub*. Jah Warrior Records/Shiver, 1996.

Keith Leblanc & Tim Simenon, *Malcolm X: Stop the Confusion*. Island, 1993.

Linton Kwesi Johnson, *Dread Beat an' Blood*. Virgin, 1978; Heartbeat, 1989.

Linton Kwesi Johnson, *Forces of Victory*. Island, 1979.

Linton Kwesi Johnson, *Bass Culture*. Island, 1980.

Linton Kwesi Johnson, *LKJ in Dub*. Island, 1980.

Linton Kwesi Johnson, *Making History*. Island, 1983.

Linton Kwesi Johnson, *Reggae Greats*. Island, 1985.

Linton Kwesi Johnson, *LKJ in Concert with the Dub Band*. LKJ Records, 1985.

Linton Kwesi Johnson, *LKJ in Dub: Volume Two*. LKJ Records, 1992.

Linton Kwesi Johnson, *Independent Intavenshan: The Island Anthology*. Island, 1998.

Linton Kwesi Johnson, *More Time*. LKJ Records, 1998.

Linton Kwesi Johnson, *LKJ in Dub: Volume Three*. LKJ Records, 2002.

Janet Kay, *The Ultimate Collection*. Arawak, 1995.

Killing Joke, *Laugh? I Nearly Bought One!* Caroline, 1992.

Killing Joke, *The Malicious Singles*. Malicious Damage, 2008 – MP3 release only.

King Tubby and Lee Perry, *King Tubby Meets the Upsetter at the Grass Roots of Dub*. Fay, 1974.

King Tubby, *Creation of Dub*. Total Sound, 1975.

King Tubby, *Dub From the Roots*. Total Sound, 1975.

King Tubby, *Natty Dub*. Attack, 1975.

King Tubby, *The Roots of Dub*. Total Sound, 1975.

King Tubby, *Shalom Dub*. Klik, 1975.

King Tubby & Friends, *Dub Like Dirt*. Blood & Fire, 1999.

King Tubby, *Dub Gone Crazy: The Evolution of Dub at King Tubby's 1975–1979*. Blood & Fire, 1994.

King Tubby and Prince Jammy, *Dub Gone 2 Crazy: In Fine Style (1975–1979)*. Blood & Fire, 1996.

King Tubby and Roots Radics, *King Tubby Meets Roots Radics: Dangerous Dub*. Copasetic, 1981; Greensleeves, 1996.

The Last Poets, *Chastisement*. Douglas, 1972.

Ijahman Levi, *Haile I Hymn: Chapter 1*. Island, 1978.

Little Axe, *The Wolf That House Built*. Wired Recordings, 1994.

Little Axe, *Slow Fuse*. M & G Records, 1996.

Little Axe, *Hard Grind*. On-U Sound, 2002.

Fred Locks, *Black Star Liner*. VP, 1975.

Herman Chin Loy, *Aquarius Dub*. Aquarius, 1973.

Mad Professor, *Dub Me Crazy*. Ariwa, 1982.

Mad Professor, *Dub Me Crazy 2: Beyond the Realms of Dub*. Ariwa, 1982.

Mad Professor, *Dub Me Crazy 3: The African Connection*. Ariwa, 1983.

Mad Professor, *Dub Me Crazy 4: Escape to the Asylum of Dub*. Ariwa, 1983.

Mad Professor, *Dub Me Crazy 5: Who Knows the Secret of the Master Tapes?* Ariwa, 1985.

Mad Professor, *Dub Me Crazy 6: Schizophrenic Dub*. Ariwa, 1986.

Mad Professor, *Dub Me Crazy 7: The Adventures of a Dub Sampler*. Ariwa, 1987.

Mad Professor, *Dub Me Crazy 8: Experiments of the Aural Kind*. Ariwa, 1988.

Mad Professor, *The Inspirational Sounds of Mad Professor*. Universal Egg, 1999.

Malcolm X, *No Sell Out*. Island, 1983.

Mark Stewart and the Maffia, *Learning to Cope with Cowardice*. On-U Sound, 1983.

Bob Marley & the Wailers, *Catch a Fire*. Island, 1973.

Bob Marley & the Wailers, *Natty Dread*. Island, 1974.

Bob Marley & the Wailers, *Exodus*. Island, 1976.

Bob Marley & the Wailers, *Survival*. Tuff Gong, Island, 1979.

Bob Marley & the Wailers, *Uprising*. Tuff Gong, Island, 1980.

Bob Marley & the Wailers, *Confrontation*. Tuff Gong, Island, 1983.

Bob Marley & the Wailers, *Rebel Music*. Tuff Gong, Island, 1986.

Bob Marley & the Wailers, *Simmer Down at Studio One*, Vol. 1. Heartbeat, 1994.

Bob Marley & the Wailers, *Wailing Wailers at Studio One*, Vol. 2. Heartbeat, 1994.

John Martyn, *Solid Air*. Island, 1973.

John Martyn, *Inside Out*. Island, 1973.

John Martyn, *Sunday's Child*. Island, 1974.

John Martyn, *One World*. Island, 1977.

Massive Attack & Mad Professor, *No Protection*. Wild Bunch Records, 1995.

Matumbi, *Dub Planet Orbit 1*. Extinguish, 1980.

Linda McCartney, *Wide Prairie*. Parlophone, 1998.

Missing Brazilians, *Warzone*. On-U Sound, 1984.

Misty in Roots, *Wise and Foolish*. People Unite, 1982.

Sylvan Morris, *Morris on Dub*. Jaywax, 1975.

Sylvan Morris & Harry J. *Cultural Dub*. Harry J, 1978.

The Mount Vernon Arts Lab, *Gummy Twinkle*. Via Satellite Recordings, 1998.

Mr Scruff, *Heavyweight Rib Ticklers*. Unfold, 2002.

Muslimgauze, *The Inspirational Sounds of Muslimgauze*. Universal Egg, 2000.

The Observer, *Sledgehammer Dub*. Observer, 1975.

Observer All Stars & King Tubby, *Dubbing with the Observer*. Attack, 1975.

Oku Onuora, *I A Tell ... Dubwise & Otherwise*. ROIR, 1982.

Oku Onuora, *Overdub: A Tribute to King Tubby*. Ion Records, 2000.

Augustus Pablo, *Ital Dub*. Starapple, 1974.

Augustus Pablo, *King Tubbys Meets the Rockers Uptown*. Clocktower, 1977; Rockers/Jet Star, 1998.

Augustus Pablo, *East of the River Nile.* Message, 1977; Shanachie, 2002.

Augustus Pablo, *Pablo Meets Mr. Bassie: Original Rockers Vol. 2.* Shanachie, 1991.

Augustus Pablo and Lee Perry, *Augustus Pablo Meets Lee Perry at the Black Ark.* Rhino, 2001.

Robert Palmer, *Double Fun.* Island, 1978.

Dawn Penn, *No, No, No.* Big Beat Records, 1994.

Lee Perry, *Return of the Django.* Upsetter/Trojan, 1969.

Lee Perry, *Rhythm Shower.* Upsetter, 1973.

Lee Perry, *Cloak and Dagger.* Rhino, 1973.

Lee Perry, *Upsetters 14 Dub Blackboard Jungle.* Upsetter, 1973.

Lee Perry, *Revolution Dub.* Cactus, 1975.

Lee Perry, *Kung Fu Meets the Dragon.* DIP, 1975.

Lee Perry, *Return of the Wax.* DIP, 1975.

Lee Perry, *Musical Bones.* DIP, 1975.

Lee Perry, *Super Ape.* Upsetter/Island, 1976.

Lee Perry, *Return of the Super Ape.* Lion of Judah, 1977.

Lee Perry, *Megaton Dub Vols I & II.* Seven Leaves, 1978.

Lee Perry, *Judgement in Babylon.* Lion of Judah Records, 1985.

Lee Perry, *Build the Ark.* Trojan, 1990.

Lee Perry, *Rastafari Liveth Itinually.* Justice League, 1996.

Lee Perry, *Technomajikal.* ROIR, 1997.

Lee Perry, *Arkology.* Island, 1997.

Lee Perry, *Complete UK Upsetter Singles Collection*, Vols. 1-4. Trojan, 1998–2002.

Lee Perry, *Archive.* Rialto, 2002.

Lee Perry, *Dub-Triptych.* Trojan, 2004.

Lee Perry & Dub Syndicate, *Time Boom De Devil Dead.* On-U Sound, 2002.

Lee Perry & the Whitebellyrats, *Panic in Babylon.* Damp Music, 2004/Narnack, 2006.

The Power Steppers, *Bass Enforcement.* Universal Egg, 1995.

The Power Steppers, *Bass Re-Enforcement.* Universal Egg, 1996.

Pink Floyd, *The Piper at the Gates of Dawn.* Columbia, 1967.

Pink Floyd, *A Saucerful of Secrets.* EMI, 1968.

Pink Floyd, *Wish You Were Here.* EMI, 1975.

Primal Scream, *Vanishing Point.* Creation Records, 1997.

Primal Scream, *Echo Dek.* Creation Records, 1997.

Prince Buster, *The Message Dubwise.* Fab UK, 1974 [1973].

Prince Far I, *Message From the King.* Carib Gems, 1977.

Prince Far I and the Arabs, *Cry Tuff Encounter: Chapter 1.* Hitrun Records, 1978; Pressure Sounds, 1997.

Prince Far I, *Cry Tuff Dub Encounter: Chapter 2.* Virgin, 1979.

Prince Far I, *Cry Tuff Dub Encounter: Chapter 3.* Daddy Cool, 1980; Pressure Sounds, 1996.

Prince Far I, *Cry Tuff Dub Encounter: Chapter 4.* Trojan, 1981.

Prince Far I and the Arabs, *Dub to Africa.* Hitrun Records, 1979.

Prince Jammy, *Kamikaze Dub.* Trojan, 1979.

Public Image Ltd., *Metal Box.* Virgin, 1979.

Public Image Ltd., *The Flowers of Romance.* Virgin, 1981.

Public Image Ltd., *Album.* Virgin, 1986.

Public Image Ltd., *The Greatest Hits, So Far.* Virgin, 1990.

Reverberation and Muslimgauze, *New Soul: Reverberation Remixes by Muslimgauze*. Third Stone, 2000.

The Revolutionaries, *Green Bay Dub*. Burning Vibrations, 1979.

Winston Riley, *Meditation Dub*. Techniques, 1976.

Rhythm & Sound, *The Versions*. Burial Mix, 2003.

Rhythm & Sound, *See Mi Yah*. Burial Mix, 2005.

Max Romeo & the Upsetters, *War ina Babylon*. Island, 1976.

The Rootsman, *Koyaanisqatsi*. Soundclash, 1994.

The Rootsman, *In Dub We Trust*. Third Eye Music, 1995.

The Rootsman, *Realms of the Unseen*. Third Eye Music, 1999.

The Rootsman, *New Testament*. Meteosound, 2002.

The Rootsman meets Celtarabia, *Union of Souls*. Third Eye Music, 1998.

The Rootsman meets Muslimgauze, *Al Aqsa Intifada*. Third Eye Music, 2002.

The Ruts, *The Crack*. Virgin, 1979.

The Ruts, *Babylon's Burning Reconstructed: Dub Drenched Soundscapes*. Collision, 2006.

The Ruts DC, *Present Rhythm Collision*. Bohemian, 1982.

The Ruts DC, *Rhythm Collision Remix*. Echo Beach, 1999.

Scientist, *Scientist Heavyweight Dub Champion*. Greensleeves, 1980.

Scientist, *Scientist Rids the World of the Evil Curse of the Vampires*. Greensleeves, 1981.

Scientist & Culture, *Scientist Dubs Culture into a Parallel Universe*. RAS, 2000.

Scientist & Prince Jammy, *Scientist v Prince Jammy: Big Showdown*. Greensleeves, 1980.

B. B. Seaton, *Gun Court Dub*. Love, 1976.

The Sex Pistols, *Never Mind the Bollocks, Here's The Sex Pistols*. Virgin, 1977.

Singers & Players featuring Bim Sherman, *War of Words*. On-U Sound, 1982.

Singers & Players, *Staggering Heights*. On-U Sound, 1983.

The Slits, *Cut*. Island, 1979 – Island reissue, 2000.

The Slits, *The Return of the Giant Slits*. CBS, 1981 – CBS reissue, 2006.

Michael Smith, *Mi Cyaan Believe It*. Island, 1982.

Smith and Mighty, *Bass is Maternal*. More Rockers/STUD!O K7, 1995.

Mark E. Smith, *The Post Nearly Man*. Artful Records, 1998.

Mark E. Smith, *Pander! Panda! Panzer!* Action Records, 2002.

Wayne Smith and Prince Jammy, *Sleng Teng/Prince Jammy's Computerised Dub*. Greensleeves, 1985.

Stamper Doctor, *Dub Zone*. Teams, 1979.

Steel Pulse, *Handsworth Revolution*. Island, 1978.

Sub Oslo, *The Rites of Dub*. Glitterhouse, 1998.

Suicide, *Suicide*. Ariola, 1977.

Symarip, *Skinhead Moonstomp*. Trojan, 1970.

Tackhead, *Friendly as a Hand Grenade*. World Records, 1989.

Tad's Logic Dub Band, *Chapter 1 Dub Mix*. Tad's, 1984.

Talking Heads, *Remain in Light*. Sire, 1980.

Tangerine Dream, *Electronic Meditation*. Ohr, 1970.

Tappa Zukie, *Musical Intimidator*. Trojan, 2004.

Terrorists, *Forces 1977–1982*. ROIR, 2001.

Thievery Corporation, *Sounds from the Thievery Hi-Fi*. ESL Music, 1996.

Thievery Corporation, *The Richest Man in Babylon*. ESL Music, 2002.

Thievery Corporation, *Babylon Unwound*. ESL Music, 2004.
Thievery Corporation, *Versions*. ESL Music, 2006.
Tom Tom Club, *Tom Tom Club*. Island, 1981.
Toots and the Maytals, *In the Dark*. Trojan, 1974.
Toots and the Maytals, *Funky Kingston*. Trojan, 1975.
Toyan, *How the West Was Won*. Greensleeves, 1981.
Twinkle Brothers & the Trebunia-Tutka Family, *Higher Heights*. Twinkle Records, 1992.
Twinkle Brothers & the Trebunia-Tutka Family, *Dub with Strings*. Twinkle Records, 1992.
UB40, *Signing Off*. Graduate, 1980.
The Upsetters, *Clint Eastwood*. Trojan, 1969.
The Upsetters, *Eastwood Rides Again*. Trojan, 1970.
The Upsetters, *The Good, the Bad and the Upsetters*. Trojan, 1970.
U Roy, *U Roy*. Attack, 1974.
U Roy, *Dread in a Babylon*. Virgin, 1975.
U Roy, *Natty Rebel*. Virgin, 1976.
U Roy, *The Lost Album – Right Time Rockers*. Heartbeat, 2002.
Adrian Utley and Mount Vernon Arts Lab, *Warminster*. Ochre Records, 1999.
Van Der Graaf Generator, *World Record*. Charisma, 1976.
Various artists, *Hot Shots*. Trojan, 1970.
Various artists, *The Harder They Come*. Island/Mango, 1972.
Various artists, *The Roxy London WC2: Jan-April 77*. EMI, 1977.
Various artists, *Green Bay Killing*. Pantomime, 1978.
Various artists, *Joe Gibbs Original DJ Classics*. Rocky One, 1979/1990.
Various artists, *Countryman*. Island, 1982.
Various artists, *Drums of Defiance: Maroon Music from the Earliest Free Black Communities of Jamaica*. Smithsonian Folkways, 1992.
Various artists, *Dubitamin*. Roundtrip Records, 1996.
Various artists, *Roots of Innovation: 15 and X Years On-U Sound*. On-U Sound, 1996.
Various artists, *Churchical Chants of the Nyabingi*. Heartbeat, 1997.
Various artists, *Producer Series: Trojan Box Set*. Trojan, 1999.
Various artists, *Dread Meets the Rockers Uptown: Social Classics Vol. 2*. EMI/Heavenly, 2001.
Various artists, *Wild Dub: Dread Meets Punk Rocker Downtown*. Select Cuts, 2003.
Various artists, *Trojan Nyahbinghi Box Set*. Trojan, 2003.
Various artists, *Ire Feelings: Reggae Chart Hits 1969-1976*. One Stop Records, 2003.
Various artists, *Babylon is Ours: The USA in Dub*. Select Cuts, 2003.
Various artists, *Mento Madness: Motta's Jamaican Mento: 1951–1956*. V2 Music, 2004.
Various artists, *Death Disco: Songs From Under the Dance Floor, 1978–1984*. EMI, 2004.
Various artists, *Dub Stories*. Uncivilized World, 2006.
The Wailers, *Burnin'*. Island, 1973.
Wingless Angels, *Wingless Angels*. Mindless Records/Island Jamaica, 1997.
Jah Wobble, *The Legend Lives On... Jah Wobble in Betrayal*. Virgin, 1990.
Yellowman & Josey Wales, *Two Giants Clash: Yellowman Versus Josey Wales*. Greensleeves, 1984.
Benjamin Zephaniah & The Hazardous Dub Company, *Back to Roots*. Acid Jazz Roots, 1995.
Zion Train, *Grow Together*. China Records, 1996.

Filmography

Babylon. 1980. Director: Franco Rosso.
Countryman. 1982. Director: Dickie Jobson.
Dub Echoes. 2009. Director: Bruno Natal.
Dub Stories. 2006. Director: Nathalie Valet.
The Guns of Navarone. 1961. Director: J. Lee Thompson.
The Harder They Come. 1972. Director: Perry Henzell.
In einem Jahr mit 13 Monden. 1978. Director: Rainer Werner Fassbinder.
Punk Rock Movie. 1978. Director: Don Letts.
Reggae in a Babylon. 1978. Director: Wolfgang Büld.
Wild at Heart. 1990. Director: David Lynch.
Woodstock. 1970. Director: Michael Wadleigh.

Index of Subjects

Index of Names